Praise for *A New Way for Mothers*

"A true change maker."

—Global Invest Her

"The air of calm, grace, and joy that Louise brings to a room is echoed in this book with its thoughtful and realistic approach to motherhood. Rather than seeing motherhood as a separate stage in a woman's life, Louise's approach brings in all of our life before it and asks: who are we as a whole person? This revolutionary concept not only encourages mothers to bring all their skills to their new lives, but it also highlights the importance of learning and growing as you go. Most importantly, it emphasises kindness to yourself, patience with yourself, and apprecia-tion of yourself—and we all need more of that."

—HARRIET MINTER, journalist, broadcaster, and female leadership expert

"More diverse boards bring better perspectives, challenges, and out-comes. To achieve this, businesses need to actively encourage and develop diversity at all levels, particularly at senior management. However, alongside this, we desperately need to encourage more women back into the workplace by helping them balance caregiving with careers. In this book, Louise Webster challenges our thinking and demonstrates there is no one simple solution. She encourages us to stop the judgement, to start supporting one another, and to honour individual journeys. As a father of seven-year-old twin girls, I have also become increasingly aware of the need to more actively create a world where everybody receives support and encouragement in developing their capabilities and achieving their aspirations. The world is a better place when we have authors like Louise making us think more deeply on this topic."

—DR. DAVID KELLY, Board Director

A NEW WAY for MOTHERS

FAMILIUS

Published by Familius LLC, www.familius.com

Familius books are available at special discounts for bulk purchases, whether for sales promotions or for family or corporate use. For more information, contact Familius Sales at 559-876-2170 or email orders@familius.com.

Library of Congress Cataloging-in-Publication Data
2017935340

Print ISBN 9781945547171
Ebook ISBN 9781945547553

Printed in the United States of America

Edited by DeAnna Acker
Cover design by David Miles
Book design by Brooke Jorden

10 9 8 7 6 5 4 3 2 1
First Edition

A NEW WAY for MOTHERS

A Revolutionary Approach for Mothers
to Use Their Skills and Talents While
Their Kids Are at School

LOUISE WEBSTER

For all mothers—connecting you to your skills, well-being, and happiness in the hours available.

Contents

Introduction

The world will be saved by the Western woman.

—Dalai Lama XIV

W elcome to this book! You have taken your first step by picking it up; this is the start of an exciting journey together. This book is an idea—and an action plan—for you to make a new way for yourself in the world. I hope you find this book is filled with love, wisdom, and inspiration. My hope is that it will lead you to greater well-being, happiness, strength, and peace.

Before writing this book, I created beyondtheschoolrun.com, a website to inspire, engage, and connect parents with their skills and talents in the hours available to them. What does BeyondTheSchoolRun mean? To me, it refers to the moment in time when a mother creates space in her mind to start to think about her life beyond caring for her children. I have met some mothers who, after years of looking very happy, have started to question where they are. They wonder, *What has happened to my job?* This doesn't mean your children are necessarily at school. My children weren't when I felt this moment. It doesn't matter when this moment happens, but I believe many of us reach this point. This is the BeyondTheSchoolRun moment. And this is the moment I have written this book for. I hope that the new way presented in this book can provide a starting place for you to find answers, steps, connections, and inspiration.

I believe we can care for our children and still utilise our skills in the hours available to us. I believe that by combining our well-being and our talents, we can work towards a healthy, long-term connection between work and caregiving and in doing so we can create a new way not only for ourselves but also for future generations.

And I believe this journey isn't exclusive to me. It is available to all of us. In this book, I will share with you what steps I took, who inspired me, what I read, and the wisdom and guidance I received from others I met along the way.

A Bit about Me

I am a mother of two children (ages six and ten). But like most of us, I had a *before children* story and life.

I worked in public relations. I began by working for others, both at agencies and within a corporation, but I knew I wanted to have kids and would need more flexible hours. So I started my own agency, Rare Communications, which I ran for five years.

Shortly after having my first child, I unexpectedly hit a wall. I think it was a combination of exhaustion and a lot of people around me having personal issues. I had always been someone who had helped solve other people's problems, but this was a big wake-up call. I needed to focus on myself and, most importantly, my baby. I also realised the life I had created didn't fit and that I needed to reassess. So I decided it was time to end the business, which thankfully I sold to another business owner, and as a family, we decided to move out of the city.

I didn't know at the time that this was to be one of the greatest, although most challenging, turning points in my life. It led me to explore a new way, a way that combined work and family, well-being and earning, and passions and dreams.

It was after I had my second child that I desperately felt the need to reconnect and work again. I found that not working hugely impacted how I felt and my well-being. But I began to see the barriers in returning to the workplace flexibly. And I also understood the difficulty of returning to work after a period of time focused solely on caregiving.

When my son started school, I became very aware of just how many women had given up careers to care for their children. Lawyers, human resources professionals, marketers, and so much more. It just seemed to me that, like myself, so many of those women had skills to offer and yet were restricted by their roles as main caregivers. I can't tell you the amount of times I heard women say that they were always told they could achieve whatever they dreamt but that they didn't know that as soon as they had children that would all change. I kept questioning, *Why could this talent not be utilised without compromising caring for our children?* What value it would be to businesses, and also what value it would be to the well-being of parents and their children? I became acutely aware of the need to create change, not only for myself but also to ensure I could look my daughter in the eye and say with all honesty that she could work towards her dreams.

So, with all that in mind, and with a growing awareness of the level of inequality for women and girls, I set about to establish www.beyondtheschoolrun.com—a place to inspire, engage, and connect parents with their skills in the hours available to them. I wanted to create everything I myself was looking for. Most especially, I wanted to meet a community of people who wanted the same things and understood the challenges of combining caregiving and work.

What I didn't realise in creating BeyondTheSchoolRun was that I would unlock skills I never knew I had. If anyone had ever told me I would write a book, I would never have believed them. I would never have imagined attending events at No. 10 Downing Street three times either. But here I am, and I am so grateful. And the step-by-step journey I share with you in this book took me on this extraordinary journey.

What I also didn't realise is that I have been on a journey to find me—the authentic me—through wellness, fitness, work, and happiness. I have become much more closely connected to who I am, what I can achieve, and what my dreams and passions are. And I truly and deeply believe that together we can make the greatest difference in our lives and the lives of others—one step at a time.

I hope this book is a message that you can do what you are meant to. Life doesn't have to stop when you have children, and you can take steps towards your individual dreams in the time that is available to you. It's just about finding a new way, and part of that journey is finding yourself. Here I am connecting with a dream that I had forgotten and lost. Thirty years later, I have found it at the very place I think I lost it—at school.

I hope wherever you are in your life right now, this book can be the light, support, and wisdom that I was once searching for. I know how hard it is, I truly do, and wherever you are right now, this is for you.

Who Is This Book For?

This book is for any mother who has felt that BeyondTheSchoolRun moment and is searching for a purpose and a way to use her skills outside of caregiving. Your history might resemble mine in a lot of ways, or it might not. It doesn't matter your exact path or your past. What I do believe matters is that we need to come together, without divide. We are all working, whether we are caring or breadwinning. Whatever our paths, they are individual to us. But what unites us is that we are parents and we love our children and that we are passionate about the world and their future. I think it is so important as mothers to bridge the divide between the terms "working" and "non-working." It needs to come from us. We need to stop the judgement; we need to start supporting one another by honouring our individual journeys and working together for ourselves and our children. Together, our combination is strong; separate, we are all weaker.

This book recognises that our journeys are all different. Despite all being parents, we are still individual. Since creating beyondtheschoolrun.com, I have seen mothers taking different paths that work for them, based on their needs for earnings, their time, their support, and their passions.

Whatever your circumstances, wherever you come from, and wherever you are going, I truly hope you find some wisdom from my journey that can support you.

This book is written with a very open heart and a passion for us, as parents and mothers, to lift one another and help unlock one another's potential. Because when we do, I think this world will shine.

Creating a New Way

I hope this book will support you on your journey beyond motherhood. My hope is to empower you, your children, and others around you with the tools and inspiration to live a life connected to the power of your natural skills. This is about setting the foundations for your future life—a life filled with well-being, growth, and success alongside your children, without sacrifices or pressure.

This isn't about updating your CV or finding career advisors—that is the previous way. This is about recognizing ourselves as whole people and understanding that our well-being is connected to our work. It is about recognizing that our children can teach us and about understanding that this is a long journey to finding the natural talents which light us up rather than wear us down. This is about digging deep to find our true, authentic selves that lead us on a journey to self-fulfilment, empowerment, and happiness.

This is not saying that everyone needs to go back to work. Because this isn't about going "back." This is about moving forward and creating a new way that works for us all. This is about recognizing that we all have skills and talents, and when we utilise them, it will benefit us, our children, and the world.

As with anything new, it takes time, commitment, and focus, but with every step you take, you will want to take more. After you've had a baby, every step back into the world is a new one—even if it's just getting on a train or a plane or going out for a meal. So, in many ways, you are already creating a new way for yourself; this is just an extension of that.

How the Book Works

This book has ten chapters. One possible way to work through the book is by doing one chapter a month. This is how I did it, and I found the focus worked well for me. Or you might decide to do the chapters in your own selected order. There is no right or wrong; just follow your intuition. The book has been created for you to use in the way that best works for you; turn to the pages that you need or follow it step-by-step. I hope that it can be with you and support you when needed.

I speak a lot about steps, because this really is a step-by-step process, individual to each of us. It's like starting to exercise—you will realise that each step gives you such a great feeling, a feeling of movement towards your dreams whilst having the love and support of your very own family behind you. Like learning how to eat well to nourish ourselves, this process isn't necessarily easy. We have old habits and programming, so it takes time. But each step takes us closer. We are starting fresh, creating a new way that will be sustainable, enjoyable, and healthy.

I am still learning, I am still growing, and I am not an expert, but I hope that my experiences, my journey, and the wisdom of many others can be of great value to you. The book is made up of my experiences, my learnings, interviews with experts I have met along the way, and tips and teachings from mothers I have connected with on my journey. Here is some of what you will find inside the chapters:

Wise Women

I am really happy to include the voices and wisdom of wise women throughout the book. The reason I include each one is that each, in some way, has inspired me on my journey. I hope their stories, experiences, and knowledge can do the same for you.

Experts

Similar to the wise women, the experts I have interviewed for this book have guided me in some way, whether I had the honour of meeting them in person or was inspired by their work, books, or messages.

Resources

I have included at the end of each chapter the resources, websites, and blogs that I regularly referred to (and still do) for inspiration, wisdom, and focus.

Steps Beyond

In each chapter, I include suggestions for steps you can take to implement the ideas. These are all based on my own steps and experiences, so I hope they work for you too.

CHAPTER ONE

First Steps

All you really need to do is accept this moment fully. You are then at ease in the here and now and at ease with yourself.

—Eckhart Tolle, *The Power of Now*

This chapter focuses on our mind—the importance of connecting with it and how we do this on a regular basis to make the greatest difference. I explore connecting with our minds again, clearing our minds of what we don't need, and the amazing feeling of connection with ourselves when we do. This ultimately leads us to the inner wisdom our minds hold—of our skills, talents, and what we can achieve. The information we need is available to us all, either stored within us or around us—we just need to access it. Here I provide you with the steps to do just that. This is an exciting first step and one that I hope will reshape your life the way it has mine. So, let's start . . .

Being Present

I think one of the key starting points on my journey was learning the importance of the present moment. This really was life changing. I think it is easy as parents to spend a lot of time focusing on "life before children"—I certainly did. So it is an important starting point to acknowledge where we are right now. This is your starting point, your place to grow and take your steps from—the present moment.

The early years of parenting really take us back to a slower pace. We need to cocoon ourselves, which may seem hard, but in this process, we can find patterns that we never knew of before. I started to explore the power of being in the present through small things, like taking a walk with my daughter and discovering the beauty of nature. I think one of the greatest gifts our babies bring us is this opportunity to become truly present. They provide a regular, daily practice of connecting with this part of life, a part that might have been lost very early on. And by staying in the present ourselves, we also keep our children in the present moment for as long as possible. We can avoid saying what we are doing tomorrow or later and just live right there and right then.

It also became clear to me that the greatest time to connect with the present is when we have young children. They come into the world fully in the present moment. They are not thinking about the past or looking into the future. They live there and then, in that very moment. And look at the joy they experience as a result. This really is a gift from our children.

I came from a culture that was "busy busy" all the time. If you asked someone how they were, generally the answer would be "busy." To be honest, it always felt slightly uneasy, the whole idea that "busy" represented a form of success and a better kind of day. So when I was forced out of this mentality when I had children, I felt like I started to connect with myself again, my own flow. Children slow you right down, even though there is so much to do. The ongoing practice of breastfeeding and stepping out of the hustle and bustle has taught me so much that I think it has changed my outlook forever.

I found that once I started to connect with the present moment, I could start to see all that I already had and then the steps I could follow from there. All the anxiety, tension, and questioning about where you are melts away when you start to focus on the present moment. I found that I could stop searching and questioning and start to enjoy where I was instead.

I can say all this now, but it wasn't an easy conclusion to come to. There were days and days when I envied my husband going into the office while I was at home wondering how on earth I could manage another day of entertaining, feeding, and cleaning up after two young children. What I came to appreciate, though, in that very present moment was that I could find the calmness and peace that I really needed to enjoy the day with the children. It took me out of my head and put me into the moment, and there is such power in that. I truly started to accept where I was at that point and that it was where I was meant to be. From that point, I could grow. I just needed to work out how.

So how do we connect with the present? I found a lot of inspiration in the words of Eckhart Tolle in *The Power of Now*. When I read it, I consumed it so quickly, it was like I drank up every single word. I recognised how to just stop and be present and enjoy the moment. And when you do that, the magic appears, the wonder of life emerges, and opportunities unfold.

Steps Beyond

- ► Let go of the old habit of "busy." It is very different from being productive, progressive, and growing. Focus on getting to where you need to go and achieving what you need to throughout the day, but not in a rushed way.
- ► Limit talk about what is happening later or tomorrow. Concentrate on right there and then.

Children Are Our Greatest Teachers

Once we have learnt to be present, I believe that children can show us the way as much as we can guide them. They can help us grow the way we can with them. But we need to be aware of it; we need to recognise the moment. All too often, we view children as being difficult, when in fact they are just nudging us to grow.

I am sure that our children's need for us is balanced with our need for them to reshape our lives and future patterns. As I was exploring this concept, I came across the work of Dr Shefali Tsabary, author of *The Conscious Parent*. This is what she had to say about learning from our children:

> While we believe we hold the power to raise our children, the reality is that our children hold the power to raise us into the parents they need us to become. For this reason, the parenting experience isn't one of parent versus child but of parent with child. The road to wholeness sits in our children's lap, and all we need to do is take a seat. As our children show us our way back to our own essence, they become our greatest awakeners. If we fail to hold their hand and follow their lead as they usher us through the gateway of increased consciousness, we lose the chance to walk towards our own enlightenment.

Although it can seem like children are stopping us from moving forward, I think in many ways they are doing the very opposite—they are freeing us from the patterns and routines we create that are stopping us from living our authentic, free lives. Stepping out can be so freeing, but like any habit, you may feel drawn back to it for a long time. The early years of full-time caregiving forces you out of these patterns. And when the intensity of caregiving lessens, many women realise they no longer want to go back to the old way of life. This is when we can start to see the potential of how we can live and how we can shape our own lives with work, well-being, and happiness.

Once you put your ego aside and start to live in the present, what becomes very clear is that children are here to teach us. If you listen hard enough, you will learn the very lessons that will help you grow, develop your work, improve your well-being, and find your dreams and passions again—all through your children.

One way children teach us is by reconnecting us to the need for flexibility. The early years make you realise that although routine is important, being flexible and open to plans changing at any time is not only necessary but in many ways good for us. Children also connect us with our communities. It becomes harder to travel, so spending time locally can become so important and remind you of the value of local communities. Children show you as well that there is no such thing as perfection. We can strive, and we can learn and grow, but perfection does not exist. Another thing children can teach us is that there is so much beauty and happiness in the simple parts of life. They have also taught me that it feels good to care for another and that it is important to care for myself in order to do that. Ultimately, these lessons show up when you are not showing up as your true self. I don't think anyone else will make these lessons clearer to you, and this is truly valuable information.

Steps Beyond

- ▶ Connect with the flow of your children. Align as closely as possible with their daily rhythm (e.g., running around outside with them, going to bed early as possible).
- ▶ Watch your children and how they are when they are living in the moment—see the wonder and joy. Store that feeling of wonder and joy, to remind you.

Working the Mind Again

Engaging the mind again was one of the key first steps in my personal journey. The moment I started to focus on my brain again after the years of caring for my children was a defining moment. I can't tell you how great it felt when I started to pay attention to the importance of working my mind. I found it had really disconnected, although I never fully realised the impact of how this was making me feel. I felt disconnected and disengaged, and, as a result, I felt a huge sense of apathy. I had never given any thought to the importance of working my mind in the past, because it was just something I did when I was working in an office on a daily basis. But after years of intense caregiving, I realised quite how important it was to my well-being, motivation, and ability to move forward.

I somehow knew I needed to work on this, and every time I did, I felt more and more alive, more engaged, and more inspired. So, as much as possible, this became a daily practice. I would watch TED talks, which I found stimulated a part of my consciousness. They made me think and develop my thoughts and opinions, and, with that, they brought confidence in myself. I sought out talks that were different from my day-to-day life, that connected my thoughts and brain with a different part of life. I watched TED talks on well-being, education, and so much more. I started to read articles connected to women and work, and I found the more I read, the more I started to unlock my natural passions.

I found that this not only needed to be a regular practice but it needed to happen as early in the day as possible. In the very early years with my daughter, I always used to work, read, and connect with the wider world via email or social media in the hours that she slept. The more I engaged my mind, the more I realised how much I needed it. The smallest amount made all the difference in re-engaging myself. Just as we fire up our metabolisms through exercise in the morning, we can fire up our brains through mental exercise. I find my brain functions so much more efficiently when I kickstart it as early in the day as possible. Even now, if I don't start my day with some "brain work," it is much harder to find my flow throughout the rest of the day.

Starting with my brain was so powerful—it really was. It made me start to understand myself and find confidence in myself. It is so important to keep searching for the right content to engage you, whether it's a talk, a blog, or something else—keep working your brain as a priority.

Here are a few of the TED talks that really got me thinking and helped ignite a flame in my mind:

- ▶ Ken Robinson, "Changing Education Paradigms." This talk reminded me about how our natural skills can be lost and how if we keep searching, we can find them. They are in us, but maybe the school system has not unlocked them.
- ▶ Steve Jobs, "How to Live Before You Die." This talk ignited a flame in me. This was really about following your own journey, having the courage to follow your heart, and not wasting time living anyone else's life.

Steps Beyond

- ▶ Start the day by utilizing your brain (even in the smallest form).
- ▶ Leave the less complex jobs (like admin or washing) until later in the day. Write your plans, write blog posts, or do whatever you need to do to engage your brain first.
- ▶ Make it a priority to find talks, vlogs, websites, or other resources that inspire you.
- ▶ Notice how you feel when you connect with content you need and that will help you grow.

Clearing Your Mind

I found that an important element to working my mind was that I had to clear it of content that wasn't serving me. After becoming a mother, I became increasingly concerned about the content, media, and information projected towards mothers. I felt the implication that the moment you become a mother, you lose your individual identity. I found this message in media (advertisements), general content, and just day-to-day living. I didn't feel fed with anything that inspired or engaged me. I longed for those moments in the supermarket (my one visit out for the day with a young baby) that I could come away from having connected with the wider world. I desired in those moments to stretch my mind, learn, or engage. Instead, I found the messages disempowering and dumbed down. They filled my mind in a way that I didn't want.

In the short moments that my mind wasn't focused on caring for my baby, I wanted it to be filled with positivity, inspiration, and wisdom. My dream was to create a place that would provide everything that I searched for after becoming a mother—inspiring information, opportunities to grow, well-being advice, and support. This is one of the reasons I created beyondtheschoolrun.com.

I remember thinking, *Why can't the receipts at tills have interesting facts on them?* Why couldn't the messages on posters not try and sell something but share with me something new and informative, so that I felt I had taken a step forward?

So I selectively decided to disconnect from this information. If it meant limiting myself from media, so be it. I was so emotionally highly tuned after having children that the information that I processed needed to be pure, authentic, and beneficial to my growth or learnings as a parent. Also, my time to connect with content was limited, so the content needed to be positive, engaging, and empowering.

I would turn the radio off when the news came on, not only to shelter my children's clear, positive minds from the negativity but also to shelter my own mind. I started to filter information that was creating such negativity. The little time I did engage with external content, I was very selective. I sought only information to grow, strengthen, and develop my mind. I craved engaging information when I was out with my children, information that would spark a light in my mind, so I looked for it. I started to read, and I found the very people who inspired me with wisdom, insight, and ideas.

Early on in my journey with BeyondTheSchoolRun, I was invited to a screening of *Miss Representation*. I went with little understanding of what I was about to see, but it became very clear that I had been fed with many "stories" throughout the years as a woman. Along with a group of women at the screening, I was shocked to learn how much cultural stereotyping had gone into my subconscious without question. I think it has become so ingrained in us as a society that we don't even really understand that some of the messages and beliefs are there. And in so many ways, they are limiting our potential.

I experienced this on the way to my first meeting at No. 10 Downing Street. It was during the school holidays, and I remember taking both children on the train to drop them off at my husband's office so I could go to the meeting whilst he looked after them. I remember two nice gentlemen helped me with the buggy on the train and we started chatting. They asked me where I was going, but before I answered, they assumed I was off shopping. I didn't tell them I was in fact off to meet the Prime Minister's advisor, but what struck me was their assumption that because I was a mother, I was most likely going shopping rather than working. I doubt very much that if my husband had been the one with the children, they would have made the same assumption. I think that, over time, that mindset—those day-to-day conversations, thoughts, and assumptions—impacts women.

I dreamt, instead, of creating places on every high street where mothers could pop in and be inspired, engaged, and connected. They could watch a TED talk whilst their children slept, read about the latest world developments, or hear about changes in the working world. All in a bright, inspiring space that felt so exciting. When mothers give birth, they have done the most creative thing on this planet. To give birth and not nurture this newfound potential and strength would be a loss to families and the world. The places I dreamt of would do this nurturing step-by-step. I imagined a mother relighting the spark every time she stepped into this environment where she had the space to explore her potential, opportunities, and talents. I longed for this kind of space, and I hope I can bring it into the world one day.

In the meantime, I've learnt a few things. I learnt I needed to filter the information that was coming at me. Newspapers no longer provided what I needed. In fact, the content was all too often so negative that it didn't help engage my thoughts. I selectively decided to not watch so much TV in the evenings. Instead I sought content that filled me with positivity and inspiration and developed my thoughts. This came from content like TED, books by Brené Brown, and new up-and-coming role models such as Ella Woodward.

Steps Beyond

- ▶ Become your own editor. Turn off the radio or TV when negative stories come on.
- ▶ Question the information that is coming at you and your children.

Finding Your Element

I believe the next key step in your journey is recognizing that we all have skills and talents that we can start utilizing once we unlock them. I passionately believe that the point at which we have children is an opportunity to explore our natural skills and talents again. Those skills may have gotten lost or hidden away, but they become available to us again at this time.

The early years of having a child, the time focused purely on caregiving, can really shed a lot of what we don't need. The time we have available becomes so limited that it is a valuable time to think deeply about what works for you and what doesn't and about what truly makes you happy. I think working this out—really identifying what we truly love doing, what lifts and empowers us—is so valuable to us going forward. This also applies to work. The time out of the workplace can force us out of the pattern that has been created over many years, often since we were in the education system. In many ways, we have been institutionalised into the nine-to-five working pattern from very early on, and removing ourselves from that pattern can be hard. However, I think the intense early period of parenting can do this, and therefore it can leave us clear and free to choose a new path—one that will provide us with a long-term approach to life and work.

For many, the way we worked before no longer fits alongside caring for young children, so we are forced to reassess our choices. We can dig deep and start to follow a new path. Even though we know that this new way is right for us, we may not know where it is leading. This type of work often doesn't provide the framework that our previous jobs gave us—but it just might give us purpose and happiness and might lead us to far greater places than we ever imagined.

I also think our children can remind us of our own childhood. They can remind us of times or opportunities that we would never have revisited otherwise. This may happen when your children start sports, or ballet, or whatever their new interest is. It will bring to the surface what you explored and connected with as a child. For children, the dream is infinite, and yet many of our dreams diminish over time. But when you start to find what you love to do, what fills you, then your dreams start to come to life again. I think it is important for our children to see us living this way. It is showing them that our skills, dreams, and passions are all linked, that they are with us forever, that they can provide us with happiness and well-being, and that we can support others, the world, and the economy.

For example, when I was younger, I used to see advertisements in the newspaper about writing courses and was always drawn to them. Yet I thought there was no way I could write. I wasn't particularly good at English in school, and I even lost one of my early jobs in a big PR agency because they said I couldn't write! On my journey with BeyondTheSchoolRun, I have realised it isn't about writing—it is about you, your voice, your passion, and your values. Once you are clear about these, whatever platform you choose—whether that is a book, a website, or something else—this will shine through.

I think it is so important to go back to when there were no limits or barriers to your dreams, when you were free to connect with whatever felt right. Go back to before the limiting beliefs crept in. My story of losing an early job because they said I couldn't write is a perfect example. This removed me from what was clearly a deep passion. So do not be put off or distracted. It is much more about our own deep belief that we can do what we dream of.

The book I first read on this topic is by Sir Ken Robinson. Reading *Finding Your Element* was a defining moment for me. In it, Robinson writes: "I believe passionately that we are all born with tremendous natural capacities, and that we lose touch with many of them as we spend time in the world. Ironically, one of the main reasons this happens is education. The result is that too many people never connect with their true talents and therefore don't know what they're really capable of achieving."

In the intensity of caregiving, we often need to disconnect from the wider world. This gives us space to remove ourselves from the labels and the stories we have previously relied on, and we can reconnect with and unlock our natural skills and talents. We can truly find what we were always meant to do; we can rediscover our dreams and purpose. We just need to start taking steps towards it.

When I started to really explore this for myself, I realised that returning to the work I did before I had children required a lot of energy, and I wondered if it was something that truly lit me up. As I started to develop the idea for beyondtheschoolrun.com, I found it gave me something I never realised I could receive from work—it gave me vision, energy, and purpose. The more I worked on the website, the more it became part of me. There was no divide between work and BeyondTheSchoolRun—it was part of who I was. It created a space for me to understand and unlock my skills and talents while doing the same for others.

I am not saying, in any way, that it is easy. Many of us have been programmed in many different ways, conditioned by society about what is deemed as success and what isn't. But this journey is about creating a new legacy for future generations to live by. It is a way to collectively utilise skills and talents and to work together rather than in isolation. It recognises that we all have individual talents and that when those talents are found, we can work alongside caregiving, healing, and other key elements of life.

Looking back at the days when I worked in PR, I did well. I was even running my own business. But what stands out to me now is that I never felt truly authentic. I was good at it, and I believe I am still good at PR, because I have much experience with it. But there is a difference in what I do now in my work with BeyondTheSchoolRun—it feels truly and deeply natural, like it is part of me. And although the path isn't clear, the feeling it gives me is so different from anything I knew before in terms of work. Robinson writes about this in *Finding Your Element*. He says that "when people are in their Element, they connect with something fundamental to their sense of identity, purpose, and well-being."

When I worked in PR, if someone asked what I did, I almost felt uneasy answering. I had to take a deep breath before explaining, as if there was a detachment between work and leisure or home life. I found public speaking so incredibly difficult, and yet I never questioned that this wasn't my path. I love it now when people speak to me about BeyondTheSchoolRun. There is no divide between myself and my work. I think that, as women, we crave authenticity in what we are doing. That doesn't mean we can't sell, grow businesses, and thrive; it just means we have to dig deep, remove the labels, and be clear about who we are.

I think it is like fitness. The more you practice this part of you, the stronger and more natural it becomes. You will connect with these talents more quickly and feel daily benefits from tapping into them. That amazing feeling you get from moving your body is there when you use your skills and talents, too. It isn't easy. Ideally, we would all grow into our "element" throughout the school years whilst nurtured and supported by our parents, so that by the time we step into the wider world, we are ready and prepared to share and earn from our gifts. All too often, this hasn't happened, and in your current situation, you are unlikely to have that support in place. But you can still make it happen. You just need to find your own way. And I really believe that at any point when you are open, you can take the steps to do this.

It can take time to rediscover what you are meant to do. It is a transition process. For some, the result may seem so unlikely. But if someone had said to me before I had children that I would develop an online business based on supporting mothers and would be invited to No. 10 Downing Street, I would never have believed them. It was a step-by-step process of believing in myself and unravelling and testing out my passions and skills. I have met a lot of mothers who have transitioned or are transitioning into careers that they feel are more "them" and add more meaning to their lives. I hear so many say that they can't go back. And I think for many, finding what was more natural could have been done with much greater ease while raising a family.

So what seems at the time to be a loss of self through becoming a mother can in fact be a finding of ourselves. As we slowly unravel each element of who we really are, the reward of this keeps us going and focused. The finding of self is one of the greatest gifts, and I believe we don't have to travel far to find it; it is right here in the parenting process.

If we didn't unlock it first as children, I believe we have a second chance during our journey as parents.

Steps Beyond

- ▶ Dream big, not small.
- ▶ Look back on your early years. What was it that you always wanted to do?
- ▶ Reconnect with passions you had as a child. Share them with others, and don't doubt them.
- ▶ Try different things and watch how they make you feel. Do they light you up inside?
- ▶ When you do find what lights you up, keep trying to find it again.
- ▶ Explore information about your talents and passions. Look for books and resources that you are drawn to.
- ▶ Watch your children as they follow their instincts and connect with what they love.

- ▶ Find what you love. Even if it's different from others, follow your path. Follow your heart and keep going.
- ▶ Be open to new opportunities in terms of work, utilizing your skills, and connecting with the wider world.
- ▶ Ask yourself these questions to determine if your work is right for you: Do you stop noticing time? When you are done, do you feel inspired and happy? Do you want to work in this area at any given time?

Resources

Miss Representation: http://therepresentationproject.org/film/miss-representation

Robinson, Ken. *Finding Your Element: How to Discover Your Talents and Passions and Transform Your Life.* New York: Viking, 2013. Find more information at www.sirkenrobinson.com.

TED: www.ted.com

Tolle, Eckhart. *The Power of Now.* Vancouver: Namaste Publishing, 1999. Find more information at www.eckharttolle.com/books/now.

Tsabary, Shefali. *The Conscious Parent: Transforming Ourselves, Empowering Our Children.* Vancouver: Namaste Publishing, 2010. Find more information at https://drshefali.com.

CHAPTER TWO

Making the Connection

The most terrible poverty is loneliness.

—Mother Teresa

I n the early years of caring for my children, I often felt an incredible sense of isolation. It doesn't seem to make sense, when you are regularly, all day, with another human being. And yet not connecting with the outside world felt like a loss for me. What I came to realise was that I didn't need to make a lot of connections throughout the day but that the ones I did make needed to feel right and fill me. This is what we explore in detail in this chapter.

Whilst caring for your children, you may have only small windows of time available, and those windows may be unpredictable and limited. So you need to become very clear about how to connect, and who you need to connect with, to take steps forward.

I learnt that the starting point of each day has to be connecting with yourself, because once you have done that, your connections with others will happen far more naturally. Then I think making authentic connections throughout the day is so important. They fill you up, the way that great food does. Anything else will just leave you searching for more.

Connecting with Yourself

It's so easy to lose yourself in the journey of parenthood, and in the intensity of caregiving, and in everything else that goes with it. I remember my mind feeling so full and yet so empty of inspiration. I love my children so much, but I needed to work out what I loved beyond them in order to be a better, stronger mother who could then treasure my time with them so much more.

I don't think the sense of isolation comes from not being around others. I think it comes from a lack of connection with our true selves. This lack of connection with ourselves then leads to connections with others that don't feel authentic—where people don't see or understand the true you. So we need to start with ourselves before others can connect with us. We need to know our true self and bring this into the world. Then any connection, whether online or face to face, will feel fulfilling.

By connecting with yourself, you start to unlock your values. Your values have always been with you, but they may have been slightly tucked away over time for various reasons. I have always found working in a kind and compassionate way fits well with me, and yet when I entered the workplace, I was told that I couldn't be both nice and successful in business. At one of my early jobs in a large PR firm, they told me that I would either sink or swim. But I now find myself really aligned with my truest values; they are a core part of who I am.

I had never really thought about my dreams and personal purpose before starting this journey, but now I can see how incredibly important they are in our lives. They guide us, set us free, fill us with joy, and connect us to others and ourselves. Only when you lose the connection with yourself do you realise quite how important it is.

When I first started BeyondTheSchoolRun, I found very few people talking about the subject of women and equality. But each time I read an article or saw someone doing something in this area, it took me a step closer to believing in my vision and, ultimately, myself. I remember when I first tweeted Anne-Marie Slaughter and she responded so positively to BeyondTheSchoolRun. You may not be connecting with someone face to face, but the connection with their words and thoughts can help you connect with yourself. These connections, whether online, face to face, or just an awareness, are so important in supporting us in connecting with ourselves. I soon started to see an industry emerge with more and more people speaking out and supporting and empowering mothers and parents.

What I realised is there are no barriers to us following our dreams—the only thing stopping us is ourselves. The labels we put on ourselves and on others are what stop us. As with everything, we need to start with ourselves, without judgment for others. When you start with yourself, the world truly changes around you. When you focus on your own self-growth, you no longer compare and contrast because you understand that we all have our own stories; we all have our own journeys lived and yet to be lived. When you are kind to yourself, you are kind to others. Start with you, and the rest will follow.

The more you can connect with your true, authentic self, the more you will empower others to do the same.

As part of connecting with yourself and your values, I think finding your true voice is really important in supporting your growth and your work. This, for me, means speaking from a very authentic place and not compromising my values.

I think that as a woman, there is no doubt that communication is so important, but taking the time to look at what information you share through words is also important. Really starting to speak based on your true values can feel very different from just speaking. This means speaking from an authentic part of yourself and sharing your ideas, views, and intentions with a clear voice.

How do you find your values? Many of us have worked for organisations where we take on their company values. But this is about finding our own values, which can then guide our work moving forward. Your values have always been with you, but I have found they have often become tucked away over time. For example, I was always passionate about supporting others, collaboration, and kindness. When I entered the workplace, this was always seen as a weakness, so I tucked it away. Now I am very clear that this is a core part of who I am. On this journey, I have also unlocked values I was never aware of consciously. For example, authenticity is important to me—people speaking their truth, being open and honest and true to themselves—and I apply this to all of my work. Once we start to align with our values, I think our work becomes much clearer and who we work with becomes clearer along with our vision.

Take time to notice how you feel when you are speaking your truth and are aligned with your values. You will find it feels right and that you don't leave the conversation questioning anything you said. When your voice is out of alignment, it often feels strange and lacks connection. Test your voice out. It may take time to find your authentic voice, but once you focus on it, you will see the difference.

I only gradually started to speak out. It was daunting to me. I would feel so nervous every time, but the more I did it, the stronger I felt. And what was amazing was that people connected with me when I spoke about what I believed in and my intentions with BeyondTheSchoolRun! I didn't need to pursue or convince; I just spoke from the heart. The more you share your message and the more you find your voice, the more you find out about yourself.

Steps Beyond

▶ Work out your values. Think back over your career and look at the values that have been important to you.

- ► Look at your behaviour and when you are most comfortable with yourself. This may show your values.
- ► Make connecting with yourself a key part of each day. Find the ways that help you do that.
- ► When you start to find them, write them down, focus on them, and stay true to them.
- ► Start connecting with your dreams. Write them down. Create a vision for yourself.
- ► Speak daily about what you believe in or are working towards.
- ► If you don't connect with a particular conversation, don't engage; just listen.
- ► Don't engage in gossip.
- ► Put your hand up at lectures or talks. Don't be afraid to talk about what you are doing or ask questions.
- ► Don't be thrown off course by people who don't get you or what you are saying. Focus on the ones that do.

Connecting at the School Gates

I think it's also important not to underestimate the potential of the school gates community. For me, the school gates community are the people you are in contact with on a regular basis through your children—this could be people at nursery or school that you see on a regular basis through your children's routine. In the early days of setting up BeyondTheSchoolRun, I had little time to interact outside my community and the school gates, so I found the connection there so valuable. The whole reason for creating BeyondTheSchoolRun was that I was surprised by the amount of talent being wasted at the school gates every day.

I found that by opening up the conversation to topics beyond our children and really engaging in work, I gained some great expertise that I am very grateful for. I remember speaking with one dad, Rob, whom I had never spoken with before. We had that usual small window of time at pickup, and in that time, I asked him about his work and told him about mine. It turned out that he was a specialist in customer web usability and was on a break between jobs. He offered his wisdom and provided such invaluable guidance for me when I was at the point of relaunching the second phase of beyondtheschoolrun.com. If I had only spoken about the children and not focused on us as individuals and our work, we may never have gotten to that point of connection, which was transformative for my work. It was all there—the information and knowledge was right where I was. I just had to see it.

This was such an important realization for me that I wrote an article about it for *The Guardian* (12 May 2014):

Why Does No One Ask What I Did before Having Children?

Since I became a parent and took some time out from work, there is one question that is asked of me less and less: "What did you do before you had children?"

Before children, our careers, skills, training and everything in between were a pivotal part of our lives and our identities, but for some reason, after children, they are rarely spoken about.

I set up beyondtheschoolrun.com in March 2012 because I came aware of the amount of skills drifting away from the school gates each day and the impact this was having on mothers, families, society and the economy at large.

Since launching the enterprise, I have spoken with a huge number of mothers about the challenges of returning to the workplace in the hours available to them. There have been some notable steps forward in recent years when it comes to opening up these issues, but to me there is still a significant piece of the puzzle missing. Together, we can take a giant leap towards completing that puzzle by starting to ask the question: "What did you do before having children?"

Why is this question so rarely asked? I was recently speaking to a local mother about this very subject and why we don't talk about it. For her, it was just too painful to look back. She loved her job, but now that she has children and her husband has a successful career, she finds it hard to justify working in the same way.

Another mother looked shocked and said she hadn't been asked this question for over 10 years. Another wrote to me via the website, telling me how she found her way back into the workplace by setting up her own business to fit around school hours. In her last sentence, she said, "I am amazed at how we don't seem to ask each other what we did before we had kids or what we are passionate about. Firstly, I am mum, but behind that, I am me, and that person is pretty interesting too!"

What is holding us back? Is it our own mindsets? At the point at which a woman becomes a mother, do the unspoken barriers set in, both in our minds and in the minds of others? I have often found myself in situations where my husband is asked what he does but no one asks me the same question.

Yet asking this very simple, sometimes painful question can also be extremely positive. If I hadn't asked, I would never have found the two very people who helped me to set up BTSR: a lawyer I met at the school gates and a local mother running a website business.

I have come to realise that this very question could be incredibly powerful in collectively unlocking our talents and skills, at the very place that we started our journeys in the first place: the school gates! Just imagine what this could lead to. New business partnerships, mentoring, start-ups, inspiration, childcare solutions, improvements in the education system . . . the potential is huge.

So shall we give it a go? Next time you have a coffee with another parent or stop to chat at the school gates, ask the question, "What did you do before kids?" Let's see where the journey takes us. I for one think it could be very exciting for us all.

We can get very caught up in the idea that everything needs to be created in agencies in the cities, but really, the skills are in us. Whether you are in an office in the city or at the school gates, the knowledge is still there. You just need to unlock it. When I was first planning to set up beyondtheschoolrun.com, I was still of the mindset that I needed the expertise of agencies with recognised reputations. I went to see one based in London who had been referred to me. As my budget was small but my dream big, I didn't question that someone wouldn't get it. The owner of the agency said she didn't think they could help and didn't think there was much hope for the concept. That very conversation could have stopped me in my tracks, but instead it made me realise that I needed to do exactly what I was proposing with BeyondTheSchoolRun. I needed to work with the parent talent. That is exactly what I have done, and it has been the best decision ever. It has kept my costs low, the flexibility is great, and the expertise is incredible.

Steps Beyond

- ► Ask to meet with people who may be able to advise or guide you. Be proactive and approach people you wish to connect with.
- ► Ask about work. Ask what people did before, what they are doing now, or what plans they have for the future.
- ► Don't judge or make assumptions.
- ► Be present. It doesn't matter how long or little time you are at the school gates; be present.
- ► Steer conversations at the school gates away from the children and towards work, business, or areas of interest.

Connecting with the Working World

Whether you are coming to this as a parent who is already working but wanting to find another way or you are a parent who is coming from full-time caregiving, the starting point is to explore what is right for you. Again, we are all different, but what connects us is the need to nurture our children while still utilizing and sharing our skills.

For me, I had to really work out who I was in terms of work. I had set up a business before, but was I truly an entrepreneur? I knew the journey wasn't an easy one. But once you work it out, you can settle into who you truly are and stop resisting it. Whether you work best within an organization, by running your own business with support, or as freelancer, creating a level of flexibility and freedom is key to all human beings.

So how do we work this out? We start to explore. The first step is connecting with other people. I really think connecting with the right people is like joining the dots. You don't have time to attend lots of meetings or networking events, so finding a way to connect with the right people for you and your work is so important.

Sometimes it can seem like so much effort to leave the house, arrange childcare, and remove yourself from the home. And yet it is so important to connect again with the wider world, to engage and explore. It can be invigorating, and it can remind you of parts of yourself you had forgotten. Recognizing the right events to go to is important, but it is just as important to actually go and not come up with excuses not to take that step.

I know how comfortable it can become to just stay home, and yet at times the comfort can become stifling. That is the point at which you need to step out, explore a little. You may not need much—a meeting, a networking event, whatever it is—but it will stretch you and you will return feeling more fulfilled than before. I sometimes found I could go to an event and be back in only a couple of hours and feel like I had achieved so much in that short time.

You don't always have to meet face-to-face to make a connection. A connection is made easily when it is with the right person and your values are aligned. So being proactive is important, but pushing is not. There will be people who get what you are doing and others who really don't. Hold onto the feeling when people do get it, and don't be dismayed by those who don't. I found this a challenge, as I was so keen to share my passion for BeyondTheSchoolRun that when I spoke with someone that didn't understand, it could throw me off course. I learnt to focus on those times people did understand and recognise the fact that not everyone would—and that was OK.

There is no doubt we need others to help us move forward, but doing that from where you are whilst caring for your children requires a new approach. It is easy to keep going on your own, but, just like your children, others challenge you to grow and move forward. It took me a while to work this out. For a long time, I just kept going on my own when I really needed to reach out to others.

It's not about knowing a lot of people, though. It is about connecting with the right ones for you. It's not about arranging a lot of meetings; it's about arranging the right ones for you. It's about finding a new way of connecting—authentically with ease, flow, and purpose.

When you are working this way, you need to tune into your intuition. If something doesn't fill you with excitement and you don't feel drawn to make it happen, it's likely not the right thing. Meeting less people can be more productive—it's more important to connect with the right ones.

Steps Beyond

- ▶ Be yourself. Be authentic, whether in person or online.
- ▶ Follow your instincts about who to connect with. You don't have to follow up on every lead. Wait until the right person comes along.
- ▶ Don't attach yourself to an outcome with a person. One conversation or meeting may be all that's necessary to gather the information or lessons you need.
- ▶ Share your news and developments with other people.

- ▶ Don't attend every networking event. Wait until you feel a real pull to attend.
- ▶ Don't create the outcome in your head before the event.

Connecting on Social Media

Once you have explored your authentic voice in day-to-day conversation, you can start looking at your public voice and testing it. One way to do this and to connect is on social media. For me, this has been life changing. Before I started the website, I knew very little about social media. Setting up BeyondTheSchoolRun forced me to connect with it and learn.

I think when you are out of the workplace for a period of time, it is easy to feel like the digital world has moved on beyond you. I think it is also then challenging to see our place on it. It is easy to feel we are not connected with it. But it takes us to make that connection and to recognise that this world is available to us as it is everyone else. I know this can seem like a big barrier when you have had time away from the workplace, but it really isn't. In fact, I think that the digital age has been created for people like us—mothers who need to make their lives work for them. Once you engage with it, you will understand the freedom and opportunities it will bring to you. Whether you are growing a business, looking for a flexible role, or wanting to retrain, the digital world is a gift to us all.

I asked **Fiona Flintham**, online marketing strategist, for her top tips on connecting with social media and how to make it really work for you.

Find Your Tribe

A great first step to developing your confidence in this online world is to find an existing, active, and engaged community on Facebook. One of the most powerful benefits of Facebook is the active communities that are being built every day. Just

Google "best Facebook groups for . . ." and you'll find masses of round-up posts directing you to the best communities in your field. These are places to fine-tune and hone your social media skills whilst getting support and encouragement in a topic area that matters to you.

Get Savvy Support

It is worth spending time in these Facebook groups. Introduce yourself and spend time listening to what others are saying. Get involved and start to post when you feel you have something to share. Whether it be a sympathetic "virtual ear" or active encouragement and advice, you'll be amazed at how responsive these communities are.

Spread Your Wings

I often hear from small business owners that they don't know what to post on social media. By starting out in an active Facebook Group, either as a support network or as research (or both), you'll see the sorts of things that get a lot of interaction. It's an invaluable insight into what people are looking for in terms of products, services, and support, and you'll learn what people love to see and engage with on social media. This will give you the confidence to start to build up your own social media presence online.

Start Simple

When you're ready to build your own presence on social media as a new business or as an expert or consultant, focus on just one platform. Facebook might seem like the obvious choice, but because it is mainstream, it's also very crowded. If your target market is also on Twitter, Instagram, or Pinterest, then you're likely to find it easier to build a following there.

Get Good at It

Commit to mastering just one platform. Take a shortcut and do an online course to learn what you need (rather than trying to figure it all out on your own). Lynda.com and Udemy.com have masses of high-quality, low-price courses to help you get started.

The first step is to just commit to opening your mind to connecting with social media. It doesn't require a lot of time spent. My first step was setting up an account on Twitter and starting to establish my voice and opinions and connect with others. It felt so empowering to go beyond my kitchen table and meet and engage with others, albeit through Twitter. I think that initial connection can empower you to explore other social media platforms. I then went on to set up the Facebook page for BeyondTheSchoolRun and engage with a community. This gave me so much strength in what I was doing. I gained confidence in my work every time someone acknowledged or agreed with a post. It took me a while to set up on Instagram, but when I did, it again opened me up to another world. I found I could really discover the people and the businesses that shared the same values and ethos, my "tribe," and share a little more from my heart. Each platform is so valuable and is available to us all, free and completely empowering.

Steps Beyond

- ▶ Embrace social media! Don't make excuses.
- ▶ Ask someone you know to help get you set up if you aren't familiar with a platform.
- ▶ Be open to learning.

> ► Explore different platforms to find the ones most useful and empowering for you.

Connecting with Your Skills

For many mothers who have taken time out of the workplace, or who are currently in a job that isn't fulfilling, finding space to re-skill is important. I have spent much time in my work with BeyondTheSchoolRun doing just that. This doesn't require days or a lot of money. You really can skill yourself for no cost in the hours and places free to you.

There are certain people I started to read about when I created BeyondTheSchoolRun, and they have provided me with such incredible wisdom and learnings through their vlogs, blogs, and content. For example, whenever possible, I would watch the videos at MarieForleo.com to train myself daily, step-by-step. The information is out there and available to you when you need it. And you don't need to spend hours in the classroom; five minutes a day can be enough.

Volunteering is another way to gain skills. I think we view volunteering only as giving time to a charity, but in my experience, sharing your work for free can also change and benefit people's lives, including your own. When I started BeyondTheSchoolRun, I didn't have any specific experience in creating a social enterprise, so I went out and shared what I had for free. I spoke at events when I could. I wrote blogs and shared what I had learnt on my journey. I think at these times, when you are learning your trade again or you are simply discovering your own confidence to do what you do naturally, offering your services for free can give you as much back as you are giving away.

I learnt and rediscovered skills that I never knew I had by working this way. I started writing a monthly newsletter. My husband asked why I was writing this newsletter, and I remember thinking that I didn't know why, but I just felt I needed to. It was each of those newsletters that provided the framework for this book. I didn't know that at the time, but it gave me the passion again to write, and it also stored information about what I was thinking and learning.

I think the power of volunteering goes beyond us giving our time. It can really help us start to connect again with ourselves, with the workplace, and with our talents. I think by volunteering, we can start to rediscover our skills and purpose. It doesn't matter how long or how little time you offer; it can give you what you need to take your steps. Especially if you are moving into a new sector, you are on a learning path. You need to unlock your skills, but it takes time to do so and to have true belief in them. And in my experience, volunteering is a great way to do it. Just go out and share what you love, whatever it is.

I think at any stage of our lives, when we are looking for what we are meant to do, volunteering our skills can be invaluable to others. But each of us will connect differently to different causes. So, again, this is very individual to you and very specific to igniting your passion and your soul's purpose. Stay focused on what really works. Be careful not to see this as charity. This is a skill exchange—which I think is an incredibly powerful idea and will be what, in time, creates the real change we need to see in the world. My long-term dream for BeyondTheSchoolRun is to create a mothers' skill exchange across the world. That one piece of advice, that one contact from a mother in the Western world, could change the path for another mother in the undeveloped world. So keep taking those steps; we need your talents and skills.

You will be learning your craft for free but getting so much in exchange. I remember doing a talk for International Women's Day. The theme of the talk was "Making It Happen," and I spoke about my experiences in making work and caregiving happen. I felt a feeling I had never experienced before. Sharing my story and experiences authentically with the audience created an incredible connection. I felt so empowered, and I remember walking away thinking I wanted to do this more. I needed to feel that to know that this was the right path for me. By volunteering to do this, I gained so much in exchange. It connected me with a part of myself I didn't know existed.

You also need to know when you are ready to move beyond volunteering and start using your skills professionally. This doesn't mean you won't still be giving to or supporting others in need, but you will be able to do this in a much stronger and more powerful way when you develop yourself. You will be able to give and contribute on a bigger scale as you grow and develop your pursuits and your own self because you will inspire others in your home and your community. I am sure we can achieve more than we ever imagined. Just think of that moment you saw your child for the first time and wondered how you managed to create such a miracle. This is our potential as human beings, but it doesn't need to stop at having children. You can take this incredible achievement beyond parenting.

Steps Beyond

- ► Find the areas that interest you and skills you may need to work on. Be honest with yourself.
- ► Find volunteering that is right for you, whether that is with a charity or by offering your services for free. Follow your own path.
- ► Learn a little each day, step by step.
- ► After each experience, make a note in your mind of how it felt. Store this for the future.

Resources

Fiona Flintham: www.fionaflintham.com

Lynda: www.lynda.com

Marie Forleo: www.marieforleo.com

Slaughter, Anne-Marie. *Unfinished Business: Women Men Work Family*. New York: Random House, 2015.

Udemy: www.udemy.com

CHAPTER THREE

A New Way of Working

It is not true that people stop pursuing dreams because they grow old; they grow old because they stop pursuing dreams.

—Gabriel García Márquez

I think it is important to recognise that in many ways, this is a new way of working. Up until now, work has often been all or nothing, so creating a new way does take time. It takes an awareness that you will have challenges, that you may be drawn to old ways, and that you need reminders to stay focused on why you are doing it. You may find you don't have many others working the way you are, and it can often be hard to stay focused on your path.

I think we may find we are following passions that we can't quite define. For many, I think, the jobs we are working on, we can't say exactly what they are going to be nor can we describe in one short sentence what we do—as in "I am a doctor." We generally like a title or a definition, but often, I believe, as we grow and follow our purpose, our jobs unravel. What maybe never existed before is now relevant and needed in the world.

I remember receiving an email from one mother who explained that she used to work in marketing, had children, and then developed a passion for the tech world and finding a way to protect children in the digital space. She explained she didn't know where this would lead or whether she could define the job specifically, but she was clear about the areas she was passionate about. I recommended she started taking her first step and see where it led. Shortly after, I received an email about a flexible job opportunity at a tech organization for children. I shared this with her, and she got the job.

We are creating a whole new way of working. For many of us, up until this point, work has always been full time, five days a week. So we need to develop ways to really make this new way work. We need to create routines both flexible and productive, and we also need places to work that will nurture us. Remember that this is a new journey for you and for many others. So keep reviewing, developing, and looking for ways to improve. But the main thing is to stay focused on your purpose and dreams, because each day will make a great difference, and each step will take you closer.

Setting Up a Business the Female Way

There are many ways to create flexible work for yourself. I think it is important to spend time working out what form of flexible working you want, and this may require some experimenting or exploring. You may want a flexible role in a corporation, to freelance, to create a business with a bigger platform behind you, or to set up your own business.

Whatever you choose to do, it is important to be true to yourself. I think an important first step is to recognise if you are an entrepreneur. If starting a business is something you are considering, it is worth exploring whether you are an entrepreneur. If being an entrepreneur isn't right for you, that is fine too.

I remember that I tried hard not to set up another business, but I found I was naturally drawn to it. It wasn't so much the concept of creating a business but rather solving a social issue that I was drawn to. And the only way I knew I could help support the change that I wished to see was through the creation of a business. I can remember very clearly when I was invited to the Silicon Valley Comes to the UK 2014 Summit as one of their CEOs. Although I was by far the smallest business amongst the group selected, I felt like I truly belonged. I didn't feel out of place; I felt like I was meant to be there, amongst kindred spirits. I came home with such an incredible feeling—that this was me, that this was my environment. It was a moment of clarity, and it felt fantastic.

No one tells you if you are an entrepreneur. I think you have to find this out for yourself. There is no "badge" or qualification, but I do believe there is a knowing, and once you recognise this, then you can truly embrace the potential in you as a natural entrepreneur. I think once you recognise and acknowledge this part of yourself, it becomes much easier to move forward, to stop resisting and start creating.

A really important part of my work in setting up Beyond The School Run was, and still is, to establish and work out for myself what it means to grow a business in an authentically female way. It has been incredibly important to me, and when I am not aligned to it, my decisions feel wrong.

I truly believe what keeps women from following their entrepreneurial spirit is exactly what I struggled with. I thought that it was all or nothing, that I had to give all the hours and all my energy to my work. But now I believe there is another way. And this way is led by purpose, passion, compassion, and a desire for change. I think there is a way that will enable mothers to create incredible businesses and world change, all within the hours available to them. The empathy, wisdom, and experience mothers gain after having children will lead the way to great businesses. I hope my journey can ignite this possibility in you and support you on your journey.

What has stood out for me the most in developing BeyondTheSchoolRun is that it is a true expression of myself. When people get it, they get me. Debbie Wosskow, entrepreneur and founder of Lovehomeswap.com, says: "There is no one type of female entrepreneur; we are all very different and individual."

Skills that I never knew I had (writing a book, creating vlogs) have been unlocked because of my passion for BeyondTheSchoolRun, and I have created a life that I love that combines work and caregiving.

As women, we have adapted, without really knowing it, to operate in a working world that is more led by the male way. Finding your female way is important. When I first saw the documentary *Miss Representation*, I couldn't believe some of the messages about women that had sunk into my mind, and I didn't realise they were there.

I still find the judgement we place on mothers in society to be so disempowering. When I first launched the website, one person told me that it was a great idea but suggested I write it in the style of *The Sun* newspaper. This was my very point. Why would we try to suppress and patronise mothers, who had gone through the most life-changing and empowering experience? We should be channelling and supporting and nurturing their creativity, empathy, and power. So I wanted to change the story. When those mothers were ready, I wanted to support their growth. I wanted to create a place where they could find themselves again, where they could be even stronger and more authentic, and where they could unlock natural skills that would sustain them throughout their lives. I could see mothers finding their skills and, in turn, helping other mothers. I imagined an exchange of skills for greater well-being and happiness.

I asked **Carrie Green**, founder of the Female Entrepreneur Association, her thoughts on creating a business the female way and what keeps us aligned with female values and our true selves.

CG: From the beginning, I became very clear on what my mission was for the business. My big vision is to inspire and empower many female entrepreneurs around the world to create great businesses. My website is a membership site, and at the beginning, so many people kept saying, *Why don't you charge more?* I don't think people understood that I wanted to reach and help as many female entrepreneurs as possible, and if I charged more, I would reach less.

This is so important—this is like my kind of guide on how to make the best decisions to move forward in the right direction. I call it my "entrepreneurial north star," always there, shining bright, guiding me to make the right decisions. It is so easy to get distracted, with people suggesting, giving ideas. If you don't have that clear vision, it is so easy to go off track.

If you focus on how you are serving your audience, then I think what you create is so impactful, and I feel like that is more of the feminine way to go. You are nurturing something, and I think that is a really feminine quality. As you serve an audience, you are nurturing them, taking care of them to your best ability, no matter what you do, what service or product you have.

I think we are seeing more and more of that, less people following the money and more people following their heart. And following the need and desire to help people.

What I have learnt from developing BeyondTheSchoolRun is that I am able to keep moving forward because the primary goal for me is to create positive change. This is my starting point, what inspires me, and what keeps me focused. I feel also this is a feminine way. We clearly need money and revenue, but for me, that isn't what drives me—my vision does. Now I need to prove that it can be done, that my vision can be the guiding force, and that money will help me continue with my work, create jobs, and grow.

I still find the work of turning this passion and vision into a growing and thriving business such a challenge. But I will work it out, and I will share what I discover. I truly hope, as women, we can grow and show others that we can create great businesses led from the heart.

I know for me, the entrepreneurial journey with BeyondTheSchoolRun has been very much led by my heart and intuition and the absolute desire to be part of creating the change I want to see in the world. The foundations for me are now set; my vision and dreams are clear. Now I just need to be open to the creative possibilities, find the support I need to grow, and create financial growth so I can grow the business and myself. I need to keep taking my steps, following these guidelines, and digging deep to ensure that I follow the path aligned to my true femininity. But I do believe we can do this, each one of us.

Steps Beyond

- ► Explore whether you are entrepreneurial.
- ► Keep searching for the right type of work for you. Finding the right business or opportunity can be like finding an incredible treasure tucked away inside of you.
- ► Don't compare yourself to others. Create your own vision. Be led by your heart.
- ► Work with your intuition, empathy, and compassion.
- ► Work out what your bigger vision is, your "north star."
- ► Don't be taken off track by other people's comments and views.
- ► Work hard, but don't push.
- ► Embrace collaboration.

Other Flexible Work Options

There are other ways of creating a flexible work life too. While being an entrepreneur isn't for everyone, setting up a business *is* a way of creating the flexibility that you want at this stage of your life. There are a lot of options when running a business with support behind you. Here are just a couple of different areas you can look at:

- ► Freelancing
- ► Social selling

Elizabeth Mary Hancock, business success coach, explains that you need to decide: "Do you want a job, a flexible one, or do you want to have your own business?"

I also spoke with **Nancy Cruickshank** from Myshowcase.com, which provides social selling opportunities for women. She shared that "what is really important, beyond earning money, for most women, is being part of a community; training, recognition at all levels and stages of development, and collaborative work supporting and championing each other."

I think that up until now, social selling has had a blurred reputation. But I have explored the interest and heard mothers speak about how empowering it has been for them to create a business around school hours. I think, as Nancy also mentioned, it is about finding a category you are truly passionate about, one that you want to share amongst your friends, family, and community because you believe wholeheartedly in it. I think it's similar to charities—we will all connect with different ones, so just focus on what resonates with you deeply. The rest will then follow.

Nancy says that "we are seeing a genuine desire for women to look after their family and find work that is fulfilling. And they care about the type of business they are part of."

I also spoke with **Simona Barbieri**, founder of Hub Dot. Hub Dot is a global platform disrupting the way women network by creating a space for authentic connection. I asked Simona about her journey to creating Hub Dot, how to make authentic connections, and how to connect with the right people in a short period of time.

LW: You are busy sharing other people's stories. Can you share yours with me, about your experience as a mother?

SB: I really enjoyed the early years of focusing solely on looking after the children, learning what I needed, reading about parenting, and going to coffee mornings. The coffee mornings provided me with incredible support during those years. But I can remember very clearly, after a few years, going to a coffee morning surrounded by a group of wonderful ladies and thinking, *This isn't it anymore; I need to do more.*

LW: So this was your "beyond the school run" moment. We are all different, needing the space and time to learn and do what we need. But when that moment comes, we then need to know and have the tools and support to go beyond. So what did you do next?

SB: I tried a few flexible jobs, but I had this idea in my head for a long time about connecting people through their authentic stories. There was one morning when I was in my kitchen (where it all started) chatting to some mothers, and one said to me, "But you have it all, Simona." This was a real defining moment. She didn't know my real story. She didn't know the postnatal depression, the miscarriage, the heartache. That was when I realised I needed to bring people together to share their true stories. And that's when people make an authentic connection.

LW: I believe that to truly connect with others, we need to connect with ourselves first. Then once we've done that, we can go on and connect with others. You can meet hundreds of people throughout the day and never make a real connection, ultimately creating a sense of isolation. And yet, when you are in your true self, one conversation can be enough. So when we are connecting with others, what can be the barriers?

SB: Labels, for sure. Any label, being a mother, where you live. It struck me when I was out with my band one evening. I love music, and this had kept me engaged throughout the years when I was solely focused on the children. One evening we were out, and one of my bandmates asked where I lived. I said Fulham [an affluent part of London]. Instantly he started making negative comments about this, when before, when we were just connected through playing music, we had no labels, no assumptions or judgement of one another. It was at that point I realised how these labels can be a huge barrier to connecting. That is why Hub Dot is about the story, the real story, right now.

I think the "conventional" form of networking doesn't work because, often, we are living the "label." So you can never come away feeling truly connected.

LW: I absolutely agree. I think the labels we create can become such a barrier from us connecting with ourselves and with others. It can really limit our potential.

SB: I remember when I was at a dinner party once, the person next to me asked me what I did. I said, "I am a mother, and I look after my children." I could see instantly the interest dropped. Why couldn't they say, *What did you do before? And what are your plans and dreams for the future?* We really limit ourselves at that point. That's also where the idea of Hub Dot came from, that there is so much more about a person than their labels. Their stories are very powerful.

LW: So how did Hub Dot go from idea to where it is now?

SB: I really didn't know where it was going. I knew I was a good connector, but I never thought I would run a business. I had to learn how to let go of the monkeys in my head who kept telling me *Why would you grow a business?* and *What makes you think anyone would be interested?* When I did that, then the business grew. It came from me finding a feminine way to create a business. Every step has needed to feel authentic to me. For example, when we secured funding and I took on the role of CEO, I found it really hard to own it. It was when one of the people that works at Hub Dot said "Well, it just means 'Chief Energy Officer'" that it clicked into place.

It's about feeling fully authentic and connected with every part of what you are doing, and then the magic happens and the dots will join.

If creating a business, entrepreneurial or otherwise, doesn't light you up, there are other options. I have been part of quite a few discussions amongst parents about work and children, and one of the most popular questions I am asked is about flexible working within a corporation. Parents ask, *How do I approach flexible working within my organization? I want to work flexibly, but I don't know how to find the right job.* And there are many more questions. The one thing I am sure of is that we each have a role to play in creating this new way. One way you can do this is by speaking out and asking for what you need within your company. This will change the future for mothers and parents going forward. The more you shape work to what is right for you and your children, the quicker we will create the change we wish to see.

I asked flexible recruitment specialists for their advice on finding flexible job opportunities. **Stephanie Dillon**, founder of Inclusivity Partners, says:

SD: Firstly, *don't limit your job search* to finding roles that say "flexible" or "part time." If you have the right skill set for a job, even if it is full time, then *apply to it.*

Nine out of ten hiring managers say they would consider flexible working for the best person. So it is best to get yourself in front of them to begin with and negotiate flexible working if you are the candidate they prefer. It's important that you are seen as the solution to the problem the business has—this then places you in a much stronger position to negotiate flexibility.

Do your research. Know in advance whether the company has flexible working policies or people working in part-time positions. A lot of this will be available on their website. If they don't, then research what their competitors are doing and use this information as a powerful tool to help influence them on why they need to consider flexible workers.

Don't just ask for flexibility. Have a *well-thought-out plan* as to how it will work for both parties. Give details, preempt any concerns they may have, and address them with how you will make it work. If you've worked flexibly before and made it work, then explain to them how it worked. If you haven't got personal experience of working flexibly and making it work, then use relevant case studies.

Steps Beyond

- ► Keep searching for the right type of work for you. Finding the right business or opportunity can be like finding an incredible treasure tucked away inside of you.
- ► Don't compare yourself to others. Create your own vision. Be led by your heart.
- ► Work with your intuition, empathy, and compassion.
- ► Don't be taken off track by other people's comments and views.

Letting Go of the Old Way

You may start out inspired by your new plans, but it is so easy to be drawn back into the old way of working—and I just want to tell you to hold on. This is especially the case at the beginning, when you may be questioning your new path. I know how challenging it can be at times. Maybe the hours versus salary don't quite add up yet, and you are not entirely sure where this path is leading you. I felt this so many times. Letting go of the old way is hard. But creating a new way means that each step you take is new. I think it is important to recognise this, especially when it may seem challenging, and you may be tempted to be drawn back into the old way of working.

We have been programmed from such a young age, through school and beyond, about what work and success are supposed to look like. So it takes time. For example, I kept thinking I needed to be working in London in an office in order to be productive. It eventually became clear, though, that the time it took to travel to London didn't make sense on a long-term, regular basis and that I needed to find a way to really maximise my work time. What I really needed wasn't a London office but just my brain and a computer.

These old patterns are hard to shift, and you need to work it out for yourself. And if something you need in your community doesn't exist, you need to find a way to create it or find a way around it. For example, I found I really wanted to meet with other like-minded mothers working in the same way, so I set up opportunities, inviting women I knew to a local group get-together. The more you remove the barriers, the more you simplify your life so you can then focus on what you want to do and what makes you happy.

Steps Beyond

- ▶ Be aware of those nagging feelings and questions that make it hard to transition to a new way of working.
- ▶ Look at the bigger picture to stay on track. Remind yourself why you are doing this. How do you see your life in the future?
- ▶ If you are finding there is a barrier to something, question yourself. There are no true barriers to what you are meant to do.

Transitioning from Old Job to New

No matter what type of job you are transitioning from or to, it can take time to rediscover what you are meant to do. It is a process. And you aren't the only one that may take time to get used to it—others around you have to adjust too. I have met a lot of mothers who have transitioned from careers in fields like law to careers as life and career coaches. These women often say they have found it is more "them." Many of them are exploring new paths and developing new jobs that have never been created before. I hear so many mothers say they couldn't go back to their old job or business. I think it is often because the previous job took so much energy that finding a more natural career is easier and makes much more sense when also raising a family.

I found that I hung on to my previous career for a long time until I was ready to transition. I kept my website live and my email address, until one day I just realised I didn't need it anymore. It was a sort of bridge to my new role. And my experience in PR has been invaluable in setting up BeyondTheSchoolRun. It is likely that your pre-kids skill set will help a lot too.

Bridging between jobs can also help support financially. One way to do this might be to utilise your current skills in a freelance role. This can work well alongside your planning for transitioning to your new career and passion.

I met **Fiona Clark**, founder of Inspired Mums, a coaching business for mothers, when I first set up BeyondTheSchoolRun. She was one of the first businesses I came across that resonated with my work. I asked Fiona about her experiences in transitioning from one job to another and what she learnt:

FC: The year 2005 was a life-changing year for me. It was the year I got married and realised that I wanted a completely different career. I'd fallen into sales as a graduate and was no longer enjoying it. I felt unmotivated and disillusioned with my role and knew that I wasn't playing to my strengths. I could feel my confidence ebbing away as each day passed, so I decided something had to change. I knew I wanted children, but I didn't want to wait until I had them to work out a plan.

On paper, I had a successful career with ten years' experience doing commercial roles, but inside, I felt lost and stuck in a rut. I couldn't see a path out—I had completely lost sight of who I was and what I wanted. Eventually I plucked up the courage to book three sessions with a career coach, which was a massive turning point for me. In a very short space of time, I had my light-bulb moment—I realised what truly motivated me and gave me a sense of fulfilment was helping people. It made complete sense and also explained why I felt so unfulfilled in my previous sales roles. I decided to re-train as a coach, and by 2006, I was fully qualified and ready to set up on my own. I felt a real sense of elation coupled with nerves as I embarked upon the next exciting stage in my career.

When people ask me what was the most challenging part of changing careers, I always say how easy it would have been to get put off early on. So many people questioned why I was giving up a successful and well-paid career in a big company (with all the perks that went with that—company car, pension, healthcare, and so on). Well-meaning friends would constantly ask me questions like "But how are you going to get clients?" and "Aren't you worried about the insecurity of being self-employed?". . . and that was my first lesson: *Don't let people talk you out of a good idea before you have even researched it or got started.* I felt strongly they were missing the point—I knew I had to do something I loved, and this meant that I was willing to make significant financial sacrifices in the short term to get my business off the ground.

Thankfully mine is a business with no big start-up costs or overheads. I could work from home and simply needed a phone and laptop to get going. So, in 2006, with my business cards printed, website live, pricing and services sorted—I just needed the phone to ring! By this point, I was pregnant with my first child and extremely excited at the thought of having a flexible career.

My first big break came when I was quoted for an article in the national magazine *Mother & Baby*. This prompted me to set up a dedicated business line and pay a monthly subscription for a call-answering service. Naively, I expected the phone to ring constantly following this feature. But no, not one single phone call. I didn't even experience a significant spike in visits to my website, despite it featuring at the end of the article. So I learnt my second extremely important lesson: *Stay positive and resilient despite any setbacks. And it takes time to establish a successful business.*

Once my son arrived in November 2006, my life became very baby focused for a few months as I muddled through in a fog of sleep deprivation. After about four months, I was ready to start coaching again, but all I could think was *Help! How am I going to find childcare that is flexible and just a few hours a week?* I started to panic—we had recently moved house and had no local friends or family that could help out. Without childcare, it would be impossible to network and drum up clients, so I knew that if I didn't invest in childcare, I wouldn't even get my business off the ground. I calmed myself down and tried to think more creatively. I decided to put the word out there to see if I could find a flexible childminder, and before I knew it, I'd found a great lady who lived right around the corner who was super flexible. So my third lesson would be: *Stay creative and open minded—there is always a solution.*

I must confess that at some point in those first twelve months, I had moments of real doubt that I was doing the right thing. It was tough getting individual clients, and I felt guilty paying for childcare unless I was actually running a coaching session. At this point, I even started trawling job adverts on the internet for part-time/flexible/work-from-home type of roles. I figured I could earn a base salary and pay for childcare and then my coaching business could build up alongside this. My wake-up call came from my brother who simply said one day, "If you put this much effort into building your business, the clients will come." This proved invaluable advice, so my fourth lesson is: *Don't panic and do plan B before you've given plan A a really good chance.*

I decided to redouble my efforts in my business. In my first year, I was positioning myself as a general life coach and didn't have a clear target market. It was only after becoming a mum myself and spending time with other mums that I got real insight and a clear sense of direction. There were so many talented mums out there who wanted to work but needed help finding a new career path, more flexible roles, or ways to increase their confidence. I decided to rebrand my business to focus on providing career and confidence coaching for mums, and Inspired Mums was born. Having a specific picture of my target market gave me a much clearer direction for my marketing, PR, and communications efforts. My messages were really resonating with people, and clients started to flow much more easily. With this in mind, lesson number five is: *Be courageous and know when to change your offering to make it more compelling.*

During that first year of business, I experienced something that I hadn't even taken into consideration . . . working on my own was lonely and tough going at times. I'd presumed working from home would be the perfect solution— flexible, enjoyable, time effective, with no commuting. But I discovered that I missed the social aspect of work and having people to bounce ideas off of. I found I got cabin fever on the days that I was on my own working from home and looking after a child. It also became abundantly clear that it was impossible to be the master of everything—finance, marketing, sales, IT, and comms. My saving grace was building an informal network of other like-minded mums and business owners to share ideas with. I also appointed a good accountant and hired freelancers to work with, such as other coaches, a PR and comms specialist, and a virtual assistant to help me run my business. At the time, it felt like a financially brave decision, but it has made a massive difference to my energy levels and ability to focus on the right things to grow my business. So based on my personal experience of being a new business owner, my final lesson would be: *Get support as early as you can—don't try to be a superhero and do everything yourself!*

In summary, the key lessons I have taken with me from my first year as a business owner are:

- ► Don't let people talk you out of a good idea before you have even researched it or got started (that includes yourself, by the way).
- ► Stay positive and resilient despite any setbacks. And it takes time to establish a successful business.
- ► Stay creative and open minded—there is always a solution.
- ► Don't panic and do plan B before you've given plan A a really good chance.
- ► Be courageous and know when to change your offering to make it more compelling.
- ► Get support as early as you can—don't try to be a superhero and do everything yourself!

I also share with you the journey of **Elizabeth Hancock**, wealth and financial freedom coach, in part because it is so interesting how closely we are all linked. Liz set up the Happy Family World Summit and was introduced to me via a local friend. It turned out Liz lived very near me, and she asked me to become a speaker for her Summit. As a result of that Summit, I am now writing this book. The publishers contacted some of the speakers at the Summit to ask if we had any ideas for a book. My initial reaction was *Absolutely not*, but then I found myself agreeing and putting together a proposal. Liz had been on her own journey in transitioning from one career to another.

EH: I had a corporate career working in human resources in the City of London. I loved it, but I wanted to move out of London when we had our children and take a break from work. After a while, though, I realised I needed something for me that would give me my own income. I still wanted to be there for my children, so commuting in to London again was out.

My path led me to discover EFT Tapping, due to the traumatic birth I had with my first child. Through this, not only did I get my dream birth, but I also started my journey into the holistic well-being world. Having trained initially in EFT just to help myself and my friends, I loved it so much I took further training, and then I set up a business in it.

That was OK—I started to make a bit of pocket money. Networking got me used to talking about my business, but it was a lot of time and effort for very little profit. I had to decide whether to accept this as a "hobby job" or return to a corporate career if I wanted to make decent money again. One New Year's Eve, my husband and I sat down and decided that I would keep my business as a hobby and that he would need to continue as the main earner. A few days later, however, I heard a coach speaking on a webinar. I found myself booking a call and speaking with her the next day. I said I'd think about the investment she was asking for, speak to my husband, and speak to her the next day. I didn't speak to my husband—I didn't want anyone to put doubt on the fire that conversation had started. I knew I had to just bite the bullet, invest the money, and go for it. So I did!

I then went on to set up the Happy Family World Summit Interview Series (through which I met the wonderful Louise; how fab is that)! Putting myself out there was scary, though, as was investing all this money, so at the same time, I trained to become a "Tapping into Wealth" Accredited Coach, mainly because the training we got ourselves was amazing (obviously, breaking through my own barriers, blocks, and limitations was key to being able to do the work on others).

Because the Tapping Into Wealth processes had such a profound effect on my own life and business, I now use it within my own programs to take entrepreneurs and small business owners from fearful to fabulous, average to amazing—freeing them financially AND emotionally. I combine all the skills and experience I've learnt over the years to help them build the strongest of foundations and then use that as a platform to really take things to the next level—all without the doubts, nerves, and often overwhelming fears that so often limit us, especially women returning to work after having children. In one year, I was earning as much as I did in my corporate career, and my income will have doubled again by the end of my second year! Thank goodness I trusted, took a deep breath, and just went for it! I hope you do too!

Steps Beyond

- ▶ Keep going—it may seem challenging at times, but keep focused.
- ▶ Test out new areas. See what lights you up and brings you energy and joy.
- ▶ Gather learnings and wisdom from others that are also working towards finding a new way.
- ▶ Stay focused—each step will take you closer to your dreams.

Finding Places to Work

One part of your new working arrangement that you may struggle with is finding *where* you want to work. Many of you may work at home, but there are other options too. And the transition to your new place of work isn't always easy. A few things happened before I became at ease with working at home. First, a kind friend offered me a space in his flexible working office in London. This helped me so much because I needed to remember how it felt to be back in the workplace again after being detached from it in the early years of parenting. I loved walking back into an office, engaging my thoughts, and focusing on work.

Then I realised I needed to be more efficient with my time and that commuting into London was taking up time that I could be working. So I started to find places to work closer to home—hotels where I could sit for a few hours whilst my daughter was sleeping. I could engage with others, soak up the atmosphere, and work. I found the contrast between concentrating on the children at home and being engaged with the wider world helped me focus and inspired me so much.

I truly believe embracing the freedom available to us is important. I am so grateful to those beautiful places that supported me and the staff who regularly chatted with me. I shared my idea and vision for BeyondTheSchoolRun when I really wasn't sure where it was leading. You can search out these places too. They are wonderful, and they can support you so well. A lot of my thoughts and my work was developed that way.

But working from home can be just as valuable. When you are ready to work from home and it's a possibility, how do you make it work? How do you truly utilise your time and feel engaged, connected, and inspired in the space?

I think, for me, there are two crucial elements to this. First, find a routine that works for you, a routine that ignites your energy and flow before you even enter your office space. Second, create a dedicated space in your home that is just for your work, where you have what you need around you and you are not distracted by anything else. I love the space I have created. It took time to slowly clear the space, but now it feels like me. I love everything I see in the room, and I keep it entirely clear of anything other than content for my work and personal growth.

By creating an office at home, I found I could work whenever possible—when windows opened up, I could just tuck myself away and work. This created the absolute flexibility that I needed, especially during the school holidays.

Often, after a long school holiday or a weekend, I would cherish that first day that I walked back into my office and shut the door to just work, work, work. It is amazing when you realise how valuable work is to us. It becomes more clear when it is not available. In all those years of seeing it as a necessary task or a journey to retirement, we forget that it is a part of everyday life, necessary for our well-being. It connects us, engages us, and unlocks our talents. I had always enjoyed working, but I hadn't always realised how incredibly important it is to us as people.

The benefits of working from home have been so valuable for me. I can fit in more work and more of what makes me better at work (exercise). But it took time to become comfortable with it. One important element of becoming comfortable is finding your flow. In my experience, once you have found that flow, it doesn't matter where you work. But creating your flow takes work (read the next chapter for more on finding your flow).

I want to touch on the issue of living and working outside of the city, because it is something that had an impact on my life and the way I worked. Like many, we decided to move outside London once we had children. When we lived and worked in the city, everything was accessible. Not only was the city inspiring, but attending meetings was quicker and there were more people to connect and engage with. And although it may seem like it—and it did to me at first—working outside the city isn't a barrier. Just remember that there are no barriers to connecting with the right people for you and your work. While you may feel you have lost something by moving out of the city, you have also gained by moving into a new community. Perhaps your move will allow you to be more connected to nature and will nurture you. Or perhaps there is something else you have gained. You just need to be able to recognise this and make it work for you. If you can't find what you need where you are living, try and recreate it for yourself (e.g., if you are looking for people to engage with, create a networking group).

I also think finding what environments you best work in is important, whether having a quiet environment makes you thrive or being surrounded by others energises you. I found much wisdom in the

Quiet Revolution, started by Susan Cain, but each person is different in this regard. I love having my own space and time, especially since my other hours are focused on the children, their activities, and their friends. I look at what that requires of me and what I need to create in my work environment to offset it. So a quieter environment is personally right for me now. You should focus on what is right for you at this time, and I believe your work and business will grow from there. Because if you are nourished and nurtured, your business and work will flourish.

Understanding what environments nourish you will enable you to structure your day. I, for example, do not thrive in morning coffee environments. It just doesn't work for me. So when the children are at school and I am working, it is really important that I am clear about what to I say yes and no to. You can graciously decline opportunities. Just because you work from home doesn't mean you have to say yes to everything. Dedicate your work hours to your work and personal growth and find your own best way to use them towards your goals and well-being.

Steps Beyond

▶ Follow your own patterns and routines that keep you focused.

▶ Look at where you are now and decide if you need to adapt anything to keep from feeling stuck. Maybe work outside the home or start working from home.

▶ If possible, create a small space at home just for your work.

▶ Declutter if necessary. The more you do, the more space will open up to you.

▶ Create boundaries that make it clear that it is your work space.

▶ Focus on the best aspects of wherever you live (e.g., nature, change of pace).

Making Meetings Work

Meetings are also a challenge for those working outside of an office. In the early years, I was forced to learn how to be selective about meetings—arranging childcare and travel time makes you rethink things. But learning to be selective has been so valuable. It helps me focus in on the right people and opportunities that are key to moving me forward.

Initially, when I started working this way, I thought I needed to meet people face-to-face like before. I soon learnt how important it was for me to be wise about who I met with directly—the time and energy it took was so valuable. I started to trust my intuition and to trust that it was best for both parties not to waste time meeting in person if it wasn't worth it. I now always suggest a phone call, and most of the time what we need to achieve can be done that way. I then reserve my face-to-face meeting time for meetings that I am certain will require my physical presence.

Be selective about which events you attend in person. It is very easy to get drawn into coffee mornings and other events, and your connections are important, but creating your boundaries is important too. Apply this idea as you would in an office environment, being clear about which meetings you will attend and which you won't. The time your children are in school is valuable to you, so treasure it.

Finding the right events to attend is the most important step. It's very easy to attend every event in the hope that the outcome will be a positive step, but we have to be realistic that some will be a waste of time and energy. So it's really important to think about this wisely. The approach I now take is to think about the event, and if I am really drawn to it, then it is right. If I start telling myself I should, convincing myself that maybe there will be someone there that would be great to meet, then it isn't right. Similar to clothes, either it works straight away and it is completely right for you or it doesn't—don't try to make it fit. I really think this is about connecting with your intuition. When you do attend those events that you feel are right, be fully present, and I really think you will appreciate and enjoy them more.

You can also use other creative strategies to make meetings work better. I decided this year to invite all those I wanted to meet (who were relevant to BeyondTheSchoolRun) to a morning breakfast. I got to meet everyone I needed in one morning, they all made new connections, and it worked for everyone.

When you are being very careful about the time you spend attending meetings, it can often feel like there are long periods of time in between. It can seem that nothing is happening in between meetings. But stay focused on your work and on moving forward. We come from a culture where having more meetings is viewed as productive, so it can take a while to get used to being selective and wise about who you meet with.

I remember getting ready for meetings and thinking, *This feels so uncomfortable.* I was so used to jeans that just dressing for a meeting felt alien. In particular, this was difficult during the school holidays when my mind was so focused on the children that it would take time to adjust to the idea of attending a meeting. But you will keep evolving and it will become more and more seamless, because the divide between work and caregiving will lessen. In the meantime, just be kind to yourself—tell yourself positive messages and try not to compare yourself to others in the workplace.

One way to ease the transition between caregiving and a meeting is by having the things you need for a work meeting at your fingertips. I remember, in the early days, turning up to meetings without a pen in my bag (but lots of baby wipes!) and just feeling so removed by that lack of preparation.

Steps Beyond

- ▶ Don't attend meetings or events unless you feel a real pull to meet with that person.
- ▶ Try a phone call as a first meeting, then see if you need to meet face to face.

- ▶ Be selective with the meetings you accept and how you spend your time.
- ▶ Follow your intuition and your instinct about what events and meetings to attend.
- ▶ Be prepared. Have one bag with your work things, ready to take whenever you go to a meeting—with a PEN (lesson learnt!), pad, and business cards.

Resources

Beauty Counter: www.beautycounter.com

Brendon Burchard: www.brendon.com

Elizabeth Hancock: www.elizabethmaryhancock.com

Female Entrepreneur Association: www.femaleentrepreneurassociation.com

Hub Dot: www.hubdot.com

Inspired Mums: www.inspiredmums.co.uk

Myshowcase.com: www.myshowcase.com

Stella & Dot: www.stelladot.co.uk

CHAPTER FOUR

Finding Your Flow

I attribute my success to this: I never gave or took
an excuse.

—Florence Nightingale

really think finding and maintaining your flow is key to sustained
energy, focus, and productivity. In my experience, flow is when you
are fully immersed in an element of your work and you become
unaware of time or all else. It is a truly amazing feeling and not something I was aware of previously. I really had no idea what flow was
before I started developing BeyondTheSchoolRun. I just thought of
work as something that took focus, attention, and discipline. Although
that is required, creating flow within your working day is incredibly
valuable. Your mind becomes clear of anything other than what you
are doing. It is almost like a meditative state, and when you are in it,
you can work with far greater ease. Your body doesn't feel strained,
and you are not forcing yourself to achieve something. It is almost as if

you are being carried along. That said, I find it must be a daily practice to harness it. And there are challenges to maintaining it.

Finding your flow is so valuable to working in short periods of time, and it is also valuable to our sense of ease with our work. Which is why I explore it more here, including how to unlock it, how to sustain it, and how to regain it when moving between work and caring.

We need to set practices that work for us individually, and we need to sustain them on a regular basis. This is what I learnt gets me in my flow:

► Morning rituals

► Exercise

► Nutrition

► Positive mindset

► Finding my feminine way

When I am not in my flow:

► I question my work a lot

► I look for external reassurance

► Everything takes much longer, with strain instead of ease

So how do we find our flow and keep it?

I think it's already in us, but it needs unlocking, and it is individual to each of us. I think we can get taken out of it from an early age, with the structure of the school system and other influences. So really, our job is to find it and make it a daily practice until it becomes second nature again. It may be natural, but until it is achieved without consciousness, it requires a conscious effort to make it a daily practice. Recognise that whatever you need to do to achieve it each day is so worth it.

Taking time to look at your habits, ones that aren't supporting or nurturing you, is really important. Many are just embedded in our daily lives. We don't even give them a thought, but once you take a moment to look at those that no longer serve you, you make way for new patterns that will. As an example, the moment I stopped multitasking was such a relief. After so many years of doing it, I decided one day that it didn't work for me. And the more I focused on one task at a time, the more efficient I became.

For me, exercise and what I eat are key parts in finding and maintaining my flow. How I start my day is also very important. I looked for new habits I could create to make me feel strong and ready to take charge. So that meant exercising early, often before the kids were up—which also meant going to bed earlier. I changed my habit from just having a coffee to always having my vitamins with my coffee. These changes made all the difference. The start of your day can really determine the rest of it, so take time to develop a routine that works for you.

The thing about habits is they are often hard to let go of—they have been set in our system, so it does take a conscious period of time to reset them. There are so many reasons why, as women, we may have picked up these habits—from our mothers, from our friends, or from our own disconnect with our bodies' needs. And to change a habit, you do need to consciously do it for a period of time. One strategy is to write a note on your desk to remind you, until one day, you will just do it without thought. Keep testing and exploring your own needs, then make them a daily practice, until one day you will wake up and realise it is happening without conscious thought—and that will be an amazing day!

It is important to align our flow with the world around us too. As with the changing seasons, I think the school calendar year can be a good guide for us in the flow of our work. As the school holidays begin, it can be time to remove ourselves slightly from the routine and structure of the day to think more freely, connect again with nature, and ground ourselves again. This preparation can serve us so well when the school term starts again, giving us renewed energy, focus, and clarity.

Steps Beyond

- ► Look at your habits and see how you can change them to nurture you more. Do you need to exercise, or eat healthier, or take vitamins, or have some quiet time each day?

- ▶ Don't ignore the small habits that often get overlooked. Sometimes the smallest habits can make the biggest difference.
- ▶ Stick with the change—it takes time to make the habit stick.
- ▶ Try different strategies to help you remember your new habit.
- ▶ Remember to take your family's natural flow into account when creating your own flow.

Creating a Flexible Routine

I have found that creating some form of routine, however flexible it needs to be, is really important in maintaining a workflow. This is especially the case when you are moving between caregiving and working because the routine will help you in establishing yourself when you have those hours to work. But remember that this will always keep changing. As your children go from nursery to school, more hours will open up to you. But if you establish a routine that works for you, you will find you will be able to adapt it to work as opportunities change.

I came to a point, when both my children started school, that I had a longer period of time to work. Creating a work routine became really important because it was no longer just two or three hours to work; it was nine a.m. to three p.m. This initially seemed very daunting, but once I developed a routine that worked, it felt great. It is really empowering to have this time open for work. So I established myself as working from my office at home, and I really found this space to be so valuable for focusing in those hours.

Your work also needs to allow for school holidays. Finding this flexibility is important in balancing your work as a parent and your work in the wider world. I do believe the children's calendar can support us too and help create a balance. The holidays are for spending more time outside in society, and then once the school term starts, you can return to your regular routine. This ability to adapt is important; it keeps us flexible. It can be so incredibly easy to get stuck in a set routine again, one that determines our days and doesn't allow our minds to open to other ways and opportunities. But the one key thing children teach us is that change is part of life. They experience it all the time: new year, new teacher, new school, new skills. We, too, can learn from this and keep ourselves open to new ways and new options. Creating routines is important to maintaining productivity and flow, but keep an open mind and be flexible.

Steps Beyond

- ► Develop a routine that works. It should make you feel vibrant and motivated.
- ► Maintain your routine, but also keep it flexible.
- ► Your windows to work may come at different times. Be ready.
- ► Create structure and discipline similar to being in an office— even if you are working from home.
- ► During your working hours, focus on your work and do not be distracted by other jobs. Use your windows of time wisely—they all add up.

Making Weekends Work

One common challenge to maintaining your flow is the weekend. I often found weekends very exhausting, and by Monday, I didn't feel focused and ready for work. I have learnt that making weekends work takes some time, but it is important to focus on it.

As a starting point, I have found that making sure I am working during the week is important. I had to find ways to create hours to work and really focus on making sure I was not spending the hours of a working day socialising or going shopping (unless that was part of caring for the children). Then, on the weekend, I felt ready for the reward of the weekend. I think the sense of a reward for work accomplished is such a great feeling. But for a long time after having children, I didn't feel like the weekend was any different from the week. So I had to create the difference. I had to ensure I was saving some things for just the weekend.

On Fridays, try celebrating the work you achieved throughout the week. The weeks and weekends can merge into one when you are at home with children, but trying to create a distinct pattern will make such a difference. Do all your work during the week, and you will really feel like you have best utilised the hours available. Once you feel you have taken steps forward in the week, you will feel ready to let go more on the weekend. Otherwise, you will be searching on the weekend for something to fill you.

This is particularly important when your children are at school. If they are learning and growing during those hours, then you should be too. Then you all feel the same sense of achievement at the end of the week.

You can use your weekends wisely too. Try keeping Sunday as a day to prepare for the week ahead, as you would when/if you used to work in an office. For myself, I make sure I use Sunday to organise the house, take care of clothes, and do the washing. It means that Monday feels like a fresh start for me. It took me time to work out that weekends are really valuable to how my week runs, and it has made such a difference to my energy and my focus as soon as the week starts.

Steps Beyond

- ► Be disciplined with your work week so that you feel the reward at the end.
- ► Prepare for the week ahead on Sunday. Sort out the shopping, prepare food for the week, and write your work to-do list.

Making Mondays Work

Once you have found a weekend routine that works, getting started on Mondays is the next challenge. I have found that Mondays are important days for setting the framework and intention for your week. It is so tempting after a weekend to start searching outside for contentment. But I have found Monday is a really important day to engage with yourself and focus your mind on your work. I know how hard it can be. You feel so removed from the "work" part of yourself again, but staying committed to this will honestly make all the difference. So many times, I have sat in my office, wondering how to start and what to do. But staying committed and finding a way to focus on my work completely reshapes how I feel, and my work, for the whole week.

If, like me, you need inspiration on a Monday morning to shift your mind away from family time, then look for a vlog (or some other content) that will spark you. If I need to get my brain and mind focused again, I often turn to the vlogs by Marie Forleo or Gabrielle Bernstein to provide me with motivation.

I also learnt that if I can't find inspiration around me when I need it, then I can create it myself. So, one Monday morning, I launched the beyondtheschoolrun.com Monday morning video vlogs, and I have committed to doing those every Monday. Create your own routine that really keeps you focused. Have one part of your work that you complete every single Monday. That way, you will feel a sense of achievement and be clear about what to start with each week.

Steps Beyond

- ▶ Look for ways to create your own inspiration.
- ▶ Create a work task that you have to achieve every Monday— and stick to it.

Taking Steps during School Holidays

School holidays are also something to be mindful of with our flow and routine. We need to prepare for the transition in focus between caregiving and work. This is when we need to bring together everything we have learnt up to now.

It is so important to prepare, to stay focused, and to learn from each holiday what you need to do to improve for the next one. You can still keep taking great steps during the holidays, and you can prepare yourself for when the children go back to school. Then you are ready to go back to work straight away. They key for me has been keeping all of the elements going as much as possible, including some exercise, healthy eating, engaging with my brain and mind, and bringing in support so I can increase my time.

I think the best way to prepare is to learn from each holiday experience. I keep learning, and I find preparing in advance is really important, especially for the longer breaks, such as the summer. I prepare for the holidays by looking for the support that I need, preparing in advance for playdates, and speaking to my husband about what areas he can take on, such as meal planning. I also try and stick to a routine that works. I find that if I start my day the right way, then the rest will follow well. It's so easy to forget yourself again in the holidays, and then it can take time once they return to school to find your rhythm and flow. But once you have established a routine that helps you connect with your own flow, then you can try to introduce it into your days during the holidays as much as possible. So try and focus on this and see this as a part of your work.

I have also found the change of routine during holidays is beneficial in many ways. It allows me to move away from the structure of the school day and towards a more flexible one. This can give you freedom to focus on different areas of your work. I often carry a note pad in my bag with me to write down ideas and thoughts whilst I am out with the children. You can stay connected with your work and use this time to work on different areas that you might not focus on during a more structured working day.

The more you maintain your natural flow during the school holidays, the easier you will engage with it again once the time becomes available to you to work again. Also, when you stay focused during your hours in the weekdays throughout, you will enjoy the weekend and holidays so much more.

Steps Beyond

- ► Use your parent network to find and provide mutual support.
- ► Try combining work and childcare. For example, have meetings with others mums/parents while you are at your children's play or while at a playdate.
- ► Look for ways to incorporate your normal routine into the school holidays.
- ► Find ways to stay connected to your work during holidays. Try taking a few minutes to write down new ideas, or read something related to your work.

Starting New in September

It is important for us to remember that no matter how wonderful our routine is, there are always new beginnings. Schedules shift, children grow older, and our situations sometimes change. With that in mind, I think one way to keep our flow aligned to our changing lives is to prepare for September and back to school. New school years can provide a time for us to start afresh. I find this time of year very exciting. In many ways, it feels like the real "New Year." It's a great time to start putting plans into action, to start creating, and to move forward. I also find it a great time to set new intentions, almost like a New Year's resolution.

We can use this time wisely to move forward and take brave steps. We can use the space of the summer holiday to prepare us for our next steps. With the energy of the summer behind us, and with children often starting school or nursery, we can move forward in new ways. It can, like most changes, feel daunting. But with new beginnings come new opportunities—opportunities for change and growth. This can feel difficult, because you may have spent a long time in the routine you have been in. It can often feel safe and comfortable, but small changes can make a great difference.

Think about what you need in your life. As I write this, it is September 2016, and I have realised how focused I am on the kids, work, and home and that I really desire to have more fun again. I have set that as my intention. It doesn't take me away from my everyday; it just means that in those moments, I can choose to have fun. I can stop "sweating the small stuff" and—as the children do—laugh, play, and feel light.

Steps Beyond

► Focus on setting your intentions at the beginning of each new school year. Prepare for your "new year" and think about your routine and who can support you.

Pace, Not Race

Even though finding your flow is important to accomplishing your work, I think it's really important to remember that it isn't a race. When we pace ourselves, we will get to where we are hoping to go. This is about working for the long-term. It's a way that recognises the role of caregiving as well as the importance of maintaining and utilizing our skills throughout our lifetime. This is about creating a pattern for life— an ebb and flow of working and caregiving. It is a pattern of life that keeps you engaged and connected and creates a great sense of wellness throughout your full life without a need to retire from a life you love. So there is no race—just enjoy the steps.

Steps Beyond

► Set a healthy pace for your work.

Resources

Gabby Bernstein: http://gabbybernstein.com/

Jess Lively: www.jesslively.com

Marie Forleo: www.marieforleo.com/

CHAPTER FIVE

Money Matters

Money won't create success; the freedom to make it will.
—Nelson Mandela

I have to say, this is a big subject—maybe a whole book's worth. But I have only a chapter, so I'll tell you what's most important. What I have come to realise is that finding your own authentic connection with money—a connection that helps you live and thrive with purpose—takes some understanding. As with everything linked to the parenting journey, we have an opportunity to start fresh, to clear out the old, and to make true, authentic connections.

When you have been through an intense period of time focused on caregiving, it can take you away from your connection to earning money. That, I found, can lead to various emotions and disconnections, because our connection with money is deeply rooted in our connection with our own sense of worth. What I realised, after years of not earning a salary, was that I felt incredibly disempowered by it. If I wasn't the one earning it, it felt very different, and I felt disconnected from a part of myself. The lack of independence I felt from this was stifling.

This is not about the actual amounts of money but about the independence it gives you to make your own choices and not have to be accountable. I think for every single one of us, there is the opportunity, our birthright, to earn money to live the life we choose. Once we connect with money, start learning about it, and, MOST importantly, start taking charge of it, we can collectively make the greatest difference. But we can also do this in a feminine way—one that resonates deeply with our core values as women. As **Hannah Martin**, cofounder of Talentedladiesclub.com, says: "for most mothers, this is about regaining financial independence, not necessarily about earning for a new car."

I found the impact of not earning my own money wasn't something that happened overnight; it was gradual. I had sold my previous business, and the money from that supported me whilst I was on my maternity and in the early stages of BeyondTheSchoolRun. However, being home to care for the children, I needed to rely more on my husband's income. As Hannah says, "This isn't something that happens overnight. You have babies, and then many women find themselves in a situation where they are asking their husbands for money, and this is very hard."

So I started really looking at our connection with money on so many levels. I realised that we have all been programmed from a young age with messages about what money means, and these emotions can have an impact on how we respond and how we earn money. I think one key factor is how the other part of our work within society is valued—the time spent caring for our children. All too often, we can feel like this isn't recognised, and this can have a long-term impact on our own self-worth. Because when half, or more than half, of your working day is spent caring for and nurturing others but your effort isn't valued, your sense of self-worth suffers. I hope that together, as a society, we can engage with money in a clear, authentic way that provides a long-term path to earning, sharing, and caring. It's all a work in progress, but I really think it works step-by-step. As society starts to evolve and recognises the value of caregiving, our self-value will grow as well. We need society to value caregiving as much as we do bread-winning. But until that happens, it is important to work on your own self-worth (more about that in the next chapter).

Taking steps towards earning a salary again, within school hours (and outside school holidays!), can have its challenges. It can seem almost impossible. I am here to say it's not. And taking those steps now can really pay off later, when more hours become available to you. I came to realise that earning money again isn't just about working; it is closely linked to connecting with ourselves and to finding self-love and self-worth. However little or great, earning money is so important to us as people—both female and male. It can be very exciting, and you can find that the two—family and work—can work well together.

I also think we need to find our feminine connection with money—what it means to us and how we use and earn it is so import-ant. In my money journey, the very first person I came across was Kate Northrup, and I have loved her work ever since. I connected with her work because she focuses on our own belief system, how and where we work, and all the areas where you may not connect with the traditional discussion of money. It made me want to learn more, engage with money, and commit to my own path. It felt very feminine and exciting.

I also believe women have been removed from the conversation of money, and we need to reconnect with it again. I have found myself in many situations with my husband when a conversation about money has come up and it has been directed to him and not to me. I have started a conversation with someone about business and work only to be looked at as though I wouldn't know anything. My son talks to me regularly about sport, and as a result, I am so much more informed and engaged with sport. Because of his drip feed of information, I am increasing my connection with a subject I had little connection with before. We need to do the same for money. It doesn't matter whether you are an entrepreneur, a freelancer, a full-time caregiver, or work-ing for an organization. If we want to grow our money, then we need to talk about it, we need to connect with it, and together we need to empower ourselves to earn, save, and grow.

Steps Beyond

- ▶ Commit yourself to connecting with money again, step by step.
- ▶ Notice your communications about money. What you are saying about money that may be limiting you?
- ▶ Think about how you felt around money when you were younger.
- ▶ Try decluttering. This will bring you greater awareness of what you spend.
- ▶ Be kind to yourself. You have worked hard, even if it may not have been recognised through a wage.
- ▶ Say out loud how you are keen to start working and earning again.
- ▶ Look after it, from the money in your wallet to your own bank account. Open bank statements and read financial information.
- ▶ Connect with those who are empowering women and money.
- ▶ Join groups or communities where money is discussed.

Earning Again

To find your connection with money again, you have to start earning it. So let's start the financial journey. Let's create your money story—how you feel around money, what it means to you, and how you can take steps to earn it.

Having less of my own money to spend has made me very cautious and selective about how I spend and taught me that I need less to be happy than I thought. However, I also aspire to a lot—I dream of buying beautiful clothes and of earning to create balance for myself and my husband. This is, however, step by step.

For me, creating a long-term vision and plan keeps me focused. I realised I needed to re-skill and regain belief in myself. I have found that with a long-term vision and a big dream, I can find peace with where I am right now because I know what I am working towards. Accessing your dreams and not settling for anything less is so important. For some, your passion may be growing a business. However, whilst it grows, you may need to create income through additional work. Whatever it might be, become clear on what your purpose is first and then how you can achieve this.

I have also learnt to be open to financial opportunities that I never imagined possible. I entered a competition called Britain's Top Real Role Model in 2014, never imagining for a moment I would win it. But I did, and the winner received funds to move their business to the next level, which is exactly what I needed at the time.

I am still learning and certainly hope to be able to give more guidance on this in the future, but in the meantime, I asked for wisdom from others on taking financial steps forward. First, I asked **Debbie Wosskow**, an entrepreneur and the CEO of Lovehomeswap.com for her thoughts.

> DW: I grew up around female entrepreneurs—my mother and grandma (who worked into her nineties). Everyone in my family is an entrepreneur—a typical third-generation Jewish family. I always had jobs, starting from the age of eleven, working for my mother, folding jumpers in Benetton. Financial independence and an independent lifestyle were always part of my upbringing.
>
> Two things my mother said to me have always stayed:
> - Always have your own money.
> - If you like nice things, then you need to earn to have them.
>
> When it comes to money:
> - I am very structured about it.
> - I take charge of it and stay focused on it.

▶ I like to know where it is. I have always run my money.
If you are running anything, you have to learn about and understand money. I talk to my son and daughter regularly and equally about money.

It gives you confidence to understand it. You don't need to be super rich—start with what you have and take charge of it. Focus on it. Think about investing. Only you can make this happen—no one else. You can do it.

A proverb says *What you put your attention to grows*. And Debbie confirms this, although she came from a background where it was the norm to take charge of your own money. This is open to everyone—all you need to do is start.

I also asked **Carrie Green**, founder of the Female Entrepreneur Association, about how you take your passion and start making money and growing your business. I know how hard it is, because often, the possibilities aren't clear.

CG: I had a struggle with this. When I started my first business, I made more money than I needed, but it left me feeling hollow and empty. So when I launched FEA, all I wanted to do was give and serve my audience. But when I reached a low point and couldn't even afford Christmas presents, I realised I needed to do something about this. A good friend of mine suggested that I do a visualisation around money and helped me create a financial visualisation tape. Within days of doing this, a series of strange events happened. I was asked to collaborate on a seminar with a lady I had admired for a long time. I was so nervous, but that seminar earnt me $2,000. What I learnt from this was that I could be of greater service by charging. I used to think charging someone for something was taking, when in fact you are giving because you can serve more. For example, if I had put my creative energy in to making a jewellery range, I wouldn't dream of not charging for it, so why should this be any different?

I find visualisations and affirmations and paying attention to my thoughts is so helpful in [sending] my thoughts in a positive direction. It is really focusing on retraining your brain.

I also think it is really important to stop undervaluing yourself, to stop focusing on the doubts and fears. It really is all about mindset and what we are thinking.

I keep a dream jar. In there I have my individual dreams, and I pick out one and visualise how this will be. I have a board with my dreams and visions on it so that I see it regularly. I remind myself and keep programming my mind and brain. I also have on the board the word *trust*. I think this is really important, because it does get hard. There are so many times on the journey when you question yourself and what you are doing, and just seeing this word, *trust*, can remind you to relax into the journey and really trust the process. I keep this quote to remind myself: "Successful people hang on when everyone else has let go."

Really focusing on your thoughts and mind is so important. I remember once having dropped the kids off at school and just thinking, *I don't know how I can find the inspiration to move forward with work.* I looked on Instagram, and one of the younger female entrepreneurs I follow had left a message on there: *Be brave.* Those two words were enough to get me going. My mindset shifted, and I went on and had a great day. It was incredible how powerful this was. I think surrounding ourselves with these messages, in whichever form—on our walls, in our wallets, anywhere that we will look regularly—is so important. If you are not receiving these encouraging words from others, create that encouragement yourself and surround yourself with it. And trust.

Steps Beyond

- ► Be open to what you want to achieve long term, and dream big.
- ► Share your vision with your family. Talk positively about your financial plans and intentions, where you wish to be, and how you want to contribute.

- ► Look at what your work is giving you right now, other than money—independence, confidence, connections.
- ► Explore ways you can use your current skills to earn while freelancing.
- ► Surround yourself with positive messages.
- ► Create a vision board with the word *trust* on it to remind you to trust the journey.
- ► Create a visualization tape and affirmations.
- ► Stay focused.

Resources

Female Entrepreneur Association:
  femaleentrepreneurassociation.com

Global Invest Her: www.globalinvesther.com

Kate Northrup: www.katenorthrup.com

Talented Ladies Club: www.talentedladiesclub.com

CHAPTER SIX

Happiness

In identifying one's mental state as the prime factor in achieving happiness, of course that doesn't deny that our basic physical needs for food, clothing, and shelter must be met. But once these basic needs are met, the message is clear: *we don't need more money, we don't need greater success or fame, we don't need the perfect body or even the perfect mate— right now, at this very moment, we have a mind, which is all the basic equipment we need to achieve complete happiness.*

—Dalai Lama XIV, *The Art of Happiness: A Handbook for Living*

For me, this BeyondTheSchoolRun journey is deeply linked with happiness. It is so important to explore what truly and individually makes us happy and to find our personal steps. We should not be defined by others, or by society, in making those choices. We should understand for ourselves what it is that makes us, as individuals, happy. This, like all other parts of this book, is a journey, but I found that it was an important step in my journey.

Finding and following your passion is so greatly linked to your happiness. When we start to find what we love, it becomes a part of who we are. In this chapter, I want to explore finding happiness with where we are right now, not with where we came from or where we are going. At any given moment, we can choose happiness and we can choose positivity, because it is in reach for all of us.

This is very different for each of us, but we share in the potential happiness, joy, and growth that can come from understanding ourselves more fully. And I believe when you become a parent is a great time to do this. So let's go . . .

Making Peace with Where You Are Right Now

We need to start with where we are right now. That begins with recognizing what got you to this point and recognizing the potential going forward. Even when you find yourself somewhere you hadn't planned or imagined. For me, finding myself outside the city and no longer working was a shock. I felt a huge sense of disconnect, but I needed to find a way that acknowledged where I was and then took steps forward. This can be a really challenging part of the journey, but once you arrive, you realise everything you need is where you are right now.

Much of our work when we become mothers is very practical—cleaning, washing, running errands, etc.—and for me, this was, and still sometimes is, very frustrating. But again, I learnt that when I was taking steps forward in the hours available to me, I could find peace in the housework. It's a bit like when you are in the office and you need a rest from thinking, so you focus on admin instead. If you are still taking your steps forward, when you come to the housework, it will be a welcome rest that is very grounding. I know this is often far easier said than done, especially when there is endless washing. But try to use your time doing housework to plan, dream, and envision your next steps. Or you can use it to remove all thoughts, to clear your head.

I think you will come to a point where you understand that you need to be where you are right now. Where you are may change, but for right now, this is what you need. I have often thought that the grounding connection with nature and community is what I needed, much more than my husband needed it, and that is what I have gained by being home with the children. Can we revisit what we missed and be nourished by it through the parenting journey? I think so. I never really understood my need for connecting with nature, the outdoors, and regular exercise, but being with the children forced me to recognise this. And what a gift!

The ethos of this book, and of my work with BeyondTheSchoolRun, is not about running from where we are now but about recognizing that the here and now has a purpose. And about taking steps forward when you can, to reach your infinite possibilities.

So how do we find peace with the day to day? Here are three ways:

1. Positive thinking
2. Being kind to yourself
3. Forgiving

Positive thinking made a significant difference in my life once I started to focus on my thoughts. I started to enjoy and appreciate the time with the children at home, and I also started to attract positive people and support. When I took a moment to acknowledge my daily thoughts, I realised how negative I was being about myself. I also came to realise those negative thoughts were not necessary or productive, and they were not feeding me in a beneficial way. It is so powerful and so simple, and it is amazing how different your day can be. You just need to take a moment and choose a different way.

So how do we start to create a positive mindset? The first step is to start to listen. Take a moment to hear what you are telling yourself. When you start to tune in, you can recognise when those thoughts are negative and let them go or reshape them with positive ones. At any given moment, you can check in. If, all of a sudden, you feel less confident or positive, then listen in to what you are telling yourself and what messages you are giving your body. Then decide whether you want to reshape them. It can take a while to become conscious of your thoughts. But once you shift those negative thoughts to positive ones, you will feel significantly happier.

Another way to find day-to-day peace is by being kind to yourself. You have done an amazing job in bringing children into the world. Remember and recognise those achievements. It is easy to focus on what you have lost or given up or on how different your life is now. Instead of looking back on what has been, look forward to what you have gained in becoming a parent. What parts of yourself have you unlocked—strength, wisdom, compassion? And so much more. Parenting is incredibly intense, so be kind to yourself daily.

I signed up for Dr. David Hamilton's daily self-love newsletters and found them such a support at the start of each day—mainly in connecting with myself and reminding myself of my worth, which can get lost in the day-to-day role of caregiver. So take time to focus on your self-love. Find ways to support and praise yourself; then you won't feel the need to seek it externally. Make it a daily practice.

I also wanted to mention forgiveness here, because it plays such an important part in our lives. In particular, it is important to us as parents, because I think the emotions we carry around impact not only us but also our children.

I think we each have our own individual journey. We all have different stories and experiences, but what unites us is the human desire for peace—peace within and peace on earth. And I truly believe that, as families, we are key to this human development. If we can find our own peace, then we can individually and collectively make great strides.

So where do we start? The path of forgiveness is difficult. It's not something I had explored before, but when I did, I found it hugely enlightening. I found that it needs to be a daily practice, sometimes for even the smallest moments. Those small moments often leave us feeling stuck in our day. Forgiving yourself, instead of holding on to those small moments (for example, forgetting something for the children's school or eating something that made you unwell), is so important.

This is especially true for us mothers, because there are always times when you feel you aren't getting it right.

Beyond these small moments, I think we need to look at our bigger picture. Are we holding on to resentment towards another, and how is it making us feel? Often, these emotions can be difficult, but letting them go can be life changing, a true gift to yourself.

I found exploring that bigger picture really helpful, especially in regards to where I came from and what experiences that led to. I learnt a lot by recognizing my own family line. My mother's great-grandparents were Jewish during the Second World War, and their painful experiences greatly impacted both of my mother's parents. These painful experiences, I believe, manifest themselves throughout generations, just in different forms. And the route to stopping this is forgiveness. My parents divorced when I was very little, and as a sensitive child, I felt a lot of disruption and sadness. It is easy to focus solely on your own experiences, but once you start to trace them back, you can find clarity, understanding, and a level of empathy. This isn't an easy process, but it is a giant step towards peace within ourselves and within the world. I think once we collectively achieve this, whatever our individual stories and experiences are, we will make huge developments in our human evolution.

Steps Beyond

- ► Make positive thinking a daily practice.
- ► Meditate to clear your mind of negative thoughts.
- ► Catch your thoughts and choose to change them.
- ► Focus on gratitude.
- ► Read a positive quote or affirmation.
- ► Be kind to yourself. Take time to cherish yourself. Buy yourself a gift or take a long bath. Just say thank you to you.
- ► Forgive yourself daily. Every moment is an opportunity to start fresh.

► Take a moment to recognise what or whom you need to forgive. How is this making you feel?

► Decide you want to forgive, even if you don't know how. That alone will make you feel lighter.

► Say out loud that you want to forgive. Put it out there and follow the journey.

Being Present

One of the challenges of working this way is transitioning between caring for the kids and work. It feels like there is such a disconnect between the two. Your life caring for the children (tidying the house, playing at the playground) can feel a million miles away from sitting in meetings. But it is important that we keep ourselves prepared for both so we can move between the two with ease and kindness towards ourselves.

It's very easy to spend the time that you are with the children feeling like you should be working. But this won't serve us. Work and family should complement each other, as yin and yang. The hours you work, you should challenge yourself to take bold steps forward. And in the hours you are with your children, you should be present with them, connected again to nature and grounded in day-to-day life.

The turning point for me, and it helped my work so much, was when I acknowledged that the two—work and family—worked together. I learnt to work as hard as I could in my working hours, but I didn't want it to eat into our time together. I wanted to treasure that time together. And I found much inspiration in the hours that I switched off work to be with the children.

It has taken me a while to see the importance of this, but I am reminded, when I go to a meeting or when I am stretching myself with work, that what I then need more than anything is the simplicity of everyday life. This really has been transformative to my work and to my well-being, and I can't emphasise enough how important the two are together. On this journey, they go hand in hand.

I also think it is important to remember that you are still "working" when caring for your children. Both parts are work—both require you to be fully engaged, just with different parts of yourself. Making this a fluid transition is key, but learning that they are interconnected and complementary is what is going to be valuable to our work, our families, and our long-term well-being.

Steps Beyond

▶ Schedule your day so you are clear about when you are changing from work to caring for the children.

▶ Remember that the time spent caring for your children is a valuable part of your work and that work and caregiving go hand in hand.

▶ If you start to become distracted, just remind yourself to return to the present moment.

Five Ways to Have a Fulfilled Day

When you no longer have a typical workplace structure, you need to start developing your own. And you need one that is flexible—as your baby grows and more time opens up, one routine may need to evolve into another. It's really important to look at how to develop your day in order for you to feel good, strong, and empowered to move from work to caregiving.

A real turning point in how I shaped my day came from a meeting I had with a wonderful lady, **Harriet Minter**, former Head of Women in Leadership at *The Guardian* and speaker and writer on the subject of women. What she said to me made such a difference to my day. She shared some advice she had been given about the five things you need to do to have a fulfilled day:

1. Exercise.
2. Connect with your community.
3. Give.

4. Develop a form of mindfulness.

5. Learn.

For me, as a parent, I had already become very connected with my community, and I was likely to be exercising running around in the playground already. And giving is a given! What can more easily be missed is mindfulness and learning. Many mothers would say they just need "headspace" when sometimes we don't even recognise that the need is for personal learning and growth.

For a long time, I was really drawn to my previous framework of an office in the city for work. I searched for ways in which child-care could support this, but I came to realise that I needed to find another way. This framework didn't work in combining what made me happy—being there for the children but also moving forward with my passions. Instead, I discovered I felt content when I focused on moving BeyondTheSchoolRun forward. Those steps were enough for me to feel fulfilled throughout my day without needing to go anywhere other than my home office or close by. This isn't always the case, but in the limited amount of time I had for work, I learnt that it was what fulfilled me the most.

Steps Beyond

- ► Look for the things that help you feel fulfilled. The specifics are unique to you.
- ► Consider exercise as a way to clear your mind and refocus yourself.
- ► Make sure you are connecting with your community regularly.
- ► Try mindfulness practices and keep going. It takes time to get used to it, but once you do, you will see why it is so important to your day.
- ► Look for ways, even small ones, to learn, grow, or stretch your mind each day.

Happiness Starts with Me

What became very clear to me on this journey is that happiness had to come from me. No one else could make me happy until I knew what it was that truly made me happy in the first place. They could support my happiness, but they couldn't fundamentally make me happy—not my husband or my children. It was my responsibility to find this.

Once I started to discover what made me happy, I realised I had everything already there to achieve this. I just needed to be clear so I didn't waste time doing something that didn't truly make me happy. For example, I used to think I loved shopping for clothes, but I came to realise this didn't make me happy. If I had a lot of time, then maybe it was an additional benefit, but it wasn't the core of my happiness. I started to realise, however, that exercise did make me happy, and so did using my skills. These were the core elements to making me feel fulfilled, so I prioritised these. These made me feel like I was moving forward. And as more time opened up, I could then explore other things. But I first needed to know what was at the core of my happiness.

You may find you discover things that make you happy that you never realised. I have come to love decluttering—it makes me feel like things are changing, moving forward. So keep searching; the things that make you happy may not be obvious (and they may not require any money either).

Once you understand what the core elements are that truly make you happy, you can ensure those are a priority in your day. It means decluttering other elements of your life, but whilst your time is limited, it will ensure you concentrate solely on the things that work for you. Caring for yourself is so important when you are so focused on caring for others. And if the window of time available to you is only thirty minutes a day, you need to be clear about what it is that will light you up, what will make you feel strong and content when you return to caregiving again.

Steps Beyond

- ► Work out what core elements make you happy.
- ► Be clear and prioritise these core elements.
- ► Share what makes you happy with the people you love. It will make it so much easier for them to support you.

Redefining Success

For so many of us, success has been defined by the hours spent working, the money made, or the items bought. I think after having children, there can be a search for more fulfilment, meaning, and purpose. I certainly felt this, and I wanted to really look at what success meant to me. Ambition is positive, but what used to define my daily sense of achievement was very different than it is now. My sense of success now combines work and wellness, growth and giving, dreams and the present moment.

I was so relieved to read Arianna Huffington's book *Thrive*. It really looked at reshaping our approach to work, combining it with wellness, and also pacing ourselves while maintaining a vision and purpose. We should be looking at our journey as exactly that—a journey, not a race, and not in isolation but one where working together and supporting others leads to a greater sense of success. I almost think the word "success" seems empty in itself. I like the word "thrive," because this is what I think we need to work towards, individually and collectively as a world. Success might be very different from one person to another, but for most, it is a purpose to work towards and a daily sense of achievement while enjoying each day.

Steps Beyond

- ► Think about what success means to you. Create your own definition and stay true to that.
- ► Look at what achievements make you feel the happiest.

► Seek wisdom and learnings from those who are also seeking to redefine success for themselves.

Resources

Action for Happiness: www.actionforhappiness.org

Anthony Seldon, author of *Beyond Happiness*:
www.anthonyseldon.co.uk

Dalai Lama XIV and Howard C. Cutler. *The Art of Happiness: A Handbook for Living*. New York: Penguin, 2009.

Dr. David Hamilton: http://drdavidhamilton.com

Gretchen Rubin, author of *The Happiness Project*:
www.gretchenrubin.com

Huffington, Arianna. *Thrive: The Third Metric to Redefining Success and Creating a Life of Well-Being, Wisdom, and Wonder*. New York: Harmony Books, 2014.

CHAPTER SEVEN

Vitality

The best six doctors anywhere
And no one can deny it
Are sunshine, water, rest, and air
Exercise and diet.

—Nursery rhyme quoted by Wayne Fields, *What the River Knows*

I have come to realise that well-being is like wealth. The more you invest in it and understand it, the more you get back. Focusing on our well-being is an investment, not only in the present but also in our future. The early years of parenting can be so exhausting that we need to take time to make sure we are at our strongest and healthiest. As with everything, this takes a step-by-step approach. For mothers, it is very easy to just keep going. But taking time to focus on our health is so important and can give us so much more back.

I find there are times I can move forward and give my well-being less focus and other times where I know I need to reassess, learn a bit more, explore, and change. But I do know that including well-being as a part of your life and your work is important. I really think one of our greatest journeys is understanding our own individual bodies, taking full responsibility for them, and listening to their warning signs and messages. Then we will be strong human beings and will truly create a new way for future girls and boys.

I have loved seeing the well-being movement unfold over the last few years. There is now so much information and so many brilliant people exploring for themselves and for the benefit of others. These people have also helped inform me. Here I share with you the wisdom of some of the great people I have met as well as the resources that have fuelled and fed me with great knowledge.

Nutrition

The first step I took was to consult a nutritionist. I sometimes think it doesn't make sense that we need support in the most fundamental parts of life—like eating—but we often do. So many patterns and emotions are built up, and so many messages from society are ingrained. I found wisdom in meeting nutritionist Amelia Freer. I wanted to understand why my energy was so inconsistent. I also wanted to ensure I wasn't holding on to any unhealthy eating habits that I wouldn't want to pass on to my daughter. This, for me, was a life-changing step.

What I Learnt

- ► I had many food intolerances, and these were draining my energy.
- ► Although I considered myself a healthy eater, I was very reliant on sugar.
- ► I did have patterns that I needed to let go of, like skipping meals.
- ► This may seem obvious, but I was incredibly dehydrated and needed to drink more water regularly.

What I Did

- ► I eliminated the intolerant foods until they were cleared from my system.
- ► I started the process of cutting sugar and learnt what a journey it is.
- ► I focused on drinking more water—often you are not hungry but thirsty.
- ► By doing the above, I started to regulate my eating patterns and settle into three meals a day.

Each of us and our requirements are different. You may have to address completely different nutritional habits. And I really don't think any of this can be achieved quickly. It really is a step-by-step process. The starting point is just to commit yourself to exploring it. If you would like professional support, ask for recommendations and find the best person for you. Then start to feel the incredible long-term changes.

One area I think many of us struggle with is sugar. Cutting refined sugar was a major part of improving my vitality. Before I started to explore my well-being, I hadn't realised the impact of sugar at all. For so many years, I had snacked on high-sugar carbohydrates. Although I was always interested in natural well-being, I had never learnt to truly nourish myself through food, and I found it very confusing. In becoming a mother and spending hours nurturing and feeding another person, I realised it can't be so strained. It should be more natural to fuel ourselves, to enable us to enjoy and embrace our day. And yet I felt very consumed by old patterns and emotional ties as well as by all the media messages towards women about size and shape instead of strength, individuality, and nourishment. For that very reason, it is a process, but it is one of the most important journeys we will take. So the starting point is to recognise that you need to learn, and perhaps gain expert advice.

Once you cut down on eating refined sugar, it starts to create a whole new way of eating because you start to identify when you are hungry or not and you start to regulate your energy. I also watched the impact of sugar on my children—how it changes their moods and energy levels. I realised it was having the same impact on me, even if it was less obvious. I wanted to feel strong and nourished, and I knew sugar was not supporting me in doing that. So an important step for me was to explore how to remove it. I realised it really needed to be gradual. First, I looked at what I was eating at breakfast and when were the times I was most drawn to sugar. Then I looked at the best way to replace refined sugars with natural sugars like Medjool dates and maple syrup. I know many would say this is still sugar, but for me, making this transition made the process stick. I think it would be very hard to go straight to nothing. I also made sure we started to make our own sweet treats. We found a recipe in Gywneth Paltrow's book, *It's All Good*, for healthy muffins and made them weekly for us and the kids. I think making sure you have an alternative is really important.

I kept researching and reading about it because it fascinated me. The more I read about it, the more I saw people exploring and sharing about this very subject. I discovered the book *I Quit Sugar*, which was hugely inspiring, as was the work of *That Sugar Film*. They shared their findings on the impact of sugar on our well-being and the well-being of our children.

Cutting sugar, or cutting any other unhealthy food habit, is not easy. These habits are ingrained in our culture. Especially with our children, every occasion or experience seems to somehow be linked to a sugar experience (a child's party, Christmas, rewards—it just goes on). Our research and reading really helped, because once you start engaging with something and see the benefits, you can find inspiration from others who are exploring this particular area too.

Steps Beyond

- ► Decide that you are going to focus on your well-being.
- ► Tell your family so they can support you.
- ► Find the well-being experts that you connect with and sign up for their newsletters.

- ▶ Remember to go step by step. Each one will create a solid foundation.
- ▶ Be persistent in creating new habits. Old habits take a while to turn into new ones.
- ▶ Don't try to change everything at once. When you and your body are adjusted to a new change, then you can create another one.
- ▶ Focus on the long-term. This is about creating the strongest possible body and habits for the future.
- ▶ Be kind to, but also honest with, yourself.
- ▶ Eat regular meals. Deprivation will have its consequences (adrenal fatigue).
- ▶ Try and align your eating schedule with your children's. Being surrounded by children who need regular meals can be a good reminder to yourself.
- ▶ Water, water, water!

Exercise

I want to share my journey with fitness because, all too often, we see the people who are already fit and connected with the joy of it and don't see what it takes to get there.

And fitness is a big area for me, for many reasons. I had lost my connection with fitness very early on when I was diagnosed with asthma as a child. This then led to a disconnect with the outdoors and natural fitness. I have come to understand now that is an important part of my energy, happiness, and creativity.

After I had my daughter, a mum at my son's school was setting up a small group of mothers to do an exercise class. I hadn't exercised for so long and felt so trapped in the cycle of feeling tired because of the sleepless nights. I reluctantly went along on a cold winter day and did a class. I can't tell you how hard it felt on my body; I wasn't used to focusing on my body. But it did inspire me slightly and give something back. I went again the following week, and again the following week, very slowly building up. It was really step by step. From there, I joined a gym, and I have to say, it has been a huge part of my life. I started to do classes when my daughter was in nursery or on weekends. There was one particular teacher who was so inspiring. I found her class so hard I could barely breathe, but I hadn't really pushed my body ever before. Finding a female figure who was so inspiring in her level of energy and focus pushed me. I remember being pushed along by her energy and thinking that if she could do this, then so could I.

I came to realise that every step took me closer to feeling stronger but also that it's important not to compare to others. My husband, for example, had played sport all his childhood, so his foundation level of fitness was very strong. I just needed to work on mine, be inspired by others, and in them see the potential that I could work towards.

Exercise builds the way our skills do. The feeling after working my body is like the empowering feeling of working with my skills. It makes me feel strong, when with each step I get stronger and fitter. It shows me what we can achieve as human beings, and it makes me want to keep going. Surely, this is the journey. It is about getting our bodies working at their optimum abilities for the long term.

I think this is a big subject, but what concerns me is the amount of time and energy we spend not being happy with how we look. I think the media plays a large part in this. All too often, when beautiful spring arrives, all we hear is how to create a "bikini body." For me, this doesn't work. It suggests that I need to spend hours questioning, restricting, or filling myself with negative thoughts. What does motivate me is exercising and eating to feel strong and empowered and to provide myself with a body that enables me to go on and do my work. This is why I do it—it reshapes my day. I feel stronger and more positive afterwards. And I find that removing myself from my house and work for a period of time each day is also important to my well-being, focus, and positivity. I am a kinder person and a better worker, and I feel more at peace with where I am. I have also made the best decisions and come up with the best ideas when jumping around in a class. You can change the story about the shape of your body—exercise to strengthen your mind and your body and to find your power and positivity.

If getting to a gym doesn't work for you, there are great online workouts and inspiration. I love the work of Erin Strutland. Her inspirational approach not only recognises the body but also the link with the mind. Find the rituals that work for you and set your intention each day. Mornings are important for shaping the rest of the day and your mindset, so focus on what works for you and try and make it a regular routine. This may include meditation, exercise, and vitamins.

Steps Beyond

- Commit to exercise, do it regularly, and find an exercise that you enjoy.
- When you feel tired, try some exercise. It can really make the difference.
- Don't give up. Don't give in to excuses (like the weather, etc.).
- Don't compare yourself with others—just see them as inspiration.
- Find a role model who inspires you.
- Notice the messages around you about your body.
- Move your body—not to create a "bikini body" but to create a positive mindset for the day ahead.

Energy

I realised early on in my journey that my well-being was integral to my life now as a parent. There was no opportunity to call in sick and have someone cover. So vitality had to be a priority. My energy was often so low that I couldn't get through a full day without it really dipping. I wanted to explore this, to find out what was draining me and how I could unlock more natural energy. I became fascinated by the concept of energy, and I explored every single way in which to maintain it and gain in its natural form, because I knew that energy was necessary in order to both work and care for my children.

In today's society, we value time and money, not the output of energy. And yet, what an incredibly important currency energy is. **With energy, you can do anything.**

I think there are many areas of female health and well-being that we need to focus on that are overlooked in today's society. But we need to be aware of it ourselves. I think our iron, our adrenals, and our nutrition are key areas of health to examine. I started to explore iron levels, nutrition, and exercise all in pursuit of getting stronger and fitter and sustaining my energy. Each aspect of my health plays such an important part in increasing my energy for my work.

Iron Levels

There was one simple thing I wish someone had just reminded me to do, because it could have saved me a lot of time feeling exhausted. I think, as women, it is so important to have our iron level checked. It eventually dawned on me to ask my doctor to have a check, and mine was incredibly low. It is simply sorted out, but this information is so important.

Adrenals

I am not a health professional, but this is my experience with adrenals, which I hope will help you understand them too. You know the feeling when you have had a little too much coffee and everything starts racing a little? That is your adrenals. In children, I guess we would refer to it as feeling "hyper." Adrenals are an underexplored area of well-being. It is not something I was really aware of before starting this journey, but now I am. The impact of stretching them too far leads to exhaustion and a sense of unease and disconnect. For the time spent overusing the adrenals, there is a time that must be spent resting and restoring them, so it is really important to be aware of them and keep them balanced as much as possible.

So when my adrenals are stretched, I feel less grounded and less myself. And the energy used up then needs to be paid back at another time. Now that I am aware of it, I check in. When my adrenaline is needed—for example, if I am going to do a presentation or something where it is naturally required—then that's fine. But if I am feeling it in an environment when I should be feeling calm, I have now learnt to check in.

What I came to understand is that the adrenals play a very important part in our health and well-being. That in our culture of "busy," it is very easy to dip into your adrenaline more than is needed and in circumstances for which it is not really required. It is meant to protect us from danger. I think it is really important to start to understand when you are using them and if there are times throughout your day when you feel that you are dipping into your adrenaline when it is not necessary. If you do find you are using your adrenals, look at ways to rebalance them, such as meditation or finding time for stillness. We all have only a certain amount of energy, so monitoring yourself can really help in the long term and in how you feel day to day.

For each person, it is going to be different, depending on how much their adrenals have been worked or overworked up to this point in their lives. But wherever you are, I think it is important to start to recognise yours, when they are triggered, and how you can best restore them back to balance when they are.

I have learnt a lot about listening to my body and tuning in to what it is telling me. Sometimes I miss things, and other times I catch the warning signs. This really is a balance between taking steps forward and challenging ourselves and caring for ourselves by knowing the signs our bodies give.

How People Affect Your Energy

I'm not sure we recognise the significance of other people's energy in both increasing and draining our own energy. This becomes only too clear when you first become a parent and you need every ounce of your energy to nurture your children and create a home. When you need as much energy as possible, spending time with others and coming home exhausted no longer seems to make sense. So take a moment to notice how you feel after you have been with others.

I really think this is such a valuable time to understand how people make you feel, whether they lift and inspire you or they drain you. Monitor how you feel the next day after you have spent time with someone. Do you feel tired, or are your conversations with them still in your mind? Also, if you feel you are adapting yourself in any way, this will take energy from you. One friendship or connection that allows you the space to truly be yourself is the blueprint for all other connections, so keep searching for it.

There is no doubt we need as human beings to be around others—family, friends, and community. But recognising what is right for you is important. When I first saw Susan Cain's TED talk, it felt like such an incredible relief to hear someone talking about the power of introverts. Although I love being around people, I also thrive in my own space, and her work has helped me recognise that. There will be some who are natural extroverts and find themselves energised by others and others who are introverted and need more quiet time.

The next step for me was to really identify who I should spend my spare time with. Although this may seem hard, I think that this process can truly prepare us for the rest of our lives. You may have friends you have known for years, or have recently just met at the school gates, that you come away from feeling exhausted or frustrated. Monitoring this is so important. Over time, you may become less drawn to spending time with the people you did before, but by creating this space, it will provide greater wellness and time for you to enjoy the things you love and to meet the people who truly lift and inspire you.

Nature

Nature can be a great support in boosting our energy and mood. I know it seems such a simple thing, but often I have to remind myself that nature is an incredible force and that spending time in it can feel strengthening and supportive. So make sure you spend time outside, especially during the colder months. It can be easy to tuck yourself away indoors or feel like you need to sit at your computer for all your hours of work. But embrace the flexibility this way of working provides you and take moments to feel energised by the great outdoors. I am always amazed by the difference in how it makes me feel—energised, relaxed, and, most importantly, available to everyone. If you need time to think or to gain energy, it may be the right time to step outside. Go for a walk or run or whatever activity will take you outside.

Steps Beyond

- ▶ Have your iron levels checked.
- ▶ Be mindful of your body and its responses to stress (your adrenals).
- ▶ Evaluate whether people you spend time with are inspiring you or draining you. Focus on spending your time with others wisely.
- ▶ Find opportunities to go outside and be refreshed by nature.

Aging

I felt like I went from my midthirties to my midforties in a flash as I was focused on raising the children. I didn't see it coming. Your focus for so many years turns from yourself to nurturing others, and all of a sudden, you find the years have passed you by. It was so easy to start to view myself as older and to create a negative mindset around this, but I think it is so important to move away from this. To focus your mind on your growth, happiness, and well-being whilst society views aging in such a negative way is hard, but I think we need to really work on this.

It is important for us to not succumb to the negativity of aging. So I focused on reshaping my own mindset around aging. I stopped thinking of it as negative and focused on the positivity of my journey, on the excitement of moving forward, and on connecting more and more with myself.

I do believe we can refocus and find a new way to look and feel good with the time available. Eating well and exercise is at the heart of this for me as well as refocusing on the mind and reconnecting to the journey alongside my children. Once we connect with ourselves again, I think the age of our journey and dreams no longer has a negative meaning. It is purely a length of time spent increasing wisdom.

I think we can change this forever. As parents, once we recognise that it's not a race, that we need to pace ourselves, it will extend our opportunities in work. We can focus less on the retirement story and recognise that our natural skills are part of us. By utilising those skills in whichever hours we have, they give us so much more. And then why would we want to retire from them? They give us energy, happiness, connection.

Steps Beyond

- ► Watch how you communicate about your age or birthdays. Try not to speak negatively.
- ► Switch off others' negativity towards age as well as negative messages from society.
- ► Focus on your own growth and keep the message positive.
- ► Focus on people who inspire you and on role models who are growing older with grace, power, and authenticity.

Resources

Amelia Freer: www.ameliafreer.com

Deliciously Ella: www.deliciouslyella.com

Dr. Christiane Northrup: www.drnorthrup.com

Dr. Mark Hyman: www.drhyman.com

Erin Stutland: https://erinstutland.com

Food Matters: www.foodmatters.com

Judith Raeburn, Marlow Homeopathy: www.marlowhomeopathy.com

Kris Carr: www.kriscarr.com

Madeleine Shaw: www.madeleineshaw.com

Nambudripad's Allergy Elimination Technique (NAET): www.bellequest.co.uk

Paltrow, Gwyneth, and Julia Turshen. *It's All Good: Delicious, Easy Recipes That Will Make You Look Good and Feel Great.* New York: Grand Central Life and Style, 2013.

Quiet Revolution: http://www.quietrev.com

That Sugar Film: www.thatsugarfilm.com

Wilson, Sarah. *I Quit Sugar: Your Complete 8-Week Detox Program and Cookbook.* New York: Crown Publishing, 2013. For more information, visit www.iquitsugar.com.

CHAPTER EIGHT

Support

If we value human capital as a society, we should value the array of jobs involved in caring for and educating young children—from birth through age eight—every bit as much as we value money managers or computer scientists.

—Anne-Marie Slaughter, *Unfinished Business: Women Men Work Family*

I read Hillary Clinton's *It Takes a Village,* and it really changed my whole perspective on support. It made me realise that how we are raising children isn't how it is meant to be. We are meant to have the village—the aunts, uncles, and extended family available to us. Once I acknowledged this, I realised that trying to do it all was limiting myself and my family. Finding the right support is a challenge, but focusing on it is key to your work.

Until there is a village to raise a child, we need to find ways to make it work for ourselves.

I think with so many of us working in new ways, the systems aren't quite in place yet to support us. So what creates the framework for one person may be very different for another.

Some may have parents who help, but many don't. Some may have access to great childminders, and some don't. What is important is that you keep searching for the support you need. And like your growing child, that need can change, and you need to remain flexible with that. Be able to move with the change. Recognise when the time is right to move on.

A big step for me was recognizing I couldn't do it on my own and that I needed to bring in support. I think this is one way that parenting opens your eyes to the need to work with others—that we are all human and we need support networks and communities. The work is in finding the right people for you. But stay focused on it and open to finding them.

Beyond childcare, support for me comes in so many different forms—the housework, my own personal growth and well-being, and connecting with the collective wisdom of people around me to help me evolve beyondtheschoolrun.com. I read recently that sometimes we can block the very support available to us by not recognising the fact we need it in the first place! Why we do this, I don't know, but I do know this doesn't help us move forward. The moment I recognised this was such a turning point. I became clear about what areas we could bring in help. Once you stop owning the whole job, you will be able to bring in the support you need, either from your partner or through services. Once you have created your own "village," your whole family will feel different.

Creating Flexible Childcare

Finding childcare and support that allows you to work in a flexible way is very challenging. We need to explore widely until better systems are in place. And until the childcare system supports this new way of working, it is important for you to create your own and to really focus on what and who is right for you.

Parent Networks

I think creating a group of parents whose children are friends with yours can be very valuable. You can support one another and create additional windows of time for work as the children play at one another's homes.

This can take time to build, and it is very different as it isn't based on an exchange of money for work. It is based on equal sharing, caring, and trust. It has been invaluable for me in many different ways. You will find that what you need, other parents will need too. So don't be afraid to suggest things and come up with ideas or ways in which childcare and support can be mutually beneficial. Also, other parents will have different needs and requirements, so try and keep your network broad and flexible. Working closely with the parents of your children's friends—and keeping it flexible, fluid, honest, and open—can really be a great part of your "village."

Support in Your Community and Beyond

As you start to develop your own way of working, you also need to develop the support that is right for you and your family. Again, as the way we are working is new, the support may not be a well-trodden route. I found this in the early years with my children. I needed flexible childcare but really only found full-time nannies or nurseries. At this point, we need to think differently and look for what we need. I found a nanny who was looking after children at my son's school full-time but who had hours available whilst they were in school.

We also found such amazing support in au pairs. The exchange of home for house help has been incredible. Having someone living and working with me forced me to develop my skills in delegating and to become more organised and clear about in what areas I needed support.

I remember thinking, when my children were babies, *If only we could have a system where young girls came and helped out for a few hours during the intense first six months of motherhood.* Providing them with an opportunity to see firsthand what it is like to have a baby in exchange for support for a new mother would be valuable for both. And

I have found this with the au pair system. It has supported us all in a flexible way.

Keep exploring new ways of childcare. If you need someone who is flexible, don't be afraid to ask for what you need or suggest new arrangements. Maybe ask local parents with older children whether their sons or daughters would be interested in earning some money and coming to look after your children whilst you worked. We did this one summer, and it worked so well. I was still at home working upstairs, and the children had someone to play outside with. I think we need to be creative. Often the solutions are on our doorsteps, but we need to be open to them.

Another area of society where I also think this could be of benefit is amongst the elder community. For retirees to spend time caring for young children could not only provide flexible childcare for parents but also be hugely beneficial for the elderly in keeping them connected and engaged. We found a local agency who provided babysitters, and I approached them to see if they had any evening sitters for a few hours in the day. We found a wonderful retired lady who had had children that were grown up and who was flexible and enjoyed being around the children. This support at the time the children weren't in school yet was invaluable.

And don't forget to review the other areas of daily life that it might benefit you to outsource. The housework was a big one for us. Once we found the right level of help with this, it was quite transformative. It meant that when I did have hours available, I focused solely on my work. I think this needs constant reevaluation, especially during the school holidays, but spending time focusing on this will pay off in the long term.

Steps Beyond

- ▶ Be clear about what support you need across childcare and the home, and be proactive in finding it.
- ▶ Don't wait to get support until you are too tired.

► Plan ahead for childcare and support as you would plan ahead in the workplace.

► Make your support structure a priority—whether it's getting the right cleaner, having someone iron your shirts, or arranging for an au pair.

► Be clear about how you need support. Write lists and delegate.

► If something doesn't feel right, go with your instinct. It is always the right thing to do, especially when it comes to the care of your children.

► Ask others in your community, create support networks, and share playdates to add more time for work.

► Make decisions for yourself and your family. What another parent is doing may not be right for your child.

► Stay open minded, be creative, and ask for what you need.

Fathers

If you are the main day-to-day caregiver for the children, it can often be difficult to allow the space for your husband to parent. I experienced this myself. I was so consumed by the routine of caring for the children that when the weekend came and my husband was there, I found it very difficult. Without knowing it, I would make him feel uncomfortable and uncertain about taking charge.

I think it would be like us walking into our husbands' jobs and just getting right to work, with no instruction. It's equally hard, though, when you are focused on the children all week and then another person steps in at the weekend or later in the day. You just want to make sure it all runs smoothly. At times, it works and weekends flow, and at other times, it doesn't. I know only too well that it's not easy. But I think that's okay, if we recognise this is new and it takes time. And I really think the steps we take as couples are huge steps collectively towards gender balance.

For so many of us who were used to careers, running businesses, and having financial independence, we can throw everything into the role of full-time caregiver, partly because at the beginning it is so unbelievably intense that it sets you in motion that way. I have really learnt that opening up a window to allow my husband in is so important.

As you open the way for him to be involved, the doors open for you too. His connection with the children grows, and that gives you the chance to grow and explore your own opportunities. Finding true balance between both parents is important to you, and it's important to allow the children to connect with both parents.

I do believe the role of fathers is so important for the development of our children and also for our own well-being. I think creating this balance is very individual to each couple. What is right for individual families is different because the support networks around you are different and every person's job is different. But one thing is true to us all—if we can find balance and equality in the home, it is of benefit to everyone. And if we can each find our own version of equality in the home, imagine what we can achieve in the wider world!

Making a window for fathers to step in and find their way in parenting isn't easy. When they are working full-time then readjusting to the home environment, it can be challenging. And I think the vital role of fathers hasn't been fully recognised in society—although this is changing. We have heard so many false stories, whether passed through generations, the media, or society, on how life should be for mothers and how it should be for fathers. Reconnecting with our authentic selves as parents can take time.

I first came across fathers speaking out when I saw a dad blogger, **Scott Behson**. It felt so positive that there were fathers talking about the importance of the father in a child's life, because all too often the emphasis is on the mother. I asked Scott, who is a business professor, a consultant, and the author of the book *The Working Dad's Survival Guide*, to give me some advice for this chapter on how mothers can create those spaces for fathers. Here's what he said:

LW: This book is for mothers, so I wonder whether you could possibly share any thoughts, from a father's perspective, on how women can create space for fathers to find their way in fatherhood. Often when you are the main caregiver, creating space for the other person to step in isn't easy.

SB: In many families, couples start out with egalitarian ideals in which both will maintain their careers and be equally involved parents. Unfortunately, a few barriers to these arrangements often prevent couples from arranging their family lives according to their values. The first is the workplace and the expectations for fathers to be the primary providers. Even when men have available parental leave, they tend to take far less of it than women, usually owing to concerns about being perceived as insufficiently committed at work and inviting negative career consequences.

As a result of this imbalance of initial leave taken and subsequent imbalance in time spent adapting to a newborn, many mothers become more competent in some of the basics of baby care and are more attuned to the baby's rhythms. Changing diapers really isn't hard, it's just that it requires some practice—and dads who are home for a week or two get far less practice than moms who often have months of leave. Over time, these early experiences set up a pattern in which the mom is seen as the primary parent and the dad is seen as the semi-competent helper parent. Once this pattern emerges, women's careers sometimes stall after a long leave, while men's careers (due to their truncated leaves) are relatively unaffected. This leads to greater separation in work and family roles—even when neither parent wanted it this way.

Relatedly, some families show signs of "maternal gatekeeping" in which moms, due to their role, can limit dads' access to their kids and, over time, prevent them from being involved in housework and childcare. This also involves the perceived need to micromanage dads so that they have to parent (or cook or clean) exactly the way mom does. This is obviously counterproductive as it shifts so much of the burden on mom and presents a barrier to involved fatherhood. In addition, some research shows that children benefit from being exposed to different parenting styles by the adults in their lives. Soothing and rough-and-tumble are both important.

My advice for moms would be to allow the time and space for dads to be involved parents and develop their own complementary parenting style. One can do this by intentionally leaving the home to take breaks, giving solo parenting time to dad early and often. Dads will have to be able to figure things out for themselves and find their own styles. One could also work with their spouse to establish certain rituals and responsibilities that are just for dad—maybe a dad who works late hours gets to do bath time and last bottle with baby every night before bedtime. Finally, in my house, we have a rule that my wife and I "can ask the other to do something, or tell the other how to do something, but can't do both." In this way, it is OK if I let our son pick out his outfits while my wife picks out a perfectly matching ensemble.

Steps Beyond

- ► Create a dream together, with your spouse. Whether that dream has one person working or both people sharing work and childcare, create it.
- ► Be kind to yourselves as parents.
- ► Be open to change.
- ► Remember that both you and your spouse are working hard, you are exhausted, and there is little time to yourself when you are parenting.
- ► See the steps you take with your husband as long-term. The more space you create for him, the more he can step in. Imagine the difference in a year or more.

Work Support

As with support at home, we also need to find the right support with our work. This can come in all different forms—a wise word, recognition for your work, a conversation with someone who understands what you are working on, an email, or offered support. Here we explore how you find it, remain open to it, and create a system that works.

Finding Your Tribe

I meet a lot of mothers who have transitioned from professions such as law or marketing to careers in life coaching or well-being. Whatever their transition was, what became very clear to me was that contacting and connecting with the right people was so important. If you are now working in a new area, connecting with your "tribe" can take a little time, but stay focused on it. Once you do find them, it will feel great to be connected with those dedicated to the same purpose.

When I started BeyondTheSchoolRun, I felt very much on my own. And yet as time went on, I connected with more and more people who were working towards similar goals of improving and changing the way for mothers and empowering women and girls. When I started to connect with those people, it felt like there was a real industry, and that felt great. Together, and in our own ways, we could contribute, collaborate, and move forward, each with an individual approach to our work. It really dawned on me when I was invited to speak at The Work and Family conference that I had become a part of an "industry."

When you find those people whom you connect with, reach out to them. The feeling that comes when someone you admire for their work supports you is incredible. I remember when I emailed Arianna Huffington. I didn't think for a moment she would email back, but I thought, *Why not try?* I suggested writing a blog for *The Huffington Post.* I remember receiving her reply; it was such a lift, just at the point I was questioning what I was doing. She responded that they would love to hear what I had to say. Although I didn't go on and write a blog for them, it didn't matter. At that point in my journey, I needed a focus and this response did just that. It was almost a little sign to say "Keep going." I am truly grateful to those who have taken that moment to respond or encourage. Often these small connections can create the greatest difference to another person's journey.

Steps Beyond

- ▶ Approach people who might be part of your "tribe" or who might support or guide you. What is the worst that can happen?
- ▶ Be clear and concise about why you are making contact.
- ▶ Accept introductions and meetings.
- ▶ Be present when communicating about your work. Often the conversations you don't expect will provide you with the wisdom or steps you need.

Finding Your Mentors

There is no doubt we need the collective wisdom of others, but does it need to be in the form of a mentor?

I think in some ways we have become confused about mentors. We focus on somehow finding someone who will steer us through our journey. But we are all on our individual paths. What I do believe is possible is being guided by a collective group. It is not about attaching to them or having expectations but just connecting with those who will help you unlock a part of yourself. I remember in the early stages, I thought I really needed a mentor, that the business needed it. I just needed to be present, listen, and believe in myself.

Support comes in so many different forms, and welcoming it in your work is really important. I have found that there are people who will support you at the very time you need it; you just need to be open to it and say what you need. Be honest and open to others about where you are at, and the rest will follow.

I found so much wisdom, support, and guidance in a collective group of people. I came to realise that no one person could mentor me to create my dreams; however, individuals could support me in finding it in myself to move forward. No one can give you the motivation or the tools, but what they can do is ignite the spark inside of you, help you find your own inner wisdom, and build your confidence and skills. And when others believe in you, and it only takes one or two, you can climb mountains.

I have been at so many turning points with developing BeyondTheSchoolRun, times when I have thought I couldn't make this work, but at that very moment, someone has come along and helped me move forward. I am so grateful to the people who have supported me, from single conversations to meetings to support from a great advertising agency. I think it is so important not to attach an outcome to a meeting or expect anyone else to create your work. You do, however, need to find the right support for you—and it is out there.

You don't necessarily need one single person as a "mentor." Be open to support from all places. Don't expect too much from one person or attach yourself to the thought that they will be the one to create your business or work. Just be present. When I stopped looking outside of myself for the answers and started to trust in myself and my own journey, it was a big step.

Steps Beyond

- ► Don't rely on having a single "mentor." Collective wisdom may work for you.
- ► Look for support nearby. Often, you don't need to look far. The guidance you need may be on your doorstep or at the other end of the phone.

Resources

Behson, Scott. *The Working Dad's Survival Guide: How to Succeed at Work and at Home*. Melbourne, FL: Motivational Press, 2015. For more information, visit http://fathersworkandfamily.com.

Clinton, Hillary Rodham. *It Takes a Village*. New York: Simon & Schuster, 1996.

Sandberg, Sheryl. *Lean In: Women, Work, and the Will to Lead*. New York: Alfred A. Knopf, 2013.

CHAPTER NINE

Self-Care and Growth

You must do the thing you think you cannot do.

—Eleanor Roosevelt, *You Learn by Living:*
Eleven Keys for a More Fulfilling Life

I think self-care and growth is such an important part of this journey. It is so closely linked to our work, lives, and happiness. This really was a very new area to me, not something that I had explored in detail, and yet now I value my personal growth. When I grow, my perspective changes, and as a result, my whole world changes. It is truly miraculous. I have learnt that we all have lessons to learn, we all have areas of ourselves that need either letting go of or growing, and ultimately, when we do, we take steps to becoming stronger, healthier, clearer, and freer.

Creating these new patterns is about making changes for life, shifting old patterns and old behaviours that no longer serve you, and ultimately taking steps towards your greatest self—inside and out. I find this a really exciting part of the journey, although I know it can be very hard too. Being open to exploring who we are is like unlocking hidden treasures, so keep searching and seeking, because there are miracles to be found.

Being Brave

Part of the BeyondTheSchoolRun journey is about being brave—being brave to take steps that may seem challenging, being brave to follow your own path, being brave to look within. The early years of parenting are so intense and cocooning that to reemerge with this greater sense of self, wisdom, and compassion can be challenging—that's why taking steps is so important.

When we were at school and in the workplace, we were challenged regularly. Somehow, in the parenting phase of life, there is a temptation to stop being challenged and to hide. So I started to slowly accept things that would challenge me. For example, I reconnected with the digital world. And when I accepted my first presentation, I wondered why I was doing it. I could have easily said no. I felt sick all the weekend before, but I knew I needed to challenge myself. And doing the presentation felt like a milestone; I had climbed a mountain, and it was exhilarating.

I think when we stop, we age. We get stuck because it is very easy to stay where we are, hide, and stay small. But those challenges that arise take us one step closer to our dreams, and our dreams are there for a reason.

Being brave takes courage, but it should still feel right. I remember when I was invited to No. 10 Downing Street for the first time. Although I was nervous, I didn't feel for a moment that I shouldn't be there or that it wasn't my place to be there. It felt very right and authentic. And when I did my very first vlog for the YouTube channel, interviewing Nick Hurd, MP at the Cabinet Office, I was nervous, but it felt completely right. I have heard many women in the past, some very successful, say that they felt like "imposters" in their jobs. But working in this new way—unlocking your skills and following your passion, values, and flow—feels real, genuine, and right.

Being brave also takes us to places we never imagined. Every newsletter or blog post I have written has led me to a place of much more confidence in my own ability to write. I remember when Harriet Minter, Editor of Women in Leadership at *The Guardian*, asked me to write a piece about how no one asks me about my work now that I am a mother. The day I saw the piece published online, I burst into tears. I had a deep belief, from many years, that writing wasn't something I could do, and yet here I was, successfully writing a published piece. And today I am writing a book. It's not about the writing; it's about the connection with our true selves and our voices. The writing is a platform to share. So every time you are working on something and you wonder why, remember that it will lead you to where you need to go.

We need to create our own challenges in our own way—each one different, but each equally important. When you work in this way, you will find that each of the small steps you take will lead you collectively to a bigger, braver one. And, although it's challenging, it will feel incredibly right—as though you are meant to be there right in that moment.

Steps Beyond

- ► Look for a challenge, an opportunity to be brave.
- ► Don't talk yourself out of these challenges.
- ► Don't compare. Your steps are individual. Something that may seem bold to you may not be to another.
- ► Remember how you feel after you finish a challenge. Use it to help you next time.
- ► Don't dismiss the small steps. They prepare you for the big ones.
- ► Stretch yourself, but don't push yourself.

Friendship and Social Connections

For many of us, our friendships can change after having children. The hours you used to spend nurturing those relationships are no longer there. Often we have moved to different places, making meeting new friends harder. But with less time and energy available, you can start to recognise those relationships that nurture you and those that don't. I think in many ways, although it can seem isolating at times, this can lead us towards great new long-term friendships.

The starting point really has to be becoming a best friend to ourselves. We have to learn to speak to ourselves the way would expect our greatest friend to and to nurture ourselves and enjoy our own company. I know how difficult this can seem. Something that seemed so natural and effortless has to become a focus.

I have often found that what I am missing, many others are missing too. There are so many families who have moved out of London with children. With that, there are so many new relationships and a building of a new community. Those communities, however stifling they may seem at times, are so valuable. They won't be there forever, but whilst they are, they connect you with the very people that will support, inspire, and connect with you. And if you are finding you need more community, create your own. I found growing my own community via BeyondTheSchoolRun has created a place for me to engage with others on subjects that I am passionate about. And this is truly inspiring.

Find ways for friendships to work for you. Old ways, like dinners and drinks, may no longer work (in the future, maybe). If it doesn't, you will be able to find those friends who feel the same. You create the groups, the new ways—you make the suggestions and the rest will follow. Embrace walks in the park with friends and early mornings rather than late nights. It may seem like you are missing something, but in fact, this is an important time for your body to change and create new habits that will last. Your children are not restricting you or holding you back; they are helping you grow. Don't resist it. Embrace it and enjoy it.

Our first experience of creating our own networks beyond our family unit is as children. However big or small, this is a huge part of our lives. It helps us grow, be happy, and live a full life. When you watch your young children select friends in the early years, what you see is that their selection process is based on a very natural instinct to connect with the right people for them. Not everyone is going to be right, but when they are being truly themselves, which all young children are, then they naturally gravitate towards those people who will enhance them.

When you become a parent, recognizing who you need to spend the little time and energy you have with is very important. A good guide is to look for who is empowering you. Once your attention turns to caring for young children, your friendships need to be balanced, nurturing both ways, and authentic.

Create your own networks, but most importantly, be yourself. When you become a parent, it brings you back to your authentic self because there's no time or extra energy for pretending or adapting. And this is what the workplace needs; it needs the authentic you. It needs women bringing their natural female qualities. This way, you will naturally meet the people who will empower you, and you will naturally connect with friends, colleagues, and school gates support. It's as simple as being YOU.

Steps Beyond

- ► Don't compromise yourself, your values, or your authenticity when you are with others.
- ► Recognise if friends are draining you or not nurturing you.
- ► After you have been with people, see how your energy levels are. If you feel drained or tired, this is a great warning that this person has drained you.
- ► Create ways that work for you to see your friends.
- ► Tell your true friends how important they are to you, especially if you don't get to see them often.

► Spend time with people who inspire and lift you.

► You are likely to have at least one friend who really gets the true you. Use this as a magic formula for future friendships.

Feeling Good from the Outside

With so much attention and time on the children, the home, and our work, it is really easy to not focus on how we look. I know this well. I remember one Christmas, it just dawned on me that, although I looked fine, I wasn't truly happy with my external appearance. But with limited time and budget, I also felt maybe it wasn't a priority. Now I don't think it needs to take too much time. I think it is a case of acknowledging it and recognizing that you are on a journey to connecting with your natural style. I really do believe we each have a natural style, much like handwriting, and once it's unlocked, then it's with you forever. However, with so much media and information around women and how they are meant to look, it is easy to lose this personal style and focus our thoughts on comparing and contrasting. This results in us not feeling like our greatest selves.

I remember one day just saying enough was enough when it came to how I looked. I had taken my daughter out to the playground, I was in really scruffy clothes, and I hadn't done much to my hair. Basically, I didn't feel like my greatest self. I then went to the school to pick up my son. I felt like somehow I hadn't settled in to my day. Something was missing—and it was me. I hadn't taken one moment to focus on how I looked. I promised myself from that day that I would every day take a moment to make myself feel the best I could in the time I had. I promised myself that I would take steps to start to connect with my sense of style again in a way that worked.

I took three initial steps:

1. I decluttered—and decluttered more. It took time, but it was such a great process. I spent weekends clearing out my cupboards, reselling items, or taking things to charity.

2. I found a uniform that worked. For me, it was Gap skinny jeans and Gap T-shirts. This made me feel dressed enough, with little time to have to think about it in the morning.

3. I started to focus on the best way to unlock my style. I registered with fashion bloggers and starting reading about fashion again.

Being a parent forces you to cut through the clutter of everything, and I think fashion is the same. Once we recognise that we don't suit everything the shops are trying to sell us, we can find our own style that works for us as individuals. Then we can save so much money and time, and we can feel like our true selves from the outside as well as the inside.

Create a Wardrobe That Works

I find creating a "daily uniform" has worked really well for me. It is wonderful not having to spend time thinking about what to wear and just wearing something that makes me feel empowered both for work and for caring for the children. Skinny jeans and a shirt have long been an affordable staple of mine.

Everything doesn't suit us. We just need to know what works for us and how to find it. We need to start to unlock our own natural and individual style. Then we stop feeling uncomfortable in clothes that don't work, we stop spending money on clothes that don't work, and we find our true sense of self from both the inside and outside.

In the early days, I think it is so important to create a uniform so that we can remove the time and frustration spent thinking about what to wear. Then we can develop and nurture our sense of style from the starting point of a daily uniform. Our steps towards authenticity in clothes need to be simplified. We need to block out the noise and the messages, and we need to go on our individual journeys of exploration. We can gain knowledge and insight, wisdom and inspiration, from others, but ultimately, this is individual. And once we get it, we will see that where we are right now is great.

In the same way that parenting shows us the way to unlocking our natural skills, I also think there is an opportunity to unlock our natural style. With limited time, money, and energy to focus on your clothes, there needs to be another way. Finding my individual style was it for me. We don't need to be sold to by the retailers; we need to cut through the clutter and find ourselves so that each day we can dress with ease, feel our greatest, and do our jobs.

Be Kind to Yourself

You do have limited time to focus on this, and that is OK. Be gentle with where you are and what you have right now.

I remember a meeting I went to when my daughter was young. At the time, the majority of my day was focused on caring. I arrived at the meeting, having spent a long time getting to it. I was very aware of lots of young girls looking very glamorous. This felt so removed from me—fashion, makeup, dressing for a work environment. So I quickly I popped to the toilet and put some eyeliner on. I had the meeting feeling utterly exhausted and slightly uneasy. When I left, I looked in a mirror to see that all the black eyeliner had smudged all over my top eyelid! I learnt that the point was to keep it simple and to be kind to myself.

Being kind to yourself includes not comparing yourself to others. At that meeting, I didn't need any extra makeup. But I put it on because I compared myself to other women. We are all different. You may see mothers who were already connected with their individual style, and therefore it feels very natural. Just stay focused on yourself, gain inspiration from others, and keep taking your own steps.

Declutter

I have learnt from decluttering that I need less than I thought. I have also learnt that all too often in the past, my buying was emotional rather than thoughtful. This has been very empowering. I have sold and donated so many clothes, and now when and if I shop, I buy only what I really love and what will fit into my wardrobe long term. The power of decluttering is more than just creating space in your wardrobe. It is about creating new, healthy ways that free you to unlock your natural style, spend less time focused on your look, and still feel great about who you are.

Keep going with the decluttering. I have found it's a process. It doesn't happen in one go.

Find Your Style

When I started exploring this area for myself, I was introduced to **Sally Smy**, founder of Queen Bee Styling. Sally and I subsequently went on to do a few vlogs together on the BeyondTheSchoolRun YouTube channel, and I really enjoyed exploring this subject with her. I asked Sally about her advice on connecting with your style again, or for the first time, after having children and how to do this in a time- and money-efficient way.

> SS: My turning point came whilst I was on maternity leave with my first child. Prior to that, I had worked for eighteen years in fashion and was relatively comfortable with my image. I went on maternity leave—and found myself in what I refer to as "the tunnel." From the day of my daughter's birth and for a long time afterwards, I couldn't focus on anything but my little one. One day, about eight months after my daughter was born, I caught sight of myself in a shop window—I looked shockingly scruffy and was still wearing maternity clothes. I literally took a step back. It was a moment where I thought I had become someone else. I took a deep breath and decided I needed to sort it out and focus on "me" again. The prospect of my impending return to work as a fashion buyer was the "kick up the bottom" I needed.
>
> So I took a deep breath and went through the following process:
>
> ► I booked an appointment at the hairdresser's.

- ► I went and had a consultation at a makeup counter.
- ► I arranged childcare so I could go shopping.

You do need to stop to take a look at yourself. The immediate change that motherhood brings often results in changes in our appearance, body shape, and lifestyle. Before, I was focused on looking a certain way only when I worked full time in fashion. I find now, even when I am at home, I still need to feel confident in what I am wearing. It is important for me to think about clothes in the general day to day, and by this I mean at the park as well as going to work.

Here are some strategies I use:

- ► Think about the basics, e.g., jeans, shoes, a coat. Get these right first.
- ► Add one pair of cool shoes to the basics. They can make an outfit.
- ► Think about your individual tastes and just adapt them slightly (for example, if you love jeans, push yourself out of your comfort zone and try different styles).
- ► Be realistic about your body. Dress for the body you have.

I know it can seem a daunting task. Your body shape may have changed, you don't have time, and it can be overwhelming, but making the effort has such a positive effect on your confidence.

LW: One step at a time. Just acknowledging you are ready is a step. I remember, last Christmas, posting a picture on Instagram of me saying my New Year's resolution was to focus on enjoying fashion again. I never really knew why I did that at the time, but now I do. I was making a commitment to myself to take those steps.

SS: Our clothes are a message to people around us (and ourselves) that we are nurturing ourselves.

Here are some steps you can take to get started:

- Look in your wardrobe. Give yourself an appraisal of your clothes. Ask yourself—*Do I love them? Do they actually fit me? Are they out of date?*

- If possible, have a professional go through it with you, or an honest friend, to help work out what suits you and what needs to go.

- Declutter and sell unneeded clothes or give them to charity. In your wardrobe, just have what you are wearing in the week. If an item has been there for two years and you haven't worn it, get rid of it.

- Take seasonal things out of your wardrobe and pack them away. Styles like heavy knit jumpers and winter coats take up lots of room and are not needed in the summer months. (Have a practical wardrobe that you are wearing at this moment in time.)

- When you have decluttered, step back and see where the gaps are in terms of your lifestyle right now.

- Get expert help—set appointments for your hair or a makeover at a beauty counter. Make a focused list of the clothes you need and go out to buy just those items (don't be swayed; focus on what you need).

- Build a visual guide—look at fashion blogs and favourite brands. Get an idea of what you want before you go shopping. If you haven't shopped for a while, it's important to get some visual inspiration.

- Create a uniform. Start to understand your style and likes, and build from there. If you prefer wearing trousers, then just work from there—invest in the latest trouser shapes in classic colours. Don't try to change your whole look from head to toe. Find the things you like (e.g., jeans, jersey tops) and get that right first. Start with small steps and build from there.

LW: It's very easy to hide behind clothes, when in fact removing those layers and finding the essence of your style can feel so refreshing and renewing.

As you build your wardrobe, remember these three things:

- ▶ Don't worry about trends; just find the styles you like.
- ▶ Always ask yourself before you buy something: *Do I really love what I am about to buy?*
- ▶ Take one step at a time. Don't compare yourself with others—focus on you.

Steps Beyond

- ▶ Subscribe to some fashion blogs that may be right for you.
- ▶ Your clothes don't need to cost much. When you buy, buy the right items for you.
- ▶ Do a wardrobe clear-out and general decluttering.
- ▶ Explore clothes and fashion that support your sense of positivity and motivation.
- ▶ Make sure anything new that you bring into your wardrobe, or home, is what you love.

Preparation for the Colder Months

If you live in a place where the winters are particularly cold (like myself), I think it is important to spend time preparing for them so you are strong and well enough to keep taking steps forward all year round.

I really think we need to move our mindsets beyond the state of the weather. We know that winter comes each year, so preparing for it allows us to stay strong and focused and happy. As soon as I recognised that, I found I could embrace each season with much more positivity. There is no doubt that the winter months are the most challenging, but that doesn't mean they can't be great. I also think this is an important area because this is a large part of our year and we need to remain productive and engaged during these months to keep taking our steps forward. It doesn't need to take much, but a few simple steps can make all the difference.

I think learning from previous years what worked well for you and the family and what didn't is key. Those winter months, in many ways, are times to cocoon ourselves, but we also need to ensure that we have certain elements and practices in place to maintain our well-being so we can keep taking our steps and be ready to bloom in summer.

One key strategy I have used is to not speak negatively about the weather. You are not allowing it to impact your day, instead staying focused on yourself, your positive thoughts, and what you have right there and then. I also started to read about vitamin D levels and how much they decrease during the winter months. It's so easy to ignore this, but it can really impact how we feel and how we work.

I also became very aware of how important it is to go outside, during daylight hours, during the colder months. It's so tempting to stay tucked up at home, but ensuring that each day we connect with nature and get our feet on the ground outside is so important. The children are great reminders to do this, but it is easily forgotten once it gets colder. However, it will make you feel so much stronger and healthier. I can't believe what a difference it can make, and it is available to everyone, every day.

Steps Beyond

- ► Have your vitamin D level checked.
- ► Try not to speak negatively about the weather, and don't allow it to affect your day.

Letting Go of the Old to Welcome the New

In seeking opportunities for personal growth, I also experienced the opportunity to let go of emotions from the past that were potentially keeping me stuck. I think the point at which you become a parent is a really key time to do this. Opportunities to explore our emotions from the past do present themselves in the family environment and in experiencing childhood again through the growth of our own children.

I spoke with Dr. Yehudi Gordon, specialist in women's health, about this. We discussed how, on your journey as a parent, it is possible to start to experience emotions from the past that need clearing. Once you let go of those emotions, you become stronger, clearer, and healthier. And, most importantly, you are free to respond to situations as a parent in the best way possible for you.

I truly think this is an incredible opportunity, but it can be hard to identify whether the emotions you are experiencing are current or historic. I think the way I have learnt to gauge this is by checking in with myself. If I am reacting to an experience, my reaction seems very intense, and that level of emotion seems out of proportion to the current experience, then I tend to know it is historic. In my experience, when you let go of the old emotions, you take steps closer towards yourself. You become lighter, freer, and clearer about who you are.

Dr. Gordon explains that "our early life experiences before the age of three drive our behaviour. Negative experiences pre–one year old can be stored in the body in the form of rage. Our children bring these out and allow us to heal." With all there is to learn and do as a parent, this isn't easy. Often, we can be so intensely involved in the situation or the moment of parenting that it is hard to explore. I hope this section can open your mind to this theory, though. If you are experiencing emotions or feelings that you wish to address—just to feel calmer, more focused, or clearer in who you wish to be as a parent—then I truly hope this provides you with some clarity.

I hope that in time, this area is explored in prenatal work. Dr. Gordon believes that "you can start to heal yourself at the point of conception." I think it is a true gift for us all to see this as a time not only for our children to grow but for us to grow as well. So whatever it might be—old childhood experiences, labels that didn't fit, messages from society or family that didn't work for you—you can say goodbye to them.

Some of these emotions have been tucked away for such a long time, we often don't even know they are there. As Dr. Gordon explains, "Elements are hidden in your unconscious." But if we don't release them, if we don't acknowledge them, they get stuck and manifest in other forms. For many of us, patterns are created in our childhoods or throughout our school years. You may find that these patterns start to show up once you have children. I think children provide a mirror to parts of yourself that you may be able to let go of.

The reason I think this is so important is that our emotional lives are so closely linked to our work once we become parents. Our energy, our motivation, and our happiness are linked to our children and our family unit. I know how hard parenting can be, how intense, how many times you think *I can't do this anymore.* The intensity of the early years of parenting can leave us tired and bewildered and often feeling far removed from our vibrant selves. Dr. Gordon said that "we can see the mothers who will end up with depression, those who haven't explored or released their past." But I also know there is another way.

This can be hard, so explore finding the right support for you. Remember: this is a step-by-step process. It isn't something that happens in a few days, and it is individual. Each step will, however, make you stronger and wiser, and it will be another giant step closer to your authentic self.

I think we can focus on this by really tuning into our bodies on a regular basis. We can hear what our bodies are telling us both emotionally and physically so that we are ready to release those old blocks when they surface. I think when we are mindful of this process, we become aware of these emotions and the need to release them. This can be a daily process in just monitoring ourselves, our emotions, and how we are feeling.

I truly believe this is a crucial stage in our human development— one of life's greatest opportunities not yet explored. But once it is, we will evolve as parents and human beings.

Exploring these emotions is natural and healthy, and it is an opportunity for long-term well-being. But we need to know how to work with the emotion, how to release it when it arrives, and how to avoid tucking it away where it may manifest in the form of sickness. I hope to see this in the future as a subject that is openly discussed and prepared for in prenatal groups. I hope help and support becomes readily available when needed and that it is viewed as a collective growth process. I think we will see huge advances in well-being throughout the later stages of our lives as a result.

Steps Beyond

- If you are responding to a situation and your response seems out of context, explore whether this may be historic.
- Share with people close to you to see if your response to a situation or your emotions seem out of context for the current situation.
- Find the right support for you (maybe a wise person or someone who can help guide you).
- Be gentle with yourself; *it can be very difficult.*
- Research tools that can help you with your personal growth.
- At home, acknowledge your emotions, how you are responding to situations, and how that makes you feel.

Peace in Your Home

Your family environment is so important to your work and vice versa. When the family environment is peaceful, you are in a great place to work, be creative, and maintain your flow. When this is off, as a mother, the emotional drain is big. Having children really made me look at how my actions, behaviour, and thoughts impact them. I decided that I needed to take responsibility for my own personal growth. By opening my mind, and questioning myself and not others, I could create greater peace in the family.

Personal development, I believe, is a process of understanding ourselves better, working towards our greatest potential, releasing parts of ourselves not needed, and finding the parts that are making us happier, stronger, and kinder people. As we grow into adulthood, the thinking often is that we have grown up, but in my experience, there is further growth. Expanding our mindsets, releasing old unhealthy patterns, healing—all these areas add up to our own personal development. And this growth in turn will have a huge impact on our work and roles as parents because it will shape our behaviours, actions, and reactions.

One thing to address is balance in your relationship with your spouse. When my relationship with my husband was off balance, I found it draining. We both wanted to create more balance, but it takes intention. I realised that it had to start with me. When I am not connected with myself, or if I don't realise I am angry with myself about something (I haven't worked hard enough or whatever it might be), I find it hard to make a true connection with my husband. Often my anger at myself will come across as anger towards him. Also, when your partner sees you truly focusing on your steps and using your hours wisely, you will see him step into the jobs you need support with (e.g., cooking, tidying, etc.). So start with yourself and your thoughts. Confidence in yourself is beautiful and will shine through.

When things get tense in the family, our first instinct is to confront others. And yet the most powerful thing we can do is look at ourselves to see if we can learn or grow from it, because often, these experiences have been brought to us to teach us. See it, however hard it may be, as an opportunity. I know at those times it can be so hard, because everyone is upset and unsettled. And yet these are mountains to climb; once at the top, a beautiful new view will appear. Remember that there is always calm at the other side, and remember how precious these people are to you even in the toughest moments.

Now, if something is wrong at home, I often look at myself first, go inwards, and question if it has something to do with me. Is it reminding me of an experience in my childhood, and is my reaction pure or historic? You probably notice that when you become a parent, you find yourself saying things that your parents said, without thought. I think questioning these responses and thoughts can be incredibly powerful in your own self-growth, liberating you from old patterns and taking you closer to your authentic self.

Also, as mothers, I think a lot of what we are feeling impacts the mood and the flow of the whole family unit. So it is important to start with ourselves. In these moments of disruption, I have often found it is a time for change—a time to review what we are doing. Maybe we need more support, maybe the children need more independence—whatever it is, change is there to help us grow and not stay stuck.

I also sometimes notice in myself a sense of restlessness and that my body starts to feel a little stuck. This is a sign that it is time to grow, move forward, and take more steps. There will be times your routine is good and working, and other times, you will need to change or develop. It is just like our children. They are able to take a little more at a time, and they become more resilient.

In my experience, the more I have grown within myself, the more of a positive impact it has had on the children. I truly believe this is an important part not only of our journey but also of the journey of our children.

I have found tools that support my personal growth. I use tapping, also known as Emotional Freedom Technique (EFT), Nambudripad's Allergy Elimination Technique (NAET), homeopathy, and meditation. There are a great many other tools and also a great many coaches that can support our growth.

Steps Beyond

- ► Check in with yourself when there is an issue or argument. You can't change the other person, but you can change yourself.
- ► View discomfort or difficulty as a great opportunity to grow.
- ► Forgive each other in tense moments. Be kind to yourselves.

Gratitude

When you are wanting to attract more into your life and you are finding there is a block, I think a key point is focusing on gratitude. Look at what you already have and not what you don't have, and from there, you can start to grow.

The moment I started to focus on gratitude was, without a doubt, a defining moment in my journey. It changes everything. Your mentality shifts from *Why has she got that?* and *Why don't I have that?* to *Life is good* and *This is where I am meant to be*. And that is real, beautiful peace. The steps you take from there, in peace and flow, are the right ones.

I remember my last few birthdays, since turning forty, have been so emotional. I was constantly looking, in my old way, for what I would receive. Yet what dawned on me, on my forty-third birthday, was that it was about taking a moment to be grateful. I needed to reshape my thinking, as the other way wasn't working for me. So I decided my birthday would focus on what I was grateful for. I wrote a gratitude list and put a "thank you" sign up in my office—which is still there as a reminder. It is so easy to get caught up in expecting. But stopping the need for more was what I needed to enjoy life. And that is amazing.

I have to remind myself to do this. It isn't something that just happens. We live in a very consumer-focused society, but once you connect with your own gratitude, you will start to see the benefits. You stop comparing with others, something that can certainly intensify when you become a parent.

Just as we are opening ourselves to new opportunities and creating and welcoming change, I think gratitude provides us with a balance of patience and stillness. For me, it's like buying something new and then clearing something out of my wardrobe. I think the gratitude keeps us present, keeps us still, and provides us with a place to grow from.

When you are questioning or seeking more, stop and write a gratitude list. Be honest and open. I find my list reminds me yet again of what really matters. My children and husband are at the top, along with my well-being, people who support me, nature, and sunlight (oh—and avocados!). Take a moment—it doesn't take long—to write it and share it. I post it on my fridge in the lead-up to my birthday instead of a wish list.

Steps Beyond

- ► Write a list of what you are grateful for. Put it somewhere you can see it.
- ► At the times where you might be drawn to expecting gifts, focus your thoughts on gratitude.

Resources

Brown, Brené. *Daring Greatly: How the Courage to be Vulnerable Transforms the Way We Live, Love, Parent, and Lead.* New York: Avery, 2015. Find more information at www.brenebrown.com.

Dr. Yehudi Gordon: www.dryehudigordon.com

Gabby Bernstein: http://gabbybernstein.com

NAET: www.bellequest.co.uk

The Tapping Solution: www.thetappingsolution.com

CHAPTER TEN

Rest, Reflection, and Renewal

Wherever we look around the world, we see smart leaders—in politics, in business, in media—making terrible decisions. What they're lacking is not IQ, but wisdom. Which is no surprise; it has never been harder to tap into our inner wisdom, because in order to do so, we have to disconnect from all our omnipresent devices—our gadgets, our screens, our social media—and reconnect with ourselves.

—Arianna Huffington, *Thrive: The Third Metric to Redefining Success and Creating a Life of Well-Being, Wisdom, and Wonder*

 nce you have reached this point in your journey, you have discovered your flow and your passions and you are taking steps towards your dreams. It feels amazing—well done!

You have set the foundations for a new way of living. Now having spent a lot of time focusing on creating this new way, it is hard to take time to stop. I know I have often thought, *I don't want to lose what I have learnt—the new patterns and habits—by stopping.* However, taking time to rest is so important. It will enable you to restore yourself and come back stronger and clearer. So here we explore the power of disconnecting, reviewing, and resting—all hugely important steps on this journey.

Digital Detoxing

Although I am a huge fan of the benefits of the digital age, I have also become aware, over the last couple of years, of the importance of disconnecting. When we remain continually engaged with our phones or computers, it can really impact our work. I think it is key to continue to grow and unlock new parts of ourselves, our talents, and our well-being. Time away from our phones and screens provides vital space for thought and self-discovery.

The challenge in combining children and work is in being present whilst with the children and focused on work when not. When I am with the children, I try as much as possible to be disengaged from my phone. On Sundays, and most recently on holidays, I have started to disconnect altogether. I tried this once last summer, and I found myself so drawn to my phone during the quieter family moments. But I stuck to it and the outcome was so worth it—I returned home with a renewed sense of energy and focus, and I went on to launch the BeyondTheSchoolRun YouTube channel, which I had been struggling to do before we went. I cannot recommend digital detoxing enough, and I think once we make it a practice, it makes us stronger when we do connect.

This is where making authentic connections becomes really important (see Chapter Two). I found if I didn't make an authentic connection throughout the day, then I would be searching online later in the day. My husband would come home and switch off from work, and yet I was still searching for something. Making the right connections so you won't feel the need to keep searching for a connection through your phone is so important.

It is so important that we use our windows of time wisely. Connect with yourself first daily, be clear about who you want to connect with in the hours available to you, and then disconnect when you can.

Steps Beyond

- ▶ Try disconnecting from your devices for periods of time during the day and see how it feels.
- ▶ Do a digital detox on a holiday. Examine how you feel when you come home.

Decluttering

I can't tell you quite how much decluttering has been such an important part of this journey. I really can't recommend it enough. It has cleared my head and my workspace, but it has also made it easier for me to move between caregiving and meetings and so much more.

I absolutely love decluttering, and it has become a key part of the last few years for me. In the house, I've cleared areas to create space. And not just in the physical sense—it really feels like you are creating space in your mind, making room for the new. In this process, I have also become much more selective about what I bring into the house and more aware of my spending and purchasing. I really take great care to buy only items that I truly love.

On days when I wanted to feel like I was taking steps, but with ease and not focusing specifically on my work, this is what I would do. If you are feeling slightly stuck, or are at home and want to feel like you are achieving something, try decluttering. Weekends when I have been home with the children have also been a great time, and decluttering has made me feel like I have moved forward. I also found the winter months a great time to declutter, so that by the time the spring arrived, I and my home felt clear.

Also, this is the best starting point if you need a home office. The more I decluttered, the more space I created, and a small room at the top of our house became available. I made sure this space became only my workspace. I put pictures on my walls of experiences on my journey with BeyondTheSchoolRun, I set up a desk, and I made it clear this was my office. The moment I stepped in the door, it felt separate from the rest of the house. And it felt great to have a space again dedicated just to me and my work.

I have also found the power of decluttering your life, not just your home, so important when you become a parent. Look at what works, what doesn't, and who you spend time with. You can find exactly what is right for you as an individual—what things make you truly happy, which people truly nourish you, and which environments support you. The more you declutter, the more your life will flow and the more space you will make for what you need.

Another way to declutter is to clear your mind. I can't think of a group of people who need this more than mothers balancing work and children. The parenting journey is the perfect time to declutter our lives in every way. As part of this decluttering, I think our minds play a big part.

I think it's easy to hear about meditation but not easy to implement it into your life. I am still at the early stages of my own journey with it, and I am learning the potential it has to bring me back to a peaceful place, to restore energy, and to clear my thoughts. But finding space to do it can seem a challenge. As with everything new, we have to intentionally decide to commit to it each day until it becomes natural and a part of everyday life. Just ten minutes in the morning, or when your mind is full, or when your energy dips, can create a habit. It is incredible the difference it makes in reshaping your day.

I started my meditation journey by signing up for trials to both Headspace.com and Calm.com (during school holidays) and Oprah and Deepak meditations and making sure I followed them. I felt infinitely calmer and clearer, and my energy was more sustained.

Steps Beyond

► Find areas of your house that can be decluttered.

- ► Remember how it feels after you have cleared an area of your house, because it will remind you for next time.
- ► When decluttering, question whether you need something or whether you can give it to charity or sell it.
- ► Look at other areas of your life that you can make clearer— maybe your connections or your habits.
- ► Remember that decluttering is an ongoing process.
- ► Commit to try meditating.
- ► Look for free trials of meditations.

Rest

Whatever stage you are at, it is important to recognise when your body needs a rest. Your routine may be working, but sometimes we need to just pause for a bit. Don't worry; this isn't a step backwards. This is consolidation, and it is an important step in preparing you for your next stage of growth and development.

I have found it hard to recognise when I need to rest. You are gathering momentum, you have lots of plans and visions, and then your body tells you to stop. You can try and push through it, but it will keep reminding you. So there is a time to focus, plan, and stretch, and there is a time to go with the flow. Step back for a bit and let your body process all the changes, all the steps you have taken. I used to try and fit so much in when my children were not at school, and then at the times my body said rest, I sat and played Legos and Play-Doh with the kids. It was a reminder that the other things could wait. And when my energy was restored, work would come with ease, as opposed to me pushing through.

It's also a good time to remind you (as I always remind myself at these times) that it "takes a village" to raise a child. So be kind to yourself. You are working so hard. It isn't a race—when you pace yourself, there is more longevity in your work, your well-being, and your happiness.

Steps Beyond

- ▶ Remember to rest when you need it.
- ▶ Be kind when your body is consolidating.
- ▶ Remember that rest is a step forward, because it is preparing you for the next stage.

Acknowledging Progress

I found it important to take a moment to really acknowledge each of the steps I had taken, day by day, and where they had taken me. By not working in a traditional sense (hours = money), you may be missing a sense of progression or achievement. I think it is important to acknowledge and reward your own work.

Look at all areas that you have developed—not only your work but your health too. It is important to recognise the work you have done for your well-being too (your well-th!). The investment you have made has made a difference. How much stronger do you feel? Do you have more clarity, passion, and purpose? I certainly find myself feeling stronger, happier, more peaceful, less cluttered, more focused, clear about my skills, and much more connected to my authentic self. This is what drives me when I am finding it hard to motivate myself—the reminder that each one of those daily steps adds up.

Steps Beyond

- ▶ Pause and reflect on what you have achieved so far.
- ▶ Acknowledge not just the external achievements but the internal ones too.

Staying Motivated

This can be challenging at times, especially when you are working on your own and also during the colder months when there is less day-to-day interaction with others.

I can't tell you the number of times I have thought going to the shops or looking at clothes was what I needed when it really wasn't. That is a reward at the end of your work, not a distraction from continuing when it can seem hard. It's like exercise—some days you will start and you'll think you can't do it, and by the end, you are energised and feeling great again. But you have to push through the hard bit to get to the other side. You have to persist, stay focused, and not be distracted. The reward is the feeling of achievement at the end. And this is what will fill you each day. It is so easy to be distracted, especially when people around you are doing very different things and when you aren't in a workplace dedicated to motivating everyone to stay focused on work.

It is so tempting, especially towards winter, to not stay focused on taking steps. It is so tempting to join the festivities—and they start so early when you have children. When the world around you is focusing on the lead-up to Christmas, try and stay focused on your work until the "working world" finishes too. It will really pay off by the time you reach the New Year. Do not be tempted to leave things to next year. Make sure you focus on completing jobs (not starting new ones) and on planning for the new year ahead (in which you can include the new ideas and projects).

If you are flagging, look for role models who you really connect with. At those times when I find my motivation is low, I start my day by listening to someone that inspires me and whose words focus my mind and intentions. Often, this can be the very action I need to regain motivation again. There are a great many organisations now working to support mothers and women in their work, and watching a vlog or visiting their Instagram accounts can really help move you forward. I have found much inspiration in the younger generation of girls growing businesses. Their passion for kindness, authenticity, and positive messages empower other women.

I also find it is so important to stay committed to talking about your work during these times. It is easy to get distracted by conversation about the children, but when you can talk and engage with others about your work, it's amazing how empowering this can be.

And remind yourself why you are doing this—that it is about combining children and work and about a lifetime of working with your passion and skills. So it's not a race—it's a pace. You may see others who appear to be speeding ahead, but just stay focused on your journey, your growth.

Steps Beyond

- ▶ When your motivation is flagging, write a list of what you want to achieve each day and for the week.
- ▶ Seek out sources of motivation. There are many great resources online.
- ▶ If you feel restless, go for a run or a walk. This will clear your head and shift your energy.
- ▶ Speak with a friend who is working in a similar way to gain momentum and motivation.

Finishing Strong

When you are working for yourself or managing your own time, it is so easy not to finish jobs. I know this very well—I love creating and dreaming up ideas, and I need to remind myself to finish one thing before starting another. It's very easy to put our admin to one side, but this plays an important part in our work. Once this is decluttered and in order, it will help you so much. Don't see this as wasted time—just choose the right time to work on it. I often find the school holidays are good, when I have an hour or so to focus on these jobs. I also feel there is immense power in truly finishing, in putting all you have into one thing before you immerse yourself in the next.

Steps Beyond

- ▶ Create a plan of what you want to achieve by the end of the year and stay focused on it.
- ▶ Complete all administrative tasks that you can before the end of the year.
- ▶ Stay focused on completing what you have been working on so that you will be ready to start with fresh work in the new year.

Setting Positive Intentions

Planning is not something that comes naturally to me, but I have definitely found the power in it, and I think that at both the beginning of the school year and the beginning of the calendar year, it is so important to turn some of your attention towards it. I have often thought that the potential of flow doesn't fit with planning, but I have learnt that it really does. I've learnt that you need to set intentions, that you need to truly feel and see what you are going to create. When you do this, you can take steps towards your vision. You are really the only one that can see it, and you can create the place for it to happen.

Dream big, keep focused, and believe in the power of you.

Steps Beyond

- ▶ Be very clear about what you want to achieve in the coming year. What is your overall intention?
- ▶ Write down all your ideas.
- ▶ You may have lots of ideas. If they are not in your plan for this year, keep them noted for the future.
- ▶ Work on what is aligned with your overall plan for the year.

Resources

Calm: www.calm.com

Headspace: www.headspace.com

Kate Northrup: www.katenorthrup.com

Oprah & Deepak guided meditations:
www.chopracentermeditation.com

Conclusion

It has been such an honour to share all these experiences with you. I truly hope they have shaped your life in the way they have mine. This is the end of one part of the journey together but hopefully the start of another, as we keep working together to create the greatest differences in our lives and the lives of others.

The more I progressed through the writing of this book, the more I have realised that it is a journey to getting closer to who we really are. It's about finding ways to reconnect quicker with ourselves when we may be feeling removed and ultimately getting to a place where we can access our truest selves with ease. By doing that, we are giving ourselves a place to truly grow from, use our skills, and step into the world bravely and boldly, with firm foundations.

I believe that finding our greatest selves is one of the best gifts we can give ourselves and our children. That means working out what food nourishes us, what environments make us stronger, which people help us grow, and what our individual values and styles are. I hope this book has shown that we all have the potential to thrive alongside parenting. When we have children, it forces us to remove all the elements of our lives that are not aligned with this, and by doing so, it creates space for what we do need.

Parenting has to be the hardest job on this planet—but also the most important. I think we need as much shared wisdom, support, and guidance as possible—mainly to make us feel secure in our choices and encourage us in following our own intuition and instinct. I hope this book is one of many that supports, inspires, and connects you on your way.

For me, I now need to continue seeking and exploring how to take my business plans and dreams forward to create the ultimate place for all parents wishing to go beyond the school run. I want to help parents grow, connect with others and themselves, and help change the world through their skills, compassion, and love. I dream of BeyondTheSchoolRun places on each high street, a BeyondTheSchoolRun roadshow, and a great fashion brand that keeps our minds positive and focused with important messaging.

I have loved sharing this with you. Thank you so much for allowing me into your world. I truly hope that whatever you take from it, it changes your life the way it has mine.

I have had this quote on my desk since I started my work with beyondtheschoolrun.com. I hope it inspires you the way it has for me.

Your time is limited, so don't waste it living someone else's life . . . have the courage to follow your heart and intuition. They somehow already know what you truly want to become.

—Steve Jobs, 2005 Stanford Commencement Address

Together we can make the greatest difference in our lives and the lives of others.

Happiness, peace, and love to you all,

Louise

ACKNOWLEDGEMENTS

Thank you to my two shining lights, Finlay and Mila. xx

Thank you to everyone who has shared their wisdom and stories in this book and to all of you who have supported me on my journey with BeyondTheSchoolRun. I am so incredibly grateful.

About the Author

Louise Webster is a mother of two children and passionate about the potential collective talent of parents across the world. She launched BeyondTheSchoolRun.com in March 2012 to help unlock the talents and skills of parents for their well-being and the well-being of society. The enterprise has developed a strong community of parents, been featured in a range of media, and received two invitations to No.10 Downing Street. Louise won "Britain's Top Real Role Model 2014" and was invited to judge the competition in 2015.

Louise has become a spokesperson on the subject of mothers and work, speaking at conferences, commenting in press articles, and writing articles for press.

About Familius

Visit Our Website: www.familius.com

Join Our Family

There are lots of ways to connect with us! Subscribe to our newsletters at www.familius.com to receive uplifting daily inspiration, essays from our Pater Familius, a free ebook every month, and the first word on special discounts and Familius news.

Get Bulk Discounts

If you feel a few friends and family might benefit from what you've read, let us know and we'll be happy to provide you with quantity discounts. Simply email us at orders@familius.com.

Connect

- ► Facebook: www.facebook.com/paterfamilius
- ► Twitter: @familiustalk, @paterfamilius1
- ► Pinterest: www.pinterest.com/familius
- ► Instagram: @familiustalk

FAMILIUS

The most important work you ever do will be within the walls of your own home.

CPSIA information can be obtained
at www.ICGtesting.com
Printed in the USA
LVOW11s2123120517
534353LV00001B/3/P

CAMBRIDGE GEOGRAPHICAL STUDIES · 2

THE URBAN MOSAIC

TOWARDS A THEORY OF
RESIDENTIAL DIFFERENTIATION

CAMBRIDGE GEOGRAPHICAL STUDIES
Editorial board B. H. FARMER, A. T. GROVE, E. A. WRIGLEY

In this new series the editors' intention is to
include books which either describe and illustrate
the new ideas and techniques now reshaping
geographical work, or otherwise embody the
results of important new research. It will include
many books of interdisciplinary interest.

1 B. T. Robson, *Urban Analysis: a Study of City
  Structure with Special Reference to Sunderland*
2 Duncan Timms, *The Urban Mosaic: Towards a
  Theory of Residential Differentiation*

THE URBAN MOSAIC

TOWARDS A THEORY OF
RESIDENTIAL
DIFFERENTIATION

by DUNCAN TIMMS

Professor of Sociology, University of Auckland

CAMBRIDGE
AT THE UNIVERSITY PRESS 1971

Published by the Syndics of the Cambridge University Press
Bentley House, 200 Euston Road, London N.W.1
American Branch: 32 East 57th Street, New York, N.Y.10022

Library of Congress Catalogue Card Number: 70–123665

ISBN: 0 521 07964 0

Printed in Great Britain by
Alden & Mowbray Ltd
at the Alden Press, Oxford

CONTENTS

Contents

PREFACE

Well-supported theories are still in short supply in the social sciences. Observations and hunches, on the other hand, are plentiful. The task of bringing theory and observation together is rendered difficult by the imprecision of many theoretical statements in the social scientific literature and by the dubious validity of many of the observations. It will be all too apparent that both faults are characteristic of much of the argument which forms the substance of the present work. Rather than an integrated theory of the residential differentiation of the urban population, complete with supporting evidence, what is presented should be regarded more as a series of essays towards such a goal. The generalizations offered frequently go beyond the evidence. This is particularly the case when attention is paid to the non-Western or pre-modern city. In the present state of the social sciences, however, it is felt that the dangers of over-generalization are less pronounced than are those of under-generalization. If nothing else, it is hoped that the essays will throw up a number of useful 'Aunt Sallys'.

An overall summary of the book is provided in a brief last chapter. Chapters 1 and 2 are concerned with delimiting the nature and significance of residential differentiation. In the first chapter the notions of neighbourhood and of neighbourhood differences are explored in terms of a variety of human behaviours. In chapter 2 the relationship between the detailed variation in population characteristics over the sub-areas of the city and certain more general differentiating factors is examined. Chapter 3 is concerned with the relationship between these general properties and the locational behaviour of households. It is suggested that residential differentiation may be seen as an aspect of the more encompassing process of social differentiation. This theme is carried further in chapter 4, which is concerned with the relationship between the axes of differentiation and the modernization of society. In chapter 5 the implications of the multi-dimensional nature of urban residential differentiation for the spatial structure of the city are explored via certain well-known spatial models.

An interest in urban structure may derive from several sources. In my own case the initial interest was secondary rather than primary. The characteristics of the city kept intruding in studies concerned with a variety of other topics: assimilation, stratification and interaction, deviant behaviour. It became obvious that almost all facets of life in the modern society are greatly affected by the particular constellation of characteristics which forms the urban mosaic. In order to understand much social behaviour it is necessary to pay prior attention to the characteristics of the urban setting. Hence these essays.

The major part of the work reported below was carried out while I was on the staff of the University of Queensland. Several students, notably Fiona Powell, June Fielding, Eric Moore, Aubrey Everett, and Dan Hawthorne have contributed much by way of computation and discussion. The University Library produced many out-of-the-way references. An illegible manuscript was miraculously transformed into typescript by Denise Orton and Jean Cumming. Tony Wrigley, one of the editors of this series, made valuable comments on an earlier draft. To all these, my grateful thanks. To my family, who have suffered my pre-occupation, my apologies.

D.T.

CHAPTER I

THE CITY AS A MOSAIC OF
SOCIAL WORLDS

RESIDENTIAL DIFFERENTIATION

The urban community is neither an undifferentiated mass nor a haphazard collection of buildings and people. In the residential differentiation of the city the urban fabric comes to resemble a 'mosaic of social worlds'.[1] Similar populations cluster together and come to characterize their areas. As Park put it:

In the course of time every sector and quarter of the city takes on something of the character and qualities of its inhabitants. Each separate part of the city is inevitably stained with the peculiar sentiments of its population. The effect of this is to convert what was at first a mere geographical expression into a neighbourhood, that is to say, a locality with sentiments, traditions, and a history of its own.[2]

The residential differentiation of the urban population takes place in terms of many attributes and in many ways. Almost any criterion which can be used for differentiating between individuals and groups may become the basis for their physical separation. The process of separation may be accomplished through force, through a variety of sanctions, through a voluntary aggregation designed as a defence against unfamiliar ideas or customs or as an escape from persecution and discrimination, and through a selection of market forces.[3] In much early town planning residential differentiation and segregation appear as prime characteristics. In town plans by Dürer and Fürtenbach different crafts or guilds are allocated different blocks and a rough zonation in terms of wealth is envisaged.[4] In many towns of medieval Europe, and more recently in those of much of Asia and North Africa, the urban fabric is physically divided into wards and quarters. Descriptions of the characteristics of life in the various quarters form a favourite literary enterprise.[5] The place of quarters in the ecological structure of Arab cities is described by Baer:

Old districts, and even more so, the old city, are divided into quarters. In the old city they are fairly secluded from one another. The number of entrances to the

[1] L. Wirth, 'Urbanism as a way of life', *Am. J. Sociol.* 44 (1938), 1–24. Reprinted in P. K. Hatt and A.J. Reiss (eds), *Cities and Society* (New York, 1957), pp. 46–63.
[2] R. E. Park, *Human Communities* (New York, 1952), p. 17.
[3] Cf. C. S. Johnson, *Patterns of Negro Segregation* (New York, 1943), p. xvii.
[4] See R. E. Dickinson, *The West European City* (London, 1951), p. 424.
[5] E.g. *The Arabian Nights*. See also L. Mumford, *The City in History* (New York, 1961).

quarter is small, and each has a gate which may be shut, and sometimes is, even in these days. The quarter was an independent unit until recently (and in some cities still is), with its own mukhtar . . . religious functionary, night-watchman, etc. . . . In the not so distant past there used to be disputes and sometimes actual fights between groups of youths belonging to different parts of the city. In many cities there used to be much segregation of religious sects by quarter, and in some parts this remains the case . . . Perhaps even more commonly, members of a single linguistic or national group live together in a quarter.[1]

A similar theme is reported for cities south of the Sahara: 'In some parts of the West African territories . . . members of tribes other than the dominant one live customarily in separate parts of the town . . . within a distinct administrative unit with its own chief and elders.'[2] In Japan, Yazaki remarks that the divisions of the ancient castle town 'were planned by the ruler and each section of the city was occupied exclusively by members of a particular status group. Not only was the style of residences altered in the different status areas but the mode of administration differed also . . .'[3] In India the traditional social differentiation in terms of caste was mirrored in an equally rigid pattern of residential differentiation, with the outcastes being segregated beyond the city limits. The patterns of residential differentiation and segregation in the modern city may be less obvious than is generally the case in the pre-industrial community, but the absences of walls and other physical signs of demarcation by no means implies any lessening of differentiation – let alone its disappearance.[4]

Residential differentiation and the resulting segregation of populations serve many purposes. Physical isolation symbolizes social isolation and decreases the chances of undesirable and potentially embarrassing contact. Furthermore, segregation may provide a means of group support in the face of a hostile environment and it may even lead to administrative efficiency.[5] For whatever reason, residential differentiation characterizes both the pre-industrial and the industrial city, both the laissez-faire and the planned, both the capitalist and the socialist. The physical isolation of differing populations seems an inevitable concomitant of 'urbanism as a way of life'.[6]

Sociological interest in the patterns of residential differentiation and segregation in the modern city has focused on those reflecting socio-economic status and ethnic variables. Although there are considerable problems at

1 G. Baer (transl. H. Szöke), *Population and Society in the Arab East* (London, 1966), pp. 191–2.
2 UNESCO, *Urbanization in Africa South of the Sahara* (New York, 1957), p. 147.
3 T. Yazaki, *The Japanese City* (Tokyo, 1963), p. 71.
4 In times of inter-group stress physical barriers may appear even in the modern city. Northern Ireland and the United States were both replete with examples during 1969.
5 The policy of some housing administrations of concentrating their 'problem tenants' in particular streets may be rationalized in terms of the savings in travel time which it occasions for various social welfare agencies.
6 Wirth sees spatial differentiation as being the inevitable result of the size, density and heterogeneity of the urban community.

both the conceptual and operational levels in developing a valid measure of residential differentiation which can be used for comparative purposes,[1] a growing body of empirical reports is at hand. Much of the work is based on the index of dissimilarity, a measure of the net displacement necessary if one population is to reproduce the percentage distribution pattern of another.[2] Applied to data on residential distributions the index of dissimilarity shows the net percentage of one population who would have to relocate in order to reproduce the residential pattern of the other. A modification of the index of dissimilarity yields a measure of segregation defined as the degree of residential dissimilarity between the named group and the remainder of the population.[3] In the case of complete identity of distribution patterns the index of dissimilarity will be zero; in the case of complete dissimilarity – where no members of the one population live in any areas inhabited by the other – the index will be 100.

The existence of gross ethnic differences appears to be associated with relatively extreme residential differentiation. Residential dissimilarity correlates highly with social distance: the less desirable a given group is as intimate role-partners for another the greater will be their residential dissimilarity.[4] Ethnic groups separated from each other by social differences are less likely to live in similar areas than are those who differ merely say in language. Thus, in the United States, Negroes exhibit consistently higher indexes of residential dissimilarity when compared with the distribution of White Anglo-Saxon Protestants than do members of various European migrant groups. On a block-by-block basis Taeuber and Taeuber report that Negroes have indexes of residential dissimilarity of between 60 and 98 when compared with Whites in 207 U.S. cities.[5] The mean value of the index is nearly 88. In order to reproduce the block-by-block distribution pattern of White Americans at least 88 per cent of the Negroes living in the 207 cities would have to relocate. Amongst other ethnic minorities the degree of physical separation from members of the host society varies according to such factors as their similarity in terms of language, religion and occupation. In Australian cities, British-born migrants show the least degree of separation from the Australian-born, followed by other Northern European groups, then Central European migrants, Italians and Greeks and, finally, East

---

[1] A good discussion of some of the conceptual and operational problems involved is contained in K. E. Taeuber and A. F. Taeuber, *Negroes in Cities* (Chicago, 1965), Appendix A, pp. 195–246. See also O. D. Duncan and B. Duncan, 'A methodological analysis of segregation indexes', *Am. Sociol. Rev.* 20 (1955), 210–17.
[2] See D. W. G. Timms, 'Quantitative techniques in urban social geography', in R. J. Chorley and P. Haggett (eds), *Frontiers in Geographical Teaching* (London, 1965); O. D. Duncan and S. Lieberson, 'Ethnic segregation and assimilation', *Am. J. Sociol.* 64 (1959), 364–74; S. Lieberson, *Ethnic Patterns in American Cities* (New York, 1963).
[3] Timms, 'Quantitative techniques'.
[4] See D. W. G. Timms, 'The dissimilarity between overseas-born and Australian-born in Queensland', *Sociol. and Soc. Res.* 53 (1969), 363–74.
[5] Taeuber and Taeuber, *Negroes in Cities*.

3

Europeans.[1] A similar ordering of the groups is apparent in terms of inter-marriage and in that of subjective social distances estimated by the native population.[2] In Brisbane 60 per cent of the Italian migrants, 68 per cent of those from Greece, and over 75 per cent of those from Latvia, Yugoslavia, Malta, Hungary, and the Ukraine would have to move to other collectors' districts to reproduce the pattern of the Australian-born population.

The residential differentiation of socio-economic status groups within the city follows a similar pattern to that in terms of ethnicity. Again, the greater the social distance between two groups the greater is likely to be their residential dissimilarity.[3] In Brisbane some 50 per cent of the unskilled manual workers would have to relocate in order to reproduce the census collector's district distribution pattern exhibited by professional workers. The professional workers are themselves somewhat segregated from the rest of the population: 45 per cent of them would have to move to new areas if their distribution pattern were to fit that of the rest of the population. Within ethnic districts socio-economic status operates as a secondary form of differentiation: thus within the ethnic community the residential dissimi-larity between socio-economic status groups repeats that found in the wider population.[4] Little evidence is forthcoming about trends in the residential dissimilarity of socio-economic status groups although some limited data on Brisbane suggest that the degree of separation between the groups may be increasing.[5] If this is indeed the case it is likely that the explanation lies in the increased mobility of the population and in changes in the structure of the building industry. With increased mobility households have a greater opportunity to indulge their residential desires – high amongst which are several considerations closely relating to segregation. According to Keller: 'Thus the paradox: the more mobility exists and thus the more chances for equalizing statuses the less egalitarian people are as regards their houses, their addresses, and their neighbourhoods.'[6] The construction of mass housing projects serves but to accentuate the trend.

The residential differentiation of the urban community in terms of ethnicity and socio-economic status is compounded by several other factors. Different age groups occur in different areas and well-marked cyclic effects

1 Timms, 'Quantitative techniques'; J. Zubrzycki, *Immigrants in Australia* (Melbourne, 1960), pp. 79–85; F. L. Jones, 'Ethnic concentration and assimilation; an Australian case study', *Soc. Forces*, 45 (1965), 412–23.
2 Timms, 'Quantitative techniques'.
3 See O. D. Duncan and B. Duncan, 'Residential distribution and occupational stratification', *Am. J. Sociol.* 60 (1955), 493–503; P. Collison and J. Mogey, 'Residence and social class in Oxford', *Am. J. Sociol.* 64 (1959), 599–605; Timms, 'Quantitative techniques'.
4 O. D. Duncan and B. Duncan, *The Negro Population of Chicago* (Chicago, 1957).
5 In a study of South Brisbane, Moore reports a general increase in residential dissimilarity between occupation categories over the period 1954–61. Moreover, the greatest displacement was exhibited by the highest status categories. E. G. Moore, 'Residential Mobility in an Urban Context', unpublished Ph.D. dissertation, University of Queensland, 1966.
6 S. Keller, 'The role of social class in physical planning', *Internat. Soc. Sci. J.* 18 (1966), 495.

may be noted. Different parts of the city are marked by higher or lower proportions of the unmarried, the separated and divorced, and the widowed. There is a systematic patterning of criminality, mental illness, and various other forms of aberrant behaviour. Voting patterns, membership in associations and a host of other participatory phenomena vary from neighbourhood to neighbourhood. The effect of residential differentiation is to divide the urban fabric into a series of more or less distinct sub-communities. Each area is associated with a particular combination of population characteristics. In turn these characteristics become part of the local environment. 'Each area with its particular characteristics leaves its cultural stamp upon the people who reside there, and affects them in numerous and diverse ways.'[1] The city becomes a mosaic rather than an unitary phenomenon.

The major portion of the present study is concerned with the factors and processes which underlie the differential distribution of various population groups over the city, but first it is necessary to explore in more detail the relationship between population and area at the local, neighbourhood level.

NATURAL AREAS

Much of the conceptual framework of urban sociology is derived from the pioneering work of the classical human ecologists.[2] Based on their analyses of Chicago and of other rapidly growing mid-Western cities the ecologists produced a body of theory and concepts which is unparalleled in its integration and has provided the foundation of most later efforts in urban analysis. Central to the concern of the Chicago ecologists is the concept of the natural area. Writing in 1964, Burgess defines the natural area as 'a territorial unit whose distinctive characteristics – physical, economic, and cultural – are the result of the unplanned operation of ecological and social processes'.[3] Nearly forty years earlier an extended definition of the concept was provided by Zorbaugh:

The structure of the individual city ... is built about [a] framework of transportation, business organization and industry, park and boulevard systems, and topographical features. All of these break the city up into numerous smaller areas, which we may call natural areas, in that they are the unplanned, natural products of the city's growth. Railroad and industrial belts, parks and boulevard systems, rivers

[1] H. W. Dunham, Comment on article by Kohn and Clausen, *Am. J. Sociol.* 60 (1954).
[2] The label 'classical ecology' refers to the work of such Chicago students as R. E. Park, E. W. Burgess and R. D. McKenzie. The distinction between 'classical', 'orthodox', and 'neo-orthodox' versions of human ecology is developed by G. A. Theodorson, 'Human ecology and human geography', in J. S. Roucek (ed.), *Contemporary Sociology* (New York, 1959). For a general introduction to the Chicago school, see E. W. Burgess and D. Bogue (eds), *Contributions to Urban Sociology* (Chicago, 1964), pp. 2–14.
[3] E. W. Burgess, 'Natural area', in J. Gould and W. L. Kolb (eds), *A Dictionary of the Social Sciences* (New York, 1964), p. 458.

5

and rises of land acting as barriers to movements of population tend to fix the boundaries of these natural areas . . . In the competition for position the population is segregated over the natural areas of the city. Land values, characterizing the various natural areas, tend to sift and sort the population. At the same time segregation re-emphasizes trends in values. Cultural factors also play a part in this segregation, creating repulsions and attractions. From the mobile competing stream of the city's population each natural area of the city tends to collect the particular individuals pre-destined to it. These individuals, in turn, give to the area its peculiar character. And as a result of this segregation, the natural areas of the city tend to become distinct cultural areas as well – a 'black belt' or a Harlem, a Little Italy, a Chinatown, a 'stem' of the 'hobo', a rooming-house world, a 'Tower-town', or a 'Greenwich Village', a 'Gold Coast', and the like – each with its characteristic complex of institutions, customs, beliefs, standards of life, traditions, attitudes, sentiments, and interests. The physical individuality of the natural areas of the city is re-emphasized by the cultural individuality of the populations segregated over them. Natural areas and natural cultural groups tend to coincide. A natural area is a geographical area characterized both by a physical individuality and by the cultural characteristics of the people who live in it.[1]

The concept of the natural area provided the analytical base for many of the empirical studies which were produced by the University of Chicago Department of Sociology in the heyday of classical human ecology during the 1920s, 1930s and 1940s. Studies of particular types of natural area, such as the ghetto and the 'Gold Coast and the Slum', are complemented by studies of individuals and groups who are believed to be the characteristic residents of certain specified types of natural area, for example the hobo and the gang, and by analyses of the distribution of various forms of deviant behaviour considered against the natural area framework, such as suicide, juvenile delinquency, and psychiatric disorders.[2] Burgess reports that the results produced by the Chicago ecologists were so impressive that at a meeting of the Chicago City Council a resolution was passed that future census data for the city should be made available on the basis of the community areas which the Chicago School had mapped out.[3] Community Fact Books have appeared for Chicago after each U.S. Census since 1930. According to Park:

Now, the fact of primary importance here is that social statistics – births and deaths, marriage and divorce, suicide and crime – assume a new significance when they are collected and distributed in such a way as to characterize . . . natural

---

[1]
H. W. Zorbaugh, 'The natural areas of the city', *Publs. Am. Sociol. Soc.* 20 (1926), 188–97. Reprinted in G. A. Theodorson (ed.), *Studies in Human Ecology* (Evanston, Ill., 1961), pp. 45–8. Quotation from latter, pp. 46–7.

[2] L. Wirth, *The Ghetto* (Chicago, 1928); H. W. Zorbaugh, *The Gold Coast and the Slum* (Chicago, 1929); N. Anderson, *The Hobo* (Chicago, 1923); F. M. Thrasher, *The Gang* (Chicago, 1927); R. S. Cavan, *Suicide* (Chicago, 1928); C. R. Shaw and H. D. McKay, *Juvenile Delinquency and Urban Areas* (Chicago, 1942); R. E. L. Faris and H. W. Dunham, *Mental Disorders in Urban Areas* (Chicago, 1939).

[3] Reported in Burgess and Bogue, *Contributions to Urban Sociology*.

6

areas . . . It is assumed, in short, partly as a result of selection and segregation, and partly in view of the contagious character of cultural patterns, that people living in natural areas of the same general type and subject to the same social conditions will display, on the whole, the same characteristics . . . The natural areas of the city . . . constitute . . . a 'frame of reference' a conceptual order within which statistical facts gain a new and more general significance.[1]

Ambiguities in the natural area concept

The concept of the natural area has been put to many uses – yet the definition of the concept contains several ambiguities and not a little confusion. Even amongst the early Chicago ecologists there is evidence of a more than trivial disagreement concerning the referents of the natural area. Thus, while Zorbaugh appears to view it as primarily a physical phenomenon, McKenzie defines the natural area in terms of the characteristics of its population, stressing such features as race, language, income and occupation.[2] Wirth adopts a similar perspective.[3] Burgess recognizes three aspects of the natural area: an ecological dimension, in which he includes both physical and economic characteristics, a cultural dimension, which reflects the values of the population concerned, and a political dimension. None but the first aspect, however, is apparently necessary to the existence of natural areas, the others are accessory factors which come into play if the natural area becomes, in Park's terms, a 'neighbourhood', that is a locally-based social system. To Park natural areas are communities or ecological collectivities, while neighbourhoods are societies.[4]

The introduction of the concept of the neighbourhood does little to clarify the situation. Although 'neighbourhood' has been one of the most frequently used terms, not only in urban sociology, but also in planning circles, this use has been at the cost of great confusion.[5] To a large extent the concept shares with that of the natural area a basic ambiguity concerning its physical and/or social referents. According to Gould, 'Neighbourhood denotes one or more of the following: a) a small inhabited area; b) the inhabitants of such an area; c) the relations which exist between the inhabitants: the fact or quality of their nearness to each other; d) friendly relations between the inhabitants.'[6] The major disagreement is generated by the question of whether the neighbourhood forms an interacting group or whether it forms no more than a statistical aggregate, a collectivity of actors. Glass provides definitions

1 Park, *Human Communities*, pp. 197–8.
2 R. D. McKenzie, *Neighbourhood* (Chicago, 1923).
3 L. Wirth, 'Human ecology', *Am. J. Sociol.* 50 (1945), 483–8. Reprinted in Theodorson, *Studies in Human Ecology*, pp. 71–6.
4 Park, *Human Communities*.
5 See S. Keller, *The Urban Neighbourhood* (New York, 1968).
6 J. Gould, 'Neighbourhood', in Gould and Kolb, *Dictionary*, p. 464.

7

of the neighbourhood under both headings: under the first she defines it as 'a territorial group, the members of which meet on a common ground within their own area for primary social activities and for spontaneous and organized social contact'; under the second heading the neighbourhood is described as 'a distinct territorial group, distinct by virtue of the specific physical characteristics of the area and the specific social characteristics of its inhabitants'.[1] The latter definition is almost identical with the Burgess conception of the natural area, with the exception of Burgess's emphasis on the role of 'natural' as opposed to 'planned' factors in the evolution of the ecological community.

According to Morris and Mogey: 'One of the most striking features of Western urban society has been the decreasing correspondence between social and physical groupings.'[2] The functional specialization of land use, the development of secondary institutions caring for many household needs which were once informally met, greater social and physical mobility, changes in both leisure and work activities, and, more generally, changes in value orientations have all lessened the association between physical neighbourhood and social neighbourhood. The divorce between location and social behaviour should not, however, be exaggerated. For many sections of the population, notably the very young and the very old and those who have responsibility for them, the limits of time, money, and energy, are still sufficiently pronounced to effectively confine much of their social participation to the immediate neighbourhood. They may not be involved with all their neighbours, but much of their interaction is with neighbours. Writing about life in an area marked by 'physical drabness, economic stringency, and bodily contiguity' Wilson remarks that 'People courted, mated, married, quarrelled, and amused themselves in a confined area from which escape was difficult – financially, geographically, and emotionally'.[3] Even if overt contacts are few and far between, the neighbourhood may still exert considerable social influence on the individual. Thus, commenting on the importance given to material possession as an index of social rank amongst the inhabitants of Greenleigh, Young and Wilmott remark

Those are the rules of the game and they are, under strong pressure from the neighbours, almost universally observed. Indeed, one of the most striking things about Greenleigh is the great influence the neighbours have, all the greater because they are anonymous. Though people stay in their houses, they do in a sense belong to a strong and compelling group. They do not know their judge personally but her influence is continually felt.[4]

[1] R. Glass, 'The structure of neighbourhoods', in M. Lock (ed.), *Middlesbrough Survey and Plan* (Middlesbrough, 1947). See also R. Glass, *The Social Background to a Plan* (London, 1948), p. 18.
[2] R. N. Morris and J. Mogey, *The Sociology of Housing* (London, 1965), p. 145.
[3] R. Wilson, 'Difficult Housing Estates', *Tavistock Pamphlets*, No. 5 (London, 1963), p. 10.
[4] M. Young and P. Willmott, *Family and Kinship in East London* (London, 1957), pp. 135–6.

Amongst the young, the neighbourhood play-group is an important element in initial socialization[1] and may form the basis of later school groupings where school enrolments are organized on a territorial basis. Amongst the aged, neighbours act as intermediaries: providers of gossip and of help if it is needed. Townshend suggests that it is in fulfilling this role that neighbours contribute to a sense of local solidarity and identity.[2] The local community may no longer be a primary group in the sense outlined by Cooley,[3] but it is nonetheless important as a source of social contacts for a large proportion of its residents, as the site of much of the individual's early extra-familial interaction and socialization, and, most generally, as the provider of a set of reference yardsticks for the evaluation of much of his behaviour.[4] The neighbourhood may not be coterminous with the group structure of society, but it provides the framework for a great deal of social behaviour.

THE NEIGHBOURHOOD AND BEHAVIOUR

Apart from ethnographic studies of the way of life in certain specified areas of the city,[5] three major sources of material are available for an analysis of the relationship between residence and behaviour: studies of the association between propinquity and friendship, studies concerned with explicating the socio-cultural factors involved in deviant behaviour, and studies concerned with the relationship between area of residence and educational experience. We shall look at some examples of each in turn.

Propinquity and friendship

The most comprehensive analysis of the relationship between residential location and patterns of informal social relations is the study by Festinger, Schachter and Back, set in a housing estate developed for married veteran students attending the Masachusetts Institute of Technology.[6] The study is concerned with the patterns of friendship and communication at the intra-neighbourhood level. The population of the estate was highly homogeneous in terms of age, family characteristics, and socio-economic background and its inhabitants had few or no previous contacts in the community.

1 See J. S. Plant, 'The personality and an urban area', in Hatt and Reiss, *Cities and Society*, pp. 647–65.
2 P. Townshend, *The Family Life of Old People* (London, 2nd ed., 1963), p. 145.
3 C. H. Cooley, *Social Organization* (New York, 1962 ed.), pp. 23–31.
4 See M. Sherif and C. W. Sherif, *Reference Groups* (New York, 1964).
5 E.g. the work of the Institute for Community Studies.
6 L. Festinger, S. Schachter and K. Back, *Social Pressures in Informal Groups* (London, 1950).

9

In such a situation Festinger *et al.* hypothesize that 'friendships are likely to develop on the basis of the brief and passive contacts made going to and from home or walking about the neighbourhood'.[1] These passive contacts, in turn, are likely to be mediated through proximity and through those locational effects which require people to use the same paths in their movement about the estate. The influence of proximity is measured through physical distance; that of locational effects through 'functional distance', an index of 'the number of passive contacts that position and design encourage'.[2] In both cases the data obtained are in striking agreement with the hypothesis. Comparing actual friendship choices with possible choices, there is a marked inverse relationship between friendship nomination and distance. Within each of the courts into which the estate is divided the highest ratio of actual to possible friendships is reported for immediate neighbours, those respectively two and three distance units away have successively smaller ratios, while no choices at all are made to those who live four units away. There is a similar effect in the case of choices given outside the nominator's court. 'The greater the physical separation between any two points in these communities, the fewer the friendships.'[3] The effects of functional distance are revealed in the tendency for the residents of end houses to receive significantly fewer friendship nominations than those living in any other position. On the basis of their findings, the authors posit that 'The closer together a number of people live, and the greater the extent to which functional proximity factors cause contacts among these people, the greater the probability of friendships forming and the greater the probability of group formation.'[4] The groups formed on the basis of the two proximity factors not only provide the framework for informal communication within the estate, but also serve as the providers of consensual opinions and attitudes. Thus each court is reported as developing its own group standards and to possess its own machinery for sanctioning conformity. Individuals who deviate from the group norm tend to be isolated within their court. The ecological structure of the estate provides the framework for its socio-cultural structure.[5]

Festinger *et al.* point out that the locale of their study is unusual in the homogeneity of its population and suggest that ecological factors may be much less important in determining friendship and group formation in less 'artificial' communities. An analysis of a new middle-class housing

[1] *Ibid.* p. 34.
[2] *Ibid.* p. 35.
[3] *Ibid.* p. 44.   [4] *Ibid.* p. 161.
[5] Similar findings are reported by Caplow and Forman for a student housing project at the University of Minnesota. Caplow and Forman show that while length of residence is associated with number of acquaintances it has little association with number of friends. Friendship choices are overwhelmingly local. See T. Caplow and R. Forman, 'Neighbourhood interaction in a homogeneous community', *Am. Sociol. Rev.* 15 (1950), 357–67.

estate on the fringes of an Australian city, however, provides striking corroboration for their assertion of the relationship between proximity and friendship.[1]

The locale of the study is the first part of what is planned to become one of the largest private enterprise housing developments in Australia. The initial development of Waratah[2] took place in the early 1960s on a site some $7\frac{1}{2}$ miles from the centre of one of the State capitals in an area 'across the river' from some of the best-known high status residential districts in the city. The estate is designed to be a 'model suburb', with shopping facilities, golf courses, an Olympic-sized swimming pool, a sports oval and parks, primary and secondary schools. At the time of the study, however, much of this lay in the future and the immediate concern is with the sixty-six households resident on the site some two years after the estate was opened. Median length of residence is ten months.

Community participation and the goal of 'togetherness' are themes stressed by both the developers of Waratah and by its residents. The amount of friendship interaction on the estate, as ascertained by a socio-metric technique, is generally high. The fourteen women who leave Waratah for work tend to be socially isolated within the estate, but the great majority of the remainder are active participants in the local interaction system. Two-thirds of the women are members of one large network. The effects of distance on friendship interaction are marked, even though no houses are separated by more than half-a-mile.

TABLE 1.1 *The relationship between friendship choices and physical distance in Waratah*

Distance in yards	Actual choices given	Number of possible choices	Choices given Possible choices
100	156	703	0·22
200	105	1120	0·09
300	67	1046	0·06
400	17	556	0·03
500+	6	586	0·01

Table 1.1 shows the relationship between the ratio of actual to possible friendship choices made by the women on the estate and straight-line distance. Women living within a radius of 100 yards of the respondent are more than ten times as likely to be chosen as friends as are those living more than 400 yards away. More than two-thirds of all the friendship

[1] D. W. G. Timms, 'Anomia and social participation amongst suburban women' (University of Auckland, 1969), mimeo. paper.
[2] The name is fictitious.

nominations directed to estate residents involve women living in the same street as their chooser; nearly half of all reciprocal friendships involve immediate neighbours.

The emphasis given to social participation in Waratah poses a problem for those in a less-advantageous location. To a large extent the esteem accorded to a Waratah woman is a function of her participation. Those who are socially isolated tend to exhibit alienation.[1] The spatial patterning of the population, as reflected in the map of demographic potential,[2] reveals a close relationship with the patterning of alienation. Those women who are physically isolated tend also to be socially isolated – and they respond to their frustration by rejecting their rejectors. The influence of micro-geography is as pronounced in Waratah as it is in the estate studied by Festinger *et al.*, notwithstanding the differences in population character-istics. In both estates the physical arrangement is reflected not only in the patterning of the informal contacts between residents but also in the patterning of residents' attitudes.

Although proximity makes interaction easier and contact more likely, the relationship between the physical structure of the community and the pattern of its friendships should not be exaggerated. As Kuper states: 'The siting factors, with their planned and unplanned consequences, only provide a potential base for neighbour relations. There is no simple mechanical determination by the physical environment.'[3] Contact may lead to hostility rather than friendship and there are many instances of physically adjacent households who have little to do with each other. Different groups differ in their dependence on local friendship opportunities: the effects of proximity are probably more pronounced for women, especially those with young children, for the aged and for the infirm than they are for men, for the middle-aged, and for the fit. Proximity is most likely to lead to friendship when the persons concerned are similar in other ways. According to Gans, propinquity brings contact, but the development of contact into positive affect depends on social homogeneity.[4] Because the population of the city is residentially differentiated into more or less homogeneous areas, how-ever, proximity is able to exert a considerable influence on the patterning of urban social relationships, especially for those individuals and groups who for one reason or another spend much of their time within their local vicinity.

The relationship between residential differentiation, propinquity, and social interaction is further explored in a series of studies concerned with the

[1] The measure of alienation is Srole's 'Anomia Scale'. See L. Srole, 'Social integration and certain corollaries', *Am. Sociol. Rev.* 21 (1956), 709–16.
[2] Demographic potential may be interpreted as a measure of aggregate accessibility. See J. Q. Stewart, 'Demographic gravitation', *Sociometry*, 11 (1948), 31–58.
[3] L. Kuper (ed.), *Living in Towns* (London, 1953), p. 27.
[4] H. J. Gans, 'Planning and social life', *Journ. Am. Inst. Planners*, 27 (1961), 136–7.

premarital residence patterns of marriage partners. The concern here is with inter-neighbourhood rather than intra-neighbourhood patterns. In a review by Katz and Hill,[1] it is shown that the original finding by Bossard,[2] that the frequency of marriage decreases as the distance between the two parties increases, is generally supported. Katz and Hill explain the relationship in terms of a theory which combines elements of normative, segregational, and interactional perspectives. Traditional normative views of mate selection stress the role of cultural factors in delimiting a field of eligible marriage partners. Generally the emphasis in urban–industrial society is on the advantages of marrying within the group. Since groups having different cultures are residentially segregated by neighbourhood, the emphasis on endogamous marriage will be reflected in the propinquity of eventual marriage partners. Persons who deviate from the group expectations on the choice of marriage partners may be expected to show relatively greater distances to their eventual mates than will those who conform to the local norm. Katz and Hill further elaborate the theory by pointing out that the time-cost expenses of interaction vary according to distance and to the number of intervening opportunities. Drawing on Stouffer's model of intervening opportunities and interaction[3] they suggest that (*a*) marriage is subject to normative evaluations and expectations; (*b*) that within a field of normatively defined eligibles the probability of marriage varies directly with the probability of interaction; and (*c*) that the probability of interaction varies as the ratio of eligible interaction partners at a given distance to the intervening opportunities: thus the probability of marriage reflects the combined effects of the normative divisions of society, the patterns of residential differentiation, and the time-cost implications of proximity *v.* distance. In an analysis of Oslo material, Ramsøy[4] is able to show that each factor has an independent influence. Beshers[5] has suggested that recognition of the relationship between the probability of marriage and propinquity may be an important element in a family's residential location. Where there are fears that normative constraints against the choice of the 'wrong' marriage partner are breaking down, it may be necessary for the parents of eligible children to relocate in a neighbourhood which contains only the 'right' sort of potential mates. Who daughter marries reflects who daughter meets – and who daughter meets reflects where she lives. Since marriage is so closely entwined with the social stratification system and forms one of the most important dimensions for the evaluation of a family's social rank there is a

[1] A. M. Katz and R. Hill, 'Residential propinquity and marital selection', *Marr. and Fam. Living*, 20 (1958), 27–34.

[2] J. H. S. Bossard, 'Residential propinquity as a factor in marriage selection', *Am. J. Soc.* 38 (1933), 219–24.

[3] S. A. Stouffer, 'Intervening opportunities', *Am. Sociol. Rev.* 5 (1940), 845–67.

[4] N. R. Ramsøy, 'Assortative mating and the structure of cities', *Am. Sociol. Rev.* 31 (1966)773, –86.

[5] J. M. Beshers, *Urban Social Structure* (New York, 1962), pp. 104–7.

strong motivation to ensure that it is guided along the 'right' lines. Residential differentiation both allows and facilitates such guidance.

The neighbourhood and deviant behaviour

The connexion between deviant behaviour and residential location is a major element in most sociological discussions of deviancy. A large volume both of research and of theory has been directed towards the explication of the connexion, but a fully integrated and verified series of propositions relating deviancy to neighbourhood is still awaited. Rather than attempt a general synthesis all that will be attempted here is to present a selection of some of the more important work which bears on the connexion of neighbourhood to deviancy.

It has long been recognized in the scientific literature that both the total amount and the types of deviant behaviour exhibited by residents of various districts differ considerably. In the nineteenth century, Mayhew provided a detailed description of the variation in crime and other forms of proscribed behaviour which characterized the various districts of London.[1] He pointed out that the major 'rookeries' of crime in the metropolis have had a long history, such areas as St Giles and Spitalfields having been the 'nests of London's beggars, prostitutes, and thieves' for several centuries. On the basis of his interviews and observations in the field, Mayhew was impressed by the socio-cultural roots of criminality. Anticipating the Lombrosian viewpoint, in which criminality was related *inter alia* with physiologic and genetic characteristics, Mayhew states in 1862:

But crime, we repeat, is an effect with which the shape of the head and the form of the features appear to have no connexion whatever ... Again we say that the great mass of crime in this country is committed by those who have been bred and born to the business, and who make a regular trade of it.[2]

Mayhew's conclusions have been generally corroborated by later investigators.

A milestone in the development of modern criminology was reached with the publication, in 1929, of the first of a series of reports on criminality and delinquency authored by Shaw and McKay.[3] Working essentially within the Chicago ecological tradition, Shaw and McKay produced a mass of data showing the variation in 'delinquency rates' in the different natural areas

[1] H. Mayhew, *London Labour and the London Poor* (London, 1864), esp. vol. 4.
[2] H. Mayhew, *The Criminal Prisons of London* (London, 1862), p. 383.
[3] C. R. Shaw, F. M. Zorbaugh, H. D. McKay and L. Cottrell, *Delinquency Areas* (Chicago, 1929); C. R. Shaw and H. D. McKay, *Social Factors in Juvenile Delinquency* (Washington, 1931); C. R. Shaw, *The Jackroller* (Chicago, 1930); C. R. Shaw, H. D. McKay, and J. F. McDonald, *Brothers in Crime* (Chicago, 1938); C. R. Shaw, H. D. McKay, *Juvenile Delinquency and Urban Areas* (Chicago, 1942). For extended discussions of the work of Shaw and McKay, see Burgess and Bogue, *Contributions to Urban Sociology*, pp. 591–615 and T. Morris, *The Criminal Area* (London, 1957), pp. 65–91.

first of Chicago, and then of several other American cities. Aware of the dangers of ecological determinism they also pay considerable attention to the role of individual factors as intervening variables in the relationship between group characteristics and individual behaviour. The methodological concern they display with regard to 'situational analysis' and the combination of ecological data with individual case studies, a precursor of the modern emphasis on 'contextual' effects,[1] enables Shaw and McKay to avoid many of the pitfalls of ecological determinism which some writers have seen as being characteristic of all ecological research.[2] By calculating delinquency rates, the number of offenders per thousand population at risk, Shaw and McKay are able to show not only that there are gross differences in the aggregate rates for different parts of the city, but also that there are slighter but still significant differences in the distribution of the different age groups of offenders. Thus the truants and the juvenile delinquents are concentrated in the slum districts and near large industrial areas, while the adult offenders are primarily concentrated in the rooming-house areas on the fringe of the central business district. Common to all the high rate areas, however, are the facts of physical deterioration and obsolescence, taken to be symptoms of some underlying malaise which is thought to be related to the uncontrolled nature of the city's growth. Shaw and McKay show that areas which were characterized by high rates of delinquency in the late 1920s had also been so characterized in 1900, notwithstanding considerable changes in the national, ethnic, and occupational composition of their populations. They suggest that the explanation of this stability lies in the development of 'delinquent norms' in the delinquent areas and in the normative confusion which results from rapid population movements. Great stress is laid on the importance of neighbourhood play-groups and of the family in the development of the child's attitudes and behaviour tendencies. It is pointed out that in areas characterized by a confusion of values and norms many of the standards upheld by the child's peers might be antithetical to those of his parents. Case studies of individual delinquents are used to illustrate the argument. Thus, in the case of Nick,

It is clear that the parents had very little appreciation of the nature of Nick's problems and the sort of social world in which he was living. Although his behaviour was, for the most part, strictly in conformity with the socially approved standards of the playgroup and neighbourhood, it was a violation of the family traditions and expectations. He was torn between the demands and expectations of two conflicting social groups.[3]

[1] E.g. M. W. Riley, *Sociological Research* (New York, 1963), vol. 1, pp. 644–738.
[2] Cf. C. T. Jonassen, 'A revaluation and critique of some of the methods of Shaw and Mckay', *Am. Sociol. Rev.* 14 (1949), 608–15. See also R. S. Sterne, 'Components and stereotypes in ecological analyses of social problems', *Urb. Aff. Quart.* 3 (1967), 1, 3–21.
[3] Shaw and McKay, *Social Factors in Juvenile Delinquency*. Quoted in Burgess and Bogue, *Contributions to Urban Sociology*, pp. 594–5.

The urban mosaic

The social world of the juvenile growing up in a disorganized neighbourhood is vividly outlined in a chapter entitled 'The Spirit of Delinquency Areas'. An extended quote gives the flavour of the original:

Children who grow up in these deteriorated and disorganized neighborhoods of the city are not subject to the same constructive and restraining influences that surround those in the more homogeneous residential communities farther removed from the industrial and commercial centers. These disorganized neighborhoods fail to provide a consistent set of cultural standards and a wholesome social life for the development of a stable and socially acceptable form of behavior in the child. Very often the child's access to the traditions and standards of our conventional culture are restricted to his formal contacts with the police, the courts, the school, and the various social agencies. On the other hand his most vital and intimate social contacts are often limited to the spontaneous and undirected neighborhood play groups and gangs whose activities and standards of conduct may vary widely from those of his parents and the larger social order. These intimate and personal relationships, rather than the more formal and external contacts with the school, social agencies, and the authorities, become the chief sources from which he acquires his social values and conceptions of right and wrong.

In many cases, the child's relationship to his parents assumes the character of an emotional conflict which definitely complicates the problem of parental control, and greatly interferes with the child's incorporation into the social milieu of his parents. In this situation the family is rendered relatively ineffective as an agent of control and fails to serve as a medium for the transmission of cultural heritages.

Delinquency persists in these areas not only because of the absence of constructive neighborhood influences and the inefficiency of present methods of prevention and treatment, but because various forms of lawlessness have become more or less *traditional* aspects of the social life and are handed down year after year through the medium of social contacts. Delinquent and criminal patterns of behavior are prevalent in these areas and are readily accessible to a large proportion of the children.[1]

The volumes authored by Shaw and McKay contain the seeds of most of the subsequent approaches to the sociology of delinquency. Their emphasis on the role of delinquent traditions finds echoes in Cohen's theory of the delinquent contraculture, Miller's concern with the focal concerns of lower-class culture, and the Sherifs' emphasis on the role of the local neighbourhood as a reference group.[2] Their concern with the intervening effects of social integration is reflected in the Sutherland–Cressey theory of differential association[3] and in the demonstration by Maccoby *et al.* that high

---

[1] *Ibid.* pp. 595–6.
[2] A. K. Cohen, *Delinquent Boys* (New York, 1955); W. B. Miller, 'Lower class culture as a generating milieu of gang delinquency', *J. Soc. Issues*, 14 (1958), 5–19; Sherif and Sherif, *Reference Groups*. A wide selection of sociological theories relating to criminality and juvenile delinquency is contained in M. E. Wolfgang, L. Savitz and N. Johnston (eds), *The Sociology of Crime and Delinquency* (New York, 1962).
[3] D. R. Cressey, 'Epidemiology and individual conduct', *Pac. Sociol. Rev.* 3 (1960), 47–54. Reprinted in Wolfgang *et al.*, *Sociology of Crime*, pp. 81–90.

16

delinquency areas are characterized by significantly higher degrees of social disintegration than otherwise similar low delinquency areas.[1] In each case there is a clear assumption that *where* an adolescent lives will have a major effect on the chances of his becoming delinquent.

To Cohen the delinquent sub-culture is a collective innovation developed by low status youths in face of the problem of having to deal with the insecurity and feelings of inferiority which are engendered in them as a result of their unfortunate experiences at the hands of an essentially middle-class society. The conflict between neighbourhood values and those of the wider community are brought into especially sharp focus in the school system. Since their family and peer-group backgrounds ill-prepare them for successful participation in the competitive educational system designed by and for the middle classes, the lower-class youths tend to find themselves at the bottom of the school's status hierarchy. The feelings of status inferiority, combined with a general ambivalence to middle-class values, are brought together in the development of a set of group norms based on an inversion of what are perceived as being the central middle-class values. A central role in the process is played by the realization by the low-class youths that they are not alone in their situation and the consequent associational nature of their solution to their problems. There is a clear analogy with the Marxist theory of developing class interest and conflict. The new set of norms provide a new set of status dimensions based on an inversion of middle-class values. Within the local peer-group context the disenchanted low status youth may hope to achieve high rank by demonstrating his alienation from conventional, middle-class norms. The adolescent peer-group provides both the incentive and the opportunity for the disadvantaged youth to develop his own bases of value.

Cohen's emphasis on the reaction-formation nature of the delinquent contraculture has been sharply criticized by other writers. Miller, in particular, presents a theory of the relationship between lower-class culture and gang delinquency which is in sharp disagreement with the Cohen model. To Miller

the cultural system which exerts the most direct influence on (gang) behaviour is that of the lower class community itself – a long-established, distinctively patterned tradition with an integrity of its own – rather than a so-called delinquent sub-culture which has arisen through conflict with middle class culture.[2]

The bases of the lower-class culture are seen as lying in the common adaptations made by the unsuccessful immigrants and down-trodden Negroes who inhabit the central city slums. Rather than an ideological reaction-formation, Miller sees the content of the lower-class culture as an

[1] E. E. Maccoby, J. P. Johnson and R. M. Church, 'Community integration and the social control of juvenile delinquency', *J. Soc. Issues* 14 (1958).
[2] Miller, 'Lower class culture'. Quote from Wolfgang *et al.*, *Sociology of Crime*, p. 267.

effective adaptation to the local reality. Central to the culture are a series of focal concerns – trouble, toughness, smartness, excitement, autonomy, and fate. The world of the lower-class adolescent is effectively structured in terms of these concerns. Brought up in a home environment characterized by 'serial monogamy', in which effective male models are absent, the adolescent is thrown upon the company of his peers to search for a satisfactory identity and status in terms of the street group's codes. Like Thrasher before him,[1] Miller emphasizes that much of the lower-class street gang's behaviour is non-delinquent. Because of the nature of the lower-class focal concerns and the relatively easy rewards associated with some illegal activities in the lower-class community, however, the adolescent lower-class gang also provides a likely setting for the occurrence of delinquent behaviour.

A problem common to all sub-cultural theories of delinquent behaviour is that of explaining why not all inhabitants of the relevant neighbourhoods appear to become delinquent. To some extent the problem may be illusory: thus Kobrin and Mays show that there may be a very considerable difference between the 'official' delinquency rates and rates computed on more direct evidence of actual behaviour.[2] Kobrin suggests that even the more inclusive official records indicate the proportion of delinquents to be approximately two-thirds of the age eligibles in high rate areas. The proportion is presumably considerably higher if all those who are not apprehended are added. On the other hand it remains apparent that a certain proportion of juveniles in delinquent areas appear to be able to escape the coercive effects of their environment. Part of the answer probably lies in the detailed organization of the community. The work of Shaw and McKay is replete with suggestions about the effects of differences in the internal structuring of social relationships in the neighbourhood. In an analysis of two working-class neighbourhoods in Boston the main correlate of criminality is found to be the extent of integration into the ongoing interaction system of the local community.[3] In the high rate neighbourhood the inhabitants neither know nor want to know as many of their neighbours as do those in the low rate area. There is no apparent difference between the areas in beliefs about the 'wrongness' or the 'seriousness' of delinquent activities, but in the high rate neighbourhood there is a strong feeling against disciplining other people's children and 'interfering in the affairs of other people's kids'. Within the high rate neighbourhood itself the delinquent families are yet further isolated and there is little interaction between 'law-abiders' and offenders. There are few differences between the neighbourhoods in most of their characteristics, but the high rate neighbourhood is considerably less homo-

---

[1] Thrasher, *The Gang*.

[2] S. Kobrin, 'The conflict of values in delinquency areas', *Am. Sociol. Rev.* 16 (1951), 653–61; rep. in Wolfgang *et al.*, *Sociology of Crime*, pp. 295–66; J. B. Mays, *On the Threshold of Delinquency* (Liverpool, 1958).

[3] Maccoby *et al.*, 'Community integration'.

geneous in its ethnic and religious composition. A similar emphasis on the significance of local interaction networks follows from Sutherland's hypothesis about differential association. According to this view 'criminal behaviour is learned in interaction with persons in a pattern of communication'. When persons become criminals 'they do so because of an excess of definitions favourable to violation of law over definitions unfavourable to violation of law'.[1] The associations which a person has are seen as being determined in the general context of social organization. The role of locality factors is thus likely to be high. In support of the hypothesis of differential association Wootton states that, on the basis of her experience as a Juvenile Court Magistrate, she has

been very impressed by the part which casual acquaintances appear to play in determining who does and who does not step over the line in districts in which court appearances are not at all unusual. The arrival of a particular family in a particular street may have devastating consequences for the children of neighbours with hitherto blameless records.[2]

In one of the most well-known studies produced by the Chicago ecological school, Thrasher suggests that one of the factors which facilitates the evolution of the spontaneous play-group of childhood into a delinquent gang is the availability of outlets for stolen goods in certain inner city areas.[3] The presence of junk dealers and the 'no-questions-asked' attitude of many adult buyers helps to make larceny easy and profitable. Extensions of this concern with the local integration of adults and juveniles in explaining the development of different forms of delinquent behaviour have been made by Kobrin and, more generally, by Cloward and Ohlin.[4] Kobrin is particularly concerned with 'differences in the degree to which integration between the conventional and criminal value systems is achieved'. In neighbourhoods where there is a high degree of integration, adult deviancy 'tends to be systematic and organized'. Not only may the more successful violators become the administrators of organized crime but they may also maintain membership in conventional institutions such as the local church, political parties, and unions. Delinquent activity in such areas is essentially 'an apprenticeship in crime'. The contrasting type of delinquent area is one in which there is little organized adult activity in crime although many adults in these areas may commit individual violations. Frequently such areas have recently suffered from population turnover so that the carriers of conventional codes are momentarily disorganized. In such circumstances juveniles are exposed to norms favouring both violation and non-violation and, at the

[1] E. G. Sutherland and D. R. Cressey, *Principles of Criminology* (Philadelphia, 1960), pp. 74–81.
[2] B. Wootton, *Social Science and Social Pathology* (London, 1959), p. 68.
[3] Thrasher, *The Gang*.
[4] Kobrin, 'Conflict of values'; R. A. Cloward and L. E. Ohlin, *Delinquency and Opportunity* (New York, 1961).

same time, are insulated from the effective control of either sort of adult model. In these disorganized areas 'the delinquencies of juveniles tend to acquire a wild, untrammelled character . . . The escape from controls originating in any social structure, other than that provided by unstable groupings of the delinquents themselves, is complete'.[1]

The Cloward and Ohlin approach to the explanation of the different forms which may be taken by gang delinquency in the city represent a consolidation of the anomie orientation of such writers as Durkheim and Merton[2] with the socio-cultural orientation of Shaw and McKay and Sutherland. The theory which Cloward and Ohlin present is probably the most ambitious since Shaw and McKay. Expressed more formally than Kobrin's hypothesis, the 'theory of delinquency and differential opportunities' nonetheless leads to similar conclusions. Cloward and Ohlin suggest that in order to become a criminal the individual must have access to illegitimate means. As in the case of any other achieved status 'the individual must have access to appropriate environments for the acquisition of the values and skills associated with the performance of a particular role, and he must be supported in the performance of the role once he has learned it'.[3]

In the same way as legitimate opportunities, illegitimate opportunities are differentially available. Given a predisposition to deviate, resulting from a socially structured inability to reach valued ends by legitimate means, 'the nature of the delinquent response that may result will vary according to the availability of various illegitimate means'.[4] According to the availability of illegitimate means in the local community two main types of delinquent response are postulated: the criminal gang and the conflict gang. A third type, the retreatist gang, is believed to be the result of a double failure: a lack of success in both the legitimate and illegitimate structures. The criminal gang is characteristic of the integrated delinquent area in which illegitimate means are readily available in both the learning and supportive roles. Close bonds exist between adult violators and juveniles and there is a readily available infrastructure of such supportive statuses as fences, shady lawyers, junk men, and the like. In such a neighbourhood the child not only has the opportunity to perform in an illegitimate way but is likely to be shown that such performances may be highly rewarding. The delinquent sub-culture which arises in such circumstances 'is a more or less direct response to the local milieu'. A stable neighbourhood organized around illegitimate values results in stable criminality. The conflict sub-culture, on the other hand, is believed to be characteristic of disorganized low status neighbourhoods. In areas characterized by

---

[1] Kobrin, in Wolfgang *et al.*, *Sociology of Crime*, p. 264.
[2] See M. B. Clinard (ed.), *Anomie and Social Structure* (New York, 1964).
[3] Cloward and Ohlin, in Wolfgang *et al.*, *Sociology of Crime*, p. 256.
[4] *Ibid.* p. 258.

high rates of vertical and geographic mobility, massive housing projects in which 'site tenants' are not awarded priority in occupancy, so that traditional residents are dispersed and 'strangers' reassembled; and changing land use, as in the case of residential areas that are encroached upon by the expansion of adjacent commercial and industrial areas . . . transiency and instability become the over-riding features of social life.[1]

Under these conditions Cloward and Ohlin suggest that there will be many influences on the young making for violent behaviour. In the disorganized areas the adolescent is cut off from both legitimate and illegitimate opportunity structures. His chances of success in the conventional world are slight, yet there are few effective illegitimate models from which he can learn and few supportive agencies available should he attempt to use illegitimate means. The resulting discontent is subject to little social control and the adolescents must rely upon their own resources for achieving prestige: 'Under these conditions, tendencies towards aberrant behaviour become intensified and magnified.' Violence is seized upon as an avenue for the attainment of prestige not only because it expresses pent-up frustration, but also because it is an activity in which the inhabitants of disorganized areas are not at a relative disadvantage. 'The principal prerequisites for success are "guts" and the capacity to endure pain. One doesn't need "connections", "pull", or elaborate technical skills in order to achieve "rep".'[2]

As a result, in the disorganized neighbourhoods of the city, the play-groups of children become the conflict gangs of adolescence, with each gang jealously guarding its 'turf'. The third class of delinquent adaptation identified by Cloward and Ohlin is the retreatist sub-culture organized around the consumption of drugs. In essence they suggest that 'retreatist behaviour emerges among some lower-class adolescents because they have failed to find a place for themselves in criminal or conflict subcultures'.[3] Faced with the same anomic situation as others in their neighbourhood as far as legitimate opportunity structures are concerned, their attempts to use illegitimate means are unsuccessful. If they are able to adjust their aspirations downwards Cloward and Ohlin suggest they may be able to make the stable 'corner boy' adaptation outlined by Whyte;[4] 'but for those who continue to exhibit high aspirations under conditions of double failure, retreatism is the expected result'.[5] Although the empirical basis of the Cloward and Ohlin thesis is scant it remains probably the most systematic attempt yet published to relate neighbourhood socio-cultural characteristics to juvenile delinquency.

Attention so far has been concentrated almost wholly on studies relating the neighbourhood to the delinquent activity of adolescents. Work relating

[1] *Ibid.* p. 282. [2] *Ibid.* p. 283. [3] *Ibid.* p. 287.
[4] W. F. Whyte, *Street Corner Society* (Chicago, 1955).
[5] Cloward and Ohlin, in Wolfgang *et al.*, *Sociology of Crime*, p. 287.

other forms of deviant behaviour to the neighbourhood is also relevant to our purpose. In fact, however, with the exception of a few ecological studies concerned with the more severe psychiatric disorders and with suicide, there is little material available relating community characteristics to deviant behaviour other than that committed by juveniles. Adult criminals generally appear as rather shadowy figures on the fringes of the investigator's concern with delinquent youth or else are seen as merely grown-up versions of the latter. Little material is available on the community background of alcoholism or of much adult drug addiction. The oft-remarked association between 'suburban neurosis' and the consumption of barbiturates by women has little research evidence to bear it up. Analysis of the local participation of such 'deviants' and the content of local sub-cultures should be a rewarding exercise.

The classic ecological study of the residential distribution of psychotic patients is Faris and Dunham's *Mental Disorders in Urban Areas*, a study of Chicago and of Providence, Rhode Island.[1] Replication of their work in a series of other American cities,[2] and in Bristol, Luton and Derby,[3] has generally led to a corroboration of their pioneer findings. Faris and Dunham's study is based on data relating to nearly 29,000 patients admitted to four state mental hospitals during the period 1922 to 1934. The area framework for the ecological analysis consists of the sub-communities defined in the Chicago 'Community Fact Books'. Both the rates for all psychoses and those for different diagnoses show systematic variations between the various areas of the city. The general pattern is very similar to that of the delinquency rates established by Shaw and McKay: high rates are clustered around the central business district while there are progressively lower rates towards the periphery of the city. The distribution of schizophrenia, general paresis, drug addiction, and alcoholic psychoses parallels that for the total series, with the highest rates occurring in neighbourhoods characterized by low socio-economic status and rapid population turnover. With the exception of the few high rate areas most neighbourhoods have a low frequency of these psychoses. Both male and female and native-born and foreign-born populations show the same general distribution pattern. The rates of schizo-

1 R. E. L. Faris and H. W. Dunham, *Mental Disorders in Urban Areas* (Chicago, 1939).
2 E. W. Mowrer, *Disorganization, Personal and Social* (New York, 1942), chaps 15–16; H. W. Dunham, 'Current status of ecological research in mental disorder', *Soc. Forces*, 25 (1947), 321–6; S. A. Queen, 'Ecological study of mental disorders', *Am. Sociol. Rev.* 5 (1940), 201–9; C. W. Schroeder, 'Mental disorders in cities', *Am. J. Sociol.* 48 (1942), 40–7. For a general criticism of the ecological approach in the investigation of psychiatric disorders see M. L. Kohn and J. A. Clausen, 'The ecological approach in social psychiatry', *Am. J. Sociol.* 60 (1954), 140–51.
3 E. H. Hare, 'Mental illness and social conditions in Bristol', *J. Ment. Sci.* 102 (1956), 349; E. H. Hare, 'Family setting and the urban distribution of schizophrenia', *J. Ment. Sci.* 102 (1956), 753; D. W. G. Timms, 'The Distribution of Social Defectives in Two British Cities: A Study in Human Ecology', unpub. Ph.D. dissertation, University of Cambridge, 1963; D. W. G. Timms, 'The spatial distribution of social deviants in Luton, England', *Aust. N.Z. J. Sociol.* 1 (1965), 38–52.

phrenia for Whites are highest in areas where Negroes are in the majority, while those for Negroes are highest in areas where Whites are in the majority. In contrast with the findings on schizophrenia, patients diagnosed as having a manic-depressive psychosis show a virtually random residential distribution. Although the highest incidence rates occur in the inner city there is no general gradient towards the outskirts and inter-area variation is slight. The correlation between the incidence rates of schizophrenia and manic-depressive psychoses is little different from zero.

The distribution of hospitalized mental patients in the English towns of Luton and Derby closely follows the Chicago pattern.[1] In Luton the neighbourhoods within a half-mile radius of the city centre have a total first admission rate which is more than twice that of neighbourhoods located more than two miles from the centre. In Derby there is a threefold difference between neighbourhoods in the two zones. In both towns both the total rates and the rates for schizophrenia are highest in those neighbourhoods which combine low status with high residential mobility. The correlation between schizophrenia and the manic-depressive psychoses is insignificant in Luton but significant and positive in Derby. No convincing explanation of the difference in the two towns is forthcoming and the Derby pattern stands as a deviation from that reported in the majority of other analyses.

Although there is an impressive consistency in the findings on the distribution of the major psychoses in Western cities there is little evidence of consistency in the attempts which have been made to explain the findings. Faris and Dunham's preferred explanation is couched in terms of social isolation, but alternative explanations have been proposed which stress differential community attitudes and reactions to abnormal behaviour, the drift of schizophrenics (and other deviants) to disorganized communities, and differences in family socialization patterns.[2] The social isolation hypothesis has also been proposed as an explanation of suicide which has been shown to have a distribution pattern which is very similar to that of schizophrenia.[3]

In essence the social isolation hypothesis suggests 'that extended isolation of the person produces the abnormal traits of behaviour and mentality'.[4] A vicious circle of seclusion and rejection ends in the person's withdrawal from reality. 'Any factor which interferes with social contacts with other persons produces isolation. The role of an outcast has tremendous effects on the development of the personality.'[5] According to Sainsbury:

That the differential distribution of suicide rates within the city corresponds with

---

[1] Timms, 'Distribution of Social Defectives'.
[2] See S. K. Weinberg, 'Urban areas and hospitalized psychotics', in S. K. Weinberg (ed.), *The Sociology of Mental Disorders* (Chicago, 1967), pp. 22–6.
[3] P. Sainsbury, *Suicide in London* (London, 1955); J. P. Gibbs (ed.), *Suicide* (New York, 1968), esp. Introduction and chap. 2.
[4] Faris and Dunham, *Mental Disorders in Urban Areas*, p. 173.   [5] *Ibid.* p. 177.

The urban mosaic

the areas of social disorganization, mobility and isolation, seems well founded. These statistics raise the question whether social disorganization causes suicide. The evidence suggests that it does. The interpretation offered is that high mobility and social isolation preclude a stable social framework by which the individual may orientate himself, so that he pursues an anonymous and aimless existence devoid of meaning, which induces an ennui culminating in suicide.'[1]

Similarly Gibbs postulates that

disruption of social relations is *the* etiological factor in suicide, whether variation in the rate or the individual case. The general thesis is stated formally as two propositions: (1) the greater the incidence of disrupted social relations in a population, the higher the suicide rate of that population; and (2) all suicide victims have experienced a set of disrupted social relations that is not found in the history of nonvictims.[2]

The evidence in favour of the general thesis concerning the noxious effects of social isolation is strong, but there is little material available for specifying the precise effects of different types and different lengths of isolation. If both schizophrenia and suicide (as well as drug addiction and alcoholic psychosis) are seen as resulting from a disruption of social relationships, what determines which reaction takes place? Are disruptions equally significant whenever they occur? In their 1939 statement, Faris and Dunham suggest 'Normal mentality and behaviour develops over a long period of successful interaction between the person and . . . organized agencies of society. Defects in mentality and behaviour may result from serious gaps in any part of the process.'[3] In earlier statements, Faris concentrated on a postulated incongruity between intra-familial and extra-familial orientations towards the child and suggested that these could be subsumed under a model of the 'typical process' of schizophrenia which has its roots in childhood difficulties of relating to others. Parental over-solicitude produces a 'spoiled child' type of personality which is subject to persecution, discrimination or rejection by its neighbourhood peers. In the face of continued lack of success at making friends in the neighbourhood the child eventually gives up, 'from this time their interest in sociability declines and they slowly develop the seclusive personality that is characteristic of the schizophrenic'.[4] As a result of a lack of experience with interacting with others the person is deficient in his understanding of relational behaviour and may therefore be expected to react towards others in unconventional and culturally inappropriate ways. In this model Faris appears to anticipate one of the major aspects of the aetiological scheme outlined by the authors of the Stirling County study.[5]

---

[1] Sainsbury, *Suicide in London*. [2] Gibbs, *Suicide*, p. 173. Italics in original.
[3] Faris and Dunham, *Mental Disorders in Urban Areas*, p. 153.
[4] R. E. L. Faris, 'Cultural isolation and the schizophrenic personality', *Am. J. Sociol.* 40 (1937), 456–7.
[5] As of late 1969 three volumes had been published in the *Stirling County Study of Psychiatric Disorder and Sociocultural Environment*: vol. 1, *My Name is Legion*, by A. H. Leighton (New

24

In what is the most comprehensive analysis of the relationship between community characteristics and psychiatric morbidity yet published, Leighton *et al.* advance the theory that the major environmental factor in the aetiology of mental disorder is social disintegration, as indicated by such measures as poverty, cultural mixing, decline in religious behaviour, broken homes, and poor communication. The disintegrated community is one which lacks a patterned and stable network of interaction and reciprocity; it resembles a 'collectivity' rather than a society. The theory is stated strongly:

Our causal orientation may be illustrated by the following hypothetical situations. If you were to introduce a random sample of symptomatically unimpaired people into the Disintegrated Areas in numbers small enough so they produced no significant change in the socio-cultural system, we think most of these individuals would become impaired. Conversely, if you were to take people out of the Disintegrated Areas and make a place for them in a well integrated community, we believe many would show marked reduction or disappearance of impairment.[1]

Rather than a direct causal link between the experience of living in a disintegrated community and the development of disorders Leighton *et al.* suggest a more complicated two-step process. Life in communities characterized by a variety of indices suggesting social disintegration has certain noxious effects on the 'essential psychical condition', probably as a result of interference with the individual's needs for recognition and affiliation. Faced with this disturbance, the personality system may still avoid breakdown if it can substitute more gratifying objects for those causing the original maladjustment. Here again, the inhabitant of the disintegrated area is handicapped. 'The culture of the Disintegrated Areas is extremely poor in the number and complexity of objects available for this kind of adjustment.' Moreover, even if such objects are available, the breakdown of social relationships in the disintegrated neighbourhood means that the disturbed local inhabitant has little likelihood of finding them. Few guides exist

and those that do exist seem far more likely to foster than to prevent the emergence of self-defeating sequences and the ultimate emergence of symptoms. Concretely, there is not much to prevent and often much to encourage a person with a disturbed essential psychical condition seeking relief by withdrawing to daydreams, building satisfactions on paranoid systems of thought, forgetting the past and blotting out the future, sinking into chronic states of apathy, depression, and anxiety, or masking the disturbed feelings by means of alcohol, sex, fighting, stealing, and other forms of excitement.[2]

York, 1959); vol. 2, *People of Cove and Woodlot,* by C. C. Hughes, M. A. Tremblay, R. N. Rapoport and A. H. Leighton (New York, 1960); and vol. 3, *The Character of Danger,* by P. C. Leighton, J. S. Harding, D. S. Macklin, A. M. Macmillan, and A. H. Leighton (New York, 1963).
[1] Leighton *et al., Character of Danger,* p. 369.
[2] *Ibid.* p. 389.

The disintegrated areas described in the Stirling County study are small rural slums.

All are outside of towns either just or quite far. They are strings of houses stretching along the highway or along a gravel road from a cross-road. All are situated on submarginal, unproductive land, overcut, untilled ... The houses are mostly poorly built, of rough lumber, often with a tarpaper finish. Many are quite dilapidated. The interior is much like the outside – poorly furnished and poorly kept.

The inhabitants are the remnants of former industries, stranded when the latter foundered. Their ethnic and religious background is diverse. Occupationally they are unemployed or seasonal workers.

There is very little social cohesion, organisation, or leadership in any of these neighbourhoods. The prevailing attitudes toward each other are hostility and suspicion, toward the rest of the world, a rather hopeless envy; toward themselves the feeling that they are a worthless lot ... They are not acceptable socially in any circles except their own, so little visiting is done outside.[1]

Similar communities exist in the peripheral zones of many New World cities. In Australia, shanty towns containing mixed aboriginal and immigrant populations occur on the outskirts of many Queensland and New South Wales cities. Their characteristics – physical, social, and reputational – appear to be identical with those described in rural Nova Scotia.

Peripheral slums occupy one of the two major zones in transition which characterize the ecological structure of the city – zones which are in the process of major changes in function.[2] The other zone in transition, that surrounding the central business district, contains what is probably the core of the city's deviant areas. The characteristics of the rural slum have much in common with those of the unstable slums and rooming-house districts which typically occur around the borders of the city centre. The combination of low socio-economic status and high rates of population mobility appears to provide a fertile environment for deviant behaviour wherever it occurs. The association between neighbourhood characteristics concerning socio-economic status and population mobility and rates of deviant residence may be illustrated by data on the patterning of criminality and mental illness in Luton.[3]

The territorial framework for the analysis is provided by a series of indicants available on a street-by-street basis. Three variables – the jurors' index,[4] rateable value per elector, and net residential density – were used

---

[1] *Ibid.* pp. 405–6.
[2] The concept of the 'zone in transition' is developed in E. W. Burgess 'The growth of the city', in R. E. Park, E. W. Burgess and R. D. McKenzie (eds), *The City* (Chicago, 1925), pp. 47–62. Reprinted in Theodorson, *Studies in Human Ecology*, pp. 37–44.
[3] Timms, 'Spatial distribution of social deviants'.
[4] The jurors' index has been used in several British studies as an indicant of socio-economic status. See P. G. Gray, *et al.*, *The Proportion of Jurors as an Index of the Economic Status of a District* (London, 1951) and B. Robson, *Urban Analysis* (Cambridge, 1969), p. 134.

to develop a scale of socio-economic status. A trichotomous division of each variable allowed the construction of a Guttman scalogram containing seven scale types.[1] The coefficient of reproducibility was 0·92. Contiguous street units falling into the same scale type were amalgamated into natural areas. These, in turn, were combined to form seven area types. A single variable – electoral stability – was used to tap the population mobility dimension. The indicant simply shows the proportion of electors remaining at the same address on two successive electoral registers, taken one year apart. Classification of street units in terms of quartiles of the electoral stability indicant allows the construction of a two-dimensional typology of natural areas which provides the territorial framework for the calculation of various incidence rates.

The overall relationship between neighbourhood socio-economic status and electoral stability and rates of deviant residence in Luton is shown in Table 1.2. The information on deviants is gathered from two main sources: magistrates' court records and the files of the local mental hospital. The incidence rates for adult and juvenile criminality are given as the number of persons convicted resident in the relevant area per one thousand population at risk. The incidence rate for mental illness represents the number of first admissions resident in each area, again as a proportion per thousand population at risk (taken to be fifteen years of age and over).

TABLE 1.2 *Incidence rates per thousand population at risk per annum for adult criminality, juvenile delinquency, and mental hospital first admissions by social status types and electoral stability, Luton 1958–60*

| Social status type | Electoral stability | | | | | |
| | More stable than average | | | Less stable than average | | |
	Adult crim.	Juv. del.	M.H.F.Ad.	Adult crim.	Juv. del.	M.H.F.Ad.
6	0·4	3·2	1·0	0·6	6·4	1·1
5	0·8	6·3	1·7	0·5	3·9	1·6
4	1·0	9·0	1·1	2·8	10·1	1·9
3	1·5	8·0	1·8	3·7	11·8	1·7
2	3·1	17·3	2·1	5·7	15·9	2·0
1	2·2	11·1	2·6	9·9	26·4	2·6
0	2·8	11·2	2·7	11·2	29·4	2·9

Both classificatory properties are highly relevant to the distribution of Luton's labelled deviants. The lower the socio-economic status and the lower the electoral stability of a neighbourhood the higher are its rates of adult and juvenile criminals and the more likely are its residents to be admitted

[1] See Timms, 'Quantitative techniques'.

to mental hospitals. Those areas which fall into the lowest social status type and the lowest electoral stability quartile contain 10 per cent of the city's adult population and 7 per cent of its juveniles. They also provide 38 per cent of Luton's criminals, 22 per cent of its juvenile delinquents, and 18 per cent of its mental hospital first admissions. In contrast, those areas which fall into the highest social status type and the highest electoral stability quartile contain 11 per cent of Luton's adult population, 13 per cent of its juvenile population, 1 per cent of its adult criminals, 2 per cent of its juvenile delinquents and 5 per cent of its mental hospital first admissions.

Within the lowest social status type–lowest electoral stability quartile areas a clear distinction may be made between the moderately unstable slums and the highly unstable rooming-house districts. Electoral stability in the unstable slums averages 81 per cent with a range from 79 to 84. In the rooming-house districts electoral stability averages 64 per cent with a range from 44 to 75 per cent. The rooming-house areas provide an environment which is in many ways similar to that of the peripheral rural slum, albeit with less of an emphasis on family living.

The characteristic dwelling unit of the rooming-house area is the boarding house or the low-grade apartment building. The most noticeable social characteristic is a high rate of population mobility and the absence of any but the most rudimentary family structure. In Britain, rooming-house districts are closely related to the areas of nineteenth-century middle-class town houses which have become obsolescent as a result of the social and economic changes of the twentieth century. The combination of a decline in the availability of domestic servants and the changes in locational advantage wrought by the motor-car has occasioned a radical change in the function of many once-fashionable districts. As their original occupants have moved out to the outskirts of the town or further afield, so the old town villas have been invaded by institutions or by populations considerably lower in social status than the former owners. The very size of many of the villas virtually rules out their continuance as single-family dwellings and a process of sub-division and conversion is well-nigh ubiquitous. The encroachment of commercial use and the noise and crowds of the city centre effectively down-grade the appeal of even the converted property. The areas become a repository for the shiftless and the unstable.

The most extreme examples of the rooming-house type of district in Luton consist of relatively large turn-of-the-century villas built to house the town's richer merchants. In the inter-war period the merchants and manufacturers gave way to doctors and other professional men. Social status only seriously tumbled in the 1950–60 decade and at the time of the field study (1960–1) there were still one or two original inhabitants left, bitterly and bemusedly decrying the change in their surroundings. The individual houses are generally of large size, with four or more bedrooms.

Building density is moderate and the provision of gardens and other open spaces relatively generous. In their physical structure the rooming-house regions are far removed from the usual stereotype of the urban slum. In common with the slum, however, closer inspection reveals that the rooming-house regions are characterized by neglect and physical deterioration. Door and window frames are left unpainted, the stonework is cracked, broken windows are repaired with cardboard. The single-family house is very rare and most of the houses have been converted into boarding-houses or flats, many under the control of immigrant landlords. Many of the residents have names of Irish, Scots and Asian derivation. The number of West Indians also appears to be relatively high. Few families are present. The environment appears to be one of extreme social fragmentation.

The rooming-house areas contain approximately 5 per cent of the adult population of Luton and 3 per cent of its juveniles. They also contain 30 per cent of its adult criminals, 13 per cent of its juvenile delinquents and 12 per cent of its mental hospital first admissions. Details of the types of offence and diagnosis attributed to the rooming-house residents are shown in Table 1.3.

TABLE 1.3 *Incidence of deviants in the rooming-house areas of Luton by broad offence and diagnostic categories* (rates per 1,000 population at risk)

A. Adult criminals

	Against property	Against the person	Drunk and disorderly	Other	Total
Rooming-house	6·9	2·4	11·8	0·5	21·6
Luton aggregate	1·7	0·7	1·3	0·2	3·6

B. Juvenile delinquents

	Against property	Against the person	Drunk and disorderly	Other	Total
Rooming-house	25·7	7·9	12·3	2·3	48·2
Luton aggregate	9·5	1·7	1·0	0·7	12·9

C. Mental hospital first admissions

	Neuroses	Schizo-phrenia	Manic-depressive	Senile	Misc.	Total
Rooming-house	0·61	1·05	0·79	0·36	0·42	3·23
Luton aggregate	1·30	0·32	0·52	0·38	0·27	1·79

In general, the pattern of offences committed by the residents of Luton's rooming-house districts is similar to that which Cloward and Ohlin and

Kobrin posit in their discussion of unintegrated neighbourhoods in the American context. The total incidence of adult criminals in the rooming-house districts is six times the Luton aggregate and eight times that in all other areas of the city. The incidence of juvenile delinquents is four times that found in the aggregate data. Offences committed by adults against property and against the person are four times as frequent as in the aggregate figures: offences involving drunkenness and disorderly behaviour are nine times as frequent. In the juvenile data, offences against property are two-and-a-half times as common as in the aggregate figures, offences against the person are five times as frequent, and offences involving drunkenness and disorderly behaviour twelve times as frequent. The most notable feature of the mental illness data is the predominance of schizophrenia. This is diagnosed more than three times as frequently as in the aggregate data. Manic-depressive psychoses are diagnosed one-and-a-half times as frequently as in the aggregate data while the psychoneuroses are diagnosed twice as frequently in the total figures. The psychoses associated with old age are relatively under-represented.[1]

There are considerable differences in age, sex, and occupational character-istics between the deviants resident in the rooming-house districts of Luton and those living elsewhere in the city. Table 1.4 shows the relevant data.

TABLE 1.4 *Age, sex, and occupational characteristics of deviants from rooming-house areas of Luton*

A. Criminals

	Per cent male	Per cent aged			Per cent occupied as			
		8–20	21–9	30+	Unempl.	Lab-ourers	Semi-skilled	Other
Rooming-house	93	11	45	44	18	43	28	12
Luton aggregate	87	50	23	27	16	35	32	16

B. Mental hospital first admissions

	Per cent male	Per cent aged			i Per cent occupied as			
		Under 21	21–44	45+	Unempl.	Lab-ourers	Semi-skilled	Other
Rooming-house	70	2	61	37	22	25	23	30
Luton aggregate	45	4	44	52	5	26	32	38

NOTE. i Males only.

Amongst the criminals, the rooming-house districts produce relatively few young offenders and relatively many in the older age groups. Few of the

[1] Apart from difficulties in the application of diagnostic labels this finding may be an artefact of biased population estimates.

offenders are female. The ethnic background of the offenders is mixed with the Irish and Scots being well to the fore. The great majority of the offenders are either manual workers or unemployed. A relatively similar pattern of individual characteristics is exhibited by those rooming-house inhabitants who are admitted to mental hospital. In comparison with the aggregate data the major distinguishing features of the rooming-house mental patients are their masculinity – 70 per cent males as compared with 49 per cent in the total series – their relative youth, and their concentration amongst the unskilled manual occupations and unemployment.

Life in the rooming-house areas of Luton has much in common with that which Zorbaugh describes in the blighted inner city areas of Chicago.[1] Zorbaugh's description of the effects of transiency, anonymity and isolation appear equally as relevant to the Luton of the early 1960s as they did to the Chicago of the 1920s. In the fragmented and disorganized social system of the rooming-house environment,

the person accommodates himself ... by an individuation of behaviour. Old associations are cut. Under the strain of isolation with no group associations or public opinion to hold one, living in complete anonymity, old standards disintegrate and life is reduced to a more individualistic basis. The person has to live and comes to live in ways strange to the conventional world.[2]

The residential patterning of social deviants is far from random. Different areas of the city are associated with different rates of deviant behaviour and with particular forms of deviance. The criminals and mental patients residing in the rooming-house districts of the city are very different from those who live in the working-class suburbs or the traditional slums. The concentration of many of the more serious forms of deviant behaviour amongst those inhabiting areas which combine low social status with high rates of transiency suggests that there may well be a connexion between social and individual forms of disorganization. More generally the evidence argues that, for whatever the reason, there is a close association between the characteristics of the immediate residential milieu and the probability of being identified as a social 'problem'.

The neighbourhood, the child, and education

For much of the first ten or eleven years of life much of the individual's activity is confined to an area within a relatively small radius of his home. In this area he obtains most of his extra-familial social relationships, notably in play-groups. It is more likely than not that his school will be in close

[1] Zorbaugh, *The Gold Coast and the Slum.*
[2] H. W. Zorbaugh, 'The dweller in furnished rooms', in E. W. Burgess (ed.), *The Urban Community* (Chicago, 1926), pp. 98–105.

proximity and most of his school peers will be neighbours. Many of the adult models to whom he is exposed will also be drawn from his immediate vicinity. Apart from occasional family visits to out-of-neighbourhood friends and relatives and the formalized interaction with his teacher, his adult contacts are primarily with the parents of his play-group friends. There are many opportunities for a neighbourhood effect on the socialization process. In the present instance we are concerned with only one aspect of this effect – the relationship between neighbourhood and education – but the implications for the child of residence in one area rather than another extend across a very wide range of activities and attitudes.

The education of children takes place in terms of a complicated interplay of family, neighbourhood, and bureaucratic influences. Each set of influences is greatly affected by the residential differentiation of the urban population. Robson has demonstrated the close relationship which exists between neighbourhood and family attitudes towards education: 'No matter what the area, the attitudes of individual families were more similar to those prevailing around them than to those of their "objective" social class.'[1] Only where the family can isolate itself from the neighbourhood – for example by carefully controlling its children's friendships – can it hope to have an easy time maintaining attitudes or behaviours which are deviant in terms of the local norms. The fact that differences in social class provide one of the main bases of residential differentiation, however, serves to keep neighbourhood conflicts over educational values and aspirations to a minimum. Thus, in his study of seven widely different neighbourhoods in Sunderland, Robson is able to demonstrate consistent differences in family attitudes towards education.[2] Unfortunately for children from the less privileged areas of the city, however, the education system tends to be based on certain allegedly universalistic values which are primarily those of the middle and upper status groups. Educational success – as measured by such criteria as college entrance or attendance at 'academic' school – is distributed very much according to what Mays[3] terms the social geography of the city. Children coming from inner city neighbourhoods, especially those inhabited by families of low socio-economic or ethnic status, have a much lower chance of achieving high educational goals than others of similar potential living in more favoured areas.

The physical amenities and facilities offered by schools in differing areas vary considerably. In the inner city school, buildings are frequently old and may be surrounded by distracting land uses. The physical structure of the buildings may no longer be congruent with the demands of the teaching situation. Moreover there may be a tendency for obsolescent schools, particularly those in areas which have acquired a 'bad' reputation, to acquire

[1] Robson, *Urban Analysis*, p. 244.   [2] *Ibid.* pp. 187–215
[3] J. B. Mays, *Education and the Urban Child* (Liverpool, 1962).

obsolescent teachers. Prejudices about the behaviour of working-class children are not confined to those members of the middle classes who never come into contact with them. By birth or recruitment the great majority of teachers are agents of the middle-class society and they may be quite alien to the neighbourhood in which they teach. In the middle-class neighbourhood teachers and parents may be expected to agree on many of the education issues which involve the aspirations and achievements of the school child. Teachers and parents may even be friends; they are quite likely to be neighbours. In the lower-class neighbourhood, on the other hand, there may be considerable conflict between parental and teacher views and the conflict is unlikely to be mediated by cross-cutting friendships. Parental attitudes to such matters as homework, selective education, years at school, etc., show marked neighbourhood variations.[1] Interest in the child's education, perhaps the most potent variable in the dynamic of school achievement, also varies greatly from neighbourhood to neighbourhood. As Mays notes, in the suburban community it is the uninterested parent who is likely to be the deviant; in the lower-class inner city area indifference is the norm.[2] The attitudes of parents are likely to be reinforced by those of other adults in the neighbourhood. In the traditional lower-class area they may also be re-enforced by the standards of the adolescent peer-groups. Many writers have characterized the collective norm of the lower-class peer-group in terms which seem to imply a direct antipathy to the demands of educational achievement.[3] Thus Mays suggests that one of the prime causes of the disadvantaged educational position of the inner city child is the 'nature of the local social milieu itself with its emphasis on group factors, easy-going hedonism, pursuit of short-term goals and prejudice against "bookishness" '.[4] The peer-group values may well be reflected in what Wilson has termed the moral climate of the school.[5] The dominant group of children in a school tend to set the standards for the rest. Wilson is able to demonstrate the effects of such pressure on both the aspirations and achievements of youths from varying socio-economic status and ethnic backgrounds in San Francisco. In schools with a predominantly lower-class enrolment the proportion of middle-class boys who plan to go on to College is significantly lower than the proportion in schools which draw their students from predominantly middle-class neighbourhoods. Lower-class boys attending schools in middle-class areas obtain significantly better grades than similar boys with the same IQ's who attend schools with predominantly lower-class pupils. More generally Wilson suggests that 'The *de facto* segregation brought about by

[1] *Ibid.*; Robson, *Urban Analysis*; R. J. Havighurst, *Education in Metropolitan Areas* (Boston, 1966).
[2] Mays, *Education and the Urban Child*.
[3] E.g. Cohen, *Delinquent Boys*; Miller, 'Lower class culture'; Morris, *Criminal Area*.
[4] Mays, *Education and the Urban Child*, p. 189.
[5] A. B. Wilson, 'Residential segregation of social classes and aspiration of high school boys', *Am. Sociol. Rev.* 24 (1959), 836–45.

concentrations of social classes in cities results in schools with unequal moral climates which . . . affect the motivation of the child . . . by providing a different ethos in which to perceive values'.[1]

The child's conception of social reality is built up in the process of his interaction with his family, his peers, the other adults in his community, and those agencies of the wider society, particularly the school, with which he comes into contact. By comparing his experiences and his attitudes with those of his play-mates he can obtain consensual validation for his behaviour. By imitating the available adult models he can incorporate their roles into his future repertoire. By conforming with the normative expectations of those who have power over him he can gain acceptance into the group. In each case the earliest experiences may be expected to set the tone for much of what follows. The significance of neighbourhood for personality development is that most of these early experiences may be expected to take place within the bounds of the local area. Both the informal groupings of the play-group and the family and the formal groupings of the school are based on a territorial delimitation of the community. The residential differentiation of the urban population ensures that this delimitation is unlikely to throw up random aggregates. Rather, there will be certain consistent patterns. In their turn these patterns will affect the personality development of the individual. Where the child is met with congruent reactions from family, neighbours, peers, and external agents he is likely to grow up with an integrated and secure sense of his own identity and of his own worth. Where the reactions conflict, the resulting personality may also be full of ambiguities and self-doubts. The residential differentiation of the community, aided and abetted by the geographical variation in educational facilities, has significance far beyond the immediate situation of the individual.

Overview of the neighbourhood and human behaviour

The consequences for human behaviour of residence in one neighbourhood rather than another are mediated by the network of social relationships which connect the individual with his family, with peer-groups, with voluntary associations, and with a plethora of other groups. The neighbourhood is important because so many of these relationships depend on face-to-face contact and this form of interaction is particularly sensitive to spatial distance. A large variety of social processes takes place more forcefully when they occur within a face-to-face context. Although developments in communications technology have vastly increased the range over which meaningful interaction can take place it remains true that no other form of contact can approach the face-to-face meeting when evaluatively-charged

[1] *Ibid.* p.845.

material is to be transmitted. Face-to-face contact brings into play a host of ancillary communication systems – primarily gestural in form – which provide a richness of content which is lost in less intimate forms of inter-action. These ancillary systems appear to be particularly influential in the transmission of attitudinal and evaluative information. The importance of non-verbal cues for the interpretation of meaning suggests that face-to-face contact is not only the most influential form of interaction, but also that it is an essential aspect of the human socialization process. Not only is the occurrence of face-to-face contact dependent on spatial proximity, but the groups in which it occurs most frequently, notably the family and the peer group, are themselves the objects of residential segregation. A child born in one neighbourhood rather than another is likely to belong to a particular type of family and to be exposed to a particular set of extra-familial stimuli. It is because people are segregated over the neighbourhood of the city in a systematic rather than a random fashion, and that the probability of contact varies according to propinquity, that the neighbourhood has significance for human behaviour. This significance is most pronounced for those who are essentially restricted to the neighbourhood – the young, the old, and those who care for them – but the effects of neighbourhood experiences on the developing personality may be apparent throughout life. The effects of residential differentiation are far-reaching. It is for this reason that it is important to analyse the bases on which residential differentiation rests.

CHAPTER 2

ECOLOGICAL STRUCTURE AND FACTOR STRUCTURE

The neighbourhoods which comprise the residential fabric of the city and form the framework for analyses of the relationship between locality and behaviour differ on innumerable grounds. In terms of physical structure they differ in density and age of development, in geographical position, and in types of dwellings. More importantly, from a behavioural perspective, their populations differ in age and sex composition, in occupations, incomes, and styles of life, in political, ethnic, and religious allegiances, and in a wide range of attitudes and behaviours. Each of these differences contributes its portion to the patterning of the urban residential system. In any attempt to understand this system it is necessary that each of these diverse differences should in some way be taken into account. The measurement problems which this involves form the major preoccupation of the present chapter.

UNIVERSES OF CONTENT, INDICANTS AND PROPERTIES

The conceptual tools which form the basic instruments of scientific endeavour may be classified under many rubrics. For our present purposes it is only necessary to distinguish between three such constructs: universes of content, indicants, and properties. In combination these three provide the basic tools for measurement and classification.

The universe of content

The universe of content forms the subject-matter of an analysis. It consists of the set of elements to which the procedures of measurement or classification are to be applied. The validity of a scientific analysis is closely related to the clarity with which its universe of content has been specified: analyses based on an ambiguous universe of content are, at best, likely to be inefficient and, at worst, may be wholly irrelevant to the problem which they are designed to illumine.

A universe of content is defined as the set of all those phenomena which are relevant to a particular inquiry. The delineation of the universe involves the taking of decisions under three headings: one regarding the type of objects to be included in the universe, a second concerning the delimitation of the set containing the objects, and a third concerning the particular aspects of the object which are relevant to the problem under discussion.

The nature of the objects which form the population of any particular analysis reflects the division of labour amongst the various scientific disciplines. Each science tends to lay claim to its own universe of content and in many disciplines custom dictates an 'obvious' unit for study. In the social sciences, however, there is still considerable debate over the choice of basic objects for study. Studies concerned with the social structure of the city or with the aetiology of mental illness may take as their base elements such widely divergent objects as individuals, households, or neighbourhoods. In such cases it is imperative that the definition of the empirical universe of content coincides with that of the theoretical universe of content which forms the framework for the development of theory. The dangers of the ecological fallacy – arguing from aggregate data to conclusions about individuals – are well known.[1] Equally as dangerous is the individualistic fallacy – arguing from individual data to conclusions about aggregates.[2] Each fallacy illustrates the problems which arise when the objects forming the population of the empirical universe of content are inconsistent with those contained in the theoretical universe. With the development of various structural and contextual techniques of analysis it is now frequently the case that several different types of objects, perhaps occurring at different 'levels' of the social system, are combined in the same universe of content. Progress in analytical techniques, however, does not imply that any less attention needs to be given to ensuring the identity of the units contained in the empirical universe of content with those which form the substance of the theoretical systems which the empirical investigation is designed to illumine. In the present case our primary attention is directed at the inter-neighbourhood level.

All analyses have a finite range of application: the universe of content to which they refer has definite boundaries. An essential component of the definition of the universe of content is a statement concerning its limits. In the absence of such a statement it may be unclear just to what particular aggregates of objects a given set of findings is supposed to refer. Much of the argument which has been generated over the validity of certain generalizations in the field of urban sociology, notably Burgess's model of urban

---

[1] A considerable body of literature has now developed around the concept of the ecological or aggregative fallacy. See W. S. Robinson, 'Ecological correlations and behaviour of individuals', *Am. Sociol. Rev.* 15 (1950), 351–7; O. D. Duncan and B. Davis, 'An alternative to ecological correlation', *Am. Sociol. Rev.* 18 (1953), 665–6; L. A. Goodman, 'Ecological regressions and behaviour of individuals', *Am. Sociol. Rev.* 18 (1953), 663–4; H. Menzel, 'Comment on Robinson's "Ecological correlations and the behaviour of individuals"', *Am. Sociol. Rev.* 15 (1950), 674; J. Galtung, *Theory and Methods of Social Research* (London, 1967), pp. 45–8, 79–80; Riley, *Sociological Research*, vol. 1, pp. 704–7.

[2] Galtung, *Theory and Methods*; Riley, *Sociological Research*.

growth and Wirth's description of urbanism as a way of life, has resulted from the imprecision with which their originators delimited the bounds of their universe of content.[1] The exigencies of cultural relativism are such that few generalizations in the social sciences may be expected to possess universal validity. A classification or a set of measures may be perfectly valid for the universe of content on which it was developed and yet be declared invalid because it is applied outside the limits of this universe. A listing of the objects included in the universe of content or a specification of rules for assigning objects to the universe is an essential component of any measurement scheme.

No two objects are truly identical and there exists an infinity of properties which may be used to classify or order them. Any given analysis involves the selection of certain indicants and properties and the neglect of others. The universe of content thus formed does not consist of a set of 'real' objects but, rather, a set of elements formed by selectively emphasizing some characteristics of the objects at the expense of others. The choice of indicants and properties used in any analysis reflects the theoretical orientations and predilections of the investigator and the analysis which is produced in terms of the chosen characteristics is specific to them and to them alone. The results of an analysis based on a universe of content defined in terms of one set of indicants or properties cannot logically be generalized to structure the data belonging to another universe, even if these data refer to the same objects.

The choice of indicants and properties which are used in the analysis of a given universe of content inevitably involves the investigator in an implicit theory which states that the properties selected are important for the explanation of the phenomena under study. As understanding about a given subject-matter develops so it may be expected that different analytical constructs will come to be used in discussing the phenomena concerned. As Jevons stated at the end of the nineteenth century: 'Almost every classification which is proposed in the early stages of a science will be found to break down as the deeper similarities of the objects come to be recognised.'[2] Contemporary analytical properties reflect the theoretical positions of contemporary science. In an era of geographical determinism the 'obvious' property on which to base the analysis of residential differentiation might be one which emphasizes characteristics of the natural environment. In an era which is conscious of sociological influence, the 'obvious' analytical property may become one related to the social and cultural characteristics of the local population. Each property is related to the theoretical biases of the investigator and controls variance only in those criteria which belong to

---

[1] See, for example, the arguments by Schnore, Lewis and Hauser in P. M. Hauser and L. F. Schnore (eds), *The Study of Urbanization* (New York, 1965), pp. 347–98 and 491–517.

[2] W. S. Jevons, *The Principles of Science* (London, 1892), quoted in A. Kaplan, *The Conduct of Inquiry* (San Francisco, 1964), p. 53.

the same universe of content. The relativity of the choice of a particular universe of content to the general theoretical orientation of the investigator must be given considerable emphasis if theory-building and empirical analysis are to be kept in step with each other.

Urban neighbourhoods and small area statistics

Meaningful analysis of the residential differentiation of the urban population demands the availability of the right sort of data for the right sort of units. Whatever the significance of neighbourhood for human behaviour and whatever the status of the natural area and neighbourhood concepts their empirical utility is dependent on operational definitions.

Because the information required if one is to attempt an understanding of the urban community is so vast, most investigators concerned with the social aspects of the city are dependent on census material. To be useful, therefore, the concept of the natural area or of the neighbourhood has to be related to the territorial subdivisions used by the local census authorities.

Much of the research concerned with residential differentiation has been based on the census tract, the main framework used by the United States Bureau of Census for depicting small area statistics. Census tracts were first delimited for the 1910 U.S. Census in New York, Baltimore, Boston, Chicago, Cleveland, Philadelphia, Pittsburgh and St Louis. Each succeeding census has added more cities to the list for which tract data are available. By the 1960 Census, tracts had been defined for 180 urban areas, including 136 Standard Metropolitan Statistical Areas.

In a statement on the theory and the practice of planning census tracts Schmid states:

Facts in order to be really significant for studies in human ecology should conform to natural areas – units that are actual factors in the processes under examination. In addition, since census tracts are manipulated as statistical units in many types of analyses, they should be comparable and homogeneous. In actual practice, however, the theoretical requirements of homogeneity and comparability can, at best, only be approximated. The availability of truly diagnostic and measurable criteria, the necessity of adhering to a certain size of population, the desirability of conforming to certain administrative districts, as well as the requirements of following definitely defined boundaries, preferably streets, are perhaps some of the more important restricting considerations.[1]

The ambiguities in the definition of natural areas, particularly those concerning the relationship between socio-cultural and geographical

[1] C. F. Schmid, 'The theory and practice of planning census tracts', *Sociol. and Soc. Res.* 22 (1938), reprinted in J. P. Gibbs (ed.), *Urban Research Methods* (Princeton, 1961), pp. 166–75. Quote from latter, pp. 167–8.

characteristics, have inevitably been carried over into the practice of deline-
ating tracts on the ground. The responsibility for drawing up tracts usually
resides in a local committee, with members drawn from a range of professional and service bodies. The procedure followed in the actual delimitation
varies considerably from city to city although certain broad guide-lines, for
example the preferred population range of tracts, are laid down by the
Bureau of Census. The most frequent technique used in the delineation of
tracts involves the inspection and superimposition of a series of large-scale
maps showing physiographic characteristics, land use, demographic indices
and a series of socio-cultural and economic measures.[1] The choice of defining
criteria reflects administrative and *ad hoc* decisions about the importance of
particular types of information rather than any specific concern with the principles of urban structure. After the tracts are tentatively laid out on the basis
of available data they are checked in the field. The major difficulty in the
procedure lies in the allocation of weights to each criterion. The correspondence of geographical, social and demographic distribution is only true in a
relatively general sense. At the local level there may be much overlapping
of boundaries. In an analysis of Lansing, Michigan, Form *et al.* find that
there is no simple relationship between tracts drawn according to geographical, demographic, and social indices: 'Indeed, it is possible, using each
approach, to derive separate plans roughly alike in the number of sub-areas
and the size of the population contained in them.'[2] Similar findings are
reported by Myers, Hatt, and Mabry.[3] In practice the needs of administration
and of data collection generally dictate that the ultimate arbiter of census
tract boundaries shall be easily-visible physiographic features. The United
States Bureau of the Census and its allied institutions in other countries
normally require that tract boundaries be relatively permanent and clearly
defined since they must also delimit enumeration or collector's districts.
In the field phase of data collection ambiguity in boundaries could clearly
be disastrous. As Linge remarks, writing about Australian census collectors'
districts: 'For the most part CD boundaries follow obvious features on the
ground (rivers, roads, pylons, etc.) so that the collector can have little doubt
about where his bailiwick begins and ends.'[4] The significance of such
features for the distribution of population characteristics may be hard to
specify. As Form *et al.* observe, the use of demographic or social indices
in the definition of sub-areas may involve the violation of every type of

[1] *Ibid.*

[2] W. H. Form *et al.*, 'The compatibility of alternative approaches to the delimitation of urban
sub-areas', *Am. Sociol. Rev.* 19 (1954), reprinted in Gibbs, *Urban Research Methods*, pp. 176–87.

[3] J. K. Myers, 'Note on the homogeneity of census tracts', *Soc. Forces*, 32 (1954), 364–6; P. K.
Hatt, 'The concept of natural areas', *Am. Sociol. Rev.* 11 (1946), 423–8, reprinted in Theodorson,
Studies in Human Ecology, pp. 104–7; J. H. Mabry, 'Census tract variation in urban research',
Am. Sociol. Rev. 23 (1958), 193–6.

[4] G. J. R. Linge, 'The Delimitation of Urban Boundaries for Statistical Purposes' (mimeo.
Australian National University, Canberra, 1966), p. 11.

geographical barrier, including main streets, rivers, railways and factory districts.[1]

The lack of correspondence between the distribution of geographical, socio-cultural, demographic, and economic characteristics is frequently raised as a major obstacle to the use of sub-area data for analytical purposes. Such an objection is founded on the belief that, to be valid, census tracts or other small areas must be homogeneous. The precise meaning of homogeneity is rarely specified. The general treatment of the statistical properties to be possessed by small areas if they are to be used in the production of data for statistical manipulation lays great stress on the minimization of internal variance and the maximization of that between areas. As Beshers has shown, however, the use of the internal homogeneity criterion is only justified when the data to be generated are means or proportions.[2] For other types of data different procedures may have optimum statistical properties: thus if the analysis is to be concerned with estimating the degree of correlation between two variables in the population, the optimum procedure for the delineation of small areas would involve the minimization of within-area co-variance and the maximization of between-area co-variance. Where the analysis is concerned with observations which are intrinsic to the aggregate units then within-area variation has no meaning.

An emphasis on the homogeneity of neighbourhoods may also be derived from a concern with the relationship between individual and aggregate characteristics. In a critique of the ecological approach in social psychiatry, Clausen and Kohn[3] claim that one of the main assumptions in ecological explanations of differences in the rate of mental disorder over the various neighbourhoods of the city is that the known characteristics of the area adequately reflect the characteristics or conditions of life of those individuals who become ill. They go on to state that this implies that the particular individuals who become ill are either in some way typical of their local community or else are sufficiently exposed to it to be influenced by its social characteristics. The question of homogeneity would seem to be relevant only to the first of these implications. There is nothing in the concept of either the neighbourhood or the natural area which implies any necessary homogeneity in the sense of all its inhabitants or dwellings being alike. Indeed it may be anticipated that heterogeneity may be the determining characteristics of some neighbourhoods, for instance those in the 'zone in transition'. In a discussion of the relationship between the analysis of aggregate data and that of individuals, Tryon provides a probabilistic interpretation which may be used to further illumine the nature of small area statistics. Tryon suggests that an examination of the metric profile of an individual's census area

[1] Form *et al.*, 'Compatibility of alternative approaches'.
[2] J. M. Beshers, 'Statistical inferences from small area data', *Soc. Forces*, 38 (1960), 341–8.
[3] Kohn and Clausen, 'The ecological approach in social psychiatry'.

enables one to state the probability of what his own characteristics may be. If one knows that a given census tract has a 60 per cent Negro population then the average probability of an individual, X, drawn randomly from the tract belonging to the Negro category will be 0·60. Tryon goes on:

Furthermore, we know some very specific things about X; namely, what particular pattern of demographic features stimulates him as an inhabitant of his . . . area. Although he might himself be a deviant, he nevertheless constantly confronts the modal features of his neighbourhood group – and of these we have a precise description. In short, the metric description of a(n) . . . area may, on the one hand, give only approximate knowledge about a given individual in it, but on the other hand it does give specific knowledge of the social situation in which he lives.[1]

The criterion of homogeneity is not that all the people inhabiting a given area should be the same, but that the probability of their being of a particular characteristic should be alike in all parts of the area. Thus, if the characteristics of the area are given in terms of proportions, an area may be considered homogeneous in any measure, y, if on all major geographic subdivisions the value of y is the same. Using this and related arguments Tryon is able to provide convincing evidence for the homogeneity of 90 per cent of the 243 census tracts in San Francisco–East Bay.[2] The existence of differences within a census tract or any other small area is only prejudicial to the use of the area in ecological analysis if the differences relate to the proportions of the population possessing specified traits in major divisions of the area. The criticisms of such writers as Hatt, Myers and Mabry, constituted on the finding that census tracts contained heterogeneous populations rather than homogeneous ones, are believed to be misdirected.

A further problem in the use of small areas for statistical purposes relates to the problem of the reliability of areal data. This is a problem which has received little attention in recent years despite an early interest in the subject on the part of several statistical theorists.[3] The apparent trend towards the use of sampling rather than complete enumerations in census procedures is likely to make the question of the reliability of small area data more salient.[4] The computation of split-half reliability coefficients is rarely possible for small area data and the assumption of reliability is generally based on faith rather than empirical test. Even in the case of complete enumerations the instability of proportions and means based on small populations requires the investigator to give careful consideration to the reliability of his data.

Closely related to the question of reliability is the question of the optimum

[1] R. C. Tryon, *Identification of Social Areas by Cluster Analysis* (Berkeley, 1955), p. 4.
[2] *Ibid.* pp. 38–44.
[3] See D. L. Foley, 'Census tracts and urban research', *J. Am. Stat. Ass.* 48 (1953), 733–42.
[4] The decision of many census authorities to make use of 10 per cent samples in the collection of several of the more important sociological items is to be greatly regretted from this point of view.

size of census sub-areas. In practice, both the areal extent and the population included in census sub-areas reflect administrative and costing concerns rather than any more theoretical perspective. According to Linge, the collector's district, the basic unit of the Australian Census,

is thought of as the area and population that one collector can cover delivering and collecting census schedules. Under present methods this means that CD's are drawn (as far as possible) to contain about 1,000 population. They may be one-tenth of a square mile (e.g. a block of flats) in the centre of a town or 50 or 60 square miles on the periphery of a town. Until now CD's have been regarded as simply a census collecting device.[1]

In the United States the population of census tracts varies from less than 1,000 to more than 10,000 with a median of around 4,000 inhabitants. Certain types of information, primarily relating to housing characteristics, are also available for U.S. cities on a block basis. In the United Kingdom an earlier decision to inaugurate a tracting programme has been rescinded in favour of making data available on the Australian pattern, in terms of enumeration districts. In general the smaller the basic territorial unit, the better. Although as Beshers remarks, the aim should be to have no more sub-areas than are necessary to maximize the desired statistical property,[2] the existence of data at a fine scale enables the regrouping of areas to form sub-areas at any desired level. The advent of large computer facilities has effectively removed one of the major obstacles to the use of detailed small area data: their cost and unwieldiness. The decision of the British General Register Office to consider releasing data for the 1971 Census on the basis of a 100-metre grid system is to be welcomed.

Areas which may legitimately be characterized as possessing all the desirable statistical properties at one moment in time may not necessarily be so suitable at others. Although in general there is considerable stability in the residential structure of the community, local changes may be quite pronounced over time. One of the arguments advanced in favour of census tracts is that they provide a framework which can be maintained over time.[3] Why this should be so is unclear and it appears likely that it will be possible to defend the boundaries of collector's districts to greater effect than those of larger areas. Provided the initial units are small enough, the advantages of having a comparative and stable framework for historical analyses are likely to outweigh any local inefficiencies in their delineation. Where population increase or decrease necessitates the redrawing of boundaries this may be carried out in such a fashion that the new areas correspond to specifiable subdivisions or amalgamations of the old.

Even granted an optimum delineation of census small areas, the user of

[1] Linge, 'Delimitation of Urban Boundaries'.   [2] Beshers, 'Statistical inferences.'
[3] E.g. Robson, *Urban Analysis*, pp. 44–5.

census data may still be frustrated by the absence of the data he seeks. In general the material gathered by census authorities is designed for the needs of government rather than for those of researchers. Moreover, the material collected frequently shows strange changes over time which make the task of comparative research exceedingly difficult. Part of the blame for the unhappy confrontation which frequently occurs between researcher and census bureau must clearly be laid at the foot of the research professions who have been slow in making their requirements known. The establishment of liaison committees in many countries, bringing together both census officials and representatives of the research professions, should do much to rectify the gap which is commonly found between the data available and the data needed. It is frequently also the case that required data have to be gathered from several different organizations. Thus in some of the Australian material to be reported later, the collection of data involved the analysis of five different government and local government departments. It is unusual in such cases to find any correspondence in the territorial units for which data are computed or in the definition of variables. Such correspondence is devoutly to be desired. It cannot be stressed too highly that, whatever the sophistication of the analytical techniques used, the empirical results of any piece of research can be no better than the data which are available. The urban analyst is generally dependent on data which have been collected for and by others. In using these data he has to be constantly alert to the dangers which may accrue as the result of a lack of correspondence between the nominal definition of his variables and the operational definition which is forced upon him by others' efforts.

Properties and indicants

Granted a particular theoretical orientation it remains true that not all the concepts derived from that orientation possess equal utility as classificatory properties. Concepts vary widely in their significance. According to Kaplan,

What makes a concept significant is that the classification it institutes is one into which things fall, as it were, of themselves. It carves at the joints, Plato said. Less metaphorically, a significant concept so groups or divides its subject-matter that it can enter into many and important true propositions . . . The function of scientific concepts is to mark the categories which will tell us more about our subject-matter than any other categorial sets.[1]

Which analytical properties are judged to be significant and which are rejected rests ultimately on their relative efficiency in simplifying data. Those properties are most admired which institute natural divisions, that is,

[1] Kaplan, *Conduct of Inquiry*, pp. 50–2.

divisions which allow 'the discovery of many more, and more important, resemblances than those originally recognized'.[1] In traditional statistical terms the most powerful analytical property is that which possesses the greatest correlation with other properties of the objects concerned. A differentiation of humans on the basis of sex is a more powerful classification than one based on eye colour because it can be shown to be related to many more, and more important, behavioural features. Whether or not a given property produces a natural division can only be established as the result of cumulative and comparative study. Long-accepted properties and divisions are always liable to loss of prestige as further information is gained concerning any particular universe of discourse.

The properties used in the course of scientific analysis may be differentiated on many grounds. For present purposes a useful distinction is between theoretically defined properties, which we shall call constructs, and operationally defined properties, which we shall call indicants.[2]

Constructs are the building blocks for theories. The definition of a construct is in terms of its relation to other constructs; its meaning is constituted by its position in a system of constructs. In Hempel's terms a construct possesses theoretical or systematic import if, and only if, it has one or more constitutive definitions.[3]

Constructs are theoretical terms, they are not observable. They occur in latent space and not its manifest appearance. In order to relate to empirical material the meaning of a construct has to be translated according to certain laws of correspondence into operational procedures. These latter define the indicants which are taken to be indexes of the theoretical constructs. In order to develop theory it is necessary that at least some of the theoretical constructs be directly translatable into operationally-defined indicants. In order to be useful all constructs must possess constitutive meaning, but they must also possess at least indirect connexions with indicants. It must be possible to measure the relation between the constructs:

Measurement requires . . . the selecting and combining of appropriate sense data (indicants) into various measures (rating, scales, scores, indexes) that serve to translate concepts into operations. The more nearly these operations classify the case in terms of the property as defined in the conceptual model, the more valid the measure.[4]

[1] *Ibid.* p. 50.
[2] Cf. S. S. Stevens, 'Mathematics, measurement, and psychophysics', in S. S. Stevens (ed.), *Handbook of Experimental Psychology* (New York, 1951).
[3] C. G. Hempel, 'Fundamentals of concept formation in empirical science', in O. Neurath *et al.* (eds), *Internat. Encycl. of Unified Science* (Chicago, 1952), vol. 2, no. 7. See also P. F. Lazarsfeld, 'Concept formation and measurement in the behavioural sciences', in G. J. Direnzo (ed.), *Concepts, Theory, and Explanation in the Behavioural Sciences* (New York, 1966), pp. 139–202; W. S. Torgerson, *Theory and Methods of Scaling* (New York, 1958), pp. 1–12.
[4] Riley, p. 329. *Sociological Research*, vol. 1 p. 329.

In a well-developed science the connexion between indicants and constructs will be firmly established and the constructs themselves will be tied to each other by a large number of relations. The situation in the social sciences is as yet only a poor approximation to this state of affairs. A diagramatic representation might appear somewhat like that in Fig. 2.1.[1]

Fig. 2.1. Indicants and constructs in the social sciences. Solid lines indicate strong association; dashed lines indicate weak association

Although social scientific inquiry makes use of the same elements as more established sciences, the connexions between them are frequently of an inferential rather than deductive nature. The constructs in Fig. 2.1 are only loosely related to each other; systematization is present to a relatively low degree. At the same time, each is connected with its operationally defined indicants by what may best be characterized as an inferential leap. According to Torgerson: 'At best, the two are *presumed* to be monotonically related to each other. At worst, merely a positive correlation of unknown magnitude is *presumed* to exist.'[2] The indicants certainly indicate something, but what this something is and how it relates to the properties contained in the theoretical universe of the investigator, are matters of conjecture.

To be theoretically fruitful analytical properties need to straddle the theoretical-empirical continuum. The ideal situation, according to Parsons, 'is to have theoretical categories of such a character that the empirical values of the variables concerned are the immediate products of our observational procedures'.[3] Such a situation is rare in the social sciences but, in the absence of clear connexions between the theoretical conception of the analytical property and its presumed indicant, the empirical analysis which the latter institutes may possess little or no relevance to the theoretical discussion which it is designed to illumine. In this situation theory construction and empirical analysis may proceed in mutual isolation and sterility. In order

---

[1] Based on an idea by Margenau. See H. Margenau, *The Nature of Physical Reality* (New York, 1950), chaps. 5, 12.

[2] Torgerson, *Theory and Methods of Scaling*, p. 7.

[3] T. Parsons, *Essays in Sociological Theory, Pure and Applied* (New York, 1949), p. 5 (quoted in Riley, *Sociological Research*, vol. 1).

to serve effectively as means for developing theoretically fruitful analyses indicants must provide valid measures of the properties contained in the theoretical universe under consideration. The stronger the connexions between indicants and constructs the more readily can empirical data be brought to bear on the problem of verifying theory.

Measurement validity and factor analysis

The topic of measurement validity has a voluminous literature.[1] Although a general core of meaning seems established for the term, concerned with the relation between indicant and construct, detailed interpretations of measurement validity vary according to the orientation of the investigator and the theoretical development of the discipline. The commonest interpretation given to the term validity is that it refers to the extent to which the set of operations defining the indicant measure the empirical projection of the relevant construct. Effectively, is the indicant a measure of what it purports to measure? The difficulty with this interpretation is that in the social sciences at least the definition of the theoretical term used as a reference is often far from clear. In these circumstances operations may be 'floating' and their validity difficult to establish. In other cases it may appear that while an indicant does include the empirical information relating to a particular construct, it also includes some extra information. Under these circumstances the indicant can hardly be considered invalid, but it clearly provides a measure of somewhat different properties than that originally anticipated. A discussion of the validity of indicants falling into this last category may be couched more in terms of a search for the constructs assumed to account for the observed measures rather than in terms of the *a priori* assessment of whether or not they have actually measured what they purport to measure.

Probably the major tool in assessing the validity and meaning of a set of indicants is the body of techniques known as factor analysis.[2] In the words of Harman:

The principal concern of factor analysis is the resolution of a set of variables linearly in terms of (usually) a small number of categories or 'factors'. This resolution can be accomplished by the analysis of the correlations among the variables. A satisfactory solution will yield factors which convey all the essential

[1] E.g. J. Guilford, *Psychometric Methods* (New York, 1954), chaps. 1, 13, 14; L. Cronbach and P. Meehl, 'Construct validity in psychological tests', *Psych. Bull.* 52 (1955), 281–302; F. N. Kerlinger, *Foundations of Behavioural Research* (New York, 1964), pp. 444–62; J. Nunnally, *Psychometric Theory* (New York, 1967), pp. 75–102.

[2] Introductions to factor analysis are provided in Kerlinger, *Foundations of Behavioural Research*, pp. 650–87; Nunnally, *Psychometric Theory*, pp. 288–371; and B. Fruchter, *Introduction to Factor Analysis* (Princeton, N. J., 1954). More advanced treatments are provided by H. H. Harman, *Modern Factor Analysis* (Chicago, 1960) and P. Horst, *Factor Analysis of Data Matrices* (New York, 1965).

information of the original set of variables. Thus, the chief aim is to obtain scientific parsimony or economy of description.[1]

In addition, factor analysis provides a powerful technique for unravelling the connexion between manifest indicants and the underlying constructs which they represent.

Factors are mathematical constructs. Strictly speaking 'any linear combination of the variables in a data matrix is said to be a factor of that matrix'.[2] In practice, however, the formation of factors is subject to certain restrictive conditions concerning the weights to be applied to the various indicants. The computations involved in a factor analysis are frequently arduous and details of the method are outside the scope of the present work. It is necessary, however, that some brief comments be made on the characteristic outputs of a factor analysis. In order to facilitate the discussion a prior distinction must be made between *direct* and *indirect* factor solutions and between *orthogonal* and *oblique* sets of factor axes.

The distinction between the direct and the indirect approaches to factor analysis is based primarily on the purposes to which the analysis is to be put. The direct approach is the usual one when the analysis is concerned with testing an *a priori* hypothesis concerning the factorial composition of a specified set of data. According to Nunnally: 'The essence of any direct solution is that (1) it is performed so as to test hypotheses about the existence of factors and (2) the nature of linear combinations is stated in advance of obtaining the correlation matrix.'[3] If, for example, it is believed that six indicants are the empirical projection of two underlying factors and that the indicants may be grouped so that numbers 1, 2 and 3 are related to the first factor and numbers 4, 5 and 6 are related to the second factor, a direct method of factor analysis – probably the multiple-group technique – may be used to assess the extent to which this hypothesis is consistent with the observed data.[4] In the indirect, or step-wise, approach to factor analysis the goal is generally to condense a given data matrix into a much smaller factor matrix, hoping that 'meaning' will emerge in the process. The technique is usually employed in the essentially 'blind' or extensive investigation of a set of interesting but as yet unstructured indicants. In this situation the general norm of scientific parsimony suggests that the operations used should be such as to maximize the proportion of total variance accounted for by the minimum number of factors. The method of principal components is the most generally used technique since it is so defined that each factor extracted at any given stage of the analysis consists of that linear combination of indicants which accounts for the greatest possible amount of variance existing

[1] Harman, *Modern Factor Analysis*, p. 4.   [2] Nunnally, *Psychometric Theory*, p. 291.
[3] *Ibid.* p. 305.
[4] On the multiple-group method of factor analysis see Harman, *Modern Factor Analysis*, chap. 11; Nunnally, *Psychometric Theory*, pp. 342–7.

in the matrix.[1] A set of principal components accounts for the greatest possible proportion of original variance. After condensation the next step in an indirect solution is the rotation of factors in such a way as to facilitate their interpretation. The criteria of rotation are generally designed to ensure an approximation to what Thurstone has termed simple structure,[2] a situation in which the interpretation of factors is aided by the existence of a clear-cut pattern of item-factor correlations. An important aspect of the simple solution is the proposition that the resulting factors tend to be 'invariant under changes in the composition of the test battery'.[3]

Both direct and indirect factor solutions may be of either an oblique or an orthogonal form. In an oblique factor solution the factors produced are correlated with one another; in an orthogonal factor solution the factors produced are independent of each other. As will be seen shortly the full explication of an oblique factor analysis involves considerably more information than does that of an orthogonal solution. On the other hand, depending on the universe of content involved, it may well be that there are strong *a priori* grounds for believing in the lack of independence of the factors present in a given data matrix.

The typical output of an orthogonal factor analysis, whether direct or indirect, consists of a single matrix in which are shown a pattern of item-factor loadings, a_{ji}. Table 2.1 gives an example based on a combination of the principal components technique with a rotation of axes according to the varimax criterion. Frequently only the rotated matrix is shown in an actual analysis.

The square of any factor loading indicates the proportion of the variance in an indicant which is accounted for by the factor concerned.[4] The sum of squares in any column of the matrix of factor loadings indicates the total amount of original variance explained by that factor. The sum of the sums provides an indication of how successful the factors are at explaining the original data. In the case tabulated, out of an original variance of 6, 5·14 is

---

[1] On the principal components technique see Harman, *Modern Factor Analysis*, chap. 9. Principal components define the principal axes of the ellipsoids formed by the indicants in test space.

[2] Thurstone's criteria for simple structure are the following: (1) each row of the factor matrix should have at least one zero; (2) if there are *m* common factors, each column of the factor matrix should have at least *m* zeros; (3) for every pair of columns of the factor matrix there should be several variables whose entries vanish in one column but not in the other; (4) for every pair of columns of the factor matrix, a large proportion of the variables should have vanishing entries in both columns when there are four or more factors; (5) for every pair of columns of the factor matrix there should be only a small number of variables with non-vanishing entries in both columns. L. L. Thurstone, *Multiple-factor Analysis* (Chicago, 1947), p. 335.

In fact, the five criteria mentioned by Thurstone are not nearly sufficient to provide a completely satisfactory definition of simple structure. See Harman, *Modern Factor Analysis*, pp. 112–14, 290–4; Nunnally, *Psychometric Theory*, pp. 328–32.

[3] H. F. Kaiser, 'The varimax criterion for analytic rotation in factor analysis', *Psychometrika*, 23 (1958), 195.

[4] This is true only in the case of uncorrelated factors.

49

accounted for, that is 85 per cent. The sum of squared item-factor loadings in any row indicates the proportion of variance in the specified indicant which is accounted for by the factors. If a complete solution is provided, including

TABLE 2.1 *Constitution of orthogonal factor solution*

Variable	Pattern coefficients						Communality
	Factor I	. . .	Factor p	. . .	Factor m		
I	a_{I1}	. . .	a_{Ip}	. . .	a_{Im}		$h_I{}^2$
.	.		.		.		.
.	.		.		.		.
.	.		.		.		.
j	a_{j1}	. . .	a_{jp}	. . .	a_{jm}		$h_j{}^2$
.	.		.		.		.
.	.		.		.		.
n	a_{n1}	. . .	a_{np}	. . .	a_{nm}		$h_n{}^2$
Contribution of factor	V_I	. . .	V_p	. . .	V_m		

$$a_{jp} = r_{jp}$$

Indirect orthogonal factor solution for six indicants

A. Principal components

B. Orthogonal rotation

Variable	Pattern coefficients			h^2	Variable	Pattern coefficients			h^2
	I	II	III			I	II	III	
1	90	−15	−11	84	1	76	−11	−49	84
2	64	−55	44	91	2	91	−18	22	91
3	93	−16	13	90	3	89	00	−33	90
4	71	46	−01	72	4	44	44	−59	72
5	13	83	47	93	5	02	96	−07	93
6	−71	−28	51	83	6	−29	−02	87	83
V_p	3·10	1·34	0·70		V_p	2·49	1·17	1·48	

NOTE. Decimal point omitted in factor matrices.

a specific factor, the sum of squared loadings for a given row will equal unity. More generally, interest centres on that part of the variance which is accounted for by the *m* common factors. This may be termed the *communality* of the indicant ($h_j{}^2$):

Eq. 2.1.
$$\sum_{p=1}^{m} a_{jp}{}^2 = h_j{}^2.$$

The more a variable shares common factors with other indicants the higher its communality. Traditionally this is defined as the indicant's validity:

'The validity of a measure is that portion of the total variance of the measure that shares variance with other measures. Theoretically, valid variance includes no variance due to error, nor does it include variance that is specific to this measure and this measure only.'[1] Since the total variance in an indicant may be readily represented as the sum of the indicant's communality and a specific component, factor analysis provides a highly efficacious approach to the study of validity.

If as many factors as indicants are extracted from the data matrix it will be possible to use the factor loadings to reproduce the original items in precise fashion. Since it is nearly always the case that the number of factors extracted is considerably smaller than the number of indicants[2] and that a small proportion of common factor variance as well as specific variance may remain in the residual matrix, the item-factor loadings may in practice be used to provide only a best-estimate of the original data:

Eq. 2.2. $\qquad z'_j = a_{jI}F_I \ldots + a_{jp}F_p \ldots + a_{jm}F_m,$

where z'_j is the estimated standard score on j, a_{jp} are the pattern coefficients between indicant j and factor p, and F_p are standard scores on each of the m common factors. Equation 2.2 holds no matter how the factors are constituted. Even if the method used is one which leads to a very poor estimate of the original data, the regression weights used in the equation are still given by the pattern coefficients.

In the case of an orthogonal solution the set of pattern coefficients may be used by themselves to provide a best-estimate of the original correlation matrix. By an extension of equation 2.2 it may be shown that in the case of orthogonal factors the correlation between two indicants, j and k, may be calculated as the sum of the cross-products of their pattern coefficients. In a three factor case:

Eq. 2.3. $\qquad r'_{jk} = r_{jI}r_{kI} + r_{jII}r_{kII} + r_{jIII}r_{kIII}.$

Using equation 2.3 it is possible to reconstruct the original matrix of inter-item correlations. By comparing the reconstructed matrix with the original matrix, further evidence may be obtained on the extent to which the analysis has succeeded in exhausting the common-factor variance in the original data. A satisfactory solution will yield a residual matrix whose elements are small and randomly distributed.

The elements of an orthogonal factor solution possess the same mathematical qualities whether they are derived from a direct or an indirect analysis.

[1] Kerlinger, *Foundations of Behavioural Research*, p. 457.
[2] In the case of principal components analysis it is usual to retain all components with latent roots of unity or more, i.e. all those which account for more variance than does any single indicant.

The rationale for rotation rests simply on the aid it may provide in the interpretation of factors and in the estimation of factor scores. Rotation does not change the communality of an indicant. It does, however, generally lead to change in the amount of variance contributed by each factor. In the varimax method of rotation the aim is to so rotate the factor axes that the sum of variances of squared loadings in the columns of the factor matrix are maximized.[1] In each column this tends to give rise to some high loadings and some near-zero loadings. In this manner the interpretation of the factor may be aided.

In order to interpret a factor it is necessary to have information on the correlation between factors and indicants. In an orthogonal solution the indicant-factor correlations are identical with the pattern coefficients. In an oblique solution, Table 2.2, this identity no longer holds.

The matrix of item-factor correlations (r_{jp}) is termed the *factor structure*. In the case of an oblique solution a full presentation demands both a factor pattern and a factor structure.[2] Only in the case of an orthogonal solution are the elements of a structure identical with the corresponding coefficients of a pattern. In an oblique solution a full output consists of a factor structure, a factor pattern, and a matrix of inter-factor correlations. The factor structure is useful for the interpretation and identification of factors, the factor pattern shows the linear composition of indicants in terms of factors and the inter-factor correlations show the extent to which the factors are independent of each other. In conjunction with the factor pattern the matrix of inter-factor correlations allows a reconstruction of the original correlation matrix.

The identification and interpretation of factors demands an intuitive leap. Although the analysis begins with an inspection of the matrix of indicant-factor correlations given in the factor structure, the final interpretation of a factor demands knowledge of the relevant theoretical framework. The weight given to empirical and to theoretical considerations varies according to the nature of the analysis. In a blind analysis, where the investigator is simply concerned with discovering a likely factor structure, the interpretation may be almost wholly in terms of the item-factor coefficients revealed in the rotated matrix. In the example given in Table 2.1, factor I may be identified in terms of the common meaning given to variables 1, 2 and 3; factor II may be identified by its high correlation with variable 5; and factor III may be identified by its correlations with variable 4 and, more particularly, with variable 6. In the case of a direct analysis designed in conjunction with a factor hypothesis, a rather different set of procedures is suggested.

---

[1] On the varimax criterion, see Harman, *Modern Factor Analysis*, pp. 301–8; Kaiser, 'The varimax criterion'.

[2] For the functional relationship between the elements of a factor pattern and those of a factor structure, see Harman, *Modern Factor Analysis*, pp. 16–18.

TABLE 2.2
Constitution of oblique factor solution

Factor structure

Variable	Item-factor correlations		
	Factor I . . .	Factor p . . .	Factor m
I	r_{II} . . .	r_{Ip} . . .	r_{Im}
.	.	.	.
.	.	.	.
.	.	.	.
j	r_{jI} . . .	r_{jp} . . .	r_{jm}
.	.	.	.
.	.	.	.
n	r_{nI} . . .	r_{np} . . .	r_{nm}

Factor pattern

Variable	Pattern coefficients		
	Factor I . . .	Factor p . . .	Factor m
I	a_{II} . . .	a_{Ip} . . .	a_{Im}
.	.	.	.
.	.	.	.
.	.	.	.
i	a_{jI} . . .	a_{jp} . . .	a_{jm}
.	.	.	.
.	.	.	.
n	a_{nI} . . .	a_{np} . . .	a_{nm}

$$a_{jp} \neq r_{jp}$$

Factor correlations

Factor	I	p	m
I	1·000	—	—
p	r_{pI}	1·000	—
m	r_{mI}	r_{mp}	1·000

Direct multiple group factor solution for nine indicants (data from Harman, p. 229)

A. Factor structure

Variable	Item-factor correlations		
	I	II	III
1	90	52	37
2	83	61	38
3	87	56	46
4	55	96	43
5	56	86	49
6	63	86	50
7	28	39	59
8	38	40	76
9	38	39	88

B. Factor pattern

Variable	Pattern coefficients		
	I	II	III
1	98	−09	−04
2	76	14	−05
3	86	−04	08
4	−11	107	08
5	−01	84	04
6	11	77	04
7	−06	14	55
8	05	−04	76
9	03	−12	93

NOTE. Decimal point omitted in factor matrices.

Factor correlations

Factor	I	II	III
I	1·000	—	—
II	0·651	1·000	—
III	0·464	0·532	1·000

53

The main question in this latter case concerns the extent to which the indicant-factor correlations conform to a predicted pattern. Thus, in Table 2.2, a multiple-group analysis is employed to test an hypothesis about the factorial composition of nine indicants. The first set of three indicants is hypothesized to be related to one factor, the second set to a second factor, and the third set to a third factor. The identification of the factors is based on *a priori* theory, rather than on the date given. The task of the analysis is to ascertain whether the theoretically-given factors are consonant with the empirical data. In the tabulated case they clearly are.[1] The indicants assigned to each factor correlate more highly with it than they do with either of the other factors. Moreover, the computation of the residual matrix suggests that the three hypothesized factors effectively exhaust the common variance present in the data. It may therefore be concluded that the three hypothesized factors – already identified – are both necessary and sufficient to account for the observed pattern of inter-variable correlations.

The distinction between the blind and the hypothesis-testing approaches to factor analysis is important, but should not be exaggerated. The invariance of factors under the substitution of indicants implies that the results of one analysis will be comparable with those of another in spite of the differences in purpose or data input. On the other hand, the details of any factor solution reflect the constitution of the original data matrix and, even in the blindest of analyses, this is far from a random or even a representative sample of all items contained in the theoretical universe of content. The indicants which are available in any given context are usually a very restricted proportion of those theoretically possible and their use may be more a function of their accessibility and of the predilections of the investigator than of any regard for obtaining a representative sample of a specifiable universe of content. Factor analysis is not a technique which can somehow lead the investigator directly to 'underlying verities', to the 'real principles' at work in nature. It is no more and no less than an expeditious and efficient tool for examining the relationship between observed indicants and certain underlying hypothetical constructs which happen to fit the data. As in all research which attempts to leap the chasm between empirical data and theoretical constructs the use of factor analysis demands intuition as well as logic.

FACTORIAL ECOLOGY

Factorial ecology comprises the application of factor analysis to data describing the residential differentiation of the population, generally the urban

---

[1] The criteria for establishing the 'goodness of fit' of a given factor solution remain somewhat nebulous. See Nunnally, *Psychometric Theory*, pp. 346-7.

population. It may be either blind or in connexion with a specified factor hypothesis. In the present chapter we shall be concerned primarily with the former variety.

The typical study in factorial ecology consists of the application of extensive factor analytic techniques to a wide range of demographic, socio-economic, and housing data generated on a sub-area framework. The analysis is founded on the belief that it will be possible to account for the manifold variation in neighbourhood characteristics in terms of a much smaller number of underlying constructs. The aim of the analysis may be seen as the reduction of the original n-sub-area by s-variable matrix to an n-sub-area by m-factor matrix in which m, the number of significant factors, is considerably less than s. The criteria of significance reside in both the statistical properties of the factors, as accounting for a certain proportion of variance, and in their theoretical connexions.

A steadily accelerating rate of publication is apparent for studies of factorial ecology. Table 2.3 lists a selection of those analyses available to date and attempts also to summarize their main conclusions. It should be borne in mind that since the results of a factor analysis vary not only with the nature of the data input and the particular type of factor analytic technique employed, but also with the theoretical predilections of the investigators, any attempt to provide an overall summary of findings must be treated with caution. In particular it should be remembered that differences in the details of the factor structures produced in the various studies may reflect differences in data and technique as much as underlying differences in the bases of residential differentiation.

In view of the many differences in indicants, areas of study, and types of technique used in the various studies of factorial ecology the most striking feature of Table 2.3 is the general consistency of the findings. The manifold variation of sub-area populations within the great majority of the cities so far analysed appears to be reflection of no more than three or four underlying dimensions of differentiation. A factor interpreted as *socio-economic status* or *social rank* appears to be effectively universal. A set of factors which index differences in the *family types* characteristic of the population is also gener- ally apparent. Factors relating to the *ethnic composition* of the population and to its *mobility characteristics* occur rather less frequently, but still sufficiently often to warrant their inclusion as general differentiating dimensions. Although specific factors relating to the peculiar characteristics of the populations concerned may occur in any city, the basic pattern is organized around a small number of general dimensions.

The socio-economic status or social rank factor typically exhibits high correlations with indicants relating to the proportion of the workforce classified as professionals or managers, the proportion of non-manual workers, the educational and income level of the population, and the

55

TABLE 2.3 *Summary of selected studies in factorial ecology*
(for detailed references, see bibliography)

City	Reference	Number of variables	Number of factors	Names of interpreted factors (in order of importance)
A. U.S. studies				
Boston	Sweetser, 1965*a*	20	3	Socio-economic status
				Progeniture
				Urbanism
Chicago (SMSA)	Rees, 1968	57	10	Socio-economic status
				Stage in life-cycle
				Race and resources
				Immigrant and Catholic
				Size and density
				Jewish and Russian
				Built in 1940s and commute by car
				Irish and Swedes
				Mobility
				Other non-Whites and Italians
Chicago (city)	Rees, 1968	57	7	Race and resources
				Socio-economic status
				Stage in life-cycle
				Size and density
				Other non-White and commute by foot
				Jewish and Russian
				Built before 1940 and commute by rail
Chicago (suburbs)	Rees, 1968	57	10	Socio-economic status
				Stage in life-cycle
				Immigrant and Catholic
				Race and resources
				Size and density
				Poles *v.* Anglo-Saxons
				European ethnic groups
				Built in 1940s and commute by car
				Jewish and Russian
				Overcrowding and commute by rail
Newark	Janson, 1968	48	6 (fixed beforehand)	Racial slum
				Familism-residentialism
				Social rank
				Middle age
				Mobility
				Density
Seattle	Schmid, 1960	38 (20 crime 18 general)	8	Social cohesion — family status
				Social cohesion — occupational status
				Family and economic status
				Population mobility
				Atypical crime
				Stability
				Race

City	Reference	Number of variables	Number of factors	Names of interpreted factors (in order of importance)
Seattle	Schmid and Tagashira, 1964	42 21 12 10	4 3	Familial organization Socio-economic status Ethnic status Maleness — skid row Family status Socio-economic status Ethnic status
San Francisco	Tryon, 1955	33	(Clusters: 7)	Family life Assimilation (2) Socio-economic independence Socio-economic achievement (2) Female achievement
North-eastern, North-central, Southern, and Western regions of the U.S.	Borgatta and Hadden, 1964	36	6	Socio-economic status Suburb — family type Mobility Disorganization — deprivation Foreign-born Family disorganization

A large number of studies have also been carried out by students in the Center for Urban Studies at the University of Chicago. As of 1968, Berry and Rees report that some 25 U.S. cities had been analysed by members of the Urban Studies 371 Class.

B. Non-U.S. studies

City	Reference	Number of variables	Number of factors	Names of interpreted factors (in order of importance)
Cairo	Abu-Lughod, 1969	13	3	Style of life (class and family) Male dominance (migration) Social disorganization
Calcutta	Berry and Rees, 1969	37	10	Land use and familism Bengali commercial caste Non-Bengali commercial caste Substantial residential areas Literacy Muslim concentration Special land use factors (4)
Canberra	Jones, 1965	24	4	Ethnicity Demographic structure Age of area
Copenhagen	Pedersen, 1967	14	3	Family status Socio-economic status Growth and mobility
Helsinki	Sweetser, 1965a	20	3	Socio-economic status Progeniture Urbanism
	Sweetser, 1965b	42	6	Socio-economic status Progeniture Urbanism — career women Residentialism Established familism Postgeniture
Liverpool	Gittus, 1965	31 (housing variables)	5	Dwelling density Shared and rented dwellings Multiple dwellings Amenities

C

City	Reference	Number of variables	Number of factors	Names of interpreted factors (in order of importance)
Melbourne	Jones, 1968	70	3	Socio-economic status Household composition Ethnic composition
Sunderland	Robson, 1969	30	4	Social class Housing conditions Subdivided housing Poverty

NOTE. See also Table 4.5.

proportion living in above-average-value houses. Populations gaining high scores on the factor contain many professionals, few manual workers, many persons with above-average levels of education and income, and live in above-average-value houses. Conversely, populations gaining low scores on the factor contain few professionals, many manual workers, few persons with above-average educational or income levels and live in below-average-value houses. The links between each of the indicants are strong and the factor typically accounts for a major proportion of the common factor variance exhibited in urban residential differentiation. Various secondary features also show high correlations with the socio-economic status factor. Some investigators, notably Tryon, have attempted to distinguish a secondary but closely related socio-economic dimension, 'socio-economic independence', which loads highly on such variables as the proportion of own account workers.[1] In studies of cities in the developing societies the socio-economic status factor has also shown close links to such phenomena as minority group membership, as epitomized in the concept of caste, and more general differences in ways of life.[2] Whatever the external relations of the factor, however, its appearance as a unitary dimension underlying the detailed variations in occupational status, educational attainment, income, and house value, seems universal and the factor has proved highly stable in a variety of comparative analyses.[3]

The second most consistent set of factors uncovered in studies of factorial ecology is composed of a variety of indicants which appear to be related to differences in the types of family found in the various neighbourhoods of the city. Typically, factors belonging to the family cluster show high correlations with indicants relating to the demographic structure of the population and with indicants relating to such family-saturated phenomena as fertility and the proportion of never-married or widowed women. Somewhat less consistently, high correlations occur with such variables as the

---

[1] Tryon, *Identification of Social Areas*.
[2] E.g. B. J. L. Berry and P. H. Rees, 'The factorial ecology of Calcutta', *Am. J. Sociol.* 74 (1969), 447–91; J. Abu-Lughod, 'Testing the theory of social area analysis: the ecology of Cairo, Egypt', *Am. Sociol. Rev.* 34 (1969), 198–212.
[3] E.g. F. L. Sweetser, 'Ecological factors in metropolitan zones and sectors', in M. Dogan and S. Rokan (eds), *Quantitative Ecological Analysis in the Social Sciences* (Cambridge, Mass., 1969), pp. 413–56.

proportion of women employed outside the home, the proportion of separated or divorced persons, the proportion of single-family dwellings and the proportion of owner-occupiers. The dominant factor appears to be one indicating differences in what Bell has termed *familism*: a way of life characterized by a concern with family characteristics rather than with those relating to careers or consumption.[1] Differences along the factor are indexed by such variables as fertility, the proportion of large families, the youthfulness of the population, the proportion of married adults, and the proportion of single-family dwellings. Factors showing high correlations with these indicants have been variously termed 'family status', 'young family cycle', 'progeniture', and 'suburbanism'.[2] Populations scoring highly on the factor are characterized by many young children, few old people, and few unmarried adults, and occur in areas situated some distance from the inner city and characterized by single-family houses. The more indicants are included relating to the demographic and family characteristics of the population the more the single familism factor tends to break up into a series of more specific factors relating to different age groups and different stages of the family cycle. In Helsinki, Sweetser identifies three factors of this type: 'progeniture' or young familism, 'established familism' and 'postgeniture'.[3] In a study of Newark, N.J., Janson recognized two factors called, respectively, 'familism' and 'old age'.[4] The linkage of the various demographic indicants appears universal, but there is much less consistency in the relation of the familism factor or factors to such variables as the proportion of women working outside the home, the proportion of separated or divorced persons and the proportion of owner-occupiers. Where the family arrangements and types of outside work available to women are of such a nature as not to preclude the combination of large families and working women, there may be little if any correlation between family characteristics and the proportion of women in the workforce.[5] In Calcutta, Berry and Rees report that female employment is related to the differences between Hindu and Moslem areas rather than to familism.[6] Where career norms apply to women in much the same way as they do to men, a separate 'female careerism' factor may emerge.[7]

[1] W. Bell, 'The city, the suburb, and a theory of social choice', in S. Greer *et al.* (eds), *The New Urbanization* (New York, 1968), pp. 132–68.

[2] C. F. Schmid and K. Tagashira, 'Ecological and demographic indices: a methodological analysis', *Demography*, 1 (1964), 195–211; J. M. Beshers, 'Census Tract Data and Social Structure: a Methodological Analysis' (unpub. Ph.D. dissertation, Chapel Hill, University of North Carolina, 1957); F. L. Sweetser, 'Factor structure as ecological structure in Helsinki and Boston', *Acta Sociol.* 8 (1965), 205–25; E. F. Borgatta and J. K. Hadden, 'An analysis of tract data by regions' (mimeo. University of Wisconsin, 1964).

[3] F. L. Sweetser, 'Factorial ecology: Helsinki, 1960', *Demography*, 2 (1965), 372–86.
    C.-G. Janson, 'The spatial structure of Newark, New Jersey. Part I: the central city', *Acta Sociol.* 11 (1968), 144–69.

[5] Abu-Lughod, 'Testing the theory of social area analysis'.

[6] Berry and Rees, 'Factorial ecology of Calcutta'.

[7] Sweetser, 'Factorial ecology'.

Sweetser suggests that the increasing participation of women in the workforce throughout urban-industrial society may presage the emergence of a career-woman factor as a general basis for the residential differentiation of the modern city.[1] Variations in socio-cultural characteristics are also reflected in other linkages within the general set of family-related variables. In some communities there is so little variation in types of dwelling that indicants relating to such phenomena as the proportion of single-family structures or of new housing lose their discriminating power.[2] More generally, there appears some tendency for the measures relating to housing characteristics to exhibit high correlations with a secondary *family dissolution* factor, joining such variables as the proportions of unmarried, separated, or divorced persons. Rather than a single familism factor the evidence suggests that it may be more realistic to differentiate a set of related factors all of which tap certain aspects of the familism realm but all of which also possess their own specific meanings. Whether the factors collapse into one or remain distinct reflects both the set of indicants which are available and certain global socio-cultural characteristics of the society concerned.

The occurrence of a factor or factors reflecting the role of ethnicity in differentiating the urban population depends on the degree of homogeneity in the community concerned. Although ethnic heterogeneity has been posited as a general characteristic of the modern city, some cities, notably those of Scandinavia, appear to be essentially homogeneous in their ethnic composition. Not surprisingly there is no hint of an ethnic factor in their ecological structure.[3] More generally, however, ethnic factors occur wherever it is possible to mark off ethnically distinct populations. As in the case of the familism cluster of factors, the more information is input relating to the diverse ethnic groups characteristic of such heterogeneous populations as that of the United States, the more tendency there is for the unitary ethnic factor to split up into a series of distinct sub-factors reflecting the degree of assimilation reached by the particular groups concerned. In Chicago, Rees reports 'Immigrant and Catholic', 'Jewish and Russian', 'Irish and Swedes', 'Other Non-White and Italians', and 'Race and Resources' factors.[4] In Boston, Sweetser differentiates between three distinct ethnic factors: 'non-white ethnic', 'Italian ethnic', and 'Irish middle-class' factors. He also points out that in some analyses these distinct axes merge into a single bipolar factor.[5]

[1] Sweetser, 'Ecological factors'.
[2] D. C. McElrath, 'The social areas of Rome: a comparative analysis', *Am. Sociol. Rev.* 27 (1962), 376–91.
[3] E.g. the works of Sweetser cited above. See also P. O. Pedersen, *Modeller for Befolkningsstruktur og Befolkningsudvikling i Storbyområder-specielt med Henblik på Stockøbenhavn*. Danish text with English summary (Copenhagen, 1967).
[4] P. H. Rees, 'The factorial ecology of metropolitan Chicago', (mimeo. Chicago, 1968), to be published in B. J. L. Berry and F. E. Horton (eds), *Geographic Perspectives on Urban Systems* (Englewood Cliffs, N. J., forthcoming).   [5] Sweetser, 'Ecological factors'.

Evidence for the general significance of a factor reflecting the mobility characteristics of the population is much less conclusive than is that for the socio-economic status, familism, and ethnic factors. The most likely explanation for this is the usual paucity of relevant data. Until very recently few census authorities have included questions on mobility in their schedules and other sources of information are similarly uninformative. Where material on mobility has been included in factor analyses of residential differentiation the resulting factor loadings have been subject to diverse interpretations. Frequently, mobility has been taken as a component of a construct called *urbanism*, a construct which bears much similarity to the non-family/family dissolution factor discussed earlier.[1] Typical indicants exhibiting high item-factor correlations with urbanism include the proportion of owner-occupiers (negative), the proportion of unmarried, separated and divorced persons, and population mobility. In most analyses populations scoring highly on the mobility factor are characterized by an excess of males in the 21-45 age group, but in Helsinki, Sweetser reports that urbanism is associated with a surplus of women.[2] The status of the mobility factor as a major differentiating axis of urban residential structure can only be assessed when further material is at hand.

Apart from the three or four major sets of factors, factorial ecology has also thrown up a large number of more specific factors of differentiation. Some of these, for example the 'traditional commercial communities' factor in Calcutta,[3] are clearly related to the socio-cultural specific of time and place. Many others are probably a reflection of the particular mix of indicants included in the analysis. Examples of this latter group include factors labelled 'size and density' and 'built in 1940s, commute by car',[4] and 'atypical crime'.[5] In the absence of comparable studies elsewhere it is impossible to generalize the significance of these factors.

A major justification for the use of factors rather than individual indicants in the analysis of urban structure is the assumption that factors are invariant under substitution of measures. The appearance of the three or four basic sets of factors in studies of the factorial ecology of a wide-ranging variety of cities, for which a wide range of data is available, provides one test of this assumption. More direct assessments have involved analyses of the invariance of factors extracted from matrices based on different sets of data for the same community at the same point of time. Analyses by Schmid and Tagashira and by Sweetser, have produced results in strong support of the assumption. In Seattle, Schmid and Tagashira show that the basic

[1] E.g. T. R. Anderson and L. Bean, 'The Shevky-Bell social areas: confirmation of results and a reinterpretation', *Soc. Forces*, 40 (1961), 119-24.
[2] Sweetser, 'Factorial ecology'.
[3] Berry and Rees, 'Factorial ecology of Calcutta'.
[4] Rees, 'Factorial ecology of metropolitan Chicago'.
[5] C. F. Schmid, 'Urban crime areas', *Am. Sociol. Rev.* 25 (1960), 527-42, 655-78.

factors of family status, socio-economic status, and ethnic status appear in matrices containing respectively 42, 21, 12 and 10 variables. Moreover the reduced set of ten variables provides a highly satisfactory representation of the three basic dimensions existing in the original set of 42 variables.[1] Reporting similar findings for Helsinki, Sweetser concludes: 'We are encouraged, therefore, in generalizing that *ecological factors are invariant under substitution, addition, and subtraction of variables.*'[2] The major results of increasing the size of the data matrix appear to be tendencies for the emergence of new specific factors and, less clearly, for a progressive splintering of the three or four basic factors into sets of closely associated subfactors.

Factorial invariance can only be anticipated if the analyses concerned are directed at the same universe of content. One of the major problems in interpreting the results of factorial ecology lies in the doubt whether the bounds of the set of areas for which the analyses are reported are enclosing comparable systems. Sweetser has suggested that complexity of the factor structures produced in studies of the residential differentiation of metropolitan communities may be the result of the interaction of several different modes of ecological differentiation, notably those relating to the inner city or urban mode, the urban-suburban or metropolitan mode and the rural-urban mode.[3] Presenting data on the dimensions of differentiation found in different zones of Boston and Helsinki, Sweetser finds considerable empirical support for his hypothesis. In the inner-city area a greater degree of differentiation appears to occur, corroborating Kish's hypothesis that the degree of ecological differentiation varies inversely in relation to distance from the metropolitan centre.[4] In the rural-urban fringe the emergence of several 'ruralism' factors presages the change from urban to rural modes of differentiation. Sweetser concludes that great caution should be paid to the delimitation of the outer boundaries of metropolitan communities if they are to be used for comparative ecological studies.

Boundaries too narrow – geographically constrictive city limits, for example – may produce distortion through an overemphasis on the inner city mode of differentiation. Boundaries too wide – extended metropolitan regions, for example – may introduce unwanted effects of the rural-urban mode of differentiation . . . A fully objective comparative study of metropolitan ecological structures, whether inter-regional or cross-national, would appear to require that social ecologists develop some means of delimiting metropolitan communities on a uniform basis.[5]

Considerable attention has been given to the task of constructing practical guidelines for the delimitation of comparable metropolitan boundaries, and

[1] Schmid and Tagashira, 'Ecological and demographic indices'.
[2] Sweetser, 'Factorial ecology', p. 379.   [3] Sweetser, 'Ecological factors'.
[4] L. Kish, 'Differentiation in metropolitan areas', *Am. Sociol. Rev.* 19 (1954), 388–98.
[5] Sweetser, '*Ecological factors*', p. 455.

Berry *et al.* make a strong case for the use of daily commuting fields.[1] The translation of this recommendation into common practice, however, remains a vision of the future.

Although the invariance of the main differentiating factors in urban residential structure has been demonstrated over many sets of variables and many cities it should not be assumed that socio-economic status, familism, ethnicity, and mobility provide a stable framework for the analysis of all cities at all times. In detail, there are considerable differences in the factor structures revealed by the various analyses. Many specific factors, reflecting variations in the initial data input, have been recorded. The postulated mobility factor is highly inconsistent. Outside the United States, efforts to reproduce an ethnic factor have frequently proved unsuccessful. Even where ethnicity has emerged as a major ecological dimension it has shown widely varying relationships with other variables. Socio-economic status and familism have proved the most stable of the underlying factors, but even they exhibit tendencies to internal differentiation and, more importantly, exhibit varying degrees of independence. In most North American and Scandinavian studies there is virtually no correlation between familism and social rank; in Cairo, on the other hand, Abu-Lughod reports that she is unable to obtain any factorial separation between them. Rather than loading on two separate factors the indicants concerned all load on a single 'social rank-style of life' dimension.[2] Somewhat similar findings are reported for Calcutta by Berry and Rees.[3] The 'substantial residential areas' factor, which Berry and Rees equate with the social rank concept, exhibits high item-factor correlations with such variables as per cent children under five years of age, and per cent population in scheduled castes as well as a wide range of housing variables. To some extent the differences in the factor structures revealed in the various analyses may be accounted for by differences in data input and in the boundaries used for defining the universe of content. It is also apparent, however, that ecological structure is to some extent a function of certain more general characteristics of the society concerned. We shall be taking up this point in a later chapter.

THE FACTORIAL ECOLOGY OF BRISBANE, QUEENSLAND AND AUCKLAND, NEW ZEALAND

Australasian cities have much in common with those of the United States,

---

[1] B. J. L. Berry *et al.*, *Metropolitan Area Definition* (Washington, 1968).
[2] Abu-Lughod, 'Testing the theory of social area analysis'. In an earlier paper Abu-Lughod presents data which suggest that the ecological correlation between social rank and familism is also apparent at the individual level. There is a close association between occupational and educational status and size of family in Cairo. See J. Abu-Lughod, 'The emergence of differential fertility in urban Egypt', *Millbank Memorial Fund Quart.* 43 (1965), 235–53.
[3] Berry and Rees, 'Factorial ecology of Calcutta'.

particularly those of the West Coast. Their expansion has been recent and rapid, much of it occurring in the period since the Second World War. Growth has been aided by relatively massive immigration, involving several distinct ethnic groups. Physical expansion has been in terms of low density suburbs composed almost wholly of single-family dwellings on individual sections. Growth has occurred against a background of considerable affluence and in a relatively laissez-faire economic and political climate. It may be anticipated that each of these characteristics will be reflected in the ecological structure of Australasian cities and that this will be very similar to that revealed in U.S. studies. Brisbane and Auckland provide the material for case-studies.

The universe of content

Brisbane and Auckland have both shared in the rapid expansion of the urban population which has characterized the recent history of Australia and New Zealand. Both cities are characterized by young populations, high fertility rates and considerable immigration. Although Brisbane has received far fewer overseas migrants than Sydney, Melbourne or Adelaide, the non-Australian born still constitute some 12 per cent of its total population. In Auckland an almost explosive increase in the population of Maoris and Polynesian Islanders is occurring. In 1966 Maoris and Islanders comprised 9 per cent of the Auckland population. A further 1 per cent were of Indian or Chinese ancestry. The population of Brisbane increased from 402,000 in 1947 to 656,500 in 1966. In 1961, the date of the analyses, the city had a population of 593,700. The population of Auckland increased even more rapidly, more than doubling between 1945 and 1966, the date of the analyses, the 1945 figure of 263,300 increasing to 548,300 in the latter year. Each city enjoys considerable demographic prominence in its respective state and country. The population of Brisbane is 38·6 per cent of that of the whole of Queensland; the population of Auckland is 20·5 per cent of that of the whole of New Zealand and 29 per cent of that of the North Island.

Brisbane and Auckland are commercial-industrial cities. Brisbane, housing the Queensland State Legislature and the headquarters of most State departments and organizations, has approximately 58 per cent of its total workforce employed in commerce and the service industries. The equivalent figure in Auckland is 52 per cent. Just under 10 per cent of the workforce in both cities is employed in the construction industry. Females participate in the workforce to an extent roughly comparable with that reported by Duncan and Reiss for U.S. cities in the 250,000–1 million population range.[1] In the U.S. figures the percentage of males and of females

[1] O. D. Duncan and A. J. Reiss, *Social Characteristics of Urban and Rural Communities 1950* (New York, 1956).

aged 14 years and over in the workforce average 80·9 and 33·9 respectively. The equivalent figures for Brisbane are 82·5 and 29·4 per cent and for Auckland 83·1 and 25·9 per cent. Unemployment is negligible – less than 1 per cent – in both cities.

The great majority of the Brisbane and Auckland populations live in single-family dwellings which they either own or are buying. For a variety of reasons, notably the Australasian desire for a house on a reasonable-sized section, fire hazards, and the ubiquity of private transport, the single family bungalow is by far the commonest form of construction.[1] Approximately 83 per cent of Brisbane dwellings and 85 per cent of those in Auckland are detached single-family structures. Flat construction has, however, increased considerably in recent years, especially in the inner-city areas.

The territorial frameworks for the main factor analyses consist of 554 census collectors' districts (CDs) in Brisbane and 62 statistical subdivisions, boroughs, and cities in Auckland. Supplementary analyses, designed to investigate the effects of using different urban boundaries, are reported for two sub-sets of the Auckland material: the 41 inner-city divisions and the 21 boroughs and cities constituting the outer Auckland area.[2] Figures 2.2 and 2.3 show the territorial frameworks used in the various analyses.

The CD is essentially a utilitarian device rather than the reflection of any theoretical concern with the principles of urban structure.[3] CD boundaries generally follow obvious physical features and there is little evidence in their delimitation of any conscious regard for the homogeneity of either the areas or the populations which they enclose. On the other hand their small size, an average population of 1,044 (σ 354) and a median area of 102 acres, allows considerable confidence to be placed in their significance as unitary environments, especially in the sense outlined by Tryon.[4] Empirical support for the significance of CDs in the residential differentiation of the population is provided by the wide range in the values of the various indicants used in the analyses. The mean value of house and land varies from a low of $4,000 to a high of $52,000; the proportion of the male workforce in non-manual occupations ranges from zero to 92 per cent; the fertility ratio ranges from ·07 to 1·04; the proportion of foreign-born ranges from zero to 32 per cent; the proportion of single-family dwellings ranges from 7 to 100 per cent. The existence of such great inter-area variation can only be explained in terms of the relative internal consistency of the CDs.

The territorial framework used in the Auckland analyses is much coarser than that employed in Brisbane. Statistical subdivisions have been delimited only for the central-city areas comprising Auckland City and the boroughs of

[1] Cf. T. M. McGee, 'The social ecology of New Zealand cities', in J. Forster (ed.), *Social Process in New Zealand* (Auckland, 1969), pp. 151–2.
[2] The borough of Newmarket (population 1,334) is included in the inner-city series.
[3] Linge, 'Delimitation of Urban Boundaries'.
[4] Tryon, *Identification of Social Areas.*

Mt Albert, Mt Eden and Mt Roskill. Outside the central city a local authority framework is used. The statistical subdivisions are said to be based on a combination of 'traditional' and demographic considerations. On the whole,

Fig. 2.2. Sub-area framework for Brisbane, 1961

they correspond with named suburbs. Explaining the procedures and problems involved in their delimitation the Government Statistician writes that

the difficulty has invariably lain in the definition of the boundaries of the various suburbs. These were determined for population purposes by the Census and Statistics Department after consultation with the respective city authorities. The areas and their boundaries thus adopted possibly occasionally diverged in greater or lesser degree from what tradition or usage suggest but this was regarded as subordinate to giving not only a reasonably accurate division of the city into its named suburbs, but also an accurate statement of the rise or fall of population in each suburb.[1]

How accurate the correspondence is between the statistical subdivisions and

Fig. 2.3. Sub-area framework for Auckland, 1966

either demographically similar areas or named suburbs is a matter for conjecture. The average population of the 41 inner-city subdivisions in Auckland is 5,690 with a standard deviation of 3,175. The 21 boroughs and cities which constitute the territorial subdivisions of the outer-Auckland area have an average population of 13,805 with a standard deviation of 13,100. A major portion of the variance is accounted for by Manukau City, a rearrangement of several previously-independent areas on the southern fringes of the built-up area. If Manukau City is deleted from the record

[1] Department of Statistics, 1936 *Census Report* (Wellington, 1937), vol. I, p. ix.

the average population of the outer boroughs becomes 10,835 with a standard deviation of 5,465. Ideally, the Manukau material should be subdivided, but this proved impossible. In the event, the Manukau data was included with the remaining areas. An indication of the validity of the Auckland sub-areas is provided by the range of values exhibited by the indicants used. The range is considerably less than that reported for Brisbane, but compares favourably with U.S. census tract data. In the whole-of-Auckland analysis the proportion of the male population earning $3,000 or more per annum ranges between 2 per cent and 33 per cent; the proportion of the male workforce in non-manual occupations varies between 12 per cent and 74 per cent; the proportion of the population aged under 5 years ranges between 3 per cent and 19 per cent; the proportion of non-Europeans in the population varies between less than 1 per cent and 47 per cent; the proportion of single-family dwellings varies between 9 per cent and 99 per cent.

In neither main analysis are all the sub-areas which comprise the urban complex included in the computation. In Brisbane, all CDs which fall outside the 375 square mile area of the City of Brisbane are excluded on the grounds that the areas thus ignored, notably Redcliffe, are not fully integrated parts of the Brisbane housing or labour markets. Within Brisbane City only those CDs containing non-institutional populations are included; excluded are all CDs consisting of institutional populations such as those of hospitals, boarding schools and military camps. In a small number of cases, where institutional populations are included in the returns for otherwise residential CDs, it has proved necessary to delete the whole population in order to avoid gravely distorted figures. A small number of outlying rural CDs are also deleted from the analysis. In the final result the 554 residential CDs included in the analysis contain a population of 576,950 or 97·2 per cent of the 1961 total for Brisbane City. In the Auckland data, certain largely rural areas in Waitemata and Franklin Counties are excluded. The population of the subdivisions and boroughs included in the analysis, 518,820, forms 94·6 per cent of the 1966 total for the Auckland Urban Area as defined by the N.Z. Department of Statistics. The supplementary analyses for Auckland tap the same universe of sub-areas.

Indicants

It needs to be constantly stressed that the results of an extensive factor analysis are dependent on the original data matrix. The factors which eventually emerge do not necessarily exhaust the properties which are significant in any given situation but, rather, are a function of that limited set of indicants which form the initial input. In choosing the indicants to be included in any extensive analysis the attempt must be made to include as wide ranging and as representative a set of indicants as possible. This is not, however, a licence for reckless abandon, the input of any and all data which can be unearthed. Rather, it is a call for the exercise of restraint, so that the analysis will not be bedevilled by redundancies and spurious relationships.

The indicants employed in the Brisbane and Auckland analyses are shown in Tables 2.4 and 2.5. They form by no means as representative or as reliable

TABLE 2.4 *Indicants used in analyses of Brisbane CDs, 1961*

No.	Variable
	Socio-economic characteristics
1	Per cent male workforce professional and managerial
2	Per cent non-professional and managerial workforce clerical
3	Per cent manual workers skilled
4	Per cent male workforce non-manual
5	Per cent males in workforce unemployed
6	Per cent males in workforce own-account workers
7	Per cent females in workforce own-account workers
8	Ratio students: population 5–20
	Family characteristics
9	Per cent population 21–64 male
10	Per cent adult population aged 65 years and over
11	Per cent population 0–64 aged under 21 years
12	Per cent females 15 years and over never married
13	Per cent males 15 years and over never married
14	Fertility ratio (children 0–5 years: females 15–44 years)
15	Per cent females 15–64 in workforce
16	Per cent males ever-married divorced or separated
17	Per cent females ever-married divorced or separated
18	Per cent population increase 1954–61
	Ethnic characteristics
19	Per cent population Australian born
20	Per cent immigrants non-British born
21	Per cent non-British born Southern European born
22	Per cent non-Australian born resident 1–3 years
23	Per cent non-British born naturalized
24	Per cent population Roman Catholic
	Housing characteristics
25	Average sale value house and land
26	Per cent dwellings single-family structures
27	Per cent single-family dwellings owner-occupied
28	Gross population density
	Accessibility
29	Public transport time distance from GPO.

SOURCES. *i* Variables 1–4 – 1 in 6 sample of male occupations in Queensland State Electoral Rolls, 1961.

ii Variables 5–24, 26, 27 – CD tabulations, 1961 Census.

iii Variable 25 – Special tabulation by Valuer-General's Department, Queensland Government.

iv Variable 28 – CD tabulations and 30 chains to inch map.

v Variable 29 – Wilbur Smith Traffic Survey of Brisbane 1964–5 and BCC travel time map, 1951.

TABLE 2.5 *Indicants used in analyses of subdivisions and boroughs in the Auckland urban area, 1966*

No.	Variable	Whole city	Inner and outer city
	Socio-economic characteristics		
1	Per cent male workforce professional and managerial	+	+
2	Per cent male workforce non-manual workers	+	+
3	Per cent males earning $3,000 p.a. and over	+	+
4	Per cent workforce own-account workers	+	+
5	Standardized social rank index	+	
	Family and demographic characteristics		
6	Per cent population male	+	+
7	Per cent population aged 0–5 years	+	+
8	Per cent population aged 65 years and over	+	+
9	Per cent females 15 years and over never married	+	+
10	Per cent females ever-married, separated or divorced	+	+
11	Per cent females 15–64 years in workforce	+	+
12	Standardized family status index	+	
13	Per cent population increase 1961–6	+	+
	Ethnic characteristics		
14	Per cent population non-European	+	+
	Housing characteristics		
15	Per cent private dwellings single-family structures	+	+
16	Per cent private dwellings owner-occupied	+	+

SOURCES. *i* Variables 1–4 – N.Z. Department of Statistics, 1966; 6–11 – Census Reports, Auckland City Divisions; 13–16 – Central Auckland Statistical Area.

ii Variables 5, 12 – 1966 Census Reports. Data standardized according to procedures laid down by Shevky and Bell. For further details, see chapter 4.

a set as might be hoped. No data is available on such phenomena as deviant behaviour, social participation, political allegiances, or residential mobility. It may legitimately be claimed that any complete analyses of the residential structure of the city should include all such properties. The absence of material on mobility is particularly to be regretted in view of the probable status of mobility as a major differentiating factor.[1] Even in the more traditional spheres relating to the socio-economic, demographic, ethnic, and housing characteristics of the sub-area populations, both the Australian and the New Zealand data reveal several weaknesses.

Information on the socio-economic characteristics of CD populations is very poorly represented by the Australian Census. No information is available for Australian CDs on income or house rents and the only data available in the 1961 Census on the educational status of CD populations is the number of individuals engaged in full-time study. The situation with regard to the occupational characteristics of CD populations is almost equally as

[1] In an analysis of a set of South Brisbane CDs, indicants relating to population turnover and net movement correlate highly with an ethnicity-stability factor. See Moore, 'Residential Mobility in an Urban Context'.

unsatisfactory. The two main items relating to occupation available for CD populations in the census reports are industry of employment and status as a wage or salary earner, self-employed person or employer. No data are available specifying the occupational categories represented in CD populations and, although the industry data have been used as the basis for the construction of an indicant of socio-economic status,[1] it is clear that the industry of employment provides a very imperfect substitute for information on occupational characteristics. In order to improve the coverage of the socio-economic status dimension two additional sources of data have been tapped for the Brisbane analyses: the Queensland State Electoral Rolls and the average sale prices reached by houses and land as recorded by the Queensland Valuer-General's Department. The electoral rolls contain brief details of occupation and a 1-in-6 sample of all males appearing on the 1962 roll provides the basis for all the data on the occupational composition of CD populations. Some 30,000 individuals appear in the sample. All British citizens over the age of 21 years, resident in Australia for more than three months, are legally obliged to register their names with the State electoral office. Any registered voter who changes his address is obliged to notify the authorities of his new address within 14 days, under penalty of fine. House-to-house checks by police, however, are relatively infrequent and the system of fines does not appear to be enforced very strictly. Confidence in the use of the electoral data is further undermined by the formidable problem of using self-reported occupations as a valid measure of occupational status. No other sorts of data are available, however, which may be used to provide information about the occupational characteristics of CD populations.[2] The error contained in the occupational data may be expected to be considerably greater than that in most of the other Brisbane indicants. This will be especially true of the more detailed and specific occupational indices, for example that giving the proportion of manual workers who are skilled. Somewhat similar problems are involved in the data on house and land values. The material used, average sale value, was supplied by the State Valuer-General's Department and its accuracy is unknown.

The range of socio-economic information available for the statistical subdivisions and local authority areas in Auckland is considerably more satisfactory than that for Brisbane. Information is available from the census on both the occupational and income characteristics of statistical subdivision populations. No data are available, however, on education or house values. The social rank index included in the whole-of-Auckland analysis is derived from the Shevky-Bell scheme, to be discussed later, and consists of standardized scores on the non-manual workers and income indicants.[3]

---

[1] E.g. F. L. Jones, 'Social area analysis', *Brit. J. Sociol.* 19 (1968), 424–44.
[2] Exhaustive statistical checks carried out by Moore tend to support the reliability and validity of the electoral rolls as sources of data.   [3] See chapter 4.

The situation with regard to indicants relating to the age, sex, and marital characteristics of the sub-area populations is considerably better than that relating to their socio-economic composition. A generally comparable set of indicants is available for both cities. The only major exception is the unavailability of the fertility ratio in Auckland. As a substitute, the proportion of the population aged 0-5 years is included. From other analyses it is known to show a high correlation with the fertility ratio. The age characteristics of the populations are references by indicants dealing with the per cent aged 65 years and over and, in Brisbane, by the per cent of the 0-64 population aged less than 21 years. Data on the marital characteristics of the populations are provided by indicants dealing with the per cent aged 15 years and over never-married, and the per cent ever-married now divorced or separated.

The Brisbane data on marital characteristics are computed separately for males and females; in the Auckland data the material is presented for females only. Both sets of data include information on the per cent of women in the workforce. In the Brisbane series this is computed by taking women in the workforce as a percentage of the combined total of women in the workforce and women in home duties. In the Auckland data, the indicant is derived by taking women in the workforce as a percentage of females aged 15-64 years inclusive. In the Brisbane data, masculinity refers to the population aged 21-64 years; in Auckland a much cruder breakdown has to be used and the masculinity indicant refers to total population. The figures used to compute population change refer to the 1954-61 period in Brisbane and the 1961-66 period in Auckland. The family status index included in the whole-of-Auckland analysis is the mean of standardized scores on the women in the workforce, per cent population aged 0-5 years, and single-family dwelling indicants.[1]

Data on the ethnic characteristics of the populations are available from the census for both cities albeit, in each case, with several limitations. The Brisbane data share a problem which is common to all discussions of ethnic phenomena in Australia: the fact that the census data relate to birth place rather than to ethnic identity. Thus, children born to Italian parents in Brisbane are recorded as Australian-born whatever their ethnic identity. No data are available in Brisbane relating to the aboriginal population. The situation in Auckland is reversed: the New Zealand Census provides sub-area data on the proportion of Maori, Polynesian Islanders, and Asian populations, but does not distinguish between the various European groups. Nor are any data available for Auckland on rates of naturalization. In the ensuing analysis a single variable is used to reflect the ethnic domain in Auckland – the proportion non-European.

Both sets of data include indicants relating to house type and to form of occupancy. In view of the large size of the Auckland sub-areas no indicant relating to population density has been included in the Auckland analyses.

[1] See chapter 4.

Neither set of data includes information on population per room, which British studies have suggested may possess major differentiating power.[1] The public transport time-distance measure included in the Brisbane material is intended to serve as a gross measure of accessibility.

The dimensions of ecological differentiation

In each analysis, principal components are computed for the zero-order correlation matrices formed by the specified indicants. The correlation coefficients are for unweighted and untransformed variables.[2] Principal components with latent roots of more than unity are retained for subsequent rotation according to the varimax criterion. No *a priori* hypotheses about the pattern of item-factor correlations are involved in the computations, other than those necessitated by the specification of an orthogonal solution.

There is a considerable difference in the proportion of original variance accounted for by the main principal components in the two cities. In the Brisbane data the five principal components with latent roots of unity or more account for just under 60 per cent of original variance; the three most important components account for just over 52 per cent of initial variance. The Auckland data reveal a less differentiated pattern. In the aggregate material two principal components account for 83 per cent of initial variance. Similar results obtain in the inner-city and outer-city analyses: two principal components are important in each case, capturing 78 per cent and 83 per cent of original variance respectively. The higher proportions of variance accounted for in the Auckland analyses as compared with the Brisbane analyses probably result, at least in part, from differences in the reliability of the measures concerned. Many of the Brisbane indicants are based on suspect sampling procedures and are likely to contain important error components. The effects of this are exaggerated by the greater number and smaller size of the base units employed in the Brisbane analysis.

The decision when to stop factoring is a contentious one. In the whole-of-Auckland and outer-Auckland material no problem arises: the two components retained are the only ones to possess latent roots of unity or more and effectively exhaust the common factor variance present in the data. In neither case does any other component account for as much as 5 per cent of original variance. The situation with regard to the Brisbane and inner-Auckland analyses is less clear. In both cases there is a wide variation in the

[1] E.g. Robson, *Urban Analysis*; E. Gittus, 'An experiment in the definition of urban sub-areas', *Trans. Bartlett Soc.* 2 (1964), 109–35.

[2] Experiments involving the arc-sine transformation and weighting according to the population denominator used in the calculation of the indicants, carried out in connexion with Moore's analysis of South Brisbane, produced few alterations in the correlation matrix. In view of the complications which transformation and weighting involve it was decided not to use them in the present material.

proportions of original variance captured by the main principal components. In the Brisbane data five components have latent roots of unity or more, but only three account for as much as 6 per cent of initial variance. In the inner-Auckland data three components have latent roots of unity or more but, whereas the first and second components account for 48 per cent and 30 per cent of original variance respectively, the third component accounts for only 7 per cent of the variance.[1] For most practical purposes the inner-Auckland data may be represented in terms of a two-factor solution. There is little evidence in favour of the Kish-Sweetser argument concerning a

TABLE 2.6 *Rotated five-factor solution (varimax criterion) for Brisbane, 1961*

Indicant	No.	Factor loading					h^2
		I	II	III	IV	V	
Under 21	11	83	–	–	–	–	74
Working women	15	−83	–	–	–	40	85
1-family dwellings	26	78	–	–	–	−35	81
Fertility	14	77	−36	–	–	–	78
Time-distance	29	72	–	–	–	–	59
Southern Europe born	21	−63	–	–	–	–	49
Divorced/separated females	17	−63	–	–	–	55	78
Divorced/separated males	16	−62	–	–	–	57	78
Over 65	10	−61	–	–	–	–	50
At school	8	57	–	39	–	–	51
Population increase	18	55	−44	–	–	–	55
Roman Catholic	24	−52	–	–	–	–	55
Population density	28	−47	–	–	–	–	32
Australian born	19	39	−67	–	–	–	68
Non-British born	20	−35	71	–	–	–	66
Naturalized	23	–	−67	–	–	–	50
New immigrants	22	–	46	–	–	–	26
Professional/managerial	1	–	–	80	–	–	66
Non-manual	4	–	–	79	–	–	72
Clerical	2	–	–	75	–	–	68
House value	25	–	–	70	–	–	54
Skilled manual	3	–	–	44	–	–	31
Own-account males	6	–	–	36	74	–	68
Own-account females	7	–	–	–	74	–	58
Single males	13	−45	–	–	33	70	72
Owner-occupied	27	–	–	–	–	−62	62
Single females	12	−52	–	–	–	52	67
Masculinity	9	–	–	–	–	56	46
Males not at work	5	–	–	–	–	39	28
Per cent of total variance		23·0	9·4	11·4	6·0	9·7	(59·5)

NOTE. Only coefficients of ± 0·30 or more are indicated.

[1] The associated latent roots are 6·81, 4·16 and 1·04.

74

TABLE 2.7 *Rotated three-factor solution (varimax criterion) for Brisbane CDs, 1961*

Indicant	No.	Factor loading			h^2
		I	II	III	
Working women	15	−87	−	−	84
Fertility	14	82	−	−	76
Under 21	11	81	−	−	72
1-family dwellings	26	78	−	−43	80
Distance	29	70	−	−	53
Single females	12	−68	−	−	52
Separated/divorced females	17	−68	−	50	75
Separated/divorced males	16	−66	−	54	75
Single males	13	−62	−	−	48
Aged 65+	10	−60	−	−	42
Southern European	21	−56	−	−	43
Population increase	18	57	−	32	45
At school	8	56	−36	−	48
Roman Catholics	24	−51	40	−	48
Population density	28	−44	−	−	25
Professional/managerial	1	−	−75	−	62
Non-manual	4	−	−71	−33	66
House value	25	−	−69	−	55
Own-account males	6	−	−66	−	48
Clerical workers	2	−	−62	−38	59
Own-account females	7	−	−39	30	27
Skilled manual	3	−	−38	−33	28
Australian born	19	−	−	−74	64
Non-British born	20	−	−	−71	57
Naturalized	23	−	−	−64	43
Masculinity	9	−	−	50	32
Owner-occupied	27	−	−39	−46	39
Males not at work	5	−	−	39	27
New immigrants	22	−	−	38	25
Per cent of total variance		24·2	14·0	13·8	(52)

NOTE. Only coefficients of ± 0·30 or more are indicated.

postulated greater differentiation of inner-city as opened to outer-city communities. For the sake of completeness, however, further analysis of the Brisbane and inner-Auckland materials uses both the full and the partial complements of components.

Rotation of the principal component item-factor loadings, according to the varimax criterion, produces the orthogonal factor structures outlined in Tables 2.6 to 2.9. Six analyses are reported: five-factor and three-factor solutions for Brisbane, three-factor and two-factor solutions for inner-Auckland and two-factor solutions for the whole-of-Auckland and for the outer-Auckland boroughs.

Notwithstanding the differences in data input and in territorial frameworks,

TABLE 2.8 *Rotated orthogonal factor solution (varimax criterion) for whole-of-Auckland, 1966*

Indicant	No.	Factor loading		h^2
		I	II	
Family status	12	96	16	95
Working women	11	−94	−22	94
Single females	9	−94	03	88
Separated/divorced	10	−93	−23	91
1-family dwellings	15	92	−01	84
Owner-occupied	16	87	33	87
Population increase	13	81	07	67
Children	7	79	−42	80
Aged 65+	8	−76	29	67
Social rank	5	−03	97	94
Non-manual	2	−02	97	94
Professional	1	−09	96	94
Income	3	03	96	92
Own-account	4	42	79	80
Non-European	14	−27	−75	64
Males	6	06	−72	52
Per cent of total variance		45·5	37·1	(82·6)

TABLE 2.9 *Rotated orthogonal factor solutions (varimax criterion) for inner-Auckland subdivisions (three- and two-factor solutions) and outer-Auckland boroughs*

Indicant	Inner Auckland				Inner Auckland			Outer Auckland		
	Factor			h^2	Factor		h^2	Factor		h^2
	I	II	III		I	II		I	II	
Non-manual	96	11	10	94	95	08	91	97	01	95
Professional	97	01	09	95	94	00	89	93	−15	88
High income	97	09	03	94	93	09	87	94	06	89
Own-account	89	30	02	88	88	28	86	42	68	65
Non-European	−75	−31	−21	70	−81	−21	70	−84	−09	72
Masculinity	−60	−30	−45	65	−74	−09	55	−64	−47	63
1-family dwelling	−06	95	−13	92	02	91	84	−05	96	92
Single women	03	−92	19	89	−03	−91	84	05	−95	90
Working women	−31	−88	23	92	−33	−90	91	−08	−97	95
Separated/divorced	−33	−90	08	92	−39	−85	89	00	−95	87
Owner-occupier	41	82	−03	84	47	76	81	16	96	96
Population increase	42	58	−45	72	32	73	64	−12	78	62
Children	−41	39	−74	87	−57	66	76	−33	86	85
Aged 65+	10	−25	89	87	34	−61	49	29	−91	90
Per cent of total variance	37·5	34·6	37·7	(85·7)	40·4	37·6	(78·1)	30·2	53·5	(83·7)

the general impression of the factor structures revealed in the Brisbane and Auckland analyses is one of similarity. Moreover the patterns of item-factor loadings are generally consonant with those reported for other Western cities. Factors relating to neighbourhood or suburb differences in socio-economic status and family characteristics appear in both cities, while ethnicity plays an important independent role in Brisbane. For convenience the factors will be discussed serially.

Socio-economic status factors

In the five-factor solution for the Brisbane data the socio-economic status realm is tapped by two dimensions. One factor may be identified with social rank *per se*, while the other appears to have much in common with the socio-economic independence factor discussed by Tryon.[1] The social rank factor exhibits high positive correlations with the proportions of non-manual workers, of professional and managerial workers and of clerical workers, and with high house values. The socio-economic independence factor, on the other hand, centres on high correlations with the proportions of own-account workers. In each of the other analyses a single socio-economic status factor is apparent, although, as will be seen, the indicant own-account workers is somewhat unstable in its factorial identification. In the three-factor solution for Brisbane and in the solutions for the whole-of-Auckland and for the inner-Auckland subdivisions, the variables professional and managerial workers, non-manual workers, high house values or high incomes, and own-account workers all exhibit high positive item-factor correlations with a single social rank factor. In the outer-Auckland data, however, the proportion of own-account workers exhibits a higher correlation with a family type factor than it does with social rank. A likely explanation lies in the fact that the outer-city analysis includes data relating to the rural and semi-rural fringes of the urban area. In this material the inclusion of self-employed farmers and horticulturists inflates the number of own-account workers. Notable features of all four of the Auckland analyses are the high negative correlations which obtain between the social rank factor, the proportion of non-Europeans in the population, and the masculinity of the population. Subdivisions and boroughs characterized by low social rank are also characterized by high proportions of non-Europeans and by high proportions of males. Although it is dangerous to argue from the ecological to the individual level,[2] the Auckland data provide strong support for the notion that the segregation of Maoris and other Polynesians in New Zealand is closely associated with their disadvantaged position in the strati-

[1] Tryon, *Identification of Social Areas.*
[2] Cf. Robinson, 'Ecological correlations'; Riley, *Sociological Research*, vol. I.

fication hierarchy. The significance of the high item-factor correlation between masculinity and social rank is less clear.[1] With the exception of the own-account variable in the Auckland material none of the indicants exhibiting high item-factor correlations with the social rank factor have appreciable loadings on the family type factors.

Family factors

Each analysis produces sets of item-factor loadings which suggest the presence of various family type bases of residential differentiation. In the five-factor Brisbane analysis two distinct family-related factors may be recognized, one denoting a young family-suburban dimension of differentiation, the other indicating a non-family or a family dissolution factor. Indicants exhibiting a high positive correlation with the young family factor include the proportion of the population under 21 years of age, the proportion of single-family dwellings, the fertility ratio, and time-distance from the CBD. Indicants exhibiting a high negative correlation with the factor include the proportion of women in the workforce, the proportion of foreign migrants from Southern Europe, the proportion of separated and divorced persons, and the proportion of the adult population aged 65 years and over. The two indicants relating to the separated and divorced also exhibit a high positive correlation with the non-family factor. Other indicants loading positively on the non-family factor include the proportion of never-married adults and the masculinity of the population falling within the age range 21–64 years. The proportion of owner-occupiers correlates negatively with the factor.[2] In the three-factor solution for Brisbane the young family and non-family axes collapse to form a single familism dimension. Indicants relating to fertility, youthfulness, single-family dwellings, distance from the CBD, and population increase all exhibit high positive correlations with the factor. Indicants relating to women in the workforce, the never-married and the separated or divorced, the old, and the Southern Europeans, exhibit high negative correlations with the factor. The solutions for the whole-of-Auckland and outer-Auckland and the two-factor solution for inner-Auckland each exhibit a single family type factor. In the three-factor solution for the inner-city subdivisions, however, there is a split between a general family factor and a more specific factor which shows high item-

---

[1] A high negative association between masculinity and social rank is also apparent in the correlational analysis of 23 U.S. cities reported by C. F. Schmid, *et al.*, 'The ecology of the American city', *Am. Sociol. Rev.* 23 (1958), 392–401, reprinted in Theodorson, *Studies in Human Ecology*.
[2] The high negative correlation between the non-family factor and the proportion of owner-occupiers suggests that the factor may be closely associated with population mobility. Per cent owner-occupiers is one of the key variables in the model for predicting mobility developed by Moore, 'Residential Mobility in an Urban Context'.

factor correlations with the proportions of the young and of the old. The significance of the age factor is doubtful. Even after rotation it still accounts for less than 14 per cent of original variance, far less than that of the other two factors. For most purposes it would seem preferable to ignore the third factor in the inner-city data and to rest on the two-factor solution. The family factor generally apparent in the Auckland analyses is very similar to that produced in the three-factor Brisbane solution. High negative correlations are shown with women in the workforce, separated and divorced females, the never-married and the widowed, and the elderly. High positive correlations are shown with the proportion of young children, single-family dwellings, owner-occupiers, population increase and, in the whole city analysis, with the family status index.

Ethnic factors

The indicants believed to be highly saturated with ethnic considerations exhibit rather variable item-factor correlations. In the Brisbane analyses a clear ethnic factor emerges, denoted by high item-factor correlations with the proportion of non-British migrants, the proportion of migrants who have taken out naturalization papers (negative), and the proportion of the population born in Australia (negative). On the other hand, the indicant proportion of non-British migrants from Southern Europe correlates more highly with the familism factor than it does with ethnicity. This may most probably be explained in terms of the smallness of the Southern European population in Brisbane and its heavy concentration in the inner city. As of 1961 the numbers of Southern Europeans involved was insufficient to greatly affect the age and family structures of the inner city neighbourhoods. It may be expected that as the numbers of Southern European migrants increases so the indicants relating to them will tend to shift into the ethnic cluster. The nature of the indicants presently exhibiting high item-factor correlations with the ethnic factor suggest that the factor may be considered one of *assimilation* rather than of ethnicity *per se*. Populations characterized by high scores on the factor not only contain relatively large numbers of non-British migrants but are also notable for the small proportion of those eligible who have taken Australian citizenship.[1] In the Auckland analyses per cent non-European is submerged into the socio-economic status factor. The inclusion of further information relating to ethnicity in the Auckland data may have given rise to a separate ethnic factor, but it remains apparent that there is a close association in Auckland between ethnicity and social rank.

[1] Cf. S. Lieberson, 'The impact of residential segregation on ethnic assimilation', *Soc. Forces*, 40 (1961), 52–7.

Communalities

There are wide differences between the indicants in the amount of common-factor variance which the analyses uncover. In the Brisbane analyses, in particular, several of the indicants exhibit little relationship to the factors retained. The indicants relating to males not at work, immigrants resident one to three years, skilled manual workers, and gross population density have less than one-third of their variance accounted for by the five factors retained in the first analyses. In the three-factor solution these indicants are joined by own-account females and masculinity. At least a proportion of the low communalities exhibited by many of the Brisbane indicants may be explained in terms of sampling errors. This explanation is likely to apply, for example, to the data on unemployment, recent immigrants, and skilled manual workers. In each case the base population used in the computation of proportions is very small. In other cases, however, notably that of gross population density, no ready explanation of the low communality is forthcoming. Much higher degrees of communality are exhibited by the indicants relating to the proportion of women in the workforce, single-family dwellings, fertility, youthfulness, non-manual workers, and the separated or divorced. In both the five-factor and the three-factor Brisbane solutions common-factor variance accounts for at least two-thirds of the original variance in each indicant. In the Auckland analyses communalities are almost uniformly high. In the data for the whole city 14 of the 16 indicants exhibit communalities of more than 0·66 and seven have communalities of more than 0·90. In the outer-Auckland data 11 out of 14 indicants exhibit communalities of more than 0·66 and 6 have communalities of more than 0·90. In the three-factor solution for the inner-city all but one indicant, masculinity, have communalities of 0·66 or above. Masculinity exhibits a figure of 0·65. Six of the 14 indicants have communalities of more than 0·90. In the two-factor solution for the inner-Auckland subdivisions 11 of the 14 indicants have communalities of more than 0·66 but only 2 have communalities of more than 0·90. The lowest communalities, 0·53 and 0·56, are exhibited by the indicants relating to those aged 65 years and over and to masculinity. In the Auckland analyses, as a whole, masculinity is the least valid of the indicants in terms of its common-factor variance. This may most probably be accounted for in terms of its crude derivation and the small range it exhibits.[1] The most consistently high communalities are exhibited by the indicants women in the workforce, non-manual workers, separated and divorced females, and high-income earners.

Other Australian cities

Analyses of Melbourne and of Canberra have produced results broadly

[1] The extremes are 44·6 and 57·4.

consonant with those for Brisbane and Auckland.[1] Differences in technique and, more particularly, in the indicants used, however, make it difficult to assess the similarities and differences in any detail.

In Melbourne, Jones uses the principal components technique to simplify a mass of census data distributed over 611 'aggregated collectors' districts' (ACD) with average populations of 3,080. Seventy indicants are used in a two-stage design. In the initial analysis sets of indicants believed to belong to one or other of the three general domains of socio-economic status, family characteristics and ethnicity are analysed separately. A later analysis is presented for a reduced matrix of 28 indicants selected from all three domains. The socio-economic status cluster is indexed by a variety of measures relating to industry of employment, employment status and home ownership. No information is available on occupations or house values. The 24 variables belonging to the cluster are shown to contain three principal components with latent roots of unity or above, with the first, accounting for 41 per cent of initial variance, by far the most important. On the basis of its relatively high vector weights with indicants relating to the proportion of employers, of males employed in finance and property, commerce and business, and community service, and of females employed in business and community services, Jones suggests that the first component may 'be fairly confidently identified as representing the dimension of socio-economic status'.[2] Secondary components within the general socio-economic domain are geographically identified with 'transitional areas' and with the 'rural-urban fringe'. The pattern of vector weights is even clearer in the case of the 24 variables believed to index variations in household composition. Sixty per cent of the initial variance is captured by the first component. Areas with high scores on the component possess few private houses, many flats, boarding houses and shared dwellings, are characterized by low fertility, a stable or declining population and many women in the workforce, and contain many young unmarried, the permanently separated or divorced, and major concentrations of the old, the widowed and the pensioned. 'This first component, then, largely differentiates the household characteristics and associated life styles of the relatively independent (in some cases isolated) inner city dweller . . . from the family characteristics and life style of the suburbs.'[3] The similarity with the familism factor uncovered in the three-factor Brisbane solution and in the Auckland analyses is striking. Secondary components in the Melbourne family domain relate to age and sex differences. The 22 ethnic variables also produce a three-component solution, with one component being far more important than the others. In this case 45 per cent of initial variance is accounted for by a component which 'differentiates the residential distribution of the native-born from the foreign-born, British nationals from aliens,

---

[1] Jones, 'Social area analysis'; Jones, 'A social profile of Canberra, 1961', *Aust. N.Z. J. Sociol.* 1 (1965), 107-20. [2] Jones, 'Social area analysis', p. 431. [3] *Ibid.* p. 434.

established settlers from more recent arrivals. It also weighs heavily on immigrants from southern, central and eastern Europe'.[1] The 'general ethnic composition' component is joined by secondary components loading on Northwestern European settlers and Jews. 'This analysis, then, suggests that in 1961 there were in Melbourne three distinct patterns of ethnic concentrations: areas of general immigrant concentration (mainly southern Europeans), areas with immigrants from northwestern Europe, and areas of Jewish concentration.'[2] Product-moment correlation coefficients between the component scores for each of the three major principal components are 0·05 between socio-economic status and household composition, and 0·64 between socio-economic status and ethnic composition, and 0·44 between household composition and ethnic composition. A further analysis of 24 selected indicants, 8 per domain, produces a three-component pattern in which 70 per cent of initial variance

TABLE 2.10 *Principal components solution for 24 indicants, Melbourne ACDs, 1961*

Indicant	Pattern coefficients		
	I	II	III
Employers (m)	−71	46	−18
Not at work (m)	82	14	−01
In finance and property (m)	−84	34	−02
In commerce (m)	−71	42	15
In business and community services (m)	−74	39	−14
In manufacturing (f)	75	−50	06
Owner-occupiers	−53	−29	−36
Student index	−71	42	−22
Aged 0–14	−16	−93	11
Single adults	28	88	05
Masculinity	30	−26	25
Widows	08	90	06
Working women	57	74	−08
1-family dwellings	−30	−77	20
Population increase	−06	−69	−20
Population density	54	51	28
Catholic	87	−04	−03
Greek Orthodox	74	23	−24
Lutheran	08	−09	−81
Presbyterian	−87	03	−08
Hebrew	−19	70	−04
Italian-born	76	15	−25
Netherlands-born	−20	−31	−63
Alien	78	15	−50
Per cent original variance	35·4	26·3	8·1

SOURCE. Original data from Jones, 'Social area analysis' p. 437.
NOTE. (m) or (f) after an indicant denotes males or females respectively.

[1] *Ibid*. p. 436.

[2] *Ibid*.

is accounted for by components labelled socio-economic status, household composition and North-western European settlers. Table 2.10 shows the item-component correlations.[1]

The heavy loading which several of the ethnic indicants exhibit on the socio-economic status component leads Jones to suggest that almost as much explanatory power may be achieved with a two-component solution (socio-economic status/ethnicity and household composition) as with the three components extracted in the initial analyses.

The factorial ecology of Melbourne has a great deal in common with that of Brisbane and Auckland. An analysis of Canberra produces a less congruous result.[2] The analysis is based on 24 census-derived measures distributed over 51 CDs. Apart from industry of employment data, no material is available belonging to the socio-economic status domain. Four principal components with latent roots of unity or more are extracted, accounting in aggregate for 66 per cent of initial variance. Component I, accounting for 32 per cent of original variance is identified as an 'ethnicity' factor, although it also shows high item-factor correlations with the industry of employment variables. Jones cautions that 'In view of the absence of any direct measures of socio-economic status, such as income, occupation, or education, it would seem premature to label this factor "ethnicity-social rank" '.[3] The second and third components are labelled 'demographic structure/residential type' and 'age of area' factors respectively. The demographic structure/residential factor is closely similar to the familism dimension discussed in the Brisbane and Auckland analyses and to the household composition component extracted in Melbourne. The fourth component in the Canberra data appears to possess no readily-interpretable meaning. In view of the gaps in the data matrix and of the peculiar nature of Canberra as the nation's capital,[4] it is impossible to generalize the significance of the Canberra findings for the factorial ecology of the Australian city in general.

On the whole, the factorial ecology of Australasian cities appears to be very similar to that reported for those of North America and Scandinavia. Factors relating to population differences in socio-economic status or social rank, family characteristics and ethnicity effectively exhaust the common-factor variance present in a wide variety of census data. Social rank and

---

[1] Jones presents unstandardized vector weights for each component. To enable comparisons to be made, these have been standardized according to the square root of the relevant latent roots.
[2] Jones, 'A social profile'.
[3] *Ibid.* p. 115.
[4] All residential land in Canberra is owned by the Government and renting is far more common than in other Australian cities (51 per cent *v.* an Australian average of 4 per cent). Occupationally, the public service dominates the city and the workforce is overwhelmingly white-collar. Only 8 per cent of the workforce is engaged in manufacturing industry. Growth has been exceptionally rapid: both fertility and immigration are high. Over a quarter of the city's population is foreign-born.

familism are essentially independent of each other, but ethnicity shows varying degrees of relationship with the other factors. In Brisbane ethnicity shows a weak association with neighbourhood variations in family composition: in Auckland, Canberra and Melbourne it appears to be more strongly associated with social rank.

CONCLUSION – FACTOR STRUCTURE AS ECOLOGICAL STRUCTURE

The urban population is residentially differentiated in terms of many different characteristics. The social worlds of the city may be distinguished by the occupations, incomes, levels of education, political preferences, types of social participation, and housing characteristics of their populations. They may also be differentiated in terms of age and sex distributions, fertility rates, rates of marriage, separation, divorce, and widowhood, size of family, kinship activities, and in the proportions of their women employed outside the home. On top of all this, yet further differentiations may be made in terms of birth place and ethnic identity, mobility, religion, and of a wide variety of other indicants relating to characteristics of the population and to the frequency of various types of desirable or undesirable behaviour. The use of factor analytic techniques enables this plethora of differentiating indicants to be reduced to a more manageable number of underlying constructs. In the process it is revealed that the residential differentiation of the urban population may be represented in terms of the variation of a small number of basic factors. At least in the urban-industrial cities of North America, Western Europe and Australasia, much of the detailed variation in the population characteristics of different parts of the community may be accounted for in terms of the underlying variation along three or four basic differentiating factors. The stability of socio-economic status, familism, ethnicity and mobility as the major dimensions of ecological structure in cities found in many different parts of the world demands an attempt at explanation. It is to this task that the attention of the next two chapters will be directed.

CHAPTER 3

THE BASES OF RESIDENTIAL
DIFFERENTIATION

The application of factor analytic techniques to urban residential differentiation has produced relatively consistent results. It seems rather well established that, at least in the Western world, much of the detailed variation in the characteristics of urban sub-communities may be interpreted in terms of three or four underlying constructs relating to differences in socio-economic status, in family composition, in ethnicity and in mobility. The demonstration of factorial invariance, however, is not to be equated with an explanation of factor structures. Having established the empirical validity of the major axes of residential differentiation the next step is to attempt the explanation of their significance and to examine the relationship they exhibit to other facets of human behaviour and social structure. It is to this task that the attention of this and of the next chapter are directed.

As is true in the case of many other sociological phenomena, the explanation of ecological structure may be attempted at either of two levels: a micro-social and a macro-social. In the micro-social approach attention is focused on the relationship between residential differentiation and patterns of individual decisions and behaviour. In the macro-social approach attention is focused on the relationship between residential differentiation and certain global characteristics of the encompassing society. A satisfactory theory of residential differentiation must include both approaches. Neither approach is, by itself, self-sufficient: individual decisions involve the consideration of the range of alternatives made available by the overall structure of society, in turn this reflects the aggregate of previous decisions. The distinction between a micro-social and a macro-social approach to the study of residential differentiation is one of convenience rather than substance. We turn our attention first to the micro-social approach, leaving the more global matters to the following chapter. Before attempting to outline some of the elements which it is proposed a satisfactory micro-social theory of residential differentiation should include, however, it is necessary to give some prior attention to the two traditional explanations of locational behaviour which stem from the work of the Chicago ecologists and of their 'socio-cultural' critics: the 'sub-social' and the 'social values' models.

The urban mosaic

THE SUB-SOCIAL THEORY OF RESIDENTIAL DIFFERENTIATION

The prime characteristic of the classical ecological approach to problems of urban structure was the adoption of a biological analogy. Although there are considerable differences in the emphases which the various writers in the classical ecological tradition give to sub-social as opposed to socio-cultural factors in residential differentiation, the underlying model is one of biological economics.[1] The central concept is that of impersonal competition:

In the intimate economic relationships in which all people are in the city everyone is, in a sense, in competition with everyone else. It is an impersonal competition – the individual does not know his competitors. It is a competition for other values in addition to those represented by money. One of the forms it takes is competition for position in the community.[2]

Park is explicit about the importance of competition in defining ecological structure:

Competition, which is the fundamental organizing principle in the plant and animal community, plays a scarcely less important role in the human community. In the plant and animal community it has tended to bring about (1) an orderly distribution of the population and (2) a differentiation of the species within the habitat. The same principles operate in the case of the human population.[3]

Even when other factors are acknowledged as being influential in the process of residential differentiation they are generally assigned a secondary position. The major cause of the segregation of populations over the natural areas of the city is considered to be their differential ability to cope with impersonal competition. The indicant of ability is frequently taken to be wealth.

Every area of segregation is the result of the operation of a combination of forces of selection. There is usually, however, one attribute of selection that is more domin-ant than the others, and which becomes the determining factor of the particular segregation. Economic segregation is the most primary and general form. It results from economic competition and determines the basic units of the ecological distribution. Other attributes of segregation, such as language, race, or culture, function within the spheres of appropriate economic levels.[4]

The process of impersonal competition provides the main framework of ecological structure. The basic form of animate society is seen as the com-munity: a territorially defined group of individuals 'living in a relationship of mutual interdependence that is symbiotic rather than societal, in the sense in which this term applies to human beings'.[5] Within the community

---

1 See, for example, the papers by Park, McKenzie, Burgess, Wirth and Zorbaugh reprinted in Theodorson, *Studies in Human Ecology* and the collection of Park's work published in 1954 – *Human Communities* (Chicago).
2 Zorbaugh, 'The natural areas of the city', in Theodorson, pp. 46–7.
3 Park, *Human Communities*, p. 119.
4 R. D. McKenzie, 'The scope of human ecology', in Theodorson, p. 35.
5 Park, 'Human ecology', in Theodorson, p. 23.

impersonal competition is the prime mechanism for controlling the relationship between individuals. The basic process is a struggle for advantageous positions. The struggle for advantageous locations in geographical space is but one aspect of a much more general process. To the extent that some individuals or species obtain positions of maximum advantage it is possible to think of them as dominants: the same principles operate in the human community. The competition between different population groups or different land uses for favourable locations within the city may be analysed in terms of the same model used in the case of the competition between species in a plant or animal community. Competition and the emergence of a dominant category determine the basic outlines of the community.

[T]he principle of dominance operates in the human as well as in the plant or animal communities. The so-called natural or functional areas of a metropolitan community – for example, the slum, the rooming-house area, the central shopping section and the banking centre – each and all owe their existence directly to the factor of dominance, and indirectly to competition.[1]

The area of dominance is equated with the central business district, the area of highest land values. The pressure of demand at the centre, a function of its accessibility to the greatest numbers, determines the basic shape of the whole community. The higher the demand, the higher the land values. 'It is these land values that determine the location of social institutions and business enterprises.'[2] Moreover, over time, the principle of dominance is responsible for the phenomena of invasion and succession. Invasion, the encroachment of an incompatible population or land use, represents a sudden challenge to the equilibrium reached in a given natural area. It may frequently be related to the growing pressure at the centre: waves of invasions representing successive displacements from the centre set up new cycles of competition. Stable equilibrium will be reached only when the succession is completed, as for example if the invaders succeed in displacing the original inhabitants. The term succession is used

to describe and designate that orderly sequence of changes through which a biotic community passes in the course of its development from a primary and relatively unstable to a relatively permanent or climax stage ... [I]n the course of this development the community moves through a series of more or less clearly defined stages.[3]

In the climax phase of the succession all traces of the old land uses or populations may be lost.

Models are seductive. At times it seems clear that the classical ecologists

[1] *Ibid.* p. 25.   [2] *Ibid.* pp. 25–6.   [3] *Ibid.* p. 26.

mistook the biological analogy for a substantive theory.[1] At other times however they are explicit that the analogy is no more than a useful device. Thus Park points out that biological economics is not to be equated with human economics:

[E]cology (biological economics), even when it involves some sort of unconscious cooperation and a natural, spontaneous, and non-rational division of labour, is something different from the economics of commerce; something quite apart from the bargaining of the market place. Commerce, as Simmel somewhere remarks, is one of the latest and most complicated of all the social relationships into which human beings have entered.[2]

Human competition is subject to many rules and regulations and human inventiveness has given man a much greater power for remaking, controlling, and, above all, interpreting his environment than is possessed by any other animal. To cope with this human departure from the general animate model, classical ecology institutes an analytical division between the biotic and the socio-cultural aspects of human group life: '[H]uman society, as distinguished from plant and animal society, is organized on two levels, the biotic and the cultural. There is a symbiotic society based on competition and a cultural society based on communication and consensus.'[3] Within the cultural level emerging economic, political, and moral orders are recognized at increasing remove from the biotic substratum. Each emergent order acts as a regulator on the activities taking place in terms of the lower orders. Thus, 'in human society competition is limited by custom and culture. The cultural superstructure imposes itself as an instrument of direction and control upon the biotic substructure.'[4] In their discussions of population segregation the classical ecologists frequently give more weight to the role of socio-cultural factors than to those of biotic competition. Discussing the development of ethnic enclaves within the city Park states:

Such segregations of population as these take place, first upon the basis of language and culture, and second, upon the basis of race. Within these immigrant colonies and racial ghettos, however, other processes of selection inevitably take place which bring about segregation based upon vocational interests, upon intelligence, and personal ambition ... The physical or ecological organization of the community, in the long run, responds to and reflects the occupational and the cultural. Social selection and segregation, which create the natural groups, determine at the same time the natural areas of the city.[5]

Similarly, in his study of the Jewish ghetto, Wirth devotes much attention

---

[1] For criticisms, see M. A. Alihan, *Social Ecology* (New York, 1938); S. Greer, *The Emerging City* (New York, 1962); G. Sjoberg, 'Theory and research in urban sociology', and 'Cities in developing and industrial societies', in P. M. Hauser and L. F. Schnore (eds), *The Study of Urbanization* (New York, 1965), pp. 157–89, 213–63.
[2] Park, in Theodorson, *Studies in Human Ecology*, p. 27.
[3] *Ibid.* p. 28. [4] *Ibid.* p. 29. [5] Park, *Human Communities*, p. 170.

to the interaction between Jewish and Gentile views about the desirability of contact. He shows that the development of a ghetto may reflect either the voluntary segregation of Jewish populations, designed as a defence against the encroachment of Gentile ways of life, or alternatively the forced segregation of Jews by politically-dominant Gentile populations. The role of biotic factors, *per se*, is given little emphasis. According to Quinn: 'segregation, especially of population types, depends heavily on the social level of interaction. It generally carries the implication that at least one of the contrasting types of units recognizes differences between them and consciously takes steps to maintain or increase their spatial separation.'[1] In practice, the classical ecologists were by no means as guilty of reifying the biological analogy and of using it as the sole explanation of ecological structure, as some of their later critics have claimed.[2]

The implicit assumption in the classical ecological perspective of the close connexion between the accessibility of the city centre and the distribution of urban land values is given greater systematization in the work of the neo-classical ecologists, notably Hawley. Accessibility to the city centre becomes a major organizing principle. Thus, according to Hawley: 'Units of the community distribute themselves about a central point in relation to their ability to bear the time and cost of transportation to and from the central point.'[3] Land values are a function of demand and reflect the conditions of accessibility. Residential land uses are relatively unintensive and are therefore forced out of the inner city areas to districts where land values are lower. But the need to keep the time and cost of transportation within the limits puts bounds to the degree of scatter which is possible. The joint influence of the repulsive effects of industrial and commercial areas, the need to keep transportation outputs under control and the city-wide gradient in land values, is expressed in terms of rental value. In general, residential values vary inversely with land values. Residential property in the inner city, especially that adjacent to expanding commercial or industrial areas, is generally dilapidated and of low *per capita* rental value though even it may be on high value land. The speculative owners of such property are unlikely to invest much money in it if they believe they can soon convert the land to more profitable non-residential uses. The accessibility of inner-city properties, however, may become valued if a demand for such siting develops. The larger the city, the more likely is this to happen. Hence the inner-city areas may contain a mixture of run-down rental properties and high price apartments. Opposite factors apply in the case of residential properties towards the outskirts of the city. The spaciousness and newness

[1] J. A. Quinn, *Human Ecology* (New York, 1950), p. 354.
[2] Cf. Alihan, *Social Ecology*; A. B. Hollingshead, 'Community research: development and present condition', *Am. Sociol. Rev.* 13 (1948), 136–55; and 'A re-examination of ecological theory', reprinted in Theodorson, *Studies in Human Ecology*, pp. 108–14.
[3] A. H. Hawley, *Human Ecology* (New York, 1950), p. 286.

D

of the dwellings, factors giving rise to high rental values, tend to be counter-acted by their low accessibility. The relative weights of the factors vary with the coefficient contained in the equation which gives the friction of distance.[1] Where transportation facilities are poorly developed the advantages of high accessibility may outweigh the disadvantages of inner-city residential location so that high rental values are found associated with high land values. Where transportation facilities are more highly developed an upward gradient in residential rental values is predicted with increasing distance from the city centre to some 'break-even' point. Residential differentiation takes place in terms of this pattern of rental values. 'Rent, operating through income, is a most important factor in the distribution and segregation of familial units. Those with comparable incomes seek similar locations and consequently cluster together in one or two selected areas within the com-munity.'[2] Clustering is reinforced by the fact that households with similar incomes have similar locational requirements with regard to such things as access to workplaces and schools, need for public transportation services and desires about spaciousness. Clustering is also reinforced by the attraction of similar household units for one another. 'But such an attraction can operate only in a zone where the rents do not exceed the purchasing power of the familial units involved . . . Regardless of the motive for the occupancy of a site, that occupancy involves certain costs which must be paid.'[3]

The theory of residential differentiation implicit in the work of both the classical and the neo-classical ecologists involves an essentially atomistic economic determinism. The competitive status of an individual household is equated with its wealth. In a laissez-faire society the classical ecological model suggests that residential differentiation will faithfully mirror the the income and wealth characteristics of the population. In a society in which there are a variety of interventions designed to regulate the market, the relevance of the model is less clear.[4] Residential differentiation occurs in terms of many other population characteristics than wealth and, even in the realm of socio-economic status, it is apparent that social rank and pos-session of economic goods are by no means synonymous.[5] The emphasis contained in the classical and neo-classical ecological approaches on the importance of economic consideration in the process of residential differ-entiation occasions an overly-partial view of urban structure. The relevance

1 See W. Alonso, 'The form of cities in developing countries', *Papers and Proc. Reg. Sci. Ass.* 13 (1964).

2 Hawley, *Human Ecology*, p. 282.   3 *Ibid.*

4 See Sjoberg, 'Theory and research'.

5 R. Bendix and S. M. Lipset (eds), *Class, Status and Power* (New York, 1966); T. E. Lasswell, *Class and Stratum* (Boston, 1965); K. Svalastoga, *Social Differentiation* (New York, 1964). On the differential locational effects of occupation, education and income, see C. Tilly, 'Occupational rank and grade of residence in a metropolis', *Am. J. Sociol.* 67 (1961), 323–30; A. S. Feldman and C. Tilly, 'The interaction of social and physical space', *Am. Sociol. Rev.* 25 (1960), 877–84; O. D. Duncan and B. Duncan, 'Residential distribution and occupational stratification', p. 499.

of biotic or laissez-faire economic competition to the structuring of the urban residential system in terms of socio-economic status, familism, ethnicity and mobility, remains to be demonstrated.

THE SOCIAL VALUES APPROACH

In the late 1930s and early 1940s a severe reaction set in what was seen as the slavish use by the classical ecologists of concepts borrowed directly from plant and animal ecology.[1] It was claimed that 'the human ecologists have tended to promulgate a theoretical framework for their discipline which is markedly positivistic, deterministic, mechanistic, and organismic'.[2] Critics such as Alihan took the Chicago school to task for its alleged over-emphasis on the biological analogies of dominance and succession and for its artificial division of society into biotic and cultural spheres. With the benefits of hind-sight much of the argument now seems to have been misplaced. To a large extent the critics of the classical tradition directed their criticism at straw men of their own creation. The classical ecologists were by no means as wedded to a single-factor biological view of the community and its processes as their detractors appear to assume. Nor were they guilty of reification to the extent suggested. The division which Park makes, for instance, between biotic and cultural levels of society is clearly introduced as an artificial, ideal type construction. It serves as an analytical tool, rather than as a description of reality. On the other hand, it remains true that the classical ecologists do attempt a general explanation of residential differentiation which is couched largely in terms of impersonal competition. They give little more than lip service to the role of non-economic cultural factors. It is to this aspect of their work that the criticisms of the 'social values' school are most applicable.

The application of the social values approach to the problem of residential differentiation is given substance by Firey.[3] In his analysis of the patterns of land use in Boston, Firey claims that the emphasis of the classical ecologists on the differentiating power of land values is based on too rational a conception of human behaviour. In the classical model 'social systems are passive adapters to spatial distance and have no further role than one of compliance'.[4] The classical position ignores the importance of sentiment and symbolism in human affairs. Space is not just something which is differentiated in terms of economic costs, but instead can take on a variety of

---

[1] See Alihan, *Social Ecology*; Hollingshead, 'Community research'; W. E. Gettys, 'Human ecology and social theory', reprinted in Theodorson, *Studies in Human Ecology*, pp. 98–103.

[2] Gettys, *ibid.*, p. 99.

[3] W. Firey, 'Sentiment and symbolism as ecological variables', reprinted in Theodorson, *Studies in Human Ecology*, pp. 253–61; W. Firey, *Land Use in Central Boston* (Cambridge, Mass., 1947).

[4] Firey, *Land Use*, p. 30.

symbolic values and be the object of strong sentiments: 'locational activities are not only economizing agents but may also bear sentiments which can significantly influence the locational process'.[1] Firey illustrates his argument with a series of case-studies, describing areas which deviate from the classical prediction. The explanation, in each case, is said to lie in sentiment. Thus, Beacon Hill, a preferred upper-class residential district within five minutes walking distance of the central shopping area of Boston, has been able to escape economic trends which would suggest a change in character because it possesses symbolic value. It has a large number of historical associations with the literati of Boston and with the old-established families. It is a matter of pride to be able to say that one lives there. The case of Boston Common is similar in character. Here, again, more financially profitable land uses have been held at bay. Boston Common has 'become a "sacred" object, articulating and symbolizing genuine historical sentiments of a certain portion of the community. Like all such objects its sacredness derives, not from any intrinsic spatial attributes, but rather from its representation in people's minds as a symbol for collective sentiments'.[2] Nor, Firey maintains, are Beacon Hill and Boston Common ecological sports. Rather they are but two instances of a general pattern which ecology will only be able to understand if 'values are made central to ecological theory'.[3]

Support for the social values approach has come from a large number of studies dealing with the spatial patterning of various ethnic minority groups within the city. In a study of the movement of the Norwegian community in New York, Jonassen states that

this ecological behaviour arises out of the interaction of the realities of the New York environment with the immigrants' attitudes and values ... It is therefore indicated that the movement of these people must be referred to factors that are volitional, purposeful, and personal and that these factors may not be considered as mere accidental and incidental features of biotic processes and impersonal competition.[4]

A similar conclusion is reached by Myers in his study of the residential and occupational distribution of Italians in New Haven:

It is apparent that ecological dispersion cannot be understood solely in terms of 'biotic', 'subsocial', 'natural', 'impersonal', or 'strictly economic', factors. Men are not only physical beings motivated by biotic forces, but are human beings as well, motivated by culturally determined drives and values. Competition is not impersonal, but, on the contrary, quite personal and deliberate. Men compete, not as abstractions, but as human beings within a sociocultural framework in which cultural values and usages are tools which regulate the competitive process.[5]

[1] Firey, 'Sentiment and symbolism', p. 254. [2] *Ibid.*, p. 257. [3] Firey, *Land Use*, p. 93.
[4] C. T. Jonassen, 'Cultural variables in the ecology of an ethnic group', reprinted in Theodorson, *Studies in Human Ecology*, p. 269.
[5] J. K. Myers, 'Assimilation to the ecological and social systems of a community', reprinted in Theodorson, p. 279.

The residential patterning of any ethnic minority involves a host of non-economic values relating to such characteristics as preferred family forms, religious and political allegiances, and degree of acceptance by the host community.[1]

Until the late 1940s, human ecology was almost wholly American in orientation and data. The theories which were produced were based on experience and information relating primarily to the rapidly growing and laissez-faire cities of the mid-West. The limits of this experience were frequently ignored. As Caplow concludes in his study of the ecological structure of Guatemala City:

The literature of urban geography and urban sociology has a tendency to project as universals those characteristics of urbanism with which European and American students are most familiar. Thus, since a large proportion of all urban research has concerned itself with Chicago, there was until recently a tendency to ascribe to all cities characteristics which now appear to be specific to Chicago and other communities closely resembling it in history and economic function.[2]

The competition for location in the Chicago of the 1910s appeared to fit the biotic model well; the expansion of ecological studies into other areas and other times has produced material much less amenable to the sub-social level of explanation. The development of city planning on a wide scale has drawn attention to the role of professional ideologies in the determination of city structure.[3] At a national level, the beliefs of government about desirable forms of settlement may have immediate implications for the structuring of the residential fabric. The case of apartheid is but a single example.[4] Even in apparently laissez-faire situations it is clear that recourse must be had to other than the biotic model if a satisfactory explanation is to be offered for such diverse phenomena as the rigid quartering of the Japanese castle town, the tribal agglomerations of the West African city, the attraction of the plaza in Latin America and of the suburb in the Anglo-Saxon countries.

An impressive, if unsystematic, body of evidence can be marshalled in support of the contention that values play an important role in the process of residential differentiation. It should not be inferred, however, that the social values approach has superseded that developed by the classical

[1] See Lieberson, *Ethnic Patterns in American Cities*; J. Zubrzycki, 'Ethnic segregation in Australian cities', *Proc. Internat. Pop. Conf.* (Vienna, 1959), pp. 610–16; J. I. Martin, *Refugee Settlers* (Melbourne, 1965); C. A. Price, *The Study of Assimilation*; C. A. Price, *Southern Europeans in Australia* (Melbourne, 1964); M. M. Gordon, *Assimilation in American Life* (New York, 1964).
[2] T. Caplow, 'The social ecology of Guatemala City', *Soc. Forces*, 28 (1949), 132.
[3] E.g. P. Meadows, 'The urbanists: profiles of professional ideologies', *1963 Yearbook*, School of Architecture, Syracuse University (Syracuse, 1965). Reference in Sjoberg, 'Theory and Research'. See also H. J. Gans, 'Planning for people, not buildings', *Envir. and Planning*, 1 (1969), 33–46; S. M. Willhelm, *Urban Zoning and Land Use Theory* (New York, 1962).
[4] See L. Kuper *et al.*, *Durban: A Study in Racial Ecology* (London, 1958); W. H. Form, 'The place of social structure in the determination of land use', *Soc. Forces*, 32 (1954), 317–23.

ecologists. Not only may the two approaches be seen to be concerned with differing aspects of the residential system but the social values approach may itself be subjected to severe criticism.[1]

The nature of the relationship between values and social structure has rarely been spelled out by those attempting to explain ecological differentiation in terms of the social values perspective. Values are rarely consensual – especially in urban-industrial society – and, in the absence of consensus, it may be very difficult to use the social values approach in any attempt at prediction. Furthermore, it is unrealistic to anticipate a one-to-one correspondence between values and behaviours. Many intervening variables must also be taken into account. More serious, perhaps, is the conceptual confusion which accompanies the key construct of the social values approach – that of value itself.[2] It has been variously used to describe a wide variety of subjective phenomena. Very rarely has it been given a constitutive definition in terms of its connexions with general theory and equally rarely has it been the object of independent investigation. The concept of value seems frequently to have been introduced merely to fill the hiatus which has appeared when economic criteria appear to have been ineffective. In other cases, however, it has been pointed out that economic factors are themselves values.[3] The classical ecologists themselves are somewhat unclear at this point. On the one hand they give considerable emphasis to the role of central city dominance in the determination of land values and to impersonal competition in the segregation of population categories in terms of land values. On the other hand, they endorse the earlier remark made by Hurd to the effect that, 'The basis of residence values is social and not economic'.[4] On the whole, however, it is probably true to say that the classical ecologists tend to take the existing pattern of land and rental values as givens and to erect their theory of residential differentiation on the land values map. In this sense, the social values approach may be seen as being concerned with a more fundamental level of analysis.

The social values approach to urban ecology has served the necessary and useful function of stressing the importance of human motivation in residential differentiation. By itself, however, it can hardly be said to constitute a systematic theory of differentiation. Rather, it may best be seen as an adjunct to the economic model developed by the classical and neo-classical ecologists. It serves both to emphasize the role of general socio-cultural factors in determining the nature of economic competition and to provide a more limited

---

[1] See Sjoberg, 'Theory and Research'.
[2] For a review of the various meanings attached to the term, see J. Blake and K. Davis, 'Norms, values, and sanctions', in R. E. L. Faris (ed.), *Handbook of Modern Sociology* (Chicago, 1964), pp. 456–84.
[3] E.g. Willhelm, *Urban Zoning*.
[4] R. M. Hurd, *Principles of City Land Values* (New York, 1903), p. 77. For a similar point of view see E. Jones, *A Social Geography of Belfast* (London, 1960), p. 280.

insight into the role of sentiment and symbolism in the motivation of locational behaviour. Rather than being in conflict with the sub-social approach, the social values approach to residential differentiation is concerned with different levels of analysis and with different orders of generality.

Both the social values approach and, more especially, the sub-social approach to residential differentiation are concerned with relatively abstract processes. They represent attempts to discover general ecological principles. They have little to say about the characteristics of residential differentiation and provide little information relevant to a discussion of the four major axes of differentiation. In order to understand how these latter come into being it is necessary to adopt a more obviously social-psychological perspective in which the major emphasis is given to the decision-making activities of individuals, groups and institutions. The structure of the city is built about a myriad of decisions about location and about the characteristics of areas. Any attempt to explain the bases of residential differentiation must be concerned with the factors underlying the locational behaviours and decisions which characterize individual households and groups.

TOWARDS A GENERAL THEORY OF RESIDENTIAL LOCATION

The proximal cause of residential differentiation is a series of decisions concerning the characteristics of neighbourhoods and the location of households. In a wholly planned society the decisions involved may all be taken by a small elite group. In the extreme case, a single person may become the decision maker planning the community in accordance with his own standards.[1] In a wholly laissez-faire society, the decisions may be spread amongst a large number of individual households – the consumers of housing – and a somewhat smaller number of builders and developers – the suppliers of housing. In a society in which aspects of private economics and public planning are combined, the 'normal' state of most contemporary Western nations, the decisions may rest with many different sectors of the population, acting in many different roles. Analysis of the decision-making process in such a situation must involve a plethora of background variables, manifest and latent functions, individual desires and collective realities. The aspirations, knowledge and actions of the individual household, the building programmes of the estate developer, the siting plans of the industrialist and the bureaucrat, the promotion activities of the real estate seller, the planning structures envisaged by local, regional and national planning organizations and the activities of a wide range of financial institutions, all help to structure the decision-making process and the resulting residential

---

[1] This seems to have been the case in pre-modern Japan as described in Yazaki, *The Japanese City*. It was also characteristic of many early planned settlements in other parts of the world.

patterning. Moreover, the decisions taken at one level are rife with implications for those to be taken at other levels and feed-back loops exist not only between different systematic levels at one point of time, but also between the same and different levels across time. The decisions taken during any given time period reflect the evaluations given to the results of those taken earlier and provide the base for those to be taken in future. Much of the details of the decision-making process remain obscure and there are many gaps in our knowledge about the parameters of the process even within closely-defined groups. While it is necessary to take into account the decision-making activity of the numerous groups involved in residential differentiation it has to be admitted that our knowledge is far short of that necessary to allow the formulation of a coherent theory of residential behaviour.

As Wurster has pointed out, the assumption that the consumer has exercised a dominant role in the housing market has always been a myth, even in the United States.[1] On the other hand, it seems reasonable to begin the analysis of residential decision-making at the consumer level, the level of individual households.[2] The decision to locate in a particular house and a particular part of the city is one of the most important which a family has to make and has implications for a wide range of its activities. The decision reflects the evaluation by those concerned of a large number of personal and urban characteristics, the cluster of variables involved being different in each case. Very generally, however, the decision-making process may be seen as an evaluation by the family of the extent to which its needs, capabilities, and desires are met by the houses and neighbourhoods which are available and about which it has information. In order to understand residential differentiation it is necessary to pay attention to each of the factors involved in families' choice of one house and area rather than another.

Before any decision to locate a particular area has been taken some threshold of stress must have been passed in connexion with the previous residence.[3] The causes of such stress are legion, some stemming from changes in family characteristics, others from changes in the nature of the neighbourhood environment, others still from general changes in technology and values. In the first category belong such phenomena as changes in marital status, changes in family size and income, changes in the self-evaluation which the family gives itself, and changing locational needs resulting from changes in

[1] C. B. Wurster, 'Social questions in housing and community planning', in W. L. Wheaton *et al.* (eds), *Urban Housing* (New York 1966), p. 31.

[2] Differences in the decision-making process *within* the family are ignored for the sake of presentation. The approach used is very similar to those outlined in L. A. Brown and E. G. Moore, 'Intra-urban migration: an actor-oriented framework', mimeo., Northwestern University (Evanston, Ill., 1968) and M. D. Van Arsdol, *et al.*, 'Retrospective and subsequent metropolitan residential mobility', *Demography* (forthcoming).

[3] J. Wolpert, 'Behavioural aspects of the decision to migrate', *Papers Reg. Sci. Ass.* 15 (1965), 159–69; Wolpert, 'Migration as an adjustment to environmental stress', *J. Soc. Issues* 22 (1966) 92–102; Brown and Moore, 'Intra-urban migration'.

the employment or recreational activities which the family undertakes. Changes in neighbourhood characteristics may result from the encroachment of incompatible land uses or socially inferior populations or simply from an increase or decrease in population density. They may also mark simply the passing of time and its concomitant obsolescence. Developments in transport technology, involving the opening up of new areas and changes in the relative accessibility of old areas, changes in the value which is given to differing styles of building, for example flats *v*. bungalows, and changes in preferred ways of life, for example 'urban sophistication' versus suburban familism, may also profoundly affect the evaluation which is given to the present area and residence. Families differ considerably in the amount of stress which they can absorb and in the reactions which they develop as a result of stress. It seems likely, however, that some threshold exists for every family. Once passed the family must engage in an active evaluation of its needs and capabilities and either attempt to alter its present habitat in the hope of satisfying its aspirations or start searching for vacant houses and lots which might suit it.

THE ASPIRATIONS OF THE HOUSEHOLD

Given an initial decision to investigate vacancies, the aspirations of the individuals involved come to the fore. In detail these aspirations are likely to show a great variation from individual to individual, but in general it is the proposition of the present chapter that they may be seen as reflecting a small number of basic differentiating properties. More particularly, it is suggested that in the modern city these basic properties are closely related to those which have emerged in the studies of factorial ecology, that is, socio-economic status, familism, ethnicity, and mobility. It has to be admitted that direct evidence for this proposition is minimal. Very little material is available on residential aspirations and preferences. It is, however, encouraging that in a factor analytic study of residential preferences based on a set of seventeen 'objective' environmental criteria, Ellis finds three major sets of preference factors relating to socio-economic status, ethnic composition, and availability of recreational space.[1] The last dimension may be seen as part of the familism cluster.[2] The basic model used in the present analysis views residential location as the outcome of a decision-making process in which the multi-dimensional preferences of the household are brought into line with the characteristics of the neighbourhood through

[1] R. H. Ellis, 'A Behavioural Residential Location Model', mimeo. Technical Report, Northwestern University (Evanston, Ill., 1966); see also G. L. Petersen, 'A model of preference', *J. Reg. Sci.* 7 (1967), 19–32.
[2] The desire for space is closely associated with child-centred activities and orientations.

a complex of evaluative and information-seeking behaviours. In the process it is proposed that the urban population is residentially differentiated according to socio-economic status, family type, ethnicity, and mobility characteristics.

Social rank and ethnic considerations

Although social rank and ethnic status are distinct in both substantive and analytical senses their relationship to residential location is believed to be mediated through a common process. Before looking at the differing effects of social rank and ethnic status considerations the common features of their association with residential differentiation will be examined.

The basic proposition of the present agrument is that residential location and relocation may be seen as strategies for minimizing the social distance between the individual and populations which he desires to emulate and for maximizing that from groups which he wishes to leave behind. In a discussion of social status and migration Rossi points out that

Residential mobility also plays a role in 'vertical' social mobility. The location of a residence has a prestige value, and is, to some degree, a determinant of personal contact potentials. Families moving up the 'occupational ladder' are particularly sensitive to the social aspects of location and use residential mobility to bring their residences into line with their prestige needs.[1]

A similar theme is stated by Keller:

Within its physical and symbolic boundaries, a neighbourhood contains inhabitants having something in common – perhaps only the current sharing of a common environment. This gives them a certain collective character, which affects and reflects people's feelings about living there and the kinds of relationships the residents establish. It also contributes to the reputation of an area, which even more than its potential for fellowship and convenience may weigh significantly with its more status-conscious residents and determine their relative contentment with the area as a place in which to live.[2]

It may be added that it is not only families moving up the occupational ladder, or who are particularly 'status-conscious', who are likely to be sensitive to the prestige aspects of location. The same is likely to be true of any group which is or wishes to be vertically mobile in one or more of the various stratification hierarchies of society or which is concerned lest it become so. Amongst ethnic groups, residential segregation 'accentuates the

---

[1] P. H. Rossi, *Why Families Move* (New York, 1955), p. 179.
[2] Keller, *The Urban Neighbourhood*, p. 90.

differences between a group and the remainder of the population by heightening the visibility of the group, and it enables the population to keep its peculiar traits and group structure'.[1]

An address is far more than a convenient way of organizing the supply of public services or of locating an individual in physical space. It also locates him in social space. The address of a person immediately identifies him as a member of a particular social group, as a Bethnal Greener or an inhabitant of Bloomsbury. So pervasive is this effect that residential location has frequently been used as one of the measures of an individual's position in the local prestige hierarchy.[2] Ross suggests that in the absence of more detailed information about an individual knowledge of his area of residence may play an important role in identifying his social rank and ethnic identity.[3] With regard to social rank, Shevky and Williams suggest that

In urban-industrial society, the unfailing indicators of the social position of others readily accessible to everyone are houses and areas of residence. As every occupation is evaluated and generally accorded honour and esteem on a scale of prestige in society, so every residential section has a status value which is readily recognized by everyone in the city.[4]

Although Shevky and Williams probably overstate the degree of consensus present with regard to the status value of different locations, it is clear that a household's address does provide information on its likely social characteristics.[5] Moreover, various studies have suggested that the absence of a stable residential location may be related to personality disorganization.[6] It may be that a stable sense of the individual's own identity demands a stable residential identity. The anomia of the hobo may be at least in part a reflection of his lack of a stable residential identity. The anxiety of the relocated slum dweller may represent a similar hiatus between personal and residential identities. The return of the elderly rehoused to the inner-city areas of their early years may at least in part be represented as an attempt to regain their earlier self-images.

A person's identity is closely interwoven with the nature of his social relationships. Individuals who are perceived as being similar to himself, or as personifying what he would like to become, provide a major reference point

[1] Lieberson, *Ethnic Patterns in American Cities*, p. 6.
[2] E.g. W. L. Warner *et al.*, *Social Class in America* (New York, 1960); A. Congalton, *Status Ranking of Sydney Suburbs* (Sydney, 1964).
[3] H. L. Ross, 'The local community', *Am. Sociol. Rev.* 27 (1962), 75–84.
[4] E. Shevky and M. Williams, *The Social Areas of Los Angeles* (Berkeley, Calif., 1949), pp. 61–2, quoted in Ross, 'The local community'.
[5] Apart from the work of Warner *et al.*, see also the theoretical discussions in Tryon, *Identification of Social Areas by Cluster Analysis* and J. M. Beshers, *Urban Social Structure*, chaps. 5, 6.
[6] C. Tietze *et al.*, 'Personal disorders and spatial mobility', *Am. J. Sociol.* 43 (1942), 29–39; B. P. Dohrenwend, 'Social status and psychological disorder', *Am. Sociol. Rev.* 31 (1966), 14–34; M. B. Kantor (ed.), *Mobility and Mental Health* (Springfield, Ill., 1965).

for the evaluation of the individual's behaviour.[1] Moreover, a person's public identity may be largely equated with the types of associates he is seen with. This is especially true in the case of those more intimate primary relationships which imply the status-equality of the participants: 'A person is a member of that social class with which most of his participation, of this intimate kind, occurs.'[2] The principle may be extended to cover any social category, desirable or undesirable. Since association demands contact, and contact may be seen as a function of spatial propinquity, it follows that the manipulation of residential location may be regarded as a strategy for optimizing the probability of desired association. Individuals who wish to interact with each other are likely to wish to live in close proximity. In this way the time and the costs of interaction are kept to a minimum and the chance of associational identification is maximized. Individuals who do not desire to interact, on the other hand, are likely to wish to live far apart. In this way the chances of accidental contact are minimized and there is little possibility of an unwanted identification. Social distance and spatial distance may both be seen as symbols of class standing and as means of maintaining the existing distinction between ranks.[3] The more intimate the relationship the more it carries with it the possibility of identification. Friendship and marriage, in particular, are relationships which put existing differentials at risk. It is in terms of the connexion between residence and choice of marriage partner, and of the relationship between the latter and social prestige, that Beshers attempts to explain the differing justification put forward by Southern and Northern Whites in the United States, when asked to explain their support of discrimination against Negroes. Pointing out that the typical Southern response revolves around the question of who should marry one's daughter, while the typical Northern response is concerned with the characteristics of one's neighbours, Beshers goes on:

The southerner's concern for whom his daughter marries may be a reflection of a kinship-dominated society in which alliances by marriage supply the most significant prestige. The northerner's concern for his neighbours may reflect the importance of neighbourhood in determining prestige . . . Exactly why neighbourhood should become the important issue when the importance of kinship declines is by no means clear . . . We may speculate that contact with the neighbours is in fact pertinent to this issue. Who daughter marries has something to do with who daughter meets. Daughter will not come into contact with Negroes in an integrated

[1] On the importance of reference groups, see T. Shibutani, *Society and Personality* (Englewood Cliffs, N. J., 1961), chap. 8; M. Sherif and C. W. Sherif, *Reference Groups*; R. Merton, *Social Theory and Social Structure* (New York, 1957), chaps. 8, 9.

[2] A. Davis *et al.*, *Deep South* (Chicago, 1941), p. 59.

[3] 'Social distance – the aloofness and unapproachability of persons, especially those of different social strata – is both a symbol of class standing and a means of maintaining the existing distinctions in rank'. E. T. Hiller, *Principles of Sociology* (New York, 1933), p. 41.

school because residential segregation of nonwhites effectively yields segregation of school districts. Residence choice and marriage choice may be closely connected.[1]

Clearly one can substitute any other dimension of rank differentiation in Beshers' discussion of the relationship between residential propinquity and Negro-White contacts. In order to preserve social distance it may be necessary to institute physical distance.

The correlation between residential propinquity and rank identification implies that propinquity will be differentially desired according to the perspective of the individuals concerned. In order to 'rise in the world' those of inferior rank must endeavour to enter into relationships of rank-equality with those seen as possessing a more desirable position. An initial step may be to attempt to live amongst them. On the other hand, to those who already possess high rank, such association carries with it the danger of losing prestige. It may be possible to neutralize the risk by casting the migrants in the status of such obvious inferiors that the danger of identification is averted. Servants are little risk to the prestige of their masters. But if the neonate group refuses to accept this low status and can be seen as a real threat to the high-ranking group's enjoyment of prestige, then stringent entrance requirements will be required of all those attempting to join the latter's milieu. If financial restraints fail to work, more overtly prestige-linked criteria such as ethnic origin may be used in restricting potential settlers. Although the law of the land may outlaw such discrimination there is little to prevent a residents' association from purchasing vacant dwellings so that it can select its potential neighbours.[2] And if all these measures fail, there is still a wide variety of techniques available by which the members of a local group can let a newcomer know that he is not appreciated. Since power tends to go with prestige, the ability of the high ranking members of society to control the characteristics of their neighbourhood is considerable.

The association between residential differentiation and social desirability factors has been examined in several studies of the distribution of various occupational and ethnic populations. The present discussion may be illustrated by data from Brisbane.

The 1961 residential differentiation of five occupational categories in Brisbane is shown in Table 3.1. The occupations are arranged in their order of 'general social standing' as determined by a conventional ranking scale.[3] Entries above the diagonal show the index of dissimilarity between the groups, computed on the basis of the 554 residential census collectors'

---

[1] Beshers, *Urban Social Structure*, pp. 105–6.
[2] E.g. Keller, 'Social class in physical planning', pp. 494–511.
[3] The ranking is based on the responses of some 500 Brisbane residents but, at the scale used here, is no different from that used in several American and British studies.

TABLE 3.1 *Indices of residential dissimilarity for five occupational categories:*
Brisbane, 1961

	Occupational category	I	II	III	IV	V
I	Professional and managerial	–	35	40	42	46
II	Clerical and sales	16	–	26	29	32
III	Skilled manual	20	10	–	22	25
IV	Semi-skilled manual	23	15	7	–	22
V	Unskilled manual	30	20	15	10	–

NOTE. Entries above diagonal computed for 554 CDs; entries below diagonal computed for 28 electoral divisions.

districts in the Brisbane metropolitan area.[1] Entries below the diagonal
are computed on the basis of the 28 electoral divisions in Brisbane.

There is a clear correspondence between the ordering of occupational
categories in terms of their general social standing and that produced by
consideration of their residential patterning. Both orders are also reflected
in the pattern of friendship nominations which were produced in the course
of an earlier analysis of the relationship between stratification variables and
friendship choices.[2] Table 3.2 shows the proportion of each set of respond-

TABLE 3.2 *Percentage of best friends in each occupational category by*
occupation of respondent: Brisbane, 1964

A. Males

	Occupational category	I	II	III	IV	V	No. of respondents	No. of friends *i*
I	Professional/managerial	73	20	6	1	–	48	132
II	Clerical/sales	9	75	6	5	5	51	110
III	Skilled manual	10	22	49	10	9	41	87
IV	Semi-skilled manual	4	19	20	35	23	45	88
V	Unskilled manual	9	16	12	18	44	55	92

B. Females

	Occupational category	I	II	III	IV	V	No. of respondents	No. of friends *i*
I	Professional/managerial	76	16	4	2	2	50	147
II	Clerical/sales	12	61	11	11	5	62	142
III	Skilled manual	11	38	28	16	8	41	120
IV	Semi-skilled manual	7	25	17	37	15	37	86
V	Unskilled manual	8	21	19	16	35	58	85

NOTE. *i* Number of friends includes a small number of 'occupation unknown' responses. These
have been disregarded in the calculation of percentages.

[1] The index of dissimilarity is a measure of net displacement. See Timms, 'Quantitative techniques'
pp. 239–65 and references therein. In general, the smaller the size of the base units used in the
computations the higher will be the resulting index of dissimilarity.
[2] D. W. G. Timms, 'Occupational stratification and friendship nomination', *Aust. N.Z. J. Sociol.*
3 (1967), 32–43.

ents' friendship nominations which were directed to members of each of the five occupational categories.

The greater the prestige distance between two occupational populations the less likely are they to nominate each other as friends and the more dissimilar are their residential distributions.

Further support for the connexion between residential differentiation and social desirability factors is provided by consideration of the residential patterning of immigrants in Brisbane and its relationship with various other measures of their assimilation into the core society of Queensland.[1] The basic premise is that the less the members of an immigrant group differ from those of the host society, the more assimilated they are and the more desirable they will become as intimate role-partners.

The empirical focus of the study is the pattern of dissimilarity between the Australian-born members of the Queensland population and members of the eight largest overseas-born populations in the State. Three main aspects of the situation are sampled: the dissimilarity between the various migrant groups and the Australian-born in terms of their dispersion over the residential, occupational, and religious structures of Queensland, the marriage patterns which each group exhibits, and the perceived social distance of each set of migrants as viewed from the perspective of the native-born. A close relationship is posited to exist between all three areas of assimilation. Thus, knowledge of the degree of dissimilarity exhibited by a specified migrant group in one sphere, for example its residential patterning, should be highly predictive to its degree of dissimilarity in all other spheres. Table 3.3 gives the relevant information.

It is clear that the basic premise is well founded. All the indices of dissimilarity show high positive correlations. Dissimilarity in terms of residential,

TABLE 3.3 *The dissimilarity between the Australian-born and overseas-born in Queensland*

	Indexes of dissimilarity			Perceived dissimilarity 1967	Social distance index 1967	Per cent overseas grooms 1960–2	Per cent overseas brides 1960–2
Birth place group	Residential	Occupational 1961	Religious				
N.Z.	32	17	9	17	1·1	39	14
U.K.	10	6	13	22	1·2	30	22
Dutch	43	13	22	51	1·7	51	37
German	38	25	25	57	1·8	57	39
Polish	48	29	33	67	2·3	72	59
Italian	60	24	39	75	2·4	92	56
Yugoslav	77	29	30	76	2·5	88	52
Greek	68	43	42	76	2·4	85	71

[1] Timms, 'Dissimilarity between overseas-born and Australian-born in Queensland', pp. 363–74.

Zero-order correlation coefficients for measures of dissimilarity

Indexes of dissimilarity	a	b	c	d	e	f	g
a Residential dissimilarity	–	80	80	88	90	83	93
b Occupational dissimilarity	80	–	82	78	79	86	79
c Religious dissimilarity	80	82	–	95	94	98	92
d Perceived dissimilarity	88	78	95	–	99	95	95
e Social distance index	90	79	94	99	–	96	97
f Marital dissimilarity (grooms)	83	86	98	95	96	–	91
g Marital dissimilarity (brides)	93	79	92	95	97	91	–

NOTE. Decimal point omitted.

occupational and religious dispersion is closely related with marital dissimilarity and with two measures of perceived social distance.[1] The more similar the residential, occupational, and religious patterns of an immigrant group to those of the Australian-born the more likely are its members to marry Australian-born spouses and the more desirable they appear to the Australian-born as intimate role-partners. Social distance and residential distance appear to correspond.

The separation of socio-economic status and ethnicity as 'desirability' factors

Both socio-economic status and ethnic identity serve to structure the relative desirability of locating in particular neighbourhoods and associating with particular categories of people. The extent to which they serve as independent or as joint influences varies according to the degree of prejudice with which ethnic minorities are treated and the similarity or difference between the socio-economic composition of the ethnic population and that of the core society. In a situation where the members of an ethnic minority are overwhelmingly concentrated in a narrow range of the socio-economic status hierarchy there may be no effective discrimination between ethnic identity and socio-economic status. Areas which contain large numbers of the ethnic population will thereby be identified as being of a particular socio-economic status. This appears to have been the general position in much of the American South. It also appears to be the position in Auckland and in Helsinki, although the minority groups concerned occupy opposite ends of the social rank scale. A similar lack of independence in the ethnic component of social desirability may arise if the ethnic minority is so closely assimilated to the core society that there is no longer any vestige of prejudice

---

[1] The two measures of perceived dissimilarity are the Bogardus Social Distance Index – a measure of the desirability of members of the specified population as intimate role-partners – and a global dissimilarity judgement based on pair-comparisons with Australian-born as an anchor. For further details, see Timms, *ibid*.

or discrimination. The continued use of an ethnic label in such a situation may be related to nothing else than sentiment, as an axis of social differentiation ethnicity may have long-since disappeared. Given that ethnicity remains important as a differentiating property of persons the extent of its independence from social rank considerations will reflect the degree of prejudice which is involved. In the extreme case, where contact with a member of the minority population is considered so stigmatizing as to pollute the status of the dominant group, social distance will be maintained for the minority population regardless of its socio-economic status. The institution of caste may legitimize the invidious distinction. In such circumstances areas identified with the minority population will be undesirable even to the lowest social ranks of the core society. At the same time, the areas may be regarded as desirable by all members of the ethnic minority, regardless of their own social rank. This does not imply, however, that the social distance between different social rank positions within the ethnic population will break down. Analyses of the social and physical distance between occupational categories of the same ethnic population suggest that the degree of stratification remains marked. Within the ethnic population the patterns of social desirability and segregation tend to parallel those found in the encompassing community.[1] The ethnic population may indeed form a city-within-the-city or, more generally, an ethnic village in which the population is stratified in much the same way as in the homeland. With the passage of time it is likely that the bases of socio-economic stratification will shift into line with those held in the core society but, in the absence of assimilation, the ethnic village may long continue to hold its attractions for the ethnic population.

Family characteristics and mobility

Just as socio-economic status and ethnicity are believed to represent different aspects of the social stratification system, so it is suggested that variables relating to the family characteristics and mobility of the population may be seen as representing underlying variations in preferred life-styles. To a large extent these may be seen to be correlated with differences in life-cycle characteristics. The significance of the family life-cycle in determining residential differentiation has been most strongly stressed by Rossi in his study of 'why people move'. According to Rossi the changing housing requirements of a family as it undergoes developmental changes in structure, composition, and activities, form the most important general stimulus to residential mobility which may be regarded as 'the mechanism by which a

[1] St C. Drake and H. R. Clayton, *Black Metropolis* (New York, 1945); O. D. Duncan and B. Duncan, *Negro Population of Chicago*, esp. pp. 278–98; L. F. Schnore, 'Social class segregation among non-whites in metropolitan centres', *Demography* 2 (1965), 126–33.

family's housing is brought into adjustment with its housing needs'.[1] The recognition of changing housing needs is unlikely to be a perfect function of changes in family structure and composition. Powerful inertia factors, particularly pronounced in the later years of the family's existence, in the period when the children are leaving or have left home, introduce a rigidity of locational evaluation which is relatively independent of immediate family changes. Moreover, the definition of housing needs is likely to show considerable inter-group variation depending on the activities and beliefs followed by the families concerned. High rates of residential mobility are, nonetheless, typically found in connexion with certain transitional periods of the family cycle, notably those immediately following marriage, the initial stages of child-rearing, and the period after children have left home. To the extent that houses in different parts of the city have differential appeal to families at varying stages of the family cycle then the very existence of the latter will lead to a differentiation of the city fabric in terms of family characteristics.

Closely related to the family's evaluation of its general housing requirements is a concern for what Rodwin has termed a functionally adequate physical environment:

This physical environment will vary for different social and economic groups as well as different historical periods and stages of technology. Among the diverse conditions sought are adequate access to employment centres for the principal and secondary wage earners; convenient access to schools and shopping centres; and improved physical layouts providing adequate and attractive housing, open space, traffic safety and recreation areas ... [T]he importance of these factors will be shaped by changes in income, social organization, attitudes, technology, urban size, scale and function.[2]

It will also be shaped, of course, by changes in family composition and activities. The appeal of suburban areas to families with young children has been highlighted in several studies of suburban migration. Thus, in Bell's study of the reasons given for movement to two Chicago suburbs, 81 per cent of the respondents give a 'better-for-children' answer.[3] Associated characteristics such as the opportunity to garden and to have contact with 'nature' are also popular. What Bell terms 'familistic orientations' are stated to have affected the decision to migrate in 83 per cent of the cases studied. Although the actual percentage giving the better-for-children response is unusually high in Bell's study, it appears as the most popular of the justifications for moving to suburban areas in several other British and American studies.[4] According to Bell

[1] Rossi, *Why Families Move*, p. 178.
[2] L. Rodwin, 'The theory of residential growth and structure', *The Appraisal J.* 18 (1950), 313.
[3] Bell,'The city, the suburb, and a theory of social choice', p. 153.
[4] A summary is provided in R. N. Morris and J. Mogey, *The Sociology of Housing* (London, 1965).

the move to the suburbs expresses an attempt to find a location in which to conduct family life which is more suitable than that offered by central cities, i.e. . . . persons moving to the suburbs are principally those who have chosen Familism (investment in the family system, marriage at younger ages, short childless post-marriage span, large families) as an important element in their life styles.[1]

Not all people who move to suburban areas of the city have a heavy investment in the family system. Writers on suburban migration have also stressed such style of life characteristics as a longing for a 'domestic togetherness which gives meaning to life', a quest for personal involvement, an 'aesthetic affinity' for open living, and 'a greater sensitivity to nature and the outdoor life'.[2] To the inhabitants of a middle-class 'garden estate' in Brisbane, the appeal of the estate consisted in its rural aspect, its peacefulness and easy pace of life (a pace which was belied by the frenetic social activities of the estate population), its general convenience, especially for children, and its sense of community spirit.[3] In general, however, as Dobriner concludes in a critical review of the studies concerned with people's justifications for their move to the suburbs: 'The search for suburbia seems to focus on the good life, for the family.'[4]

The 'flight to the suburbs' and the search for a good environment in which to enact a familistic style of life appear to be essentially synonymous in the Western city. With the spread of automobile ownership and the construction of suburban estates on a mass scale, suburban residence and its associated spaciousness has been brought within the reaches of a majority of the population.[5] Both rich and poor, native born and migrant can aspire to a new house in a new suburb. Differences in socio-economic status or in ethnicity appear to introduce only minor variation in the suburban theme.

If the appeal of the suburb seems explicable in terms of a single, over-riding set of life-style preferences, that of the inner city appears to rest on a much more complex set of considerations. Some impression of these considerations may be gleaned from a description by Gans of the various types of residents to be found in the central city.[6] Five main categories are described: the 'cosmopolites', the 'unmarried or childless', the 'deprived', the 'trapped' and the 'ethnic villagers'. Each category is associated with a distinctive set of life-style preferences and has a distinctive history. The characteristics of the ethnic villagers have already been mentioned. In a sense they are in the central city, but not of it. The present concern is focused on the four remaining categories, for it is these that provide the

---

[1] Bell, 'The city, the suburb, and a theory of social choice', p. 151.
[2] E.g. W. M. Dobriner, *Class and Suburbia* (New York, 1963).
[3] Timms, 'Anomia and social participation amongst suburban women'.
[4] Dobriner, *Class and Suburbia*.
[5] See E. M. Hoover and R. Vernon, *Anatomy of a Metropolis* (Cambridge, Mass., 1959).
[6] H. J. Gans, 'Urbanism and suburbanism as ways of life', in A. M. Rose (ed.), *Human Behaviour and Social Processes* (London, 1962), pp. 652–48.

main basis for the mobility dimension of residential differentiation and contribute to the association between mobility and urbanism as a way of life.

The cosmopolites include such individuals as students, artists, writers, musicians, actors and various members of the professional cadres. They live in the inner city because they want to be near the specialized cultural facilities and excitement which can only be found in the city centre. Many are unmarried or childless. Others attempt to rear children in the city, preferably with the aid of servants, substituting the urban park for the suburban house and garden and the crèche for the neighbourhood baby-sitter. Because their way of life is unconventional a move to the suburbs is likely to be fraught with difficulty and, if attempted, is likely to be a transient affair.

The cosmopolite is urban to the core; the unmarried or childless tends to be an urban bird of passage, enjoying the benefits of urban life in the brief span between leaving the parental home and founding a new family. Typically the unmarried and childless are young white-collar workers, living within easy access not only of the entertainment facilities of the inner city, but also within easy access of their workplaces. Their sojourn in a rented apartment provides an escape from parental supervision. When they marry or, more particularly, when the marriage produces a child, they are likely to return to the suburbs. The unmarried or childless are not only the young, although these may be the majority. Others of similar characteristics may include the solo parent – separated, divorced, or unmarried – and the single person – again, separated, divorced, or unmarried. The length of their stay in the inner city, like that of the young unmarrieds or childless, depends on the permanency of their present status.

The cosmopolites and the unmarried or childless are in the inner city by choice. It is the only part of the community in which they can practise their preferred life style. The deprived and the trapped, on the other hand, live in the inner city more from necessity than by choice.

The deprived constitute the very poor, the emotionally disturbed or otherwise handicapped, the less competent or wealthy solo parents and single persons and the unstable transients. In America the majority are non-White. In Australia the deprived include many and probably the majority of the urban Aborigines. Depending on the degree of transiency they exhibit, the deprived may live in the midst of a relatively well-integrated culture of poverty,[1] or in one of confusion and anomie. The rooming-house dwellers, and to an even-greater extent the meths drinkers sleeping out in the inner-city parks, illustrate the more disintegrated category. Not all may live in such conditions through necessity: the anonymity of the rooming-

[1] E.g. O. Lewis, 'The culture of poverty', *Sci. Amer.* 215 (1966), 19–25; Young and Willmott, *Family and Kinship in East London*.

house environment may be highly attractive to anyone who wants to escape, to become invisible. Thus, amongst the unemployed, one may also find the occupants of illegitimate statuses. Most of the deprived, however, live where they do because the dilapidated houses and blighted neighbourhoods of the inner city are the only niches they can find.[1]

The final category of inner-city residents, the trapped, are the victims of change. They constitute a relic, the remnants of former occupants who have been succeeded by incompatible populations or land uses. For one reason or another – lack of money, sentimental attachment to the old home, lack of opportunity – they have stayed put while their erstwhile neighbours have fled. Frequently they are old and generally they are bewildered. In both Brisbane and Auckland the trapped are to be found interspersed with migrants in the narrow streets occupying the valley floors of the inner-city area. All around them is change.

It is clear that the style of life preferred by, or required of, each of Gans's inner-city social types has considerable implications for their location and thus for residential differentiation. For the cosmopolites and the unmarried the city centre acts as a magnet. Their way of life demands easy access to the entertainment and occupational facilities of the city centre and a loosening of the kinship ties of the family-centred suburb. They provide the forerunners of Burgess's emancipated families.[2] Urbanism is their preferred life-style. The living arrangements of the inner city, the predominance of flats, hotels, and rooming-houses, dwellings which are rented rather than owned, are 'conducive to a maximum of personal freedom from social controls and a minimum of responsibilities or physical possessions tying the individual to the home or neighbourhood'.[3] According to Freedman, the freedom which the inner city allows from customary familistic controls and the mobility which this fosters provide an ideal habitat for 'the ideal-typical urban person'.[4] Urbanism as a way of life is essentially the preferred life-style of the inner city dweller. Not surprisingly, the areas in which the mobile locate are said to be 'the most distinctly urban areas of the city. Areas with the living arrangements found in the [mobile] zone have usually been described as the locus of the secular social relations, the anonymity, and the relative freedom from group restraint typically associated with urban

---

[1] According to McKenzie the slum is the 'area of minimum choice. It is the product of compulsion rather than design. The slum, therefore, represents a homogeneous collection as far as economic competency is concerned, but a most heterogeneous aggregation in all other respects. Being an area of minimum choice, the slum serves as the reservoir for the economic wastes of the city. It also becomes the hiding-place for many services which are forbidden by the mores but which cater to the wishes of residents scattered throughout the community.' McKenzie, 'The scope of human ecology', *Pubs. Am. Sociol. Soc.* 20 (1926), 141–54; reprinted in Theodorson (1961). The quotation is from the latter source, pp. 35–6.
[2] E. W. Burgess and H. J. Locke, *The Family* (New York, 1953).
[3] R. Freedman, 'Cityward migration, urban ecology, and social theory', in E. W. Burgess and D. Bogue (eds), *Contributions to Urban Sociology* (Chicago, 1964), p. 188.
[4] *Ibid.* p. 186.

life'.[1] The fact that such areas are segregated around the fringes of the inner city and in certain resort areas enables mobility or urbanism to emerge as a distinct axis of residential differentiation. The connexion between mobility and personal disorganization, whether resulting from the attraction of the mobile areas for the 'professional' deviant or from the disorienting effects of anonymity, suggests further that the mobility dimension of residential differentiation may prove to be closely associated with certain aspects of deviant behaviour. According to Freedman, both 'the sophistication and the disorganization which are said to typify different areas of urban life may be related to mobility and its ensuing freedom'.[2]

The separation of familistic and urban ways of life

Familism and urbanism exist as virtually incompatible life-styles. The attempt to combine them, whether it be by cosmopolites living in familistic suburbs or by familistically oriented households trying to bring up children in the transient inner city, is fraught with difficulties. To this extent familism and urbanism may be seen as opposite poles of the same continuum. On the other hand, the two sets of life-style preferences may be expected to differ somewhat in their external relations. Familism may be characteristic of all socio-economic status groups; urbanism may be more characteristic of those at the top and the bottom of the social rank hierarchy. The emergence of an independent mobility dimension may depend on the availability of an external source of migrants or on a considerable degree of sophistication in the population. In the absence of more detailed studies it remains the case that the nature of the relationship between familism and urbanism life-styles is problematical.

ASPIRATIONS AND RESIDENTIAL CHOICE

Aspirations and behaviour rarely coincide. This is as true of residential aspirations and behaviour as of other kinds. As Van Arsdol *et al.* observe: 'Choice . . . may not result in a moving plan nor influence subsequent behaviour when there are limited resources and locational opportunities or desired residences are lacking.'[3] The attempt by a household to bring its residential location into congruence with its residential aspirations may be frustrated by a variety of intervening considerations. Particularly important in this regard are the range of information possessed by or available to the

[1] *Ibid.* pp. 191–2.
[2] *Ibid.*
[3] Van Arsdol *et al.*, 'Retrospective and subsequent metropolitan residential mobility', p. 5.

household, the amount of money which it can devote to housing, and the range of houses and locations which are available at the relevant time.

Information

Whatever the reasons for wanting to move, the realization of a move demands an awareness of suitable and available locations. In the search for a new residence the household is guided both by its own preconceptions about the characteristics of different types of houses and different types of area and by the information which is fed to it. Both sets of material are replete with biases.

To a greater or lesser extent, each member of the urban community possesses a 'mental map' of the city's characteristics.[1] Different areas of the city are associated with different images. The images are of whole neighbourhoods or suburbs rather than of smaller localities or individual houses.[2] The combination of images and their associated cognitive and evaluative elements, provides a framework both for the input of new information and for each household's locational behaviour. Knowledge of the characteristics of urban mental maps is a vital link in the attempt to understand the residential differentiation of the urban population. As is the case with most other aspects of residential mobility, however, there is little empirical datum to hand. A belief in the potency of mental maps is implicit in all those studies which use area of residence as an index of a person's social standing, but this belief has rarely been put to the test.[3] Even less information is available on the characteristics of mental maps, for example, the dimensions used in their construction. It is therefore no more than a tentative supposition to suggest that, to the extent that differences in social rank, ethnicity, and preferred life-style provide the major axes for determining residential desirability, so also they may be expected to provide the major dimensions of the mental maps which the population constructs for the city. A partial test of this hypothesis is provided in some data concerned with the connotations of suburban place-names to a sample of Brisbane residents.[4] The technique used in the collection of the data is based on that outlined by Ross in his study of the status-ascriptive functions of suburbs in Boston.[5]

The salience of social rank, ethnicity, and style-of-life considerations in

[1] The concept of 'mental maps' is introduced in P. R. Gould 'On Mental Maps' (mimeo. Michigan Inter-University Community of Mathematical Geographers, 1966). See also K. R. Lynch, *The Image of the City* (Cambridge, Mass., 1960).
[2] See Brown and Moore, 'Intra-urban migration'; Wolpert, 'Behavioural aspects; Lynch, *Image of the City*.
[3] Cf. Ross, 'The local community', pp. 75–84.
[4] Sample size is 301. Respondents were selected according to a two-stage cluster sampling technique.
[5] Ross, 'The local community'.

the connotations of suburban place-names is illustrated by the data in Table 3.4. The three suburbs named are of very distinct characteristics. Hamilton is amongst the highest scorers on the social rank dimension in Brisbane and has long been a home of what may be termed the 'Queensland establishment'. Its population is almost entirely Australian-born. The suburb scores relatively lowly on the familism dimension. Many of its inhabitants are elderly although there has been a recent tendency for a younger age-group to move in as the construction of high-price apartment blocks has proceeded. Mt Gravatt is an outlying and rapidly growing suburb on one of the main roads to the Queensland Gold Coast. Its population is of middling social rank, almost wholly Australian, and predominantly composed of young families. South Brisbane is a polar opposite to Mt Gravatt. It is situated immediately to the south of the central business district, is rapidly losing population, consists of obsolescent buildings, many of which are now rooming-houses, and contains a very heterogeneous mixture of migrants, including many Aborigines. Collectors' districts falling within the area have the lowest social rank scores of Brisbane.

TABLE 3.4 *Percentage of those demonstrating knowledge of area who mention social rank, ethnicity, and family or environmental characteristics*

Area	Social rank	No. mention	Ethnicity	No. mention	Family type or environment	No. mention	N
Hamilton	65	35	–	100	58	42	266
Mt Gravatt	22	78	1	99	87	13	270
South Brisbane	25	75	22	78	83	17	270

Table 3.4 is based on a very open-ended question. Respondents were simply asked to comment on the suburb as they saw it, paying particular attention to any features which made it different from other parts of Brisbane.[1] In each case the great majority of respondents were prepared to make comments. The proportion reporting no knowledge of the area, or saying that they know of nothing which makes it distinct, ranges from 12 per cent in the case of Hamilton to 10 per cent in that of Mt Gravatt and South Brisbane. Social-rank considerations are mentioned with respect to each suburb, but are especially salient in the case of Hamilton. Ethnicity is only important in the case of South Brisbane. The family type or environmental set of responses, which includes a wide range of answers pertaining to such properties as the attractiveness of the area in aesthetic terms, the age and density

[1] The question posed was: 'How about [suburb] as you see it. What kind of a place is it? What makes it different from other suburbs?'

of development, location, house types and demographic characteristics, is especially salient in the cases of Mt Gravatt and South Brisbane.

Hamilton is widely regarded as a 'beautiful, river-side suburb' which serves the 'elite of Brisbane'. Ninety-eight per cent of those respondents who characterize the suburb in social rank terms think of it in terms of high rank, employing such labels as the 'blue-ribbon area', 'upper class', 'the home of the establishment', the 'elite', the 'upper bracket', the 'fashionable', or the 'highest class' in Brisbane. Slightly less favourable comments, along similar lines, are that it is a 'flash place', a 'snob area', and the home of 'socialites'. Some suggestion is made that the recent invasion of multi-unit apartment blocks may be leading to a down-grading of prestige, but it is also pointed out that the cost of these units is 'out of reach of the average man'. Characterizations of Hamilton in the family and physical environment category stress its location, its view, the new flats and old mansions, and the stability of its population. Amongst the few negative remarks are comments about the river smog and the problems of noise associated with the area's proximity to both the docks and the airport of Brisbane.

If Hamilton is seen primarily in terms of social rank, Mt Gravatt is seen primarily in terms of the recency of its development and of its attractions for young families. The suburb has a mixed middle-class/working-class image. Two-thirds of the respondents who characterize Mt Gravatt in social rank terms use middle-class labels, one-third see it as the home of working-class families. Great stress is laid on the rapidity of the area's growth and many respondents see it as the 'up-and-coming' suburb. Its attractiveness for family living is said to lie in its 'spaciousness', 'rural atmosphere' and good facilities. The peripheral location of the suburb also comes in for a good deal of comment.

Both Mt Gravatt and Hamilton are the objects of generally favourable – often envious – comments; South Brisbane, on the other hand, is the object of almost universal vilification. A common sentiment is that it is a 'shocking place which needs demolishing'. The term 'slum' is used by 45 per cent of respondents. The inhabitants of the area are said to be the 'lowest of the low', the 'disreputable', and the 'down-and-outs'. Considerable stress is laid on the ethnic characteristics of the population and especially on the presence of Aborigines. To one respondent, 'darkies run the show', to another, South Brisbane is a 'mongrel place'. The dirtiness of the area and the roughness of its population are said to make it quite unsuitable for 'bringing up a decent family'. Instead, its inhabitants are said to be the old, the unattached, the drunks, and various migrant groups.

The responses elicited by the names of Hamilton, Mt Gravatt and South Brisbane suggest that the various dimensions of suburban evaluation differ in their salience according to the characteristics of the area concerned. The more extreme an area is in terms of one of the dimensions, the greater the weight that dimension tends to be given in the total configuration of cognitions about the area. Thus Hamilton is seen in terms of social rank, Mt Gravatt in terms of its suitability for family living, and South Brisbane in terms of its ethnicity and its disreputability. Not only may these connotations be used in assessing the desirability of locating in the named area, but, as Ross points out: 'It follows that these names are available for use in social interaction between non-intimates in defining their respective statuses.'[1]

Further evidence of the sensitivity of respondents to differences in the characteristics of areas is provided by Table 3.5. In this case the responses are generated by a forced-choice question in which respondents have to nominate which category is most representative of the area concerned under each of three headings, dealing respectively with social rank, ethnicity, and family type. The stimulus areas vary widely in characteristics along each dimension. St Lucia vies with Hamilton for the highest social rank scores in Brisbane and contains a predominance of professional and managerial workers, including a major fraction of the university faculty. A fairly wide range of age groups is represented and the suburb's collectors' districts cluster near the middle of the familism dimension in the factorial ecology of Brisbane. Ethnically, the population is overwhelmingly of British stock. Aspley is a peripheral and rapidly growing suburb designed to attract the young white-collar worker and his family. The population contains a majority of non-manual workers, especially of the sales category. There is also a sprinkling of higher rank occupational categories in one part of the suburb. Very few of the suburb's inhabitants are aged over 50 years and the fertility rate is high. As in the case of St Lucia, a few ethnic groups are represented. In contrast with Aspley and St Lucia, the three remaining stimulus areas contain major concentrations of migrants. New Farm is the centre of the Italian community of Brisbane, while West End serves a similar function for the city's Greek and Russian minorities. Inala is a peripheral housing commission area with a very heterogeneous population in terms of ethnicity, but a very homogeneous population in terms of social rank. Occupations above the skilled manual level in rank are virtually absent from the Inala collectors' districts. West End, and more particularly, New Farm, have a more heterogeneous population in social rank terms. Both areas were high rank suburbs at the end of the nineteenth century and have recently been the locale for the construction of high price and high rise apartment blocks, taking advantage of the favoured topographic features of each area. The distribution of family types in West End and New Farm also departs considerably from the young family pattern characteristic of Inala. In both suburbs a wide range of family types is present ranging from major concentration of the elderly to many young unmarrieds. The fertility rates in each suburb are low. By contrast Inala has the highest fertility rate in the city.

[1] Ross, 'The local community', p. 81.

TABLE 3.5 *Characterization of areas in terms of social rank, ethnicity, and familism variables*

Area	Social rank				Ethnicity			Family type				N
	uc	mc	wc/lc	?	Aus	for	?	old	ma	yng	?	
St Lucia	72	26	2	–	89	5	5	14	48	35	3	300
Aspley	28	56	14	2	89	6	5	3	5	91	2	296
New Farm	6	48	46	1	37	58	5	24	34	40	2	296
West End	1	14	84	1	15	80	5	12	33	50	5	260
Inala	1	5	94	–	29	67	4	–	1	97	2	284

Few respondents deny knowledge of the areas. The proportion of non-responses ranges between 14 per cent in the case of West End and less than 1 per cent in the case of St Lucia. On the whole the pattern of responses provides a close parallel with the existing population characteristics of the five suburbs. St Lucia is seen as being predominantly upper class, almost wholly Australian, and consisting of middle-aged families with grown up children and younger families with children of school age. Aspley is seen as largely middle class, predominantly Australian, and overwhelmingly composed of young families. The emphasis on young families is an exaggerated reflection of the actual composition of the population. New Farm elicits a much higher degree of dissensus. Respondents are almost evenly divided in their characterization of the suburb's population as working class or middle class. Similar confusion exists in the ethnic and family type categories. A majority associate New Farm with European migrants, primarily Italian, but a substantial minority associate the suburb with Australians. A wide range of family types is mentioned. Although evidence is lacking on the point, it may be that the dissensus in connexion with New Farm reflects differences in the characteristics of different parts of the suburb and in an associated geographic selectivity on the part of the respondents. While the 'inner' portion of the suburb is associated with an essentially working class, migrant population, the riverside portion is associated with a middle class, apartment dwelling, Australian population. West End and Inala are characterized in a much more consistent manner than is New Farm. West End is seen as being working class, migrant, and as containing young and middle-aged families. Inala is working class and low class, migrant and overwhelmingly composed of young families.

The polarization tendencies in human thoughts are associated with a stereotyping process. As it affects the construction of mental maps this is reflected in an exaggerated differentiation of the characteristics of different areas. Not only may this provide a clearly-marked map for the evaluation of different residential locations but, over time, it may act in the manner of a self-fulfilling prophecy. The attraction and repulsion of settlers in terms of existing stereotypes may be expected to bring into being the differentiation of populations which provides the content of the stereotype. Initial minor differences, subjected to selective perception, exaggeration, and evaluation, may eventually be transformed into major differences.

New information about the city is structured by that pre-existing. In the search for a new location not only is the household likely to concentrate its activities in those areas of which it was previously aware but, also, it is likely to avail itself of new information about vacancies in a highly selective fashion. Since the sources of such information are themselves associated with various biases the possibilities for selective perception and selective action are legion.

The main sources of information about residential vacancies appear to be personal contacts, the mass media, and estate agents. In his study of residential mobility in Philadelphia, Rossi provides data on the percentage of his respondents using each source: 63 per cent of the movers obtained information about vacancies from newspapers, 62 per cent obtained the information through personal contacts, 52 per cent obtained it as the result of walking or riding around, 50 per cent used real estate agents and 31 per cent obtained the information through 'windfall'.[1] The sources differ widely in their effectiveness as measured by actual movements. Thus whereas the use of personal contacts and windfall is associated with 'indexes of effectiveness' of 0·71 and 0·81, respectively, that of walking or riding around, newspapers and estate agents is associated with index values of less than 0·33. Nearly half of all moves eventuate as the result of personal contacts although they may also involve other sources of information. A further quarter are the result of 'windfalls'.

Each source of information is saturated with locational, rank and ethnic variables. Personal contacts tend to be confined to peers and information about vacancies which is passed on by informal channels therefore tends to be confined to specific strata of the social hierarchy. Similar remarks apply in the case of ethnic groups. As Hagerstrand has demonstrated, the transmission of information via personal contacts tends to amplify existing residential differentials.[2] In selecting a new residential location the potential mover is influenced to a considerable extent by the information provided by earlier movers who belong to his social categories. To the extent that the initial migrants find the new location congruent with their residential aspirations their satisfaction is likely to be reflected in an increasing flow of positive evaluations through their personal contact systems. As a result more and more of their peers are likely to become aware of the advantages of

[1] Rossi, *Why Families Move*, p. 161.
[2] T. Hagerstrand, 'Migration and area', in D. Hannerberg *et al.* (eds), *Migration in Sweden* (Lund, 1957), pp. 25–158; T. Hagerstrand 'A Monte Carlo approach to diffusion', *Arch. Europ. Sociol.* 6 (1965), 43–67.

the new area and to choose their residential locations accordingly. The effect is perhaps most apparent when the populations concerned are marked by highly-visible ethnic differences, as in the case of the chain migration of Southern European migrants to Australian cities, but as the result of the general relationship between social stratification and the desirability and opportunity of personal association it also applies to any situation in which the populations concerned are socially unequal. The biased nature of the information flow may set up a positive feed-back system in which what may initially have been almost chance differences in the characteristics of different areas eventually become highly systematic.

Both newspapers and the other media of mass communication contain their own built-in selectivities and are the object of biased sampling by those exposed to their influence. Newspapers and magazines tend to be directed at particular categories of readers, categories differentiated in terms of age structure, social rank, ethnicity and various other criteria. Vacancies advertised in one newspaper rather than another will come to the attention of only a limited segment of the population. Television advertising tends to be confined to the larger, more glamorous developments rather than dealing with the broad range of vacancies and much the same comment applies to commercial radio advertisements. Within the range of information presented by each medium it is probable that the potential mover samples according to his pre-existing mental map of the city, a map which reflects the personal knowledge he has gained through moving about the city, through personal contacts, and through previous exposure to the information put out by the mass media.

Real estate agents provide yet another source of selectivity in the dissemination and structuring of information about residential vacancies. Both branches and individual representatives of estate agents tend to specialize in particular ranges of both houses and clients. Frequently they have strong locality connexions. The combination of factors gives them a strong influence in shaping the emerging pattern of differentiation. In Brisbane, several local estate agents are run by and for members of particular immigrant groups, in some cases using overseas languages in their advertisements. The income and status connexions of particular agencies are a more general feature. The influence of a plethora of secondary considerations on the activities of real estate agents has been stressed by Taeuber and Taeuber.[1] In their study of the process of Negro segregation they point out that

the person selling or renting dwelling space is usually an agent, whose business behaviour depends not only on his personality, but also on his training, on his informal contacts with other sales agents, and on the advice and support of a series of more formal organizations, including realty boards, neighbourhood

[1] Taeuber and Taeuber, *Negroes in Cities*, p. 19.

117

improvement associations, banks, mortgagors, other financial institutions, and legal and regulatory agencies.[1]

Many of the formal and informal codes defining good business practice, for example maintenance of the 'character' of neighbourhoods and the avoidance of tenants or purchasers who might lower the sales or rental values of property, have a direct effect on the patterning of residential differentiation.

The interaction between individuals' mental maps of the city and the flow of information about residential vacancies is of such a nature as to amplify or maintain existing differentials between various residential areas. In the process of differentiation areas are likely to take on the characteristics which the population attributes to them. The differential evaluation of the residential fabric in terms of suitability for meeting the social rank, ethnic, and style of life preferences of the household provides a framework for the structuring of both old and new inputs of information concerning the characteristics of areas and the existence of vacancies. The eventual choice of residential location occurs in terms of what is thought to be the urban environment by those involved in the decision rather than in terms of any 'objective' characterization of its parts.

The economic factor

However great the desire to move to a more favoured location and however much information the household has at its disposal concerning the existence of suitable vacancies, the realization of movement reflects the availability of the necessary economic resources.

Costs are associated not only with the price or the rental of house and land, but also with their location relative to work and service places and to other locations which it is desired to visit. The time and the cost of travel may be such as to rule out what would otherwise be a highly desirable residential location. Where the time and the cost of travel exceed the savings that may inhere in the price or rent of a residence the selection process may be switched to a location which possesses perhaps a higher initial cost, but is more conveniently located. The relationship between accessibility, costs, and location is close, although its exact nature may be considerably affected by changes in transportation techniques. Alonso has suggested that the relative values of accessibility and of space are themselves functions of the ability of families to command the supply of goods and services.[2] Thus the rich may be more concerned with space than with accessibility because they can more effectively than others fill space with material goods and because they can

[1] *Ibid.* [2] Alonso, *Location and Land Use.*

command transport facilities that reduce the need for high accessibility. The rich, therefore, may be expected to pay more for space and less for accessibility than other categories of the population. In this way a gradient may be expected to eventuate, with distance from the city centre, the point of maximum accessibility, being positively correlated with wealth. Empirical tests of the gradient prediction have yielded only a moderate amount of supporting data. A similar comment may be applied to several other studies which have been concerned with the relationship between the desirability of location and various accessibility factors. Thus, Marble tests a series of hypotheses concerning the relationship of residential desirability and accessibility to the central business district, subsidiary shopping centres, and workplaces with generally negative results.[1] The crucial factor appears to be the efficiency of transport techniques. In an era when most workers had to walk to work and when the money and time available for travel was severely limited, the worker had little choice where to live. The railway towns of nineteenth-century England with their rows of workers' houses clustering around the local workshops provided little scope to all but the favoured few for the exercise of any criteria which stressed spaciousness. The situation in the modern city is very different. To those with children the advantages of spaciousness suggest a move to the suburbs. To those desiring to be near their places of work and other urban amenities alternative locations are suggested. In the same way that the events of the agricultural and industrial revolutions have enabled the population to escape or at least greatly widen the old Malthusian limits, so the events of the transportation revolution have greatly increased the range of alternative locations open to the individual and have enabled other criteria of evaluation than that of accessibility to come to the fore.[2]

The significance of housing and transport costs may be expected to decline with increasing family income. The rich can afford to locate in any area which pleases them, but the poor have little choice. It is in this sense that McKenzie describes the slum as being the area of minimum choice. It is the product of compulsion rather than design.[3] The salience of economic considerations at higher levels of the stratification system, however, should not be exaggerated. Within any specified price range there is generally a variety of available locations. For those families above some absolute minimum income there is also a range of possible decisions concerning the proportion of income to be spent on residential location. Thus Duncan and Duncan and Tilly have been able to show that clerical workers may differentiate themselves from the residential pattern of skilled manual workers by

---

[1] D. F. Marble, 'Transport inputs at urban residential sites', *Papers Reg. Sci. Ass.* 5 (1959), 253–66. Cf. D. S. Knos, 'The distribution of land values in Topeka, Kansas', in B. J. L. Berry and D. F. Marble (eds), *Spatial Analysis* (Englewood Cliffs, N. J., 1968), pp. 269–89.

[2] Hoover and Vernon, *Anatomy of a Metropolis.*

[3] McKenzie, 'The scope of human ecology'.

devoting a considerably higher proportion of their total income to housing. The high rent-income ratios which they exhibit are interpreted by the Duncans as suggesting that a 'preference for similar prestige in neighbours must accompany economic considerations in residential location'.[1] Tilly finds 'Skilled workers, on the average, have higher incomes, less education, and lower dwelling ratings than the clerical-sales group. This contradicts . . . the common assumption that income is the principal determinant of grade of residence.'[2] Social rank or style of life aspirations can apparently override many straight economic considerations.

In general it appears that economic factors are brought into play at a secondary stage of the evaluation process. They serve to discriminate between desirable locations rather than as serving as primary axes of choice. As Hawley mentions, 'If a family can pay the costs, then it may exercise any conceivable motive'.[3] If it cannot pay, then it must switch its attention to a lower price range and attempt to satisfy its desires from within this latter set of vacancies.

STRUCTURE OF THE RESIDENTIAL SYSTEM

Neither the construction of mental maps of the city nor residential differentiation occur against an undifferentiated background. Both perception and changes in location occur within a framework which is already structured. Previous evaluations of residential desirability are enshrined not only in the traditions of the city, but also in its physical plant. With the development of large-scale building organizations whole areas of the city may be blanketed by buildings specifically designed to attract particular segments of the population. The effect is the same whether the developer be a nineteenth-century factory owner, erecting cheap terraced housing for his employees adjacent to their workplace, a speculative development company, erecting a 'country club estate', or a local authority or state housing commission, erecting for those on a housing list. Even new individual developments reflect previous cultural evaluations, as Jones has shown in his discussion of the development of high status suburbs in Belfast: 'The crux of the matter . . . lies in the values already attached to the land into which expansion is taking place . . . Social values are attached not only to different urban sectors, but to tracts beyond the town limits.'[4]

Inertia factors in the evaluation and flow of information, in the provision of finance, and in the development of symbolic identification produce a remarkable stability in the urban residential system. Such changes as do

[1] Duncan and Duncan, 'Residential distribution and occupational stratification', p. 502.
[2] Tilly, 'Occupational rank', p. 328. [3] Hawley, *Human Ecology*, p. 286.
[4] Jones, *Social Geography of Belfast*, p. 278.

occur appear to result mainly from technological obsolescence or from negative reactions to invading land uses and populations. The flight of the high status inhabitants of the old town houses around city centres in the face of the invasion of low status, and especially immigrant populations, is perhaps the most extreme example of rapid change in residential characteristics. More generally it appears that the combination of individual decisions about location, the flow of information about vacancies, and the existing pattern of residential characteristics, gives rise to a system of residential differentiation which is both ordered and stable. The effects of planning rarely upset this stability. On the whole planners are drawn from and work for the more powerful and more prestigious elements of society. To some extent at least, the results of their work may be seen as a conservation and possibly even an amplification of existing residential differentials. As Gans has observed 'Although city planning has been concerned principally with improving the physical environment, it has also been planning for certain people, although only indirectly and implicitly. These people were the planner himself, his political supporters, and the upper middle class citizen in general.'[1] Enshrined in the physical plan is the planner's own ideology and his interpretation of the suitable type of environment for the given type of person. Although residential differentiation in terms of social rank, family type and ethnicity is not an inevitable result of city planning, the evidence suggests that it is at least a common occurrence.

RESIDENTIAL DIFFERENTIATION AND SOCIAL DIFFERENTIATION

Residential differentiation parallels social differentiation. The differential evaluation given to the perceived differences between individuals and groups of individuals forms the basis for much of the decision-making involved in residential location. The decision to locate in a particular neighbourhood is one of the more important which a household takes and has implications for a wide range of behaviours and sentiments. At the household level the decision may be seen as a function of a series of individual evaluations, of information flows, and of the presence or absence of suitable vacancies at the right price. At the structural level the pattern of decisions may be seen as a function of previous evaluations, of the policies followed by a wide range of political, financial and planning agencies, and of the general state of technology. In turn, each parameter reflects the specifics of place and time. The importance of social rank, ethnicity and preferred life-style in the organization of the Western city may be but a passing phase.

No difference is an inevitable basis for the residential differentiation of populations although some clusters of differences, such as those involved

1 Gans, 'Planning for people, not buildings', p. 36.

in the concept of social rank, may provide an all-but-universal axis of differentiation. It is only when a perceived difference becomes the object of differential evaluation and thus determines life chances and the desirability of interaction and identification with its possessors, that it may become a significant basis of residential differentiation. Even then its appearance as an axis of differentiation will reflect the organization of the housing market – a difference which is not recognized in the supply of houses and locations will not become an axis of ecological differentiation.

The residential movement of individuals and groups is highly systematic. As a result of the existing structure of the residential system and of the positive feed-back induced by the patterns of information flow, residential mobility is channelled in particular directions. The principal spatial effect of the complex of individual aspirations, mental maps, capabilities and decisions, information flows, the structure of the market and the activities of a wide range of housing, financial and planning institutions, is to sift and sort the population into distinct residential clusters, organized in terms of the basic social differentia considered important at the time and place concerned. The attractions and repulsions between population groups and the differences in their preferred ways of life are translated into the residential fabric of the community. The study of residential differentiation may thus be seen as but a special case of the more general study of social differentiation. At the micro-social level the understanding of residential differentiation involves the analysis of the ways in which the locational behaviour of individuals and groups is affected by the social differences extant in the community. At the macro-social level, which forms the substance of the next chapter, attention switches to the relationship between residential and social differentiation as this is affected by more general socio-cultural phenomena in the encompassing society.

CHAPTER 4

RESIDENTIAL DIFFERENTIATION AND SOCIAL CHANGE

It is characteristic of much work in urban ecology that while the fact of urban expansion is taken for granted, little attention is paid to other aspects of social or cultural change taking place in the wider society. All too frequently the urban community is taken as a phenomenon *sui generis* and considered in isolation. The hallmark of the macro-social approach to the study of residential differentiation within the city is that it attempts a rapprochement between urban ecology and the wider study of socio-cultural change. In the process an attempt is made to relate the bases of residential differentiation to the process of modernization.

Classical human ecology is a product of early twentieth-century Chicago. It is perhaps more than coincidental that the initial stimulus to the macro-social approach to urban phenomena is a product of the burgeoning mid-twentieth-century cities of the American West Coast, cities which have frequently been hailed as the harbingers of the 'new urbanization'. There is an implicit assumption in much of the work produced under the aegis of classical human ecology that in some way the Chicago of the 1920s represents the typical case of the urban community. The experiences of the new communities of the West Coast and the growth of a comparative perspective in the social sciences, a development greatly speeded by the Second World War, have undermined the simplistic assumption that any single city can be typical of urban society and have caused a more searching inquiry to be made of the socio-cultural matrix in which urban communities are embedded. The unconscious ethnocentrism of an earlier age has given way to a conscious attempt to relate the form of the urban community to the characteristics of the society in which it has developed. From this perspective the patterns of residential differentiation to be found in a given city are not to be explained in terms of specifically urban processes but, rather, must be related to a wider-ranging set of forces characteristic of the society as a whole. It is not sufficient merely to state that social rank, familism, ethnicity and urbanism form the criteria in terms of which people assess the attractiveness of residential locations; one must also show the relationship between each of these sets of characteristics and the changing nature of the encompassing society. The most concerted and influential attempt to argue along these lines is that developed by Shevky and his colleagues in connexion with the technique known as 'social area analysis'.

SOCIAL AREA ANALYSIS

The operational techniques and theoretical rationale of what has come to be known as social area analysis are presented in a series of papers and monographs published over a period of some twenty years.[1] Right from the beginning – the Shevky and Williams monograph on Los Angeles, published in 1949 – the method has been surrounded by a lively controversy. Criticisms have been directed at both the theoretical and operational aspects of the scheme. Equally impassioned defences have been produced. Modifications to the initial model, made at least partly in response to earlier criticisms, have considerably altered its scope and have made it more congruent with contemporary theories of social change and development. Like most other bodies of theory in the social sciences, social area analysis is an evolving phenomenon.

The first presentation of the social area technique is almost wholly descriptive in function: 'The study is chiefly concerned with the description and measurement of social differentiation associated with the urban phenomenon of Los Angeles.'[2] On the basis of census tract data an eighteen-celled typology is developed, each cell, or *social area*, consisting of those census tracts which exhibit a similar profile across three indexes. The indexes, termed *social rank*, *urbanization* and *segregation*, are said to be based on 'certain objective criteria or urbanization and stratification in modern society'. As critics were quick to point out, however, the referents of these criteria were by no means clear and the significance of the three indexes was left unexplained.[3] The analysis presented by Shevky and Williams is a case-study in the application of an interesting and useful but, to all appearances, theoretically-isolated technique. The theoretical rationale for social area analysis is not presented until the results of a San Francisco study are published six years later.[4] Although the authors of the San Francisco study are at pains to stress that their presentation of the theoretical rationale of social area analysis represents only a summary of that originally developed for the Los Angeles project, the lateness of the attempt has, perhaps inevitably, given rise to the suspicion that the theoretical model developed by Shevky and Bell may be little more than an *ex post facto* attempt at justifying the earlier *ad hoc* selection of indicants and properties.

[1] Shevky and Williams, *Social Areas of Los Angeles*; E. Shevky and W. Bell, *Social Area Analysis* (Stanford, 1955); D. C. McElrath, 'Urban differentiation', *Law Contemp. Probs*, 3 (1965), 103–10; W. Bell, 'Urban neighbourhoods and individual behaviour', in M. Sherif and C. W. Sherif (eds), *Problems of Youth* (Chicago, 1965), pp. 235–64; D. C. McElrath, 'Societal scale and social differentiation', in S. Greer *et al.* (eds), *The New Urbanization* (New York, 1968), pp. 33–52.
[2] Shevky and Williams, *Social Areas of Los Angeles*, p. 33.
[3] E.g. E. G. Erickson, 'Review of "The Social Areas of Los Angeles"', *Am. Sociol. Rev.* 14 (1949), 699. See also the 'Comments' by E. Greenwood and C. F. Schmid, *Am. Sociol. Rev.* 15 (1950), 108–10, and Erickson's 'Rejoinder', *Am. Sociol. Rev.* 15 (1950), 296.
[4] Shevky and Bell, *Social Area Analysis*.

Be that as it may, it is apparent that the model presented by Shevky and Bell represents a significant breakthrough in the effort to relate urban ecology to the more general study of society.

THE THEORY OF SOCIAL AREA ANALYSIS

The operational techniques used by Shevky and Williams and revised by Shevky and Bell are presented as the logical complements of a general model of social change and of the place of the large city in society. Eschewing the dangers 'of becoming bounded by the particularities of the urban frame taken in isolation',[1] Shevky and Bell assert that 'We conceive of the city as a product of the complex whole of modern society; thus the social forms of urban life are to be understood within the context of the changing character of the longer containing society.'[2]

The key construct in the Shevky–Bell theory is that of societal *scale*. According to the originators of the term, Wilson and Wilson, 'by the scale of a society [is meant] the number of people in relation and the intensity of these relations'.[3] Differences in scale are postulated as being the fundamental distinction between traditional primitive societies and modern civilized ones. As society changes in scale, from small to large, so there are a series of concomitant changes in the patterns of functional differentiation, in the complexity of organization and in the range and intensity of its relations. Taking the United States as an example, Shevky and Bell assert that

If we conceive of scale as the scope of social interaction and dependency, the past century has witnessed a vast increase in the scale of American society. Not only has the total national population become more interdependent, with a resulting increase in the scope of interaction – but American society has relations with most of the people of this earth. At the same time, the intensity of dependence on, and interaction with the immediate social environment has tended to diminish: 'national conciousness', in general, becomes more important, 'neighbourhood conciousness' less so. Such an increase in scale must, of necessity, encompass many local variationse – conomic, ethnic, regional, and the like.[4]

The results of increasing scale are identified with Wirth's propositions about urbanism as a way of life. A summary of Wirth's arguments (Table 4.1) is used to illustrate the characteristic features of large scale societies as compared with small scale societies.

Shevky and Bell argue that, although Wirth is correct in his description of the essential characteristics of modern society as distinguished from traditional agrarian societies, he is in error in assuming that the prime causal

[1] *Ibid.* p. 3.   [2] *Ibid.*
[3] G. Wilson and M. Wilson, *The Analysis of Social Change* (Cambridge, 1945), p. 25.
[4] Shevky and Bell, *Social Area Analysis*, p. 7.

TABLE 4.1 *Urbanism as a way of life in relation to the size, density, and heterogeneity of the urban population*

Postulate	Effect
SIZE An increase in the number of inhabitants of a settlement beyond a certain limit brings about changes in the relations of people and changes in the character of the community	Greater the number of people interacting, greater the potential differentiation Dependence upon a greater number of people, lesser dependence on particular persons Association with more people, knowledge of a smaller proportion, and of these, less intimate knowledge More secondary rather than primary contact; that is, increase in contacts which are face to face, yet impersonal, superficial, transitory, and segmental More freedom from the personal and emotional control of intimate groups Association in a large number of groups, no individual allegiance to a single group
DENSITY Reinforces the effects of size	Tendency to differentiation and specialization Separation of residence from workplace Functional specialization of areas – segregation of functions Segregation of people: city becomes a mosaic of social worlds
HETEROGENEITY Cities products of migration of peoples of diverse origin Heterogeneity of origin matched by heterogeneity of occupations Differentiation and specialization reinforces heterogeneity	Without common background and common activities premium is placed on visual recognition: the uniform becomes symbolic of the role No common set of values, no common ethical system to sustain them; money tends to become measure of all things for which there are no common standards Formal controls as opposed to informal controls Necessity for adhering to predictable routines Clock and the traffic signal symbolic of the basis of the social order Economic basis: mass production of goods, possible only with the standardization of processes and products Standardization of goods and facilities in terms of the average Adjustment of educational, recreational, and cultural services to mass requirements In politics success of mass appeals – growth of mass movements

SOURCE. Shevky and Bell, *Social Area Analysis*, pp. 7–8.

factors in the development of the modern way of life are the size, density and heterogeneity of the urban aggregation:

it is not the city which is an underlying 'prime mover' in the recent transformation of Western society, but the necessities of economic expansion. Size, density and heterogeneity, important in describing the urban gambit, are not the most significant structural aspects of urbanization – for urbanization is a state of a total society, as well as of its cities.[1]

[1] *Ibid.* p. 8.

To Shevky and Bell changes in the scale of society are a function of those changes in the structure of productive activity which have accompanied the application of industrial technology. Drawing heavily on the work of Clark, Shevky and Bell contend

that the postulate of increasing scale in modern society gains in analytic utility when we are able to specify that in all technological advanced modern societies the most important concomitant of changes in productivity, and changes in economic organization with the consequent alterations of social relations, has been the movement of working populations from agriculture to manufacture, and from manufacture to commerce, communication, transport, and service.[1]

The resulting increase in scale is evidenced in a variety of trends. Changes occur in the nature of income-producing property, in the growth-curves of the population and in its age and sex characteristics, in the nature of economic enterprises and in the characteristics of the professions. Increases are recorded in the proportion of the population living in cities, in the number of salaried and wage-earning employees, in the numbers of ancillary semi-professional workers and, more significantly, in the proportion of the workforce employed in managerial and supervisory positions within newly-emergent organs concerned with co-ordination, control and direction. Each of these trends is seen as being a reflexion of one or other of three major dimensions of social change:

Clark's generalization, thus, provides us with a set of structural indicators with which to approach the problem of increasing scale. We distinguish three broad and inter-related trends associated with three orders of organizational complexity: changes in the distribution of skills, changes in the structure of productive activity, and changes in the composition of population.[2]

In the Shevky–Bell model increasing societal scale is synonymous with the emergence of urban-industrial society. The prime mover is seen as changes in the economy, changes which are themselves the result of techno-logical innovations. To a large extent the model may be seen as one of economic determinism.[3] Little play is given to differences in value orientations, to power conflicts, or even to organizational matters, other than as these are seen as the necessary corollary of changes in the nature of productive activity. The logic of the model may be followed most easily with the aid of Table 4.2, which is based on a similar presentation in the Shevky-Bell monograph.

The basic social area model assumes that increasing societal scale is reflected in three sets of trends: changes in the distribution of skills, in the nature of productive activity and in the composition and distribution of the population. Statistics relating to these trends provide the substance of column 2 in the table. It is asserted that not only are these trends the

[1] *Ibid.* pp. 8–9.   [2] *Ibid.* p. 9.
[3] Cf. Sjoberg, 'Theory and research in urban sociology', p. 168.

TABLE 4.2 *Steps in the formation of the Shevky–Bell constructs*

Postulates concerning industrial society (aspects of increasing scale) (1)	Statistics of trends (2)	Changes in the structure of a given social system (3)	Constructs i (4)	Sample statistics (related to the constructs) (5)	Derived measures (from col. 5) (6)
Change in the range and intensity of relations →	Changing distribution of skills: lessening importance of manual productive operations – growing importance of clerical, supervisory management operations →	Changes in the arrangement of occupations based on function →	Social rank (economic status) →	Years of schooling Employment status Class of worker Major occupation group Value of home Rent by dwelling unit Persons per room Plumbing and repair Heating and refrigeration →	Occupation Schooling Rent } Index I
Differentiation of function →	Changing structure of productive activity: lessening importance of primary production – growing importance of relations centered in cities – lessening importance of the household as economic unit →	Changes in the ways of living – movement of women into urban occupations – spread of alternative family patterns →	Urbanization (family status) →	Age and sex Owner or tenant House structure Persons in household →	Fertility Women at work Single-family dwelling units } Index II
Complexity of organization →	Changing composition of population: increasing movement – alterations in age, sex distribution, increasing diversity →	Redistribution in space – changes in the proportion of supporting and dependent population – isolation and segregation of groups →	Segregation (ethnic status) →	Race and nativity Country of birth Citizenship →	Racial and national groups in relative isolation } Index III

NOTE. i Shevky's terms given first

SOURCE. Shevky and Bell, *Social Area Analysis*, p. 4.

structural reflections of increasing societal scale (column 3), but that they may 'serve as descriptive and analytic concepts for the study of modern social structure'.[1]

At particular points in time, given social systems can be conceived as standing in differential relationships to these three major trends . . . However, subpopulations in a particular society at a given point in time also can be conceived as standing in differential relationships to these three sets of structural changes . . . Thus, from certain broad postulates concerning modern society and from the analyis of temporal trends, we have selected three structural reflections of change which can be used as factors for the study of social differentiation and stratification at a particular time in modern society.[2]

Columns 4 to 6 of Table 4.2 identify each construct and suggest likely indicants for its measurement.

The first trend relates to changes in the bases of reward and rank:

As societies increase in scale, the nature of income-producing property is altered; land gives way to the enterprise, and ownership of the enterprise becomes less significant than position within a given enterprise. At the same time, the occupations within a society are regrouped: they become hierarchically organized into levels of skill, income, and prestige. Modern society, in contradistinction to traditional societies, is organized on an occupational basis. Only in the modern period has occupation come to have a determining influence upon status and rank; today, no other single characteristic tells us so much about the individual and his position in society.[3]

The Wilsons suggest that differentiation in terms of wealth, knowledge and skill may be expected to decrease as a society approaches maximum scale,[4] but Shevky and Bell assume a simple linear model with an increasing differentiation of occupations occurring as economic development proceeds. Differences in occupation are related to the technological requirements necessary to fulfil differing occupational roles, to the differences in their income-producing characteristics and to their function as the symbols of rank identification. Each of Weber's main aspects of social stratification – economic class, social status, and social power – is readily indexed by data on the occupational characteristics of the population.[5] Thus, 'Just as occupation has so much meaning in regard to individual position or rank, no single set of closely related facts tells us so much about a total society as do the statistics describing its working population'.[6] The structural reflection of the changing basis of rank allocation is the construct of *social rank*, indexed by data on occupation, education, and rent.[7]

[1] Shevky and Bell, *Social Area Analysis*, p. 3.   [2] *Ibid.*   [3] *Ibid.* p. 9.
[4] Wilson and Wilson, *Analysis of Social Change*, pp. 113–14.
[5] Cf. Lasswell, *Class and Stratum*; Bendix and Lipset (eds), *Class, Status and Power*.
[6] Shevky and Bell, *Social Area Analysis*, p. 10.
[7] For details of the index see below, pp. 134–5.

The analysis which Shevky and Bell provide of the changing grounds for the allocation of rewards and responsibilities in society is broadly consonant with general stratification theory.[1] Their analysis of the implications of changes in the structure of productive activity is more singular. Three aspects of social life are believed to be affected by the changing nature of production: the relationship between population and economy, the structure and function of kinship units, and the range of social relations which are centred on the city. Each is believed to be a reflection of the general underlying construct which Shevky terms *urbanization*.[2] The changing relationship between population and economic resources is analysed in terms of a scheme developed by Schultz.[3] Technological developments in modern society have allowed the population to escape from previous Malthusian constraints. With changes in the supply of food and with improvements in contraceptive techniques, population size becomes more a matter of individual decision than of ecological competition. 'Continual changes in the structure of production, creating new channels of social mobility, and . . . increased food . . . allow alternatives at the individual and group level, between family and occupational mobility. In a sense the individual still has the choice of breeding up to the food supply, or investing in property, career, etc.'[4] Once outside the Malthusian situation, however, the limits on the choice are vastly extended. At the same time, the development of large scale industrial production has led to a decline in the significance of the family as a unit of production and has allowed a widespread redefinition of kinship functions. Differences in family structure are no longer simply the reflections of differences in economic status, but, rather, reflect the choice between 'relatively fixed alternate forms of life.' The increasing importance of the co-ordination function as society increases in scale further extends the possibilities of choosing alternate life-styles. With the growth of the co-ordinating agencies a 'new middle class' is called into being: 'This class processes and communicates order; it provides services; it monopolizes relations with the customer.'[5] The combined effect of these changes is evidenced in a widespread variation in family types. There are especially striking changes in the role of women. Freedom from continual reproduction, stress on individualistic rather than familistic value-orientations, and the increased opportunity to work outside the home offered by the burgeoning service and clerical occupations, provide women with a much greater choice of

[1] Cf. Lasswell, *Class and Stratum*; Bendix and Lipset, *Class, Status and Power*.
[2] There is much in common between the Shevky concept and Wirth's view of urbanism as a way of life. For an alternative view developed by Bell, stressing familism, see below p. 135.
[3] T. W. Schultz, *The Econome Organization of Agriculture* (New York, 1953). The basis of Schultz's exposition is the proposition that the preference for children (familism) and the preference for property (mobility) have a specifiable substitution rate depending on a variety of value considerations.
[4] Shevky and Bell, *Social Area Analysis*, p. 11.   [5] *Ibid.* p. 13.

life-styles than is possible in less developed societies. The more urbanized the society, the less the emphasis on kinship-oriented values, the greater the occupational (and conjugal) freedom of women, and the greater the dominance of the metropolitan community in the co-ordination of economic and socio-political activities.

The third major trend associated with the increasing scale of society is concerned with changes in the composition and distribution of population:

As societies increase in scale, mobility increases. We distinguish three different concomitants of increased mobility: (1) redistribution of population in space, (2) alteration in the age and sex distribution, or changes in the proportion of supporting and dependent populations, and (3) an increasing diversity, with a resulting isolation of sub-groups which are functionally significant for the total society.[1]

The first aspect of increased mobility, the redistribution of the population in space, reflects a complex of changes involving the functional differentiation of the community, an increased sensitivity to economic differences and a willingness to move. The second aspect, changes in the age and sex composition of the population, is a result of the differential effects of the first. Selective migration in terms of age and sex results in considerable variations in the demographic characteristics of the population. The third aspect of increased mobility, the isolation of sub-groups, reflects the tendency of individuals sharing similar origins and positions to locate and migrate together. Particular significance is attached to visible 'ethnic' lables. Ethnic stratification is said to be general in American society: 'Related to time and origin of migration, it is reflected in variations in culture, life chances, and access to economic position, status, and power.'[2] At the structural level the changes in population composition and distribution are reflected in the construct of *segregation*.

In his revision of the social area model published in 1968, McElrath departs somewhat from the simplistic economic determinism which appears to underline the Shevky–Bell presentation. In particular, McElrath allows organizational considerations greater scope and uses a less restrictive concept of societal scale. Changes in the structure of society are presented as resulting from changes in '(1) the distribution of skills; (2) the organization of society; (3) the aggregation of population and (4) the distribution and redistribution of resources within the society. The first two are facets of industrialization; the latter two derive from the concentration of control and work in cities – urbanization'.[3] A tabular representation of the McElrath model is given in Table 4.3.

Industrialization and urbanization provide the mainsprings of the McElrath scheme. Each set of structural indexes is believed to be the

[1] *Ibid.* p. 14.   [2] *Ibid.*
[3] McElrath, 'Societal scale and social differentiation', p. 34.

TABLE 4.3 *Social differentiation and structural change: the McElrath model*

Master trend	Distributive changes		Dimensions of social differentiation	
	Historical changes	Indicants of change	Constructs	Sub-area indicants
Industrial-ization	Changing distribution and reward of skills	Literacy Further education Commerce workers Non-manual workers	Social rank	Occupation Education
	Changing structure of productive activity	Non-agricultural workers Industrial diversity Wage and salaried workers	Family status	Fertility Women in workforce
Urbanization	Aggregation of population	Urban concentration Metropolitan concentration	Migrant status	Distance: birthplace Selection: age-sex structure
	Increasing dispersion of resources	External relations Immigration rates	Ethnic status	Culturally visible minorities

SOURCE. Adapted from McElrath, 'Societal scale and social differentiation', p. 35.

reflection of one or other of the two master trends. Changes in industrial organization give rise to historical changes in the distribution and reward of skills and in the structure of productive activity. In turn these are reflected in the differentiation of the population in terms of *social rank* and *family status*. The social rank dimension is indexed by occupational status and by education. The increased demand for communication skills and the increased range and type of non-manual occupations result in a premium being paid for acquired skills. The acquisition of such skills opens the 'doors to partici-pational structures in the society. Differences in skill are the bases for the dimension of social rank'.[1] The emergence of the family status axis of differentiation is posited in changes in the organization of production. The increasing importance of commercial and clerical occupations, changes in the nature of employment contracts, the separation of home and workplace con-sequent on changes in the size and techniques of productive activity and the increasing real income which derives from industrialization, enable families to exercise much wider choice than previously in their way of life. Women may now participate in the workforce outside the home and the possession of children takes on new essentially non-economic values. 'Industrialization allows some families to eschew children and send the wife off to work, while others remain in the traditional, subsistence agricultural world.'[2] The choice

[1] *Ibid.*

[2] *Ibid.* p. 35.

of life-style provides the basis for the differentiating dimension of family status indexed by variables relating to fertility and the participation of women in the workforce. The concentration of population and of co-ordinating function in the large city serves to call into being two further dimensions of social differentiation: *migration status* and *ethnic status*. The growth of the urban population reflects a widespread redistribution. Since migrants to the city are generally in a disadvantaged position compared with the indigenes as far as access to the more prestigious urban social structure is concerned, the existence of large numbers of migrants in the developing city provides the basis for a differentiation of the population in terms of their migration experience. Migration status may be seen as an index of the individual's assimilation to the urban system and 'is based upon the extent to which movement from a place of origin to an urban centre represents a movement across important social boundaries'.[1] The construct is indexed by the birth place of the individual and by variations in the age and sex composition of the population. As the society becomes part of a world-wide economic, political and cultural network, so its extended relations are evidenced in a growing heterogeneity of its population. To the extent that the ethnic or nationality differences of its population are not only visible but are associated with differential access to the local opportunity structures, so they provide the basis for the differentiating dimension of ethnic status.

Urbanization and industrialization, then, yield four basic dimensions of social differentiation along which the rewards and resources of urban communities are distributed. In the [modern] city the range of opportunities available to an individual or family is subject to the multiple constraints of economic status (based on skills); family status (based on life style option); migration status (based on migration experience); and ethnic status (based on social visibility).[2]

THE OPERATIONAL CHARACTERISTICS OF SOCIAL AREA ANALYSIS

According to Shevky and Bell

the formulation of social trends in relation to current differentiating factors, including the typology based on these factors, in its present form has sufficient coherence, internal consistency and specificity for us to make these further claims for it: (*a*) it is simple in statement; (*b*) it serves as an organizing principle; (*c*) it is theory linked; it permits the derivation of testable propositions; (*d*) it is precise in its specifications; it permits observer agreement; (*e*) it represents a continuity with similar formulations which it aims to replace.[3]

The operational procedures which form the core of the technique of social area analysis are presented as the logical reflections of the scheme's theoretical

---

[1] McElrath, 'Urban differentiation', p. 104.   [2] *Ibid.* p. 105.
[3] Shevky and Bell, *Social Area Analysis*, p. 59.

model. Thus, the social area typology itself is introduced as the 'logically demonstrable reflection of those major changes which have produced modern, urban society.'[1] So strong a claim is almost unique in the social science literature.

The universe of content of social area analysis

In the 1949 Los Angeles study social area analysis is presented as a set of techniques for the analysis of certain aspects of the social structure of the large city. In the 1955 reformulation of the scheme Shevky and Bell suggest that it may be applied to a much wider set of units: 'There is no reason . . . why a typology based on the three social dimensions – social rank, urbanization, and segregation – could not be utilized, with specific measures in the indexes if necessary, for the study of cities with the city as the unit of analysis, for the study of regions, or even for the study of countries.'[2] Shevky and Bell admit, however, that 'the emerging characteristics of modern society' may best be exemplified in the large city or metropolis, an area of constant 'movement and expansion.'[3] The implications of this statement are not explored. If true, the constancy of structural effects across widely different scales is a remarkable property.

Indicants and properties

In the tabular representations of the 'steps in construct formation' (Tables 4.2 and 4.3), both Shevky and Bell and McElrath attempt to demonstrate the logical and statistical relationships which are assumed to exist between their various theoretical properties and the operational indicants of the social area scheme.

The first of the constructs identified by Shevky and Bell, *social rank*, is said to be related to a variety of census statistics concerning such phenomena as years of schooling, employment and occupational status, cost of housing, and the possession of various household facilities (see column 5 of Table 4.2). Each is said to be an evident element of the changing distribution of skills. In the Los Angeles study three indicants are used: the proportion of manual workers, the proportion reporting less than nine years of schooling and the proportion paying less than a specified monthly rent. Difficulties with the latter variable lead to its deletion from the San Francisco study and the suggestion that for future comparative use the index of social rank be calculated on the basis of occupational and educational measures alone. In a divergent note, Bell suggests that the term social rank be deleted in favour

---

[1] *Ibid.* p. 18.   [2] *Ibid.* p. 20.   [3] *Ibid.* p. 1.

of *economic status*. He points out that the indicants measuring the construct are essentially concerned with position or status in the economic organization of society rather than with differences in rank *per se*. The close correspondence between the two sets of positions, however, suggests that the distinction may be of little importance. In any case, it is clear that residential differentiation has more to do with general social rank considerations than with specific economic criteria.[1] In the ensuing discussion the social stratification dimension of social area analysis will therefore be considered in terms of social rank rather than economic status.

The disagreement between Shevky and Bell on the labelling of the second index, that of urbanization or *family status*, is of considerably greater moment than their argument over the social rank – economic status construct. The sample measures said to relate to urbanization – age and sex characteristics, type of tenancy and house structure – and, even more clearly the indicants used in the computation of the index – fertility, women in the workforce, and single-family dwellings – all refer to family-related phenomena. No measures are suggested which are directly related to the notion of the increasing importance of the city in the co-ordination of activities. While he admits this, Shevky argues that the referents of the indicants lie in various 'structural functional changes at a level transcending the immediate family interaction'.[2] The urbanization construct is said to be concerned primarily with the 'organizational structure of the economic system'. Bell, on the other hand, is more concerned with the immediate connotations of the suggested indicants. He suggests that they provide a relatively direct measure of a set of value-orientations concerned with *familism* – a preference for marriage and children rather than such alternatives as careers or consumption.[3] The more familistic a given population – the higher its fertility, the higher the proportion living in single-family dwellings and the lower the proportion of women working outside the home – the higher will be its family status. Family status is a more limited concept than is urbanization. Thus, it should not be assumed that populations high in family status are thereby necessarily low in urbanization. As Bell states: 'To say that family status increased for the Bay Region population from 1940 to 1950 . . . represents a generally accepted notion, but to say that the urban Bay Region population decreased in urbanization is difficult to conceive.'[4] The term status is frequently, if erroneously, associated with social rank evaluations. To avoid evaluative overtones Bell suggests in a later publication that the term family status be replaced by that of '*familism*'.[5] The two concepts are

---

[1] Cf. Tilly, 'Occupational rank and grade of residence in a metropolis', *Am. J. Soc.* 67 (1961), 323–9, and the discussion reported in chapter 3 above.
[2] Shevky and Bell, *Social Area Analysis*, p. 68.
[3] For a development of these views, see Bell, 'The city, the suburb, and a theory of social choice', pp. 132–68
[4] Shevky and Bell, *Social Area Analysis*, p. 68.   [5] Bell, 'Urban neighbourhoods', p. 242.

not, however, identical. Familism refers to a set of value preferences; family status refers to differences in family type. Although both concepts are concerned with differences in preferred life-style they reference different aspects of the decision-making process. Use of the one term does not, thereby, prejudice the use of the other. As long as the absence of rank considerations is noted, the term family status seems to have much to recommend it.

A similar, though less marked, disagreement characterizes the approaches of Shevky and Bell to the third index in their model, that concerned with the hetereogeneity of the urban population. The operational definition of the term is given as the relative concentration of specified ethnic minorities, notably non-Whites and representatives of the 'new' migration. It is pointed out that the exact composition of the index is based on the United States situation and that different cultural contexts will contain different ethnic distinctions which must be taken into account in the construction of the index. To Shevky, the referent of the minority group measure lies in the segregation believed to characterize the development of urban-industrial society. To Bell, the reference is closer at hand and the indicant becomes a measure of *ethnic status*, a population's position along the ethnic basis of social differentiation. In a later presentation, Bell suggests that it may be preferable to term the construct an index of *ethnicity*, thus avoiding any confusion with social rank factors.[1]

In his modification of the Shevky–Bell model, McElrath uses the constructs of social rank, family status and ethnic status in much the same manner as the earlier writers. Social rank is indexed by indicants relating to occupation and education, family status by fertility and the proportion of women in the workforce, and ethnic status by data on culturally and physically distinct groups (column 5 of Table 4.3). Migrant status is measured by data on locality of birth and differences in the age-sex structure. Both sets of items are mentioned by Shevky and Bell in connexion with their discussion of population mobility, but are then ignored.

The social area typology

On the basis of their scores on each of the social area indexes, the sub-units subjected to social area analysis are classified into a series of social area types.[2]

---

[1] *Ibid.* Bell notes, however, that the index of ethnicity will usually show a high correlation with social rank.

[2] On the concept of types, see P. F. Lazarsfeld, 'Some remarks on the typological procedures in social research', *Zeitschrift für Sozialforschung*, 6 (1937), 119–39; Lazarsfeld, 'Concept formation and measurement in the behavioural sciences'; P. F. Lazarsfeld and A. H. Barton, 'Qualitative measurement in the social sciences', in D. Lerner and H. Lasswell (eds), *The Policy Sciences* (New York, 1951); John C. McKinney, *Constructive Typology and Social Theory* (New York, 1966).

The construction of the typology proceeds via the construction of a social space diagram. Each dimension of the space is formed by one of the social area indexes. Populations near to each other in the space are grouped together to form social areas. Each social area is 'called social in that the properties of . . . communities dealt with are social properties. The term area is employed because a geometric space frame is utilized.'[1] It should be noted that there is no connotation of geographical space implied in the social area typology.

The division of social space into social areas is essentially arbitrary in form. Major attention is paid to the social rank and familism dimensions and the initial delineation of social areas is in terms of scores on the social rank and family status indexes. In the 1949 presentation, Shevky and Williams produce a classification system containing nine basic social areas, each of which is dichotomized in terms of its scores on the ethnic status dimension.

High

1A	2A	3A	4A
1B	2B	3B	4B
1C	2C	3C	4C
1D	2D	3D	4D

Family status (left side), Low (bottom left)
Low — Social rank — High (bottom)

Fig. 4.1. Social area diagram

The 1955 monograph envisages a more detailed subdivision of social space, with 16 social areas delimited in terms of social rank and family status and a secondary dichotomization along the ethnicity axis producing 32 eventual types. Both the social rank and family status indexes are divided into four intervals, each interval corresponding with one of the standardized score ranges 0–24, 25–50, 51–74, and 75–100. Figure 4.1 shows the resulting 16-celled typology. Social area 1D contains populations characterized by low social rank and low family status. They contain few non-manual workers, few adults with high educational qualifications, few private dwellings, many women in the workforce and few children. Populations falling into social area 1A have similar social rank characteristics to those in 1D but exhibit high scores on the familism index, i.e. they contain many single-family dwellings, few women in the workforce, and many children. In a similar fashion, social area 4A has the same constellation of family characteristics as 1A, but is of high rather than low social rank.

---

[1] Bell, 'Urban neighbourhoods', p. 243. The social space diagram is closely allied to the conception of 'property-space'. See A. H. Barton, 'The concept of property-space in social research', in P. F. Lazarsfeld and M. Rosenberg (eds), *The Language of Social Research* (New York, 1955), pp. 40–53.

The third factor, ethnicity, adds to the typology . . . by distinguishing those census tracts which contain relatively many members of American racial and nationality groups. Tract populations having high indexes of ethnicity are given an 'S' along with their social area designations . . . Tracts which have low indexes of ethnicity remain with only the designation as shown in Figure 4.1. Thus, there are thirty-two possible social areas or types of urban subcommunities.[1]

The social rank and familism indicants are standardized to their ranges in the 1940 Los Angeles data. 'A single scale is thus established for the direct comparison of census tract scores on the respective indexes for different cities at the same time or the same city at different times.'[2] Standardization to the Los Angeles range is only possible given exact comparability of the indicants. The lack of this comparability is a severe limitation on the utility of the typology for cross-societal comparisons. Ideally, it should be possible to design a set of identical and unequivocal indicants which can be used across national boundaries. In the current absence of such indicants the best that may be attempted is to standardize the variables to their ranges in the area under study. According to McElrath, 'Inter-societal comparison would then be possible under the assumption that the *range* of ratios in one city was indicative of the same implied reality as the range in another. Thus at least the relative position of a sub-area in relation to others in its city would be standard.'[3] Although the assumption is dubious, there seems little alternative possibility if the social area typology is to be used as a comparative tool in the absence of internationally available indicants.

SOCIETAL SCALE, MODERNIZATION AND THE SOCIAL AREA INDEXES

The social area model places great stress on the notion of societal scale. Increases in scale are presented as the main dynamic in the development of industrial society and provide the basis for the three or four structural concepts used in the construction of the social area typology. The historical trends said to be associated with increasing scale provide the dimensions for the differentiation of societal sub-units. The typology of social areas is presented as a logical derivative of the theory of increasing societal scale. As several critics have pointed out, however, the nature of the relationship between increasing scale and residential differentiation remains unexplained and the concept of scale is itself surrounded by considerable ambiguity.

In the Shevky–Bell presentation of the theory of social analysis the notion of scale is introduced as an intervening variable, mediating between changes in the economic structure of society – a function of technological progress – and adjustments in organizational and associational patterns. Borrowing

---

[1] Bell, 'Urban neighbourhoods', p. 244.   [2] *Ibid.* p. 258.
[3] McElrath, 'The social areas of Rome', p. 381.

from Wilson and Wilson, the notion of scale is said to refer to 'the scope of social interaction and dependency'.[1] But, in the tabular presentation of the 'steps in construct formation' which provide the link between the theory of increasing scale and the axes of residential differentiation, changes in the range and intensity of relations provide only one of the three basic postulates (column 1 of Table 4.2). What is elsewhere treated as providing the definition of changes in scale is here treated as but one aspect of them. It is unclear whether the concept of increasing scale is intended to reference an independent set of phenomena, concerned with social interaction, or whether it is merely intended as a general term to describe all those historical trends which reflect the change from traditional agrarian forms of social organization to those characteristic of modern industrial society.

Similar confusions exist in the work of the originators of the concept of societal scale. In their analysis of social change in East Africa, Wilson and Wilson define the scale of society as 'the scope and intensity of social relations' entered into by its members.[2] On the assumption that the total amount of social interdependence remains a constant, the Wilsons point out that an increase in societal scale must occasion a decline in the intensity of local relations and an increase in that of wide-ranging relations.[3] In order to measure scale it is necessary to observe a large number of indicants, notably 'the proportion of economic co-operation, of communication of ideas and feelings within and without the group; together with the relative inclusiveness of value, of dogma and of symbolism within and without the group, and the degree of social pressure exerted within and without the group'.[4] As a society increases in scale, so also it increases in complexity through the process of 'complementary differentiation'. The increasing division of labour and the decline of dogma are both indicants of this trend. With increase in scale goes a greater degree of control over the material environment and a switch from magical to scientific-rational modes of explanation and prediction. In the primitive society most relations are personal; in the large-scale society most relations are impersonal. In the large-scale society the extension in the range of relations is evidenced in a far-flung mobility. 'Complexity, control of the material environment and non-magicality, impersonality and mobility . . . are necessarily connected with one another and with largeness of scale.'[5] Again it is unclear whether the concept of scale is being introduced as a specific variable or as a general term for the change from traditional forms of society.

The ambiguity in the referents of the concept of increasing societal scale make it a poor lynch-pin for the development of a general theory of urban social structure. If the concept is viewed as a synonym for such other broad

---

[1] Shevky and Bell, *Social Area Analysis*, p. 7.
[2] Wilson and Wilson, *Analysis of Social Change*, p. 25.
[3] *Ibid.* p. 40.   [4] *Ibid.* p. 25.   [5] *Ibid.* p. 100.

processes as 'industrialization', 'urbanization' and 'modernization' it loses any distinctive character.[1] If it is intended to highlight the change from local to cosmopolitan world-views, it requires a great deal more specification.[2] In either case, the development of the concept attempted by Shevky and Bell leaves too many loose ends for it to provide a satisfactory basis for an analysis of the axes of residential differentiation.

A further hiatus in the social area model concerns the connexion between the three broad historical trends said to be aspects of increasing scale and the three differentiating constructs. In the Shevky–Bell presentation it is simply assumed that the historical changes are directly translatable into differentiating axes. In the case of social rank, Shevky and Bell state:

The construct of social rank is specified from the changing distribution of skills in the development of modern society as a significant differentiating factor among individuals and subpopulations in modern society at one point of time. Individuals and groups are seen at this point in time as being significantly differentiated with respect to one of the long-term trends which has been important in the development of the character of modern society.[3]

Similar remarks are used to introduce the constructs of urbanization – family status and segregation – ethnic status. But no attempt is made to show how the historical changes become relevant to a discussion of residential differentiation.

In one of the earliest critiques of the social area model, Hawley and Duncan claim that 'one searches in vain among these materials for a statement explaining why residential areas should differ one from the other or be internally homogeneous. The elaborate discussion of social trends accompanying urbanization is nowhere shown to be relevant to this problem.'[4] Hawley and Duncan conclude: 'In sum, it seems to us evident that "social area analysis" boasts no theory that cogently relates hypotheses about areal structure to propositions about social differentiation.'[5] In a similar, but more sympathetic vein, Udry suggests that what is presented in the Shevky–Bell scheme is not a single integrated theory, connecting residential differentiation with societal development, but, rather, two quite distinct theories which are accidentally articulated to the extent that they happen to share the same operational measures:

I suggest that the theory of the axes of differentiation of sub-areas of a society be considered in its own right, and not logically based on a theory of increasing scale

---

[1] Cf. the statement by McElrath: 'Increasing societal scale (variously labelled "modernization", "urbanization", "industrialization") creates urban settlements', McElrath 'Societal scale and social differentiation' pp. 33–4.
[2] Cf. D. Lerner, *The Passing of Traditional Society* (New York, 1958).
[3] Shevky and Bell, *Social Area Analysis*, p. 17.
[4] A. H. Hawley and O. D. Duncan, 'Social area analysis', *Land Econ.* 33 (1957), p. 340.
[5] *Ibid.* p. 344.

... I suggest that we consider these two separate but co-ordinated theories: one a theory of increasing scale; the other, using the same axes and variables, but not deducible from the first, a theory of sub-area differentiation. The two theories are logically co-ordinated through the proposition that as a society increases in scale, its sub-areas are functionally differentiated.[1]

In an attempt to meet Udry's criticism, Bell and Moskos suggest that increasing societal scale and the three axes of sub-area differentiation are related by a simple mechanism which may best be described in terms of an analogy:

The underlying logic of the procedure is simple: Take a barrel of white balls. Take repeated measures on the colours of the balls. Find that an increasing percentage of the balls are turning black. Use this trend toward turning black as a differentiating variable at a given time. Order sections of the barrel into types according to their relative percentage of white and black balls. Over-simplifying, one can say that the economic, family and ethnic characteristics of census tract populations were identified by using just such a logic.[2]

The answer is appealingly simple, but it fails to provide a satisfactory solution to the problem of the theoretical connexion between the two aspects of the social area model. Bell and Moskos appear to be suggesting a diffusion process, in which different sub-areas will exhibit greater or lesser scale according to their relative exposure to the effects of industrialization and urbanization, but the implications of this are not spelt out. As it stands the billiard ball analogy gives no clue as to why a particular combination of indicants and properties, rather than any of an infinite number of others, should be used to produce a meaningful classification of sub-area populations, nor does it help explain how it is that the three *inter-related* trends of increasing societal scale become the three *independent* axes of residential differentiation.

A more satisfactory approach to the relationship between the effects of modernization and the axes of residential differentiation is provided in McElrath's revision of the social area model.[3] McElrath sees residential differentiation as being a function of social differentiation. He asserts 'that important social differentia result in residential clustering of like populations'.[4] The processes involved in such a clustering have already been discussed.[5] The connexion between residential differentiation and changes in the characteristics of the encompassing society is made via the assertion that 'change in the organization of developing societies is accompanied by changes in the dimensions of social differentiation – those categories into

[1] J. R. Udry, 'Increasing scale and spatial differentiation', *Soc. Forces*, 42 (1964), pp. 408–9.
[2] W. Bell and C. C. Moskos, Jr., 'A comment on Udry's "Increasing scale and spatial differentiation"', *Soc. Forces*, 42 (1964), p. 415.
[3] McElrath, 'Societal scale and social differentiation'.
[4] *Ibid.* p. 40.   [5] See chapter 3.

which people are divided, and in whose terms they receive differential treatment by others'.[1] In order to understand the bases of residential differentiation, McElrath suggests that it is necessary to understand the bases of social differentiation. In their turn, these latter may be related to certain global characteristics of the society concerned. It is believed, in this connexion, that especial importance attaches to certain systematic changes accompanying social development. In particular, it is suggested that the emergence of those differentiating criteria which form the substance of the social area model may best be understood in terms of a congeries of social and individual phenomena which are associated with the phenomena of modernization.[2]

'Modernization is the process by which individuals change from a traditional way of life to a more complex, technologically advanced, and rapidly changing style of life.'[3] Basic to the occurrence of modernization is what Deutsch has termed *social mobilization*: 'the process in which major clusters of old social, economic and psychological commitments are eroded or broken and people become available for new patterns of socialization and behaviour.'[4] The breakdown of traditional commitments allows, and is associated with, changes in the organization of productive effort and in the relationship of individuals to land, the weakening of traditional extended kinship systems, commercialization of various kinds, a broader view of the world, the acquisition of new skills and the development of new goals for individual attainment.[5] In Lerner's study of modernization in the Middle East a somewhat similar role is played by the concept of *psychic mobility* or *empathy*. Lerner writes that 'the acquisition and diffusion of psychic mobility may well be the greatest characterological transformation in modern history'.[6] Rogers and Svenning, adopting a similar though more elaborate perspective, provide an extensive analysis of the communication processes which are involved in the development of social mobilization and attempt the development of a general model of modernization which connects the antecedent variables of literacy, mass media exposure and contact with the outside world (cosmopoliteness), via empathy, achievement motivation and a decline in fatalism, to changes in the willingness to innovate, in political knowledge and in basic aspirations.[7] The ability to forsake old styles for the new is a key element.

[1] McElrath, 'Societal scale and social differentiation', p. 33.
[2] The most elaborate discussion of modernization is contained in E. M. Rogers (in association with L. Svenning), *Modernization Among Peasants* (New York, 1969). See also S. N. Eisenstadt, *Modernization: Protest and Change* (Englewood Cliffs, N. J., 1966); Lerner, *Passing of Traditional Society.*
[3] Rogers and Svenning, *Modernization Among Peasants*, p. 14.
[4] K. W. Deutsch, 'Social mobilization and political development', *Am. Pol. Sci. Rev.* 55 (1961), 494–5.
[5] Eisenstadt, *Modernization*, pp. 2–11.
[6] D. Lerner, 'Toward a communication theory of modernization', in L. C. Pye (ed.), *Communications and Political Development* (Princeton, 1963), p. 332.
[7] Rogers and Svenning, *Modernization Among Peasants*, pp. 42–59.

At the societal level the effects of social mobilization are evidenced in a progressive differentiation. Traditional associations between social categories and groups are upset and the erosion of old commitments, allied with the spread of individualistic views, allows the development of new sets of categories based on new criteria. In an analysis of changes in the social structure of the Niger Republic, Van Hoey details the effects of modernization on village life. He summarizes the changes

as a differentiation and release of subgroups (slave households, conjugal households) and membership categories (slaves, youths, married women, and junior heads of households) from formerly integral structures (local groups, village groups, agnatically extended households) for participation in expanded networks of interdependence.[1]

The details of the change will vary from society to society, but differentiation – the process in which 'the main social functions or the major institutional spheres of society become disassociated from one another'[2] – is predicted as a common factor.

With the diffusion of modern values, recruitment to social categories is increasingly based on universalistic achievement-oriented criteria. What a man does becomes more relevant to the evaluation he is given and to the style of life he adopts than who he was born. Ascribed characteristics become less important, achievements become more important. According to Eisenstadt,

Perhaps the most important aspects of this differentiation and specialization of roles . . . is the *separation* between the different roles held by an individual . . . Such separation of roles [means], first, that the occupation of any given role within one institutional sphere – e.g. the occupational sphere – does not automatically entail the incumbency of a particular role in the political or cultural spheres. Second, within each institutional sphere . . . there [develops] distinctive units that [are] organized around the goals specific to each such sphere and that [are] not fused, as in more traditional societies, with other groups in a network based on family, kinship, and territorial bases.[3]

In the premodern society, there is a high degree of coalescence between the criteria of social differentiation: an individual's status in one institutional realm is highly predictive to his standing in others. Status is ascribed and differences in prestige, way of life, ethnic identity and place of residence are intimately related. With modernization this coalescence breaks down. An individual's kinship connexions no longer provide an almost perfect basis for predicting his social rank, his place of residence, or, even, his

[1] L. Van Hoey, 'The coercive process of urbanization', in Greer *et al.* (eds), *New Urbanization*, p. 24.
[2] S. N. Eisenstadt, 'Social change, differentiation and evolution', *Am. Sociol. Rev.* 29 (1964), p. 377.
[3] Eisenstadt, *Modernization*, p. 3. Tense changed from original.

ethnicity. The modernization of society causes a progressive differentiation in status-systems: new bases of differentiation appear and there is a progressive weakening of the traditional links between categories. The modernization of the individual, his social mobilization or psychic mobility, provides the dynamic which translates social change into the emerging axes of social – and thence residential – differentiation.

Changes in the bases of social differentiation – 'those categories into which people are divided, and in whose terms they receive differential treatment by others'[1] – will be reflected in the patterns of residential differentiation to the extent that they are correlated with different locational requirements and to the extent that the residential fabric of the city exhibits sufficient variety for differences in its suitability for various styles of life and its general desirability to arise. Given the operation of market forces it may be expected that differentiation of residential neighbourhoods will occur, but there may be a considerable time-lag between the emergence of new differentiating factors at an inter-individual level and their translation into residential structures. The Shevky–Bell and McElrath discussions of the relationship between the social area indexes and their component indicants assume both a marked degree of differentiation in the population concerned and the existence of a strongly variegated residential fabric. To the extent that either or both of these factors are absent, the models developed by Shevky and Bell and by McElrath will be inappropriate.

The basic social area model depicts the relationship between indicants and constructs characteristic of the modern city. Each set of indicants refers to a well-differentiated criterion of social differentiation. Linkages across the constructs are negligible: social rank is independent of family status, migration status, or ethnicity; each of these latter is independent of the others. Even if one assumes, for the moment, that this is a valid representation of the residential structuring of the modern city, it is clear that it cannot be expected to apply to cities in which modernization is less developed. Within the general realm of characteristics covered by the social area technique variations in the degree of social mobilization may be expected to result in different patterns of indicant-construct relationship. Reporting her finding that in Cairo there is no factorial separation between social rank and family status indicants, Abu-Lughod observes that

the disassociation between social rank and familism variables found in contemporary Western cities in societies at the terminal stages of the demographic transition can be attributed to the reinforcing and cumulative effects of several conditions that 'define' the nature of urban organization in such cities: (1) residential segregation according to modern ranking systems, (2) relatively low correlations between social rank and differences in fertility and family styles, (3) high differentiation of residential subareas by housing types, (4) mobility, and (5) the pre-

[1] McElrath, 'Societal scale and social differentiation', p. 33.

dominance of independent households. To the extent that these conditions are not perfectly fulfilled, the vectors will not be totally disassociated.[1]

Similar conditions may be specified for the independence of each of the other constructs. Only in the modern city possessing a diversified residential fabric and a well differentiated social structure, may it be anticipated that each construct will emerge in the manner postulated by the basic social area model. Elsewhere, variations in the patterning of the indicant-construct relationship will reflect the degree of modernization in the encompassing society. A systematization of the differing sets of relationships to be found under various conditions of modernization may, hopefully, presage the eventual development of 'a detailed theory of comparative urban ecology'.[2] Table 4.4 outlines some of the possibilities which may be envisaged.

In the modern metropolis the relationship between the social area indicants and the underlying axes of residential differentiation is relatively simple (type *a*, Table 4.4). Each construct – social rank, family status, ethnic status and migration status – is unambiguously related to its specified indicants and each indicant is a relatively 'pure' measure of its theoretical projection. The factor structure of the matrix showing the intercorrelations between the variables provides a good approximation to simple structure. Each set of indicants shows high item-factor correlations with its relevant construct and insignificant correlations with all other constructs. Each factor is relatively independent of all others.

At the opposite extreme from the multi-factor differentiation of the modern community is the situation outlined in type *b* of Table 4.4. In this example, all indicants vary together, reflecting the existence of a single basis of social and residential differentiation. Feudal cities may perhaps have been of this nature.[3] Given the heterogeneity of the urban population, however, it seems unlikely that such a structure could long survive and the various 'mixed types' outlined in types *c* to *f* of the table provide a more likely set of templates for the analysis of the pre-modern city.

The initial congruence of differentiating factors may break down in many ways and for a variety of reasons. In some cases the development of external relations resulting from trade or conquest may lead to the imposition of ethnic and/or migration differentials. It is unlikely that the minority groups will have the same access to the local opportunity structures as the members of the host society and it may therefore be anticipated that, even though ethnicity or migration status may form the cores of separate axes of differentiation, they are likely to exhibit a marked correlation with the principal axis of differentiation found in the host population. Where there is a close association between ethnicity or region of origin and the local power system, as in much of colonial society, the association between ethnic or migration indicants

[1] Abu-Lughod, 'Testing the theory of social area analysis', p. 209. [2] *Ibid.* p. 210.
[3] Cf. G. Sjoberg, *The Preindustrial City* (New York, 1960).

TABLE 4.4 *Item-construct relationships in types of city*

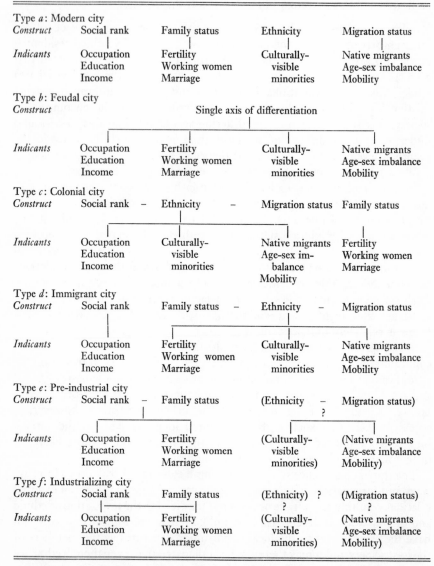

Type *a*: Modern city
Construct	Social rank	Family status	Ethnicity	Migration status
Indicants	Occupation Education Income	Fertility Working women Marriage	Culturally-visible minorities	Native migrants Age-sex imbalance Mobility

Type *b*: Feudal city
Construct — Single axis of differentiation
| *Indicants* | Occupation Education Income | Fertility Working women Marriage | Culturally-visible minorities | Native migrants Age-sex imbalance Mobility |

Type *c*: Colonial city
Construct — Social rank – Ethnicity – Migration status   Family status
| *Indicants* | Occupation Education Income | Culturally-visible minorities | Native migrants Age-sex imbalance Mobility | Fertility Working women Marriage |

Type *d*: Immigrant city
Construct — Social rank   Family status – Ethnicity – Migration status
| *Indicants* | Occupation Education Income | Fertility Working women Marriage | Culturally-visible minorities | Native migrants Age-sex imbalance Mobility |

Type *e*: Pre-industrial city
Construct — Social rank – Family status   (Ethnicity – Migration status) ?
| *Indicants* | Occupation Education Income | Fertility Working women Marriage | (Culturally-visible minorities) | (Native migrants Age-sex imbalance Mobility) |

Type *f*: Industrializing city
Construct — Social rank   Family status   (Ethnicity) ?   (Migration status) ?
| *Indicants* | Occupation Education Income | Fertility Working women Marriage | (Culturally-visible minorities) | (Native migrants Age-sex imbalance Mobility) |

and indicants relating to social rank may be so close as to suggest that they load on a single factor, with minority groups pre-empting higher or lower social strata (type *c*). Where there is a close association between style of life characteristics and ethnicity or migration status, as in many rapidly-growing cities, little separation may be expected between style of life and minority group indicants at the ecological level (type *d*).

The most systematic development accompanying modernization, however, is probably that concerning the association between social rank and familism variables. In the pre-industrial city depicted by Sjoberg, differences in family characteristics are closely associated with differences in social rank.[1] Although the extended family may be the preferred family norm, only the elite possess the necessary resources to enable its realization. The necessity to preserve inheritance and prestige is reflected in the tight control which the family exercises over the marriage of its members. With the process of modernization the nexus between rank and family is greatly attenuated. Eisenstadt observes that the separation of roles characteristic of social mobilization 'has taken place first, and perhaps most dramatically, between family and occupational roles during the industrial revolution'.[2] The individual household rather than the extended kinship system becomes the unit for the allocation of social rank and marriage and style of family life become the objects of individual choice, resting on romantic love and individual value orientations, rather than ascribed class. Changes in the distribution of resources, in medical knowledge, in the structure of productive activity and in the role of women, have further loosened the links between social rank and family characteristics. Changes in the organization of the building industry and in the nature of the housing market have created a residential fabric in which the differences in preferred ways of life can find a ready expression. It may be suggested that the dissociation between social rank and familism variables provides an index of the degree of modernization characteristic of the society concerned. In the initial pre-modern state (type *e*) both sets of indicants will load on a single style-of-life social rank factor. With the progress of social mobilization and the differentiation of status systems there will be a progressive separation of the two clusters of variables.

In transitional societies the structure outlined in type *f* may be anticipated: social rank and family status will emerge as separate dimensions of differentiation, but they will exhibit a substantial intercorrelation. It may be that some indicants of the one exhibit higher item-factor correlations with the other than they do with their own referent. Only in the modern metropolis, with its emphasis on individualism and its opportunities for expressing individual choice, may it be anticipated that social rank and familism will become fully independent factors. Even here, the degree of their independence is a problem for empirical investigation, rather than theoretical *fiat*.

McElrath suggests that the modernization of society may be associated with the emergence of an ever-increasing number of axes of differentiation.[3]

---

[1] *Ibid.* See also the summary statement by Sjoberg in 'Cities in developing and industrial societies', in Hauser and Schnore (eds), *Study of Urbanization*, pp. 216–20.

[2] Eisenstadt, *Modernization*, p. 3.

[3] McElrath, 'Societal scale and social differentiation', p. 34.

It is also apparent, however, that once-important bases for social and residential differentiation may lose their significance over time. In most modern cities this has probably already happened with religious differences.[1] Migration status may, perhaps, soon share the same fate.[2] Ethnicity, social rank, and differences in preferred life-style, on the other hand, seem to be in little immediate danger of extinction. Where ethnicity is linked with easily visible physical differences it shows little signs of disappearing as a criterion for the evaluation of social desirability. It may be expected to remain a major axis of residential differentiation and segregation for as long as it provides a basis for differentiating between persons. Differences in social rank are likely to be similarly resistant to extinction. The ranking system is replete with devices for maintaining and enhancing the social distance between classes. Family status, also, may be expected to long remain a major element in ecological differentiation. Although it is the most recent of the differentiating axes to emerge, familism bids fair to becoming perhaps the most important single dimension of ecological structure. Writing about potential changes in the nature of the market over the latter half of the twentieth century, Abrams makes the provocative comment that

In the past, and still in many fields today, total consumption patterns have been dominated by class differences . . . It is unlikely that differences of these kinds will retain their significance over the next fifty years. Almost certainly they will be replaced in importance by differences in age and differences related to consumers' position in the life-cycle. Already in some markets the consumption habits of working-class young people have more in common with those of middle-class young people than with those of their parents. Sharp differences in standards of living will in future be related to stages in life-cycle.[3]

In view of the close association between locational behaviour and other 'consumption habits' it may be anticipated that a similar structuring of the urban residential system will ensue.

Modernization is a complicated and variable process. The degree of closure in the 'modernization – residential differentiation' argument should not be exaggerated. Even given identical exposure to modernizing influences – a most unlikely assumption – differences in the initial socio-cultural matrix are likely to be reflected in the new social patterns. Although the openness and flexibility which are seen as being essential elements of the

---

[1] The example of Northern Ireland, however, suggests that caution should be exercised in such an assumption.

[2] McElrath suggests, 'The extreme form of migration status – the result of a radical shift from peasant to urban life – is likely to disappear in the next few decades. This will be due to both a diminution in the rate of rural to urban migration . . . and the continued extension of urban forms throughout [society] and the continued increase in the intensity of involvement of all people in urban life', in 'Urban differentiation', p. 110.

[3] M. Abrams, 'Consumption in the year 2000', in M. Young (ed.), *Forecasting and the Social Sciences* (London, 1968), pp. 39–40.

modernization process are posited as being dependent on the ascendance of certain universalistic criteria in the recruitment of new incumbents to key interlocking social categories, considerable variation may exist in the way these criteria are applied and in the particular sets of statuses which are involved. Similarly, although the continuation of the modernization process is likely to become part of the ideology of a new elite, there may be many variations in the relative power and status of this group as compared with more traditional or neo-traditional strata.[1] The development of new person- ality types able to take advantage of the expanding status systems is similarly likely to be affected by a variety of intervening variables. For all these reasons, it is unlikely that modernization will follow a simple pattern or that the experiences of contemporary modern societies will be reproduced exactly in those of the emergent societies. Nonetheless, it is suggested that there are sufficient similarities in the modernization process as it affects different societies to predict that it will be reflected in certain general structural considerations. More particularly, it is suggested that at the ecological level modernization will be reflected in the constellation of item-construct relationships exhibited by the social area indicants. The social area model outlined by Shevky and Bell takes for granted what is, in actuality, problem- atical. Differences in the strength and pattern of the item-construct relation- ships contained within the social area variables provide the raw material for the development of a comparative and cross-cultural theory of urban ecology. The validity of this theory forms the subject-matter of our next section.

THE EMPIRICAL VALIDITY OF THE SOCIAL AREA MODELS

Rather than the single social area model outlined by Shevky and Bell and further developed by McElrath, the consideration of modernization and differentiation suggests that it is more profitable to think in terms of a family of social area models, distinguished in terms of the factor structures revealed by the social area indicants. The original presentation of the social area indicants and indexes is that which is applicable to cities in the more developed or modern societies. In societies exhibiting a less-advanced stage of modernization, one of the less differentiated factor structures is predicted.

The technique of social area analysis has achieved a wide currency. As Table 4.5 shows, studies using various aspects of the original social area model have been reported for a large number of U.S. cities and for a growing number of urban communities in other parts of the world.

By itself, use is no guarantee of validity. Most of the studies employing the social area model – even some of those using it in pre-modern societies – have taken the validity of the basic scheme for granted. Its indicants and

[1] On the role of the modernizing elite, see Eisenstadt, *Modernization*.

The urban mosaic

TABLE 4.5 *Summary of studies using the Shevky–Bell model of social area analysis* (for full references, see bibliography)

Reference	City	Type of study
A. *U.S. studies*		
Anderson and Bean, 1961	Toledo	Factor analysis
Anderson and Egeland, 1961	Akron, Dayton, Indianapolis, Syracuse	Analysis of spatial variance
Bange, 1955	San Francisco	Organization of welfare services
Bell, 1952	Los Angeles, San Francisco	Factor analysis
Bell, 1953	San Francisco	Typology
Bell, 1955	San Francisco	Factor analysis
Bell, 1957	San Francisco	Field study of anomia
Bell, 1958	San Francisco	Sampling frame
Bell and Boat, 1957	San Francisco	Field study of neighbourhood relationships
Bell and Force, 1956a	San Francisco	Field study of formal association participation
Bell and Force, 1956b	San Francisco	Field study of formal association participation
Bell and Force, 1957	San Francisco	Religious preferences, familism, social rank
Boggs, 1965	St Louis	Crime patterns
Brody, 1962	10 U.S. cities	Analysis of spatial patterns (centralization)
Broom and Shevky, 1949	Los Angeles	Ethnic differentiation
Broom et al. 1955	Los Angeles	Characteristics of petitioners for change of name
Curtis et al. 1957	St Louis	Parishes and social areas
Goldstein and Mayer, 1964	Providence	Effects of population decline
Greer, 1956	Los Angeles	Field study of social participation
Greer, 1960	Los Angeles	Socio-political structure and suburbanism
Greer, 1962	Los Angeles	Socio-political structure and suburbanism
Greer and Kube, 1959	Los Angeles	Socio-political behaviour and the urban community
Greer and Orleans, 1962	Los Angeles	Urbanism and involvement in para-political organization
Imse and Murphy, n.d. c. 1960	Buffalo	Typology
Kaufman, 1961	Chicago, San Francisco	Factor analysis
Kaufman and Greer, 1960	St Louis	Voting patterns
McElrath, 1955	Los Angeles	Urbanization and status identification factors
McElrath and Barkey, c. 1964	Chicago	Analysis of spatial variation
Moush et al. 1960	Cleveland	Typology
Metropolitan St Louis Survey, 1956	St Louis	Typology
Polk, 1957a	San Diego	Typology
Polk, 1957b	San Diego	Distribution of delinquents
Polk, 1967	Portland	Distribution of delinquents
Schmid, 1960	Seattle	Distribution of criminals (by type of crime) and suicides

150

Sherif and Sherif, 1965	S.W. U.S. cities	Field studies of adolescent behaviour
Shevky and Bell, 1955	San Francisco	Presentation of model
Shevky and Williams, 1949	Los Angeles	Typology
Sullivan, 1961	Bronx	Parishes and social areas
Van Arsdol *et al*. 1958*a*	10 U.S. cities	Test of empirical generality of Shevky-
Van Arsdol *et al*. 1958*b*	10 U.S. cities	Bell model (factor analysis)
Van Arsdol *et al*. 1961	10 U.S. cities	Factor analysis of deviant cases
Wendling and Polk, 1958	San Diego, San Francisco Bay area	Distribution of suicides
Williamson, 1954	Seattle	Social areas and marital adjustment
Willie, 1967	Washington	Distribution of delinquents
B. *Non-U.S. studies*		
Clignet and Sween, 1968	Accra, Abidjan	Theory of increasing scale
Gagnon, 1960	Quebec	Typology
Herbert, 1967	Newcastle-under-Lyme	Typology
Hyderabad Metropolitan Research Project, 1966	Hyderabad	Typology
McElrath, 1962	Rome	Typology, analysis of spatial variance
McElrath, 1968	Accra, Kingston	Theory of increasing scale

indexes and the resulting typology have simply been used in order to generate a description of the urban population or to provide a framework for the design of social policies or social surveys. In neither case has the empirical validity of the scheme been subject to question. It need hardly be stressed, however, that the results of a classification based on an invalid selection of indicants and indexes are themselves likely to be misleading. To assess the validity of the model it is necessary to pay prior attention to the stage of modernization characteristic of the encompassing society.

It has already been emphasized that modernization is a multi-dimensional phenomenon. Measurement of the degree of modernization characteristic of a given set of societies involves a variety of unsolved problems. Very crudely, however, and following the United Nations, it is possible to make a simple twofold division of the nations of the world into the modern and the traditional, the more developed and the less developed.[1] The traditional societies include all those of the Caribbean, Latin America, Africa and Asia, with the exception of Japan and South Africa. The modern societies include all those of Anglo-America, Europe, Australia and New Zealand. Within both categories many variations in modernization exist. Thus, within the traditional group, Malaysia or Argentina exhibit a much higher degree of modernization than do, say, New Guinea or Haiti. Within the modern group,

[1] The less-developed countries are generally characterized by (*a*) relatively low *per capita* incomes, (*b*) low productivity per person, (*c*) extensive subsistence production, (*d*) high rates of illiteracy, (*e*) limited communication techniques, (*f*) high birth and death rates, (*g*) little secondary industry and (*h*) little functional differentiation.

The urban mosaic

Scandinavia, Australia and New Zealand, and parts of the United States are significantly more modern than, say, many countries of Southern or Eastern Europe.[1] A full analysis of the relationship between modernization and urban structure will demand a much more elaborate classification of societies than offered here. In the absence of a representative set of studies concerned with the ecological structure of urban communities, however, the present dichotomy will be sufficient. We shall begin our analysis by examining the validity of the social area model in the modern society.

THE VALIDITY OF THE BASIC SOCIAL AREA MODEL IN MODERN SOCIETY

The basic social area model outlined by Shevky, Bell and McElrath is founded on two beliefs: (1) that differences in social rank, family characteristics, migration status and ethnicity provide the major axes for the residential differentiation of the modern urban population, and (2) that the indicants and indexes outlined in the social area scheme provide valid measures of these constructs. The first assumption may best be assessed with the aid of factorial ecology.[2] Factor analytic studies of a variety of North American, European and Australasian cities have provided strong support for the assumed importance of social rank, familism, ethnicity and urbanism-mobility in the modern city. Although not all the factors appear to be important in all cities – reflecting differences in population composition and general socio-cultural values[3] – the pattern is sufficiently pronounced to conclude that the ecological structure of the modern city may be generally summarized in terms of the four basic constructs which the social area model has identified. The inter-relationships between the constructs are, however, more complicated than the model appears to allow. Rather than the assumed independence, the factors exhibit varying degrees of correlation, negligible in the case of social rank and familism but frequently pronounced in the case of the other associations. In order to examine the significance of these deviations from the model and to further assess the validity of the operational assumptions on which social area analysis is based it is necessary to subject the scheme to intensive hypothesis-testing forms of factor analysis.

Several analyses have been published concerned with the factorial composition of the social area indicants in U.S. cities.[4] Given that the United

---

1 As evidenced in income, educational attainments and functional differentiation.
2 See chapter 2 above. Shevky and Bell place especial emphasis on what they see as the similarity between their indexes and the results of Tryon's cluster analysis of San Francisco. See Tryon, *Identification of Social Areas by Cluster Analysis.*
3 E.g. the absence of a clearly-separate ethnic dimension in Scandinavian cities.
4 Anderson and Bean, 'The Shevky-Bell social areas', pp. 119–24; W. Bell, 'Economic, family, and ethnic status', *Am. Sociol. Rev.* 20 (1955), 45–52; W. C. Kaufman, 'Social Area Analysis: An

States is a modern society, the pattern of indicant-construct correlations revealed by the analyses should approximate to the basic social area model: indicants relating to occupational status, educational achievement and income should load on a single factor identified as social rank or economic status; indicants relating to fertility, to the proportions of single-family dwellings and of women in the workforce should load on a factor identified as urbanization or familism; indicants relating to the proportion of disadvantaged ethnic populations should load on an ethnicity factor; indicants relating to population turnover, to age and sex imbalances and to native-born migrants should load on a migration status or urbanism-mobility factor. Very few studies have included data which are relevant to the migration factor and most analyses have been concerned with the original Shevky–Bell presentation of the social area model in which three factors only are identified. The overall results of the American studies are in agreement with the Shevky–Bell presentation. Within the general consensus, however, differences in the details of the results have suggested several qualifications to the basic model. Many reflect regional differences in American society.

The first validation study to be published is Bell's analysis of the factor structure revealed in the original social area data for Los Angeles and San Francisco.[1] Using the centroid technique of factor analysis, Bell assesses the congruity between the observed pattern of item-factor correlations and two experimental hypotheses derived from the social area model. Hypothesis 1 states that social rank, familism and ethnicity represent discrete factors each of which is necessary to account for the observed differences between census tract populations in terms of a variety of social characteristics. Hypothesis 2 contains two sub-hypotheses; (*a*) that measures of occupational status, educational achievement and rent comprise an unidimensional index of social rank, and (*b*) that measures of fertility, women in the workforce and single-family detached dwellings comprise an unidimensional index of the family status of census tract populations.[2] The initial correlations between the seven indicants used are shown in Table 4.6, along with the resulting rotated centroid factors.

The data are clearly in agreement with the hypotheses: the indicants correlate with the underlying three factors in the predicted fashion and the high inter-item correlations within the clusters of measures which relate to social rank and family status respectively, provide strong support for the assumption that each index forms an unidimensional instrument. The

Explication of Theory, Methodology and Techniques and Statistical Tests of Revised Procedures, San Francisco and Chicago, 1950' (unpub. Ph.D. dissertation, Northwestern University, 1961); M. D. Van Arsdol, Jr. *et al.*, 'The generality of the Shevky social area indexes', *Am. Sociol. Rev.* 23 (1958), 277–84; Van Arsdol *et al.* 'An application of the Shevky social area indexes to a model of urban society', *Soc. Forces*, 37 (1958), 26–32.
1 Bell, 'Economic, family, and ethnic status'.
2 Since the ethnic status index is founded on a single indicant no measure of its unidimensionality is possible.

F

TABLE 4.6 *Intercorrelation of Shevky–Bell variables in Los Angeles, 1940 (below diagonal) and San Francisco, 1940 (above diagonal)*

Measures	Occ	Edu	Rnt	Fer	Wlf	Sfd	Seg
Occupation	–	78	78	68	48	19	14
Education	73	–	80	49	13	−26	49
Rent (–)	71	70	–	56	26	−05	36
Fertility	81	65	54	–	76	48	21
Women in labour force (–)	56	28	31	69	–	75	−07
Single-family dwellings	37	05	05	56	68	–	−25
Segregation index	32	65	36	38	−06	−03	–

Rotated centroid matrix

Measures	Los Angeles factors			San Francisco factors			Shevky–Bell model factors		
	I	II	III	I	II	III	I	II	III
Occ	48	19	−09	64	07	−18	+	0	0
Edu	32	−04	28	47	−11	21	+	0	0
Rnt	65	−19	−19	60	−07	−03	+	0	0
Fer	11	56	18	10	63	22	0	+	0
Wlf	15	62	−19	03	71	−03	0	+	0
Sfd	−15	73	02	−03	57	−18	0	+	0
Seg	−11	04	58	−10	11	50	0	0	+

NOTE. 0 = insignificant loading; + = significant loading.

Correlation between factors

Factors		Los Angeles			San Francisco		
		I	II	III	I	II	III
I	Social status	100	–	–	100	–	–
II	Family status	−50	100	–	−33	100	–
III	Ethnic status	−73	15	100	−62	−21	100

SOURCE. Bell, 'Economic, family, and ethnic status', pp. 46–51.

inter-factor correlations are low in the case of social rank and family status, but ethnicity is involved in relatively high correlations, especially with the social rank factor (−0·73 in Los Angeles and −0·62 in San Francisco).

Similar tests carried out by Van Arsdol et al., in a sample of ten medium-sized U.S. cities, corroborate Bell's findings in the case of a model which consists of the combined census tract data for all the cities,[1] but disclose

[1] Van Arsdol et al., 'The generality', and 'An application'.

considerable deviations from the predicted pattern when the cities are analysed individually. Using a criterion developed by McNemar,[1] Van Arsdol *et al.* find that three factors are necessary to provide a satisfactory explanation of the pattern of census tract variation in the social area indicants. Multiple-group factor analyses produce a set of item-factor correlations strikingly in agreement with the predicted structure. Table 4.7 shows the relevant details.

TABLE 4.7 *Multiple-group factor structure for ten U.S. cities combined, 1950*

Measures	Factors		
	I (Social rank)	II (Urbanization)	III (Segregation)
Occupation	92	17	16
Education	92	−17	−16
Fertility	46	−65	−09
Women in workforce	04	86	−04
Single-family dwellings	−26	−75	10
Per cent Negro	−36	15	54

Rotated factor matrix

Measures	Factors		
	I (Social rank)	II (Urbanization)	III (Segregation)
Occupation	80	10	16
Education	64	−10	−14
Fertility	25	−64	−10
Women in workforce	−05	80	−03
Single-family dwellings	−20	−66	07
Per cent Negro	03	−06	53

NOTE. The ten cities are: Akron, Atlanta, Birmingham, Kansas City, Louisville, Minneapolis, Portland, Providence, Rochester, and Seattle.
SOURCE. Van Arsdol *et al.*, 'An application', p.30.

Using Shevky's labels, Van Arsdol *et al.* name the factors social rank, which correlates 0·92 with occupational and educational indicants, urbanization, correlating −0·65 with fertility, −0·75 with single-family dwellings and 0·86 with women in the workforce, and segregation, which correlates 0·54 with per cent Negro. They conclude: 'Within the framework of the multiple-group method of factor analysis, the census tract measures for the tracts of the combined ten cities go together in the manner described by Shevky. Shevky's description of the measures and indexes, in its present

[1] Q. McNemar, 'On the number of factors', *Psychometrika*, 7 (1942), 9–18.

form, applies to the model of urban society tested in this research.'[1] The inter-factor correlations obtained in the rotated factor matrix are 0·08 between social rank and urbanization, −0·58 between segregation and social rank and 0·27 between segregation and urbanization.

The factor analyses which Van Arsdol *et al.* carry out of the individual cities produce results essentially the same as those for the combined sample in six of the ten. The four deviant cases are all Southern or near-Southern cities with a high proportion of Negroes. In each of the deviant cases the major departure from the predicted pattern involves the item-factor correlations of the fertility variable. Fertility correlates more highly with the social rank factor than indicated by the Shevky–Bell model; in two of the cities, Kansas City and Atlanta, fertility is more closely related with social rank than it is with urbanization. On the basis of this finding, the authors propose a modified factor hypothesis for the Southern cities in which social rank is indexed by the variables occupation, education, and fertility. Although they state that 'it remains to be demonstrated whether the alternative models are an artefact of the particular measures used . . . or provide a useful device for reinterpretation of the Shevky theory' they also make the observation that 'the population of these four cities include relatively larger proportions of Negroes. This fact, combined especially with the unfavourable economic position of the Negroes, may indicate that the range of family forms in these cities, as described by the fertility measure, has not yet become disassociated from social rank'.[2] It is clearly unrealistic to ignore regional differences in modernization that may occur within national boundaries.

Further modifications to the basic Shevky–Bell model are suggested in a study of the ecological structure of Toledo by Anderson and Bean.[3] In addition to the six basic social area indexes used in the Bell and Van Arsdol studies, seven additional variables are included in the analysis. Four factors are extracted from the correlation matrix using the centroid technique. Examination of residuals suggests that no other factors of any importance are contained in the matrix. Orthogonal rotation to a simple structure produces the item-factor correlations shown in Table 4.8.

The most important finding is that while the social rank and ethnic status dimensions emerge as predicted in the Shevky–Bell model, the variables relating to the family status construct appear to split into two factors. On the basis of the item-factor loadings, Anderson and Bean suggest that one of these factors may be labelled urbanization (loading on women in the workforce, multi-family dwellings, median family income (−), owner occupancy (−), ratio of families to unrelated individuals (−), per cent

---

[1] Van Arsdol *et al.*, 'An application', p. 30.
[2] Van Arsdol *et al.*, 'The generality', p. 282.
[3] Anderson and Bean, 'The Shevky-Bell social areas'.

TABLE 4.8 *Rotated orthogonal factor solution for Toledo, 1960*

Indicant	Factor			
	I	II	III	IV
Low education	−98	21	−10	02
Manual work	−93	−07	−02	09
Owner-occupiers	03	−99	05	−09
Multi-family dwellings	04	−97	07	−02
Median income	48	−78	29	−02
Families	−10	−77	20	−19
Working women	−04	73	25	−44
Married	−03	−71	−27	26
Residential stability	−32	−70	12	−11
Negro	−21	30	−70	−37
Crowding	−54	53	−59	−04
Double occupancy	−49	37	−45	−51
Fertility	03	−46	11	74
Per cent total variance	21·1	41·5	10·3	9·7

SOURCE: Adapted from Anderson and Bean, 'The Shevky-Bell social areas'.

married (−), and residential stability (−)) and the other family status (loading on fertility and double occupancy (−)). The urbanization factor differentiates populations living in rented apartment houses from those living in owner-occupied single-family dwellings. Anderson and Bean assert that the factor is concerned with an attribute of the housing character-istics of areas rather than with those of the people who live in them. The substantial loadings of the factor on items relating to population mobility, income, and the proportion of unmarried persons, counsels caution in this interpretation and the factor has much in common with the migration factor discussed by McElrath.

Outside the United States tests of the basic social area model have been reported for a mere handful of modern cities. In Europe, analyses have been published for Rome and for Newcastle-under-Lyme; in Australasia, we shall be reporting analyses for Brisbane and Auckland. For the moment our attention is focused on the two European studies. As will be apparent, neither Rome nor Newcastle-under-Lyme may be expected to match the degree of differentiation characteristic of West Coast U.S. cities.

The analysis of Rome reported by McElrath uses only two of the three Shevky–Bell constructs, social rank and family status.[1] The neglect of ethnicity is defended in terms of the ethnic homogeneity of the Roman population and, less convincingly, on the grounds that the ethnic status

[1] McElrath, 'The social areas of Rome'. McElrath points out that in terms of such 'traditional measures of the relative scale of social organization' as the proportion employed in non-agricultur-al pursuits, the proportion of salaried and wage earners, and the degree of urban concentration, 'Italy falls somewhat below the United States' (*Ibid.* p. 378).

dimension has proved to be the least independent of the constructs in American studies. Reference is made to the potential importance of migration status in the differentiation of the Roman population, but no test is made of its significance in the city's ecology. The social rank construct is measured by two indicants: the proportion of the workforce employed in non-manual occupations and the proportion of the population aged six years and over classified as illiterate. The family status construct is indexed by the fertility ratio and by the proportion of women in the workforce. McElrath suggests that both indicants are 'readily translatable to most industrial societies irrespective of the dominant value systems of these societies'.[1] The third component of the Shevky–Bell urbanization-family status index, the proportion of single-family dwelling units, is believed to be less useful in cross-national studies. McElrath points out that in many societies there may be too restricted a range of dwelling types for the proportion of single-family dwellings to become a major differentiating variable. The ecological correlations between the four indicants and the two indexes are shown in Table 4.9.

TABLE 4.9 *Intercorrelations and centroid factor loadings for social area indicants and indexes, Rome, 1951*

Indicant		Correlation coefficient						Centroid Factor Loading
		1	2	3	4	5	6	
Social rank index	1	–						94
Non-manual workers	2	94	–					89
Illiteracy (–)	3	95	79	–				89
Working women	4	65	64	59	–			83
Fertility	5	−75	−68	−74	−69	–		−89
Family status index	6	−76	−71	−73	−90	90	–	−93

As indicated in the table, the high correlation between the two indexes and the observed pattern of inter-indicant correlations, strongly suggest that a single-factor solution provides an adequate description of the data. The single centroid factor illustrated accounts for 94 per cent of the observed variance. McElrath, however, argues that the correlations between the two indexes and a set of criterion variables suggest that each index is necessary.[2] Even granted the substantive difference between social rank and family status, it remains clear that the two constructs exhibit a much closer association in the Roman data than they do in the American studies. McElrath

[1] *Ibid.* p. 380.
[2] *Ibid.* p. 384. The multiple correlations of social rank and family status with the various criterion variables are significantly higher than the equivalent zero-order correlations in 13 out of 14 cases.

suggests that this difference may be a result of the lesser degree of scale exhibited by Italian as compared with U.S. society.

The evidence from Newcastle-under-Lyme is even less in congruence with the Shevky–Bell model.[1] Newcastle is a much smaller city than any of the others for which social area analyses have been reported and it may be that the smallness of its size and its apparent homogeneity are confounding factors in its ecology.[2] The 1961 population of the city was 76,400. The territorial framework of the analysis is provided by a set of 107 census enumeration districts. The small size of each district, although an advantage in terms of potential homogeneity, is associated with a major drawback in that three of the four indicants used in the analysis are drawn from ten per cent sample data. The small sizes of the base populations raise major doubts about the reliability of both the indicants and the ensuing analysis.

TABLE 4.10 *Rank-order correlation of social area indicants for Newcastle-under-Lyme, England, 1961*

Variable		1	2	3	4
Manual workers	(1)	100			
No education after 15	(2)	81	100		
Fertility ratio	(3)	41	32	100	
Women in workforce	(4)	27	30	08	100

SOURCE. Herbert, 'Social area analysis', p. 45.

The variables used are very similar to those employed in the Rome study: social rank is indexed by the proportion of the male workforce employed in manual work and by the proportion of the population aged fifteen years and over who left school at the age of fifteen years or less; family status is believed to be indexed by the fertility ratio and by the proportion of women employed outside the home. Again in conformity with the analysis of Rome, the third indicant of the family status index, single-family dwellings, is ignored. Herbert argues that the variable 'has a particular meaning in the United States which is perhaps not found in this country or at least is not adequately expressed in the Census data'.[3] No data are used relating to the ethnic characteristics of the Newcastle population, Herbert believing that the number of immigrants in the town is too small for ethnicity to be a significant differentiating factor. He suggests that in other areas of Britain, where the proportion of immigrants in the population may be considerably higher than in Newcastle, ethnicity may become much more important in residential differentiation.

The rank-order correlations between the four social area indicants in

[1] D. T. Herbert, 'Social area analysis; a British study', *Urban Studies*, 4 (1967), 41–60.
[2] Cf. the statement by Shevky and Bell to the effect that the 'emerging characteristics of modern society' are best observed in very large cities, 'areas of movement and expansion', Shevky and Bell, *Social Area Analysis*, p. 1.   [3] Herbert, 'Social area analysis; a British study', p. 44.

Newcastle are shown in Table 4.10. The use of a non-product moment correlations technique prevents the use of factor analysis. Nonetheless, it is apparent that while the association between the occupational and educational indicants is in conformity with that postulated in the social area model, that between fertility and women in the workforce is deviant. Herbert suggests that the Shevky–Bell prediction of a negative relationship between fertility and the employment of women outside the home 'is perhaps too generalized a statement to apply to British conditions where proportions of women at work may vary with the actual size of family, with proximity to parents or in-laws, or with social class'.[1] In the absence of further material on British conditions it is impossible to assess the general validity of the Newcastle findings as characteristic of the ecological structure of British cities. The small size, working-class structure and northern location of Newcastle may well make it an unusual case.

The social area model and the axes of residential differentiation in Brisbane and Auckland

More supportive evidence on the applicability of the basic social area model to the ecology of the modern city is provided by an analysis of the pattern of indicant-construct associations in Brisbane and Auckland. The territorial framework for the analysis is the same as that used in the earlier extensive factor analytic study and consists of the 554 residential collectors' districts which constitute the metropolitan area of Brisbane and the 62 statistical subdivisions, boroughs and cities which constitute that of Auckland. The Brisbane analysis is based on data for 1961; the Auckland analysis is based on data for 1966.

The operational procedures of the Shevky–Bell presentation of social area analysis are closely linked with the data publishing programme adopted by the United States Bureau of the Census. Applications of the technique outside the United States almost invariably involve the substitution of indicants. The analyses of Brisbane and Auckland are no exception to this rule, although the number of substitutions is small and each new indicant seems clearly related to the original model. The indicants used are shown in Table 4.11.

The Shevky–Bell construct of social rank is measured variously by indicants relating to educational achievement, rent and occupational status. No data relating to education are available for either Brisbane or Auckland. In the Brisbane analysis social rank is indexed by occupational status – the proportion of non-manual workers – and by average house value.[2] In Auck-

---

1 *Ibid.* p. 46.
2 'Value of home' appears as one of the sample statistics said to be related to the social rank construct in the tabular summary of the Shevky-Bell scheme. See Table 4.2 above.

TABLE 4.11 *Definition of social area indicants, Brisbane and Auckland*

Abbreviation	Definition
WWF	Per cent females aged 15–64 years in workforce
SFD	Per cent private dwellings single-family structures
SEP	Per cent females ever married, separated or divorced
NMF	Per cent females aged 16 years and over never married
FER (Br)	Ratio of children 0–5 years: women 15–44 years
CHI (Ak)	Per cent population aged 0–5 years
65+	Per cent females aged 65 years and over
PRO	Per cent males in workforce professional or managerial
NMW	Per cent males in workforce non-manual workers
INC (Ak)	Per cent males with income of $3,000 or more p.a.
HVL (Br)	Mean selling value house and land
OAW	Per cent males own-account workers
ETH (Br)	Per cent non-British born
ETH (Ak)	Per cent non-European

SOURCES. Brisbane: All except PRO, NMW and HVL from CD tabulations, Census of the Commonwealth of Australia, 1961. PRO, NMW: 1 in 6 sample males from Queensland Electoral Register, 1961. HVL: Special tabulation by Queensland Valuer General's Department for years 1960–3.
Auckland: N.Z. Census of Population and Dwellings 1966; City Subdivision, Auckland and Central Auckland Statistical Area.

land, the occupational indicant is joined by one on the income characteristics of sub-area populations – the proportion of the male workforce earning NZ $3,000 or more per year. Related variables available for both cities are the proportion of professional and managerial workers and the proportion of males classified as employers or self-employed, i.e. own-account workers. All four indicants should be closely associated. Populations characterized as being of high social rank should contain many non-manual workers and either be housed in homes of above-average value or be characterized by a high proportion of high incomes. They should also contain relatively high proportions of professional and managerial workers and of own-account workers. Conversely, populations characterized as being of low social rank should contain few non-manual workers, and should be housed in below-average value homes or contain few persons with above average incomes. They should also contain relatively few professional and managerial workers and relatively few own-account workers.

The index of family status proposed by Shevky and Bell has three components: the fertility ratio, women in the workforce and single-family detached dwellings. Each of the indicants is available for Brisbane, but in Auckland it is necessary to substitute the proportion of the population aged 0–5 years of age for the fertility ratio. Related indicants available for both cities are the proportion of elderly persons, the proportion of never-married females 16 years and over and the proportion of the ever married now separated or divorced. Populations characterized by a high score on the

161

family status construct should have many children, few old people, few single, separated or divorced females, few women in the workforce and should be housed primarily in single-family dwellings. Populations character-ized by a low score on the construct should contain few children, many old people, many single, separated or divorced females, many working women and few single-family dwellings.

The Shevky–Bell index of ethnic status is derived from data on the proportion of Negroes and of Latin American and Southern European migrants in each census tract population. Populations with a high ethnic status, in the Bell terminology, are those which contain a high proportion of 'those groups which traditionally have held subordinate status in the dominant society'.[1] In the Australian context it is arguable whether all or only a few of the non-British migrants should be included in the index. All foreign-born migrants are 'New Australians' and, at various times, each has been the object of prejudice and discrimination. On the other hand, there is a good deal of evidence that in terms of both structural and behavioural dissimilarity and in terms of attitudinal distance, North-western European

TABLE 4.12 *Comparison of observed and predicted correlations for six social area indicants: Brisbane, 1961 and Auckland, 1961*

Indicant	FER/CHI	SFD	WWF	NMW	HVL/INC	ETH
FER/CHI	.					
SFD	+	.				
WWF	−	−	.			
NMW	o	o	o	.		
HVL/INC	o	o	o	+	.	
ETH	o	o	o	o	o	.

NOTE. + high positive *r*; o insignificant *r*; − high negative *r*.

Observed pattern

	Brisbane							Auckland					
	FER	SFD	WWF	NMW	HVL	ETH		CHI	SFD	WWF	NMW	INC	ETH
FER	.						CHI	.					
SFD	53	.					SFD	61	.				
WWF	−69	−81	.				WWF	−60	−89	.			
NMW	−17	−03	−04	.			NMW	−39	−03	−20	.		
HVL	−27	−05	04	53	.		INC	−34	−06	−26	96	.	
ETH	−18	−58	16	−18	−13	.	ETH	22	−24	43	−66	−66	

NOTE.
FER	Fertility ratio.	NMW	Proportion non-manual workers.
CHI	Proportion aged 0–5 years.	HVL	Average value house and land.
SFD	Proportion single-family dwellings.	INC	Proportion earning $3000 p.a. or more.
WWF	Proportion women in workforce.	ETH	Proportion ethnic minority.

[1] Shevky and Bell, *Social Area Analysis*, p. 25.

migrants have been effectively assimilated to the British–Australian group.[1] In view of the relatively small number of Southern and Eastern European migrants in Brisbane, however, and the small size of CDs, it was decided in the present instance to use an ethnic status index based on all non-British migrants. In the Auckland data the ethnic status dimension is represented by the proportion of the population classified as non-European.

The social area model predicts a clear pattern of relationships among the various indicants used in the scheme. Table 4.12 compares the predicted and the observed correlation matrixes between the six basic social area indicants in each city. The coefficients are derived from product-moment correlation analysis carried out on standardized but untransformed variables.[2]

The pattern of within-construct correlations is as predicted. In both cities fertility shows a high positive correlation with the proportion of single-family dwellings and a high negative correlation with the proportion of women in the workforce. Single-family dwellings correlates negatively with women in the workforce. Within the social rank cluster there is a high positive correlation between the proportion of non-manual workers and either average house value, in Brisbane, or the proportion of high income earners, in Auckland. There is less agreement with the basic social area model in the pattern of correlations between indicants belonging to different constructs. Taking a coefficient of ±0·30 as an arbitrary cut-off point, the Brisbane series exhibits a single deviation from the predicted no correlations while the Auckland data exhibit no less than five deviations. Three of the five Auckland departures from the predicted pattern and the single Brisbane 'error' involve the ethnic status indicant. The remaining Auckland deviations involve the fertility indicant. The significance of the deviations will be discussed later.

In general the pattern of intercorrelations observed in Brisbane and Auckland are similar to those reported in studies of other Western cities. Table 4.13 compares the intercorrelation coefficients obtained for five of the social area indicants – all except house value or income – in Brisbane and Auckland with those obtained in the social area analyses of Newcastle-under-Lyme, Rome and San Francisco and in the analysis of the ten-cities model constructed by Van Arsdol, *et al.*

The three measures assumed to belong to the family status construct show high intercorrelations in all the cities. The only exception from the pattern is the negligible correlation obtained in Newcastle-under-Lyme. The small population of Newcastle and the problems which Herbert has in manipulating his data render the status of the deviant finding somewhat uncertain. There is less consistency among the cities in the patterns of correlation

---

[1] E.g. Timms, 'The dissimilarity between overseas-born and Australian-born in Queensland', pp. 363–74.
[2] Standardization is to the range in the city concerned.

TABLE 4.13 *Intercorrelation of social area indicants: Auckland, Brisbane, Newcastle-under-Lyme, Rome, San Francisco and ten U.S. cities*

Indicant			SFD	WWF	NMW	Ethnic
Fertility	Auckland	1966	61	−60	−39	22
	Brisbane	1961	53	−69	−27	−18
	Newcastle	1961	.	−08	−41	.
	Rome	1951	.	−69	−68	.
	San Francisco	1940	48	−76	−68	21
	Ten cities	1950	31	−64	−55	−12
Single-family	Auckland			−89	−03	−24
dwellings	Brisbane			−81	−05	−58
	Newcastle					
	Rome			.	.	.
	San Francisco			−75	19	−25
	Ten cities			−66	11	−26
Women in	Auckland				20	43
workforce	Brisbane				04	16
	Newcastle				27	.
	Rome				64	.
	San Francisco				48	07
	Ten cities				16	11
Non-manual	Auckland					−66
workers	Brisbane					−13
	Newcastle					.
	Rome					
	San Francisco					−14
	Ten cities					−23

SOURCES. Newcastle: Herbert, 'Social area analysis'.
Rome: McElrath, 'The social areas of Rome'.
San Francisco: Bell, 'Economic, family, and ethnic status'.
Ten cities: Van Arsdol, *et al.*, 'An application'.

which obtain between the three measures of family status and those measures believed to tap the constructs of social rank and ethnicity. The correlation between fertility and the proportion of non-manual workers is always negative, but varies between −0·27 in Brisbane and −0·68 in Rome. The correlation between single-family dwellings and non-manual workers varies between −0·05 in Brisbane and 0·19 in San Francisco, and that between women in the workforce and non-manual workers between 0·04 in Brisbane and 0·64 in Rome. The Brisbane figures are, throughout, very similar to those reported for San Francisco in 1950.[1] Comparisons involving the ethnic status indicant are rendered difficult by the differences in the

[1] The 1950 San Francisco figures are referred to in McElrath's study of Rome: fertility and women in the labour-force correlate 0·69; non-manual workers and fertility correlate −0·29; and non-manual workers and women in the labour-force correlate −0·021. McElrath, 'The social areas of Rome', p. 381.

measure's definition. In Brisbane and the ten-cities data ethnicity correlates negatively with fertility; in Auckland and San Francisco the correlation is positive. In none of the four, however, does the association reach any significant level. The correlation between ethnicity and the proportion of single-family dwellings varies between −0·24 in Auckland and −0·58 in Brisbane; that between ethnicity and the proportion of women in the workforce varies between 0·07 in San Francisco and 0·43 in Auckland. All the correlations between ethnicity and the proportion of non-manual workers are negative, but they range in size from −0·13 in Brisbane to −0·66 in Auckland. Notwithstanding the differences in detail, the general impression of Table 4.13 is one of similarity and that data provide strong testimony in favour of the Shevky–Bell model as a description of the ecological structure of the modern city.

A more rigorous test of the model is provided by subjecting the Brisbane and Auckland data to multiple-group factor hypothesis. Before attempting this the various ancillary measures may be introduced. The eventual analysis relates to eleven indicants: six presumed to reflect family status, four to reflect social rank, and one to reflect ethnicity. The communalities used in the computations are derived from the principal components analyses reported earlier.[1]

The Shevky–Bell model implies a series of hypotheses about the pattern of indicant-factor correlations in the Brisbane and Auckland data which may be tested by the multiple-group method of factor analysis:

(1) At least three factors are necessary to account for the observed pattern of correlation between sub-area populations with reference to measures of fertility, single-family dwellings, women in the workforce, separated or divorced persons, never-married females, elderly persons, non-manual workers, professional and managerial workers, own-account workers house values or incomes, and ethnic characteristics.

(2 *a*) Measures of fertility, single-family dwellings, women in the workforce, separated or divorced persons, never-married females and elderly persons are highly correlated with a single factor which may be defined as familism or family status.

(2 *b*) Measures of the proportion of non-manual workers, professional and manual workers, own-account workers and either house values or incomes are highly correlated with a single social rank factor.

(2 *c*) The indicants relating to the proportion of foreign-born, in Brisbane, and to the proportion of non-Europeans in Auckland will form a specific factor which may be defined as ethnicity or ethnic status.

(3 *a*) The social rank and family status factors are effectively independent of each other.

1 See chapter 2, pages 73–80.

In the light of U.S. studies and on the assumption that the assimilation of migrants is incomplete it may also be hypothesized,

(3 *b*) That ethnic status will exhibit marked dependencies with one or other of the social rank and familism factors.

Table 4.14 shows the multiple-group factor structure produced by grouping the indicants in the manner outlined in hypothesis 2. The first six indicants are allocated to the first, family status, factor; indicants seven to ten inclusive are allocated to the social rank factor; the eleventh indicant, per cent non-British born in Brisbane and per cent non-European in Auckland, is treated as forming the basis of a specific ethnic factor.

TABLE 4.14 *Multiple-group factor structures for social area indicants, Brisbane and Auckland*

Indicant	Brisbane factors			Auckland factors		
	I	II	III	I	II	III
WWF	−93	01	20	−94	−29	−54
SFD	83	−07	−71	91	04	−30
SEP	−75	−21	−54	−90	−29	−54
NMF	−71	22	−16	−94	−04	−34
FER *i*	78	−27	−22	79	−29	28
65+	−58	15	−01	−76	15	04
PRO	−09	75	−12	−13	97	−77
NMW	−10	78	−16	−06	97	−83
HVL *ii*	−05	67	−23	−01	96	−83
OAW	−07	61	−09	37	81	−81
ETH	−26	17	81	−21	−70	80

NOTES. *i* In Auckland CHI is substituted for FER.
ii In Auckland INC is substituted for HVL.

Correlation between factors

Factor	Brisbane factors			Auckland factors		
	I	II	III	I	II	III
I	100			100		
II	−11	100		05	100	
III	−32	−21	100	−27	−87	100

In both cities the postulated factors effectively exhaust common-factor variance. In the Brisbane data over 89 per cent of original communality is captured by the three multiple-group factors and application of the McNemar criterion supports the first hypothesis. In the Auckland data, on the other hand, a third factor is statistically redundant. Over 99 per cent of original communality is exhausted by the familism and social rank factors, with the latter being extended to include the non-European indicant. Thus, hypothesis I is given only partial corroboration.

The hypothesized pattern of indicant-factor correlations involving the familism and social rank clusters is strongly supported by the multiple-group factor structures. The family status factor exhibits high negative item-factor correlations with the proportion of women in the workforce, the proportion of separated or divorced females, the proportion of never-married females, and the proportion of the population aged 65 years and over. It exhibits high positive correlations with the proportion of single-family dwellings and with the fertility indicants. Populations showing high scores on the factor have few women in the workforce, many children, few old, separated, divorced, or never-married women, and live in areas character-ized by single-family dwellings. Conversely populations showing low scores on the factor have many women in the workforce, few children, many old, separated, divorced, and never-married women, and live in areas with many multi-family dwellings. None of the indicants which have high item-factor correlations with the family type factor exhibit significant correlations with the social rank factor. In both Brisbane and Auckland this latter dimension of residential differentiation is indexed by the proportions of professional workers, non-manual workers, and own-account workers, and by either the proportion of high income earners or the average value of house and land. Each factor is easily interpretable and the factor structures provide a close approximation to the concept of simple structure. The ethnic factor is much less satisfactory as far as hypothesis 2 is concerned. In Brisbane the factor exhibits relatively high correlations with two of the indicants belonging to the familism cluster – single-family dwellings and separated or divorced persons. Collectors' districts containing high proportions of foreign-born also contain relatively few single-family dwellings and relatively many separated or divorced persons. In Auckland no separate ethnic factor is identi-fiable. Rather, the proportion of non-Europeans in the population becomes part of the general social rank factor. Statistical subdivisions characterized by relatively high proportions of non-Europeans may also be characterized as being low in social rank. Although a direct translation of the ecological finding into an assertion about the general relationship between ethnicity and social rank in the Auckland population is hazardous, the data suggest that Maori or Polynesian ethnic identity is virtually synonymous with low social rank.[1]

Given that Australia and New Zealand are examples of highly modernized societies it follows that the ecological structure of their cities should exhibit a marked degree of differentiation. In particular, according to hypothesis 3 a it may be anticipated that the social rank and family status axes of resi-dential differentiation will be essentially independent of each other. The Brisbane and Auckland data are clearly in support of this hypothesis. In

[1] Cf. E. G. Schwimmer (ed.), *The Maori People in the 1960's* (Auckland, 1968).

Brisbane the correlation between the two group factors corresponding to social rank and family status is -0.111; in Auckland the correlation is even lower, -0.046. The Brisbane and Auckland findings are virtually identical with those reported for a series of U.S. cities of similar size.[1]

The independence of familism and social rank factors appears to be an invariant characteristic of cities located in such modern societies as the Western and Northern United States, Scandinavia and Australasia. Much less consistency is apparent in the inter-factor correlations exhibited by the ethnic status dimension. Although the correlations between ethnicity and social rank are almost invariably negative they range in size from the insignificant -0.02 reported for Atlanta to -0.75 in Providence and -0.73 in Los Angeles. The Brisbane figure of -0.21 is somewhat lower than is generally reported. The Auckland figure, on the other hand, -0.87, is higher than any other reported in the literature and reinforces the assumption that ethnicity does not occur as a separate axis of differentiation among the city's statistical subdivisions. The correlations between ethnicity and family status exhibited in the Brisbane and Auckland series are virtually identical with those reported for U.S. cities. It seems wellnigh universal in the modern city that areas containing large numbers of disadvantaged ethnic minorities are also characterized by low social rank and by low family status.[2]

On the whole, the Brisbane and Auckland analyses support the assumptions of the original social area scheme as a framework for the analysis of the modern city. Family status and social rank emerge in the predicted pattern, but ethnicity is closely dependent on the other axes. While the data suggest that it is valid to consider familism and social rank as independent bases of residential differentiation, the position with regard to ethnicity remains obscure. No evidence is forthcoming from the Brisbane and Auckland materials concerning a postulated urbanism-mobility or migration status factor. The indicants which might be expected to be involved in the emergence of an urbanism factor – separated and divorced persons, old persons and never-married females – in fact correlate strongly with the general family status axis. Social rank and familism emerge as by far the most salient of the social area constructs in the modern city and the validity of the indicants used in their definition appears to be well supported.

THE VALIDITY OF THE SOCIAL AREA MODEL IN PRE-MODERN SOCIETY

Outside North America social area analyses have been reported for no more

---

[1] Van Arsdol, *et al.*, 'The generality'. The correlation between family status and social rank varies between 0.14 in Akron and -0.22 in Atlanta. Five out of ten coefficients are between zero and -0.10.

[2] This does not, however, imply that there is no conceptual distinction between ethnicity and the other social area constructs.

than a handful of cities. In the less developed parts of the world analyses are available for Abidjan and Accra, in Africa, for Hyderabad, in India, and for Kingston, in the Caribbean.[1] The Hyderabad study appears to have taken the validity of the basic social area model for granted and does not investigate its factorial relevance to local conditions. Thus, even with the addition of the factorial studies of Cairo and Calcutta it is clear that there is, as yet, far from sufficient evidence to test the validity of the 'modernization-differentiation' model in any detail. What evidence there is, however, is generally in support of the theory.

In his study of Accra, McElrath uses eight indicants, two to each of the social area constructs of social rank, family status, migration status, and ethnic status. The correlations between each measure over the 314 census sub-areas of Accra in 1960 are shown in Table 4.15.

TABLE 4.15 *Correlation of social area indicants for Accra, Ghana, 1960*

Construct	Variable		1	2	3	4	5	6	7	8
Social rank	No school	(1)	100							
	Manual workers	(2)	35	100						
Family status	Women in workforce	(3)	27	−33	100					
	Fertility ratio	(4)	35	−22	32	100				
Migration status	Region born	(5)	24	−41	46	45	100			
	Males 15–44 (−)	(6)	−34	−32	41	65	77	100		
Ethnic status	Per cent Ga	(7)	10	−38	42	36	91	66	100	
	Per cent Ewe (−)	(8)	02	−24	26	−05	36	14	45	100

SOURCE. McElrath, 'Societal scale'.

Within each construct the component variables show the predicted correlation in all except one case: the correlation between the women in the workforce variable and the fertility ratio. The predicted negative relation between these variables turns out to be positive; areas characterized by a high proportion of working women also tend to be characterized by high fertility ratios. McElrath suggests that the reason this is so is that the work which is entered into by the women is frequently of a small-scale marketing nature which is by no means incompatible with having a large family. Moreover the presence of an extended kin structure allows the care of children to be delegated. Work does not involve the women of Accra making a fundamental decision between career and family orientations: given the present structure of the market, family involvement and female

[1] R. Clignet and J. Sween, 'Accra and Abidjan: a comparative examination of the theory of increase in scale' (unpub. mimeo. paper, Northwestern University, 1968); McElrath, 'Societal scale'; Hyderabad Metropolitan Research Project, *Social Area Analysis of Metropolitan Hyderabad* (Hyderabad, 1966).

participation in the workforce are quite compatible. In the absence of an independent family status factor, McElrath states that three independent dimensions of social differentiation may be recognized in Accra: social rank, migration status, and ethnic status, with migration status being the most important axis. Multiple-group factor analysis of the Accra data suggests that this may well be the case although the item-factor loadings point to a rather different combination of variables than that suggested by McElrath (Table 4.16).

TABLE 4.16 *Multiple-group factor solutions for social area variables in Accra*

I. Oblique factor structure

Variable	Factor		
	I	II	III
No school	82	15	02
Manual work	82	−39	−24
Women in workforce	−04	66	26
Fertility	14	70	−05
Region born	−10	90	36
Males 15–44 (−)	−40	88	14
Per cent Ga	−17	84	45
Per cent Ewe (−)	−13	29	100

II. Correlation between factors

Factor	I	II	III
I	100		
II	−14	100	
III	−13	29	100

Although it does not exhaust the variance in the matrix, a three-factor solution in which the variables, women in the workforce fertility, region born, males outside the age range 15-44, and per cent Ga, load on a single group factor interpreted as migration status, leaving the variables no school and manual work to form a social rank factor, and per cent non-Ewe to form a specific factor, appears to provide the most satisfactory solution to the observed pattern of intercorrelations. Each factor is relatively independent of the others.

McElrath also presents data on the ecological correlation of social area indicants in Kingston.[1] Here, all coefficients are in the predicted direction, but the within-construct coefficients tend to be lower than predicted in the basic social area model while the between-construct coefficients tend to be

[1] McElrath, 'Societal scale'.

higher. Comparing the Accra and Kingston materials with those reported from Rome and for U.S. cities,[1] McElrath concludes that, as far as the social rank dimension is concerned:

(1) Social rank occurs as an independent dimension of social differentiation in cities of societies where the distribution of skills reveals only limited advance (Accra, Kingston). (2) This form of differentiation is increasingly independent of family status as these changes are appreciably more advanced (Rome, U.S.). (3) Some variation in the independence of social rank occurs among urban areas of the same large scale society (the ten medium sized cities and the San Francisco Bay Region).[2]

A more complex set of considerations applies to the case of family status:

(1) Family status does not operate as an independent form of sub-population differentiation in the urban area of a society where only limited changes of the structure of production have occurred (Ghana). (2) It does operate independently of social rank in a society where these changes are slightly more advanced (Jamaica). (3) The independence of family status from social rank systematically increases with societal scale and reaches its greatest independence in a society of large scale (United States). In such societies it also demonstrates some variation between urban area, with greater independence from other forms of social differentiation in large metropolitan areas (San Francisco Bay Region).[3]

The degree of differentiation parallels the degree of modernization as revealed by such statistics as per cent literacy, per cent workers in non-agriculture, per cent wage and salary earners and per cent urban.

An extension of the modernization-differentiation argument to non-urban societies may be illustrated by the situation in the Cook Islands, to the north of New Zealand. Scattered across 850,000 square miles of ocean, the 15 main islands of the Cook Group have a surface area of some 90 square miles and a 1966 population of 19,250. Over half the population live on the largest island, Rarotonga, which is the seat of government. Only twelve of the islands are permanently settled although the other three are regularly visited by copra-drying gangs or mother-of-pearl divers. According to the census report,

It may seem curious to talk of urbanization in such a context, but that in fact is what is taking place in relation to Rarotonga . . . Although several of the outer islands have small lighting sets, Aitutaki is the only island outside Rarotonga with a public electricity supply. Nearly all the factories, including the fruit juice cannery, are on Rarotonga, as also is the main secondary school and the Teachers' Training

---

[1] The Rome data is from McElrath, 'The social areas of Rome'; material on San Francisco in 1950 is derived from an unpublished paper of Bell and 'material on ten 'middle-sized' U.S. cities is taken from Van Arsdol *et al.* 'An application'.

[2] McElrath, 'Societal scale', p. 49.

[3] *Ibid.* p. 50.

College. The inadequacy of family land to support the more numerous families has also been a prime factor in the movement to Rarotonga.[1]

Outside Rarotonga, the Cook Islands exhibit an almost wholly agricultural economy, albeit generally with a cash basis. The islands of the northern group are primarily devoted to coconut trees but the southern islands produce a range of tropical fruits. Of the 600 persons in manufacturing industry 550 are in Rarotonga. Similar proportions apply to commerce and construction. Only in Rarotonga and Aitutaki of the larger islands do full-time wage and salary earners outnumber own-account workers. Population growth has been rapid, but much has been siphoned off by emigration to New Zealand, especially Auckland.[2] Within the islands there have been considerable population movements, primarily to Rarotonga, but also involving most of the other islands. The indigenous population, Cook Island Maoris, have been joined by some 600 non-Polynesians, primarily New Zealand Europeans. All but a handful of these live in Rarotonga and Aitutaki. Literacy is virtually 100 per cent.

Given the small base and relatively underdeveloped nature of the Cook Islands it is difficult to predict the bases of ecological differentiation which will characterize their population. Modernization and population movements both revolve around Rarotonga and it may be that they will provide the core dimensions of differentiation. It seems highly unlikely that independent

TABLE 4.17 *Definition of social area variables: Cook Islands, 1966*

Name	Definition
Non-manual workers	Per cent male workforce professional, administrative, clerical or sales workers
High income	Per cent population earning N.Z. $1000 p.a. or more, 'primary' income
Own-account workers	Per cent male workforce working on own account
Fertility	Per cent 0–5 years of age: women 15–14 years of age
Single females	Per cent females aged 15 years and over never married
Working women	Per cent females aged 15 years and over economically active
Local migrants	Per cent population born in other islands
Overseas migrants	Per cent population born outside Cook Islands
Full-bloods	Per cent population Cook Islands Maori full-bloods
Agriculture	Per cent male workforce employed in agriculture
Radios	Per cent dwellings with radio

SOURCE. Cook Islands *Population Census 1966*.

[1] Premier's Department, Government of the Cook Islands, *Population Census 1966* (Rarotonga, 1968), p.3.
[2] Between 1961 and 1966 the annual net outflow averaged approximately 500. In 1966 there were 6,240 full-blood Cook Island Maoris and 2,423 Cook Island Maoris of mixed-blood in New Zealand. The great majority of these lived in the Auckland metropolitan area, especially in the inner city.

social rank and family status factors will arise. Both are more likely to belong to a modernization-migration cluster.

The indicants available for the Cook Islands are shown in Table 4.17. Although it would be desirable to break the Rarotonga figures down to villages this was not possible given the material to hand. Wherever possible, indicants equivalent to those used in the New Zealand and Australian analyses have been employed.

The social rank construct of the basic social area model is tapped by three indicants: non-manual workers, high-income earners (more than NZ $1,000 p.a.) and own-account workers. The family status construct is tapped by indicants relating to fertility, women in the workforce, and never-married females. Migration status is indexed by per cent inter-island migrants and ethnicity by per cent full-bloods and per cent overseas-born. Two measures of modernization are included: the per cent of dwellings possessing a radio and the per cent of male workers employed in agriculture. The product-moment correlation coefficients between the indicants are shown in Table 4.18.[1]

TABLE 4.18 *Product-moment correlation coefficients for 11 social area indicants, Cook Islands, 1966*

Indicants		1	2	3	4	5	6	7	8	9	10	11
Non-manual workers	1	–										
High income	2	73	–				$n = 12$					
Own-account workers	3	−77	−93	–								
Fertility	4	−33	−65	59	–							
Single females	5	60	92	−83	−74	–						
Working women	6	−36	−27	33	−29	−16	–					
Local migrants	7	−60	−14	28	02	−23	47	–				
Overseas migrants	8	60	68	−71	−42	52	−19	−06	–			
Full-bloods	9	−54	−70	58	83	−72	−09	21	−23	–		
Agriculture	10	−81	−89	91	42	−79	35	28	−52	44	–	
Radios	11	49	58	−67	−12	42	−41	−17	82	01	−66	–

It is immediately apparent that the predictions of the basic social area model do not apply to the Cook Islands data. Cross-construct correlations are as important as within-construct correlations. Within the social rank set of indicants per cent non-manual workers and per cent high-income earners

[1] The coefficients are for untransformed variables. The small number of base units used in the computations is reflected in a critical value of r of ± 0.576 at the $+0.05$ level. Since the analysis is based on a full enumeration, however, rather than a sample, the usual sampling criteria for significance do not apply.

correlate in the expected fashion, but per cent own-account workers exhibits a high negative correlation with both. In the Cook Islands, as in most other underdeveloped countries, own-account workers are generally subsistence or small-scale farmers. Islands characterized by high proportions of own-account workers have lower incomes and fewer non-manual workers than those with a lower proportion of self-employed. High correlations exist between the occupational and income data and agricultural employment. The higher the proportion of farmers, the lower the income. The family status indicants exhibit negative correlations with non-manual workers and high-income earners. Within the family status set, fertility and never-married women correlate as predicted, but there is little relationship between either and the per cent of women in the workforce. This latter variable exhibits relatively low correlation coefficients with all other indicants, its highest associations being with local migrants and agricultural workers. Far from being an 'urban' variable, the Cook Islands data suggest that the percentage of women in the workforce may be related to agricultural ways of life. High correlations occur between fertility and the per cent of Maori full-bloods (positive) and between never-married women and per cent full-bloods, and never-married women and per cent agricultural workers (negative). The per cent of inter-island migrants exhibits generally low correlations apart from a moderately high negative correlation with per cent non-manual workers. Overseas migrants, on the other hand, exhibit high correlations with the occupational and income variables, and with the proportion of radio-ownership. The per cent of full-bloods shows high correlations with fertility, never-married women (negative) and high incomes (negative). The per cent of agricultural workers exhibits high correlations with non-manual workers, high incomes, and never-married women (negative), and with own-account workers (positive). The proportion of dwellings with radios shows a reverse pattern of correlations.

No attempt to interpret the Cook Islands data using multiple-group factors predicted by the basic social area model is likely to be successful. Instead, a 'blind' analysis using the technique of principal components, followed by rotation, is suggested. Table 4.19 shows the resulting pattern of item-construct loadings.

A tentative interpretation of the factors labels factor I 'modernization', factor II 'traditional way of life', and factor III 'migration status'. The modernization factor is identified by high positive item-factor loadings with per cent of dwellings with radios, per cent overseas migrants and per cent earning more than $1,000 p.a. and by high negative item-factor loadings with per cent employed in agriculture and per cent own-account workers. The traditional factor is, to some extent, a mirror image of factor I. It is identified by a high negative correlation with high income earners and moderately high positive correlations with own-account workers and agri-

TABLE 4.19 *Rotated orthogonal factor solution (varimax criterion) for Cook Islands, 1966*

Indicant	Factor			h^2
	I	II	III	
Radios	93	05	−16	89
Overseas migrants	89	−23	01	85
Agriculture	−76	47	30	89
Own-account workers	−71	59	27	93
High income	66	−69	−17	94
Full-bloods	00	95	12	92
Fertility	−16	90	−21	89
Single females	46	−79	−16	86
Local migrants	05	15	90	84
Working women	−35	−24	74	73
Non-manual workers	49	−48	−60	82
Per cent total variance	34·4	34·2	18·3	(86·9)

culture. More central to the factor, however, are the high item-factor correlations exhibited by per cent full-bloods, fertility, and per cent never-married females (negative). Islands which score highly on factor I are characterized by high radio-ownership, relatively many overseas-born and males earning more than $1,000 p.a., and by relatively few workers in agriculture or classified as self-employed. Islands which score highly on factor II are characterized by high proportions of Maori full-bloods, high fertility ratios, many agricultural workers and own-account workers, few never-married women and low incomes. Factor III is less easy to interpret, but appears similar to McElrath's migration status. Mobility is its key element. Islands scoring highly on the factor are characterized by many inter-island migrants, many women in the workforce and few non-manual workers. Inter-island migration appears to have little association with modernization but the other indicants loading on the migration factor also exhibit moderate item-factor correlations with factor I.

Neither family status nor social rank emerge as differentiating factors in the ecological structure of the Cook Islands. Indicants belonging to the social area constructs of social rank and family status are evenly split between the three major factors of the Cook Islands ecology. Modernization, centred on Rarotonga, and traditional ways of life, characteristic of the outer islands, compete as the major dimensions of the Island's ecological structure. Modernization, emanating from outside the Cook Islands and closely associated with overseas-born populations and overseas communication,[1] has yet to usher in widespread social differentiation. As it does so, however,

[1] Cf. the stress which Rogers and Svenning place on the role of communications in the modernization process.

so it may be predicted that those who accept modern values will pre-empt the higher social ranks in island society. The modernization factor will thus tend to become a social rank factor. Conversely, the factor relating to the traditional way of life, with its emphasis on family variables, may give birth to a separate family status dimension. Migration status seems already established, while ethnicity may lie dormant. It may be anticipated that the modernization of Cook Island society will lead to a growing similarity between its ecological structure and that outlined in the basic social area model.

The paucity of the evidence notwithstanding, it seems well established that the emergence and independence of the social area axes is closely related to the degree of modernization found in the community concerned. The basic social area model outlined by Shevky and Bell is valid only in the case of the most modern cities. Elsewhere, different patterns of item–construct association reflect the socio-cultural matrix and pace of modernization characteristic of the society concerned. With the progress of modernization and its associated social mobilization it may be predicted that the ecological structure of the less-developed societies will come to resemble those already characteristic of the modern metropolis.

THE STABILITY OF THE SOCIAL AREA AXES ACROSS CHANGES IN BASE UNITS AND TIME

The reliability of the social area axes across different orders of base units and across varying periods of time has received relatively little attention. Shevky and Bell claim not only that the social area typology is suitable for the analysis of social aggregates at any scale but that it may also be used for comparative analyses of a community at different time periods. In either case the stability of the underlying item-construct relationships is essential. In the absence of this stability, comparison is impossible. In the absence of sufficiently detailed material from underdeveloped countries assessment of the reliability of the social area scheme across changes in territorial and temporal frameworks must presently be confined to the stability of the basic model in modern societies.

The social area axes and different scales of base units

It is somewhat unclear in the Shevky-Bell statement about the applicability of the social area model to different orders of sub-units whether an identity is assumed between indicants and indexes used at the various scales. The general assumption, however, appears to be that, regardless of scale, social rank, family status and ethnic status will provide the main dimensions of ecological differentiation and that they will be related to the empirical indicants in similar fashion. Data relevant to this assumption are presented by Udry in a study of the bases of differentiation among nine U.S. sub-regions and 89 standard metropolitan areas.[1] Udry also reports the results of a factorial study by Jonassen and Peres concerned with the factors of differentiation among Ohio counties.[2] Although the variables used in none of the analyses are identical with those specified by Shevky and Bell, Udry considers them interchangeable. He justifies the substitution by claiming that the new variables are selected 'from "higher up the theory" when possible (i.e. we have used variables the fewest logical steps removed from the postulates)'.[3]

The extent to which the pattern of intercorrelations obtained follows the Shevky-Bell model varies considerably according to the territorial sub-units being analysed. Table 4.20 gives the relevant details.

TABLE 4.20 *Intercorrelations between variables used in analyses of the differentiation between U.S. Census sub-regions (below diagonal) and standard metropolitan areas (above diagonal)*

	Education	White-collar	Income	Working women	Fertility	Owners	Primary	Migrants	Non-workers
Education	–	53	36						
White-collar	77	–	45	43				40	−37
Income	42	87	–	35					−54
Working women				–	i	i	i		−73
Fertility				−75	–	i	i	i	54
Owners				−52	75	–	i		
Primary		60		41	79	71	–		41
Migrants					54			–	i
Non-workers	−53	−65			87	52	79	50	–

SOURCE. Adapted from Udry, 'Increasing scale and spatial differentiation', p. 411.
NOTES. i Predicted correlation not significant in data.
   ii *Definition of variables*

Education: per cent high school grades
White-collar: per cent white-collar
Income: median family income
Working women: per cent women in workforce
Fertility: cumulative fertility

Owners: per cent owner-occupied
Primary; per cent primary production workers
Migrants: per cent migrant
Non-workers: non-worker : worker ratio

For the nine census sub-regions both the social rank and urbanization-family status dimensions can be discerned, although Udry suggests that

[1] Udry, 'Increasing scale and spatial differentiation'.
[2] C. T. Jonassen and S. H. Peres, *Interrelationships of Dimensions of Community Systems* (Columbus, Ohio, 1960).
[3] Udry, 'Increasing scale and spatial differentiation', p. 409.

they are more highly intercorrelated than might be expected. There is little evidence of the existence of an independent ethnicity axis. The Shevky–Bell model is still less satisfactory for the standard metropolitan area data. The three variables belonging to the social rank set intercorrelate as desired, although the size of the coefficients is small. Urbanization-family status and segregation-ethnic status, however, fail to appear at all as independent axes. None of the inter-correlations between the four presumed indicants of family status is more than ±0·34, and the non-worker ratio, which Udry believes to belong to the ethnic status-segregation cluster, shows high correlations only with variables in the family status and social rank sets. Udry suggests that 'the urbanization axis may not be discernable because only the 89 largest SMA's were studied, all of which may be so far along the urbanization axis as to have removed its relevance for discriminating among them'.[1] If this should prove to be the case, then the general utility of the social area scheme for the analysis of inter-city differences is open to considerable question. Similar doubts about the applicability of the Shevky–Bell model are prompted by the results of the Jonassen and Peres study of 88 counties in the State of Ohio. The seven basic factors extracted coincide very imperfectly with the Shevky–Bell constructs. Thus, the Jonassen and Peres 'urbanization' factor includes high item-factor correlations for per cent white collar, per cent high school graduate and median income, from the Shevky–Bell social rank set; per cent women in the workforce, from the latter's urbanization construct; and mobility. Fertility is independent of the other variables in the urbanization factor and the per cent of owner-occupiers shows no significant loading on any axis. Udry concludes: 'In sum, the axes of differentiation of sub-areas shift as the sub-area unit changes. The Shevky–Bell model is not applicable as a general theory of the differentiation of sub-areas.'[2]

In a comment on Udry's findings, Bell and Moskos deny that his conclusions are as prejudicial to the validity of the social area axes as a general classificatory tool as he claims.[3] They point out that a casual inspection of the higher inter-correlations in a set of data is no substitute for a more formal factor analysis which can take account also of the pattern of inter-variable relationships. They also query the selection of variables which Udry believes to relate to the segregation-ethnic status construct. They suggest that the failures of the second and third axes to appear in areas larger than census tracts may be in part a statistical artefact resulting from the small number of base units involved in the analysis. Finally they assert that even in the case of factor analysis there are many ways of presenting the same data and the final decision as to whether or not particular axes of differentiation are conceptually distinct must involve not just statistical considerations,

---

[1] *Ibid.* p. 411.   [2] *Ibid.* p. 413.
[3] Bell and Moskos, 'A comment on Udry's "Increasing scale and spacial differentiation" '.

but also the researcher's judgement as to which alternative achieves the greater analytical utility. Thus, although social rank and ethnic status may prove to be highly intercorrelated in a given population, they suggest it is still justifiable and even necessary to keep the two constructs analytically distinct.

A further test of the utility of the social area model at different scales is provided by three sets of data for varying orders of sub-units in New Zealand. Each set of data refers to 1966. The areal frameworks used in the analyses are (1) the 18 urban areas of New Zealand, (2) the 21 cities and boroughs which are included in the Auckland urban area, and (3) the 62 statistical sub-divisions into which the latter are divided for census purposes. The average population of the base unit varies between 92,900, in the case of the first framework, to 7,305 in the case of the last. Ten variables are used for each analysis: six relating to the urbanization-family status construct, three to social rank and one to ethnicity. No information is available which would allow the construction of any indicant directly relating to mobility or to migration status. The definition of the indicants used is given in Table 4.21.

TABLE 4.21 *Definition of social area variables, New Zealand urban areas and Auckland, 1966*

Name	Abbreviation	Definition
Children	CHI	Per cent population 0–4 years inclusive
Age	AGE	Per cent population 65 years and over
Change	CHA	Per cent population increase 1961–6
Owner-occupiers	OWN	Per cent dwellings owned or buying
Single-family dwelling	SFD	Per cent dwellings single-family homes
Working women	WWF	Per cent females aged 15 years and over in workforce
Professional/Managerial	PMW	Per cent male workforce professional or managerial
Non-manual workers	NMW	Per cent male workforce non-manual
Income	INC	Per cent males with income $3,000 p.a. or more
Non-European	NEU	Per cent population non-European

The initial step in the analysis, the computation of ten-by-ten correlation matrixes for each set of data produces the results shown in Table 4.22. The coefficients are for unweighted untransformed variables.

It is immediately apparent that there are very considerable differences in the pattern of intercorrelations revealed by the ten indicants across the various sets of base units. The most marked difference concerns the pattern of correlation coefficients revealed by the six indicants believed to reference the urbanization-family status construct. While they give every indication of being closely related to each other in the two Auckland matrixes they separate into two distinct clusters in the urban areas data. Secondary differences between the matrixes involve the pattern of coefficients exhibited by

179

The urban mosaic

TABLE 4.22 *Correlations between social area variables for New Zealand urban areas, cities and boroughs in the Auckland metropolitan area, and census subdivisions in the Auckland metropolitan area, 1966*

New Zealand urban areas

	CHI	AGE(−)	CHA	OWN	SFD	WWF(−)	PMW	NMW	INC	NEU
CHI	100									
AGE(−)	−88	100				Critical value of *r* at 0·05 level 0·456				
CHA	73	78	100							
OWN	−18	−32	−05	100						
SFD	06	−16	−07	81	100					
WWF(−)	−07	−28	06	84	81	100				
PMW	−02	35	15	−46	−49	−58	100			
NMW	−10	24	−06	−54	−55	−66	94	100		
INC	27	55	27	−67	−74	−73	63	67	100	
NEU	80	64	66	−29	−11	−10	−15	−22	10	100

Auckland metropolitan area – cities, boroughs

	CHI	AGE(−)	CHA	OWN	SFD	WWF(−)	PMW	NMW	INC	NEU
CHI	100									
AGE(−)	87	100				Critical value of *r* at 0·05 level 0·433				
CHA	89	77	100							
OWN	74	76	69	100						
SFD	78	89	53	91	100					
WWF(−)	81	83	77	95	93	100				
PMW	−35	−26	04	06	−08	06	100			
NMW	−33	−32	−06	02	−18	−02	96	100		
INC	−20	−13	03	18	−01	16	94	91	100	
NEU	24	06	14	−28	−09	−27	−65	−67	−66	100

Auckland metropolitan area – census subdivisions

	CHI	AGE(−)	CHA	OWN	SFD	WWF(−)	PMW	NMW	INC	NEU
CHI	100									
AGE(−)	85	100				Critical value of *r* at 0·05 level 0·250				
CHA	77	69	100							
OWN	54	46	71	100						
SFD	61	64	59	80	100					
WWF(−)	60	63	72	87	89	100				
PMW	−40	−27	02	22	−12	12	100			
NMW	−39	−24	06	27	−03	20	97	100		
INC	−34	−16	11	30	−06	26	96	96	100	
NEU	22	03	−29	−44	−24	−43	−62	−66	−66	100

the income and non-European variables. There is a marked similarity between the two sets of Auckland data. The urban areas matrix, on the other hand, is highly divergent.

If the Shevky–Bell argument applies across different scales of analysis it follows that the pattern of indicant-construct correlations implied in the basic social area model should be equally applicable to each of the three sets of New Zealand data. The strange behaviour of the familism indicants in the urban areas data already suggests that their relationship with the postulated family status construct is unlikely to reproduce that found in the basic model. A more rigorous test of this assumption is provided by the results of a series of multiple-group factor analyses. The initial hypotheses are (1) that three factors will be both necessary and sufficient to account for the observed pattern of inter-variable correlations in each set of data, and (2) that each analysis will produce factors exhibiting a pattern of item-factor correlations such that (*a*) the variables relating to children, old people, population increase, owner-occupiers, single-family dwellings and house-wives will define a familism factor, (*b*) the variables proportion professional and managerial workers, proportion non-manual workers, and proportion earning more than $3,000 p.a. will form a separate social rank dimension, and (*c*) the variable proportion non-European will form the basis of a

TABLE 4.23 *Three-factor multiple group solutions for New Zealand urban areas, Auckland boroughs and Auckland subdivisions data*

I. Oblique factor structures

Variable	N.Z. urban areas Factor			Auckland boroughs Factor			Auckland subdivisions Factor		
	I	II	III	I	II	III	I	II	III
CHI	65	05	80	93	−30	24	85	−38	22
AGE(−)	51	42	64	93	−24	06	83	−23	03
CHA	66	13	66	85	00	14	87	06	−29
OWN	57	−61	29	92	09	28	85	27	44
SFD	66	−65	11	92	−09	09	88	−07	24
WWF(−)	64	−72	10	96	07	27	91	20	43
PMW	−28	94	−15	−10	99	−65	−08	99	−62
NMW	−45	95	−22	−16	98	−67	−03	99	−66
INC	−28	84	10	01	97	−66	02	99	−66
NEU	43	−10	100	−04	−67	100	−22	−65	100

II. Correlations between factors

Factor	I	II	III	I	II	III	I	II	III
I	100	−	−	100	−	−	100	−	−
II	−37	100	−	−08	100	−	−03	100	−
III	43	−10	100	−04	−67	100	−22	−65	100

specific ethnic factor. Table 4.23 gives the oblique factor structures and inter-factor correlations produced by subjecting the data to analysis in accordance with the hypotheses.

Hypothesis 1 may be tested by applying McNemar's criterion to the matrix of residuals produced by comparing the original correlation matrices with those reproduced by the hypothesized factor solutions.[1] The three-factor solutions for the Auckland boroughs and Auckland subdivisions matrices provide an excellent fit to the observed data. The New Zealand urban areas matrix, on the other hand, requires a more elaborate solution. A similar set of results occurs in connexion with hypothesis 2. The item-factor correlations exhibited by the social area indicants in the two Auckland analyses fit the predicted pattern almost perfectly: the first six indicants load on a single familism factor, the occupational and income indicants load on a social rank factor and the proportion non-European, although loading highly on the social rank factor, exhibits sufficient independence to be considered a separate specific factor. The urban areas data reveal a much more confused pattern. The postulated familism factor is poorly represented. Two of the family status indicants – owner-occupiers and housewives – exhibit higher item-factor correlations with the social rank dimension than they do with the group factor based on the initial hypothesis. A further two, children and

TABLE 4.24 *Four-factor multiple group solution for New Zealand urban areas*

I. Oblique factor structure

Variable	Factor			
	I	II	III	IV
CHI	94	−06	05	80
AGE(−)	95	−27	42	64
CHA	90	−02	13	66
OWN	−20	94	−61	−29
SFD	−06	93	−65	−11
WWF (−)	−10	94	−72	−10
PMW	17	−54	94	−15
NMW	03	−62	95	−22
INC	39	−76	84	10
NEU	75	−18	−10	100

II. Correlations between factors

Factor	I	II	III	IV
I	100	–	–	–
II	−36	100	–	–
III	59	−70	100	–
IV	75	−18	−10	100

[1] McNemar, 'On the number of factors'.

elderly persons, exhibit higher item-factor correlations with the ethnicity factor than with the postulated familism axis. Differences in the pattern of item-factor correlations exhibited by the six familism indicants in the urban areas data suggest that no attempt to subsume them under a general label is likely to be satisfactory. Instead, the data suggest a division of the familism indicants into two sets, each forming the basis of a separate factor. Table 4.24 gives the oblique factor structures and inter-factor correlations produced by dividing the first six indicants in such a manner that those relating to age structure and population increase form the basis of one factor and those relating to housing and way of life characteristics form the basis of another. The social rank and ethnicity factors are untouched.

The four-factor solution provides an excellent fit to the original data. Indeed, a satisfactory solution is provided by collapsing the factors to three, combining ethnicity with the first familism factor. In view of the substantive differences between the constructs, however, such a course is probably unwise. The first familism factor in the urban areas data may tentatively be considered an index of growth. With the exception of the Hutt Valley, all the urban areas possessing high scores on the factor are in the north of the North Island of New Zealand (Rotorua, Whangarei, Hamilton, Hutt, Tauranga, Auckland). The factor gives witness to the strong northwards trend in the recent development of New Zealand. Both Maori and pakeha migration is oriented towards the northern centres.[1] The close association between the growth factor and the proportion of Maoris reinforces this interpretation. The urban areas which have been growing fastest and which have the youngest populations, are also those which are the most attractive targets of Maori migration. The second group factor amongst the family status indicants is interpreted as being similar to the urbanization axis discussed by Anderson and Bean, albeit in inverted form.[2] It shows high item-factor correlations with each of the variables relating to the employment of women, type of tenancy and type of dwelling. The urban areas which score highest on the factor (Invercargill, Nelson, New Plymouth, Tauranga, Whangarei, and Timaru) are amongst the smallest in the set; none has a population of as much as 50,000. Conversely, the two areas which score lowest on the factor (Wellington and Auckland) are the two most cosmopolitan 'urban' communities in New Zealand. The factor is conceived as reflecting the concentration in the large city of those forms of family living which stress independence and career-oriented values. The opportunities for women to work outside the home are generally restricted in the New Zealand town; only the large city, with its centralized organizational functions, provides an opportunity of gainful employment for more than a few. Similarly it is only in the large city that a sufficiently diversified residential

---

[1] Cf. J. Metge, *A New Maori Migration* (Melbourne, 1964).
[2] The sign of a factor is immaterial.

fabric exists for the exercise of choice in type of house and type of tenancy. The urbanization factor correlates highly (0·59) with factor III, the social rank factor. The larger, more urban centres have, on the whole, the greatest proportion of professional and managerial workers, the greatest proportion of non-manual workers and the higher incomes. Wellington has by far the highest score on the social rank factor followed by Hamilton, Palmerston North and the Hutt Valley. There is little relationship between the distribution of social rank among the urban areas and the rapidity of their growth or the youthfulness of their population. Somewhat surprisingly, however, there is a moderately high negative relationship between social rank and the proportion of elderly persons. There is no consequential relationship between social rank and the proportion of Maoris in the urban areas or between the latter and the urbanization factor.

The differentiation and coalescence of the indicants belonging to the familism cluster in the various New Zealand analyses once again brings into question the exact meaning of the urbanization-family status construct. Not only do urbanization and family status have different shades of meaning, but it appears that under certain circumstances they may become empirically distinct. In most studies using the social area framework a low value on the family status index has been interpreted as implying a high degree of urbanization, but there seems no inherent reason why this should be so. When the level of analysis is at an inter-city scale, with cities as the base units, the concept of urbanization may have direct meaning. The concept of family status, on the other hand, may become simply a label for certain general demographic characteristics, losing its value connotations. At the intra-city level, the significance of urbanization is less obvious. The fact that the constituent items of the construct have been shown to possess high correlations with mobility in those few studies which have included a measure of the latter suggest that, at the intra-city level, urbanization is synonymous with urbanism – a way of life stressing such urban values as mobility and individuality. It may be anticipated that it is only in the largest cities that urbanism and family status will become dissociated.

The results of both the New Zealand study and of those reported by Udry seem agreed that the Shevky–Bell scheme is not suitable as a general framework for the analysis of areal differentiation. Even in modern society, it is clear that the pattern of item-factor correlations which the basic social area model presupposes is not common to all levels of analysis. Such a finding is hardly unexpected. Residential differentiation rests on the movement of populations and it has been pointed out several times that the motives for migration differ according to the distance involved.[1] Given this

---

[1] E.g W. Petersen, 'A general typology of migration', *Am. Sociol. Rev.* 23 (1958), 256–66; W. Isard (with G. A. P. Carrothers), 'Migration estimation', in W. Isard, *Methods of Regional Analysis* (Cambridge, Mass., 1960), pp. 53–79

difference it is highly unlikely that the resulting patterns of differentiation will be structured by the same considerations. The social area model provides many insights into the nature of the axes of residential differentiation, but it provides little material relevant to any discussion of the relationship between the axes at different scales of analysis. In the absence of further information or theory about the effects of different orders of base units it seems prudent to restrict the social area model to the analysis of differences at the urban sub-community or neighbourhood level.

The stability of the social area axes over time

To the extent that the social area model has correctly identified the base differentiating factors in the ecology of the modern community it follows that the pattern of indicant-construct loadings revealed in successive analyses of the same community over a period of time should exhibit considerable reliability. On the other hand, it may be anticipated that changes in the degree of modernization characteristic of the encompassing society will be reflected in changes in the ecological structure of the city. Over a long period of time, it must be anticipated that there will be considerable changes in the factorial composition of social area indicants. Over a short period of time – the difference between short and long depending on the pace of social change – there should be little change.

In San Francisco, Bell has demonstrated virtual identity in the underlying factor structures revealed by the social area indicants in 1940 and 1950.[1] A more extended assessment of the stability of the social area factor structures is made possible by the availability of some Auckland data on the characteristics of the urban area's constituent cities and boroughs over the time period 1926 to 1966.[2] The dates involved are 1926, 1936, 1951 and 1966.

In 1926 New Zealand had more or less recovered from the effects of the First World War although the country was experiencing a preliminary exposure to the traumas of the economic depression that was to grip the country in the 1930s. The effects of this latter were very apparent in 1936. In 1951 the country was yet again recovering from the dislocations resulting from war. The one and a half decades between 1951 and 1966 were times of considerable prosperity and development, the latter year marking the end of the era, as doubts and uncertainties about the country's external trade position built up.

Forty years represents a considerable fraction of the history of European settlement in New Zealand, but it is clear that even in 1926 New Zealand

---

[1] Bell, 'Economic, family, and ethnic status'.
[2] Although it is recognized that boroughs are much larger than is desirable for social area analysis, the similarity between the factor structures of the 1966 boroughs' data and those for the inner-Auckland statistical subdivisions provides evidence in favour of their utility.

G

185

was far removed from the ideal type of the undifferentiated primitive society. Indeed, on practically all measures of modernity the New Zealand of 1926 was more advanced than are all but a handful of present-day developing societies. Thirty per cent of the 1926 workforce was employed in primary industries. For comparison the 1950s figure in Ceylon and the Philippines was over 50 per cent while in many West African nations the percentage employed in agriculture alone was over 70. Over half the 1926 population of New Zealand was classified as urban, a greater percentage than in practically any of the countries of Latin America, Black Africa, or Asia in the 1960s. Literacy was effectively universal amongst the 1926 adult population of New Zealand whereas in many contemporary developing nations literacy rates still fall below 25 per cent. Thus, while the total population of New Zealand in 1926 was still that of a very small society, its stage of development was well advanced. The differences in residential structure which are predicted as following on the progress of modernization are, therefore, unlikely to be marked.

Modernization is by no means necessarily a smooth, linear process. Its progress may be interrupted by innumerable contingencies. The economic and political upheavals of the 1930s are likely to have had their repercussions in most developed societies and New Zealand is no exception. Unemployment, rioting, and political change were characteristic reactions.[1] It would be surprising if such momentous events were not reflected in the contemporary structure of the country's largest city.

Although there are detailed differences in the constitution of the cities and boroughs which constitute the Auckland urban area over the forty years of the study period the general pattern is sufficiently similar for them to be used as a comparative framework. In 1926 the average population of the constituent units was 9,700. The smallest unit, Howick, contained 522 inhabitants; the largest, Auckland City, had 88,429, or 43·4 per cent of the total. With the exception of Auckland City, no unit had a population of 20,000 or more. In 1966 the average population of the 21 cities and boroughs was 23,474. The smallest borough, Newmarket, had a population of 1,334 while Auckland City contained 149,989, 30·3 per cent of the total. Five other areas had populations of more than 20,000. Despite the great variation in the size of the units, the knowledge that the 1966 data produce a pattern of ecological factors closely similar to that found in the more detailed subdivisional data for Auckland and virtually identical with that reported for the census collectors' districts of Brisbane, gives confidence in the significance of the boroughs and cities framework.

The definition of the variables used in the analyses is shown in Table 4.25.

The family status dimension is tapped by six indicants, four of which are common to all the analyses, while the other two undergo redefinition in the

[1] Cf. W. B. Sutch, *Poverty and Progress in New Zealand* (Wellington, 1969).

TABLE 4.25 *Definition of social area variables Auckland cities and boroughs, 1966-26*

Name	Definition
1966	
Children	Per cent population 0–4 inclusive
Married	Per cent females 16 years and over ever-married
Sep. + divorced	Per cent females ever-married, separated or divorced
Widowed	Per cent females ever-married, widowed
Single-family	Per cent dwellings single-family homes
Owner-occupiers	Per cent dwellings owned or buying
Non-manual	Per cent males in labour force non-manual
Income	Per cent males with income $3,000 p.a. or more
Maori	Per cent population Maori
i Working women	Per cent females 15–59 years in labour force
i Aged 65+	Per cent population aged 65 years and over
i Masculinity	Per cent population male
1951	
Children	As 1966
Married	As 1966
Div. + widowed	Per cent females ever-married, divorced or widowed
Separated	Per cent females ever-married, separated
Single-family	As 1966
Owner-occupiers	As 1966
Weekly rent	Per cent rented 4-room dwellings letting at 25s. p.w. or more
Maori	As 1966
i Masculinity	As 1966
1936	
Children	As 1966
Married	As 1966
Sep. + divorced	As 1966
Widowed	As 1966
Single-family	As 1966
Owner-occupiers	As 1966
Weekly rent	Per cent rented 4-room dwellings letting at 15s. p.w. or more
Maori	As 1966
i Employed	Per cent male work force at work
i N.Z. born	Per cent non-Maori population N.Z. born
i Masculinity	As 1966
1926	
Children	As 1966
Married	As 1966
Sep. + divorced	As 1966
Widowed	As 1966
Single-family	As 1966
Owner-occupiers	As 1966
Weekly rent	Average weekly rent of unfurnished 4-room dwelling
Value	Average rental value of owner-occupied 5-room dwelling
Maori	As 1966
i N.Z. born	As 1936
i Masculinity	As 1966

NOTE. *i* Variables used in principal components analysis only.

1951 data. The common variables relate to the proportion of young children 0-5 years in the population, the proportion of women 16 years of age and over ever-married, the proportion of private dwellings classified as single-family structures, and the proportion of private dwellings owner-occupied. In 1926, 1936 and 1966 the two additional indicants are the proportion of the ever-married now divorced or separated, and the proportion widowed. In 1951 an unexplained change in census reporting yields indicants which relate, respectively, to the proportion of the ever-married now divorced or widowed, and the proportion separated.

Differences in the data available for the four study years makes it impossible to include comparable indicants for the social rank dimension. Confidence that the underlying factors will be invariant is further weakened by the small number of items available which may be expected to tap the social rank dimension. In the 1936 and 1951 data only one indicant is available which may be expected to relate to social rank: the weekly rental of unfurnished property. An indicant relating to weekly rent is also included in the 1926 series along with data on the average value of owner-occupied dwellings. For 1966, indicants relating to occupational status and income are available.

The single indicant believed to relate to the ethnic status dimension, the proportion of the population classified as Maori, is identical for the four dates. During the forty years of the study period the proportion of the Auckland population classified as Maori increased from 0·6 per cent in 1926, to 0·8 per cent in 1936, 2·3 per cent in 1951 and 6·2 per cent in 1966.

The multiple-group factor structures obtained from the correlation matrixes for the various indicants at the four dates are shown in Table 4.26. The items are grouped as suggested above.

The general impression is one of similarity. The six variables believed to tap the family status construct show consistently high item-factor correlations with the first group factor; the variables believed to tap social rank exhibit considerable independence of the familism variables and, in 1966 and 1926, clearly form a separate social rank dimension. The proportion of Maoris in the population also maintains a consistent independence of the other factors. Changes in the correlation between the factors are too slight and too much at the mercy of the differences in data input to provide any firm evidence concerning the postulated increase in factorial independence with the passage of time.

A more rigorous factorial test involves the use of principal components analysis followed by rotation using the varimax criterion. The rotated orthogonal solutions are shown in Table 4.27. It should be noted that extra variables have been included in the analyses.

The orthogonal factor structures produced for the 1966, 1951 and 1926 data are very similar to those forthcoming in the multiple-group analysis.

TABLE 4.26 *Multiple group factor structures for Auckland cities and boroughs, 1966-26*

1966

Indicant	Factor		
	I	II	III *i*
Children	86	−27	−07
Married	95	−10	08
Sep.+divorced	−96	−00	07
Widowed	−95	21	−01
Single-family	97	−10	−05
Owner-occupiers	94	10	−08
Non-manual	−19	98	−24
Income	−01	98	−11
Maori	−03	−18	100

1951

Indicant	Factor		
	I	II	III *i*
Children	82	−26	43
Married	80	−54	−15
Div.+widowed	−83	34	−14
Separated	−94	42	−35
Single-family	91	−45	40
Owner-occupiers	75	−55	−12
Weekly rent	−51	100	−09
Maori	20	−09	100

1936

Indicant	Factor		
	I	II *i*	III *i*
Children	82	−30	19
Married	80	−40	10
Sep.+divorced	−86	30	−12
Widowed	−83	17	−35
Single-family	91	−32	15
Owner-occupiers	65	−27	32
Weekly rent	−36	100	−32
Maori	25	−32	100

1926

Indicant	Factor		
	I	II	III *i*
Children	85	−30	−06
Married	77	−34	−11
Sep.+divorced	−76	−30	−20
Widowed	−85	−10	−11
Single-family	76	−59	15
Owner-occupiers	83	−17	17
Weekly rent	−21	97	−23
House value	−19	97	−22
Maori	09	−23	100

NOTE. *i* Single indicant.

Correlation between factors

	1966			1951			1936			1926		
	I	II	III	I	II	III	I	II	III	I	II	III
I	100			100			100			100		
II	−10	100		−51	100		−36	100		−21	100	
III	−03	−18	100	20	−09	100	25	−32	100	09	−23	100

Family status, social rank, and ethnic status emerge clearly as distinct, independent factors. The item-factor correlations are especially clear in 1966 when the rotated solution provides a very good approximation to simple structure. The 1936 data, however, produce a four-factor solution,

TABLE 4.27 *Orthogonal factor solution* (*varimax criterion*) *for Auckland cities and boroughs, 1966-26*

1966

Indicant	Factor			h^2
	I	II	III	
Working women	−99	−06	−02	98
Sep.+divorced	−96	−02	01	91
Single-family	96	−08	−03	93
Owner-occupier	95	13	−02	92
Married	95	−11	13	93
Widowed	−94	26	11	95
Aged 65+	−90	27	13	89
Children	84	−30	−11	81
Non-manual	−08	97	−12	95
Income	11	95	03	91
Males	46	−71	11	73
Maoris	−04	−12	98	98
Per cent total variance	60·2	21·9	8·7	91·7

1951

Indicant	Factor			h^2
	I	II	III	
Single-family	88	23	14	84
Div.+widowed	−87	−22	−37	95
Separated	−84	−11	−07	72
Children	80	04	47	85
Married	72	43	−15	72
Owner-occcupier	71	39	−32	76
Weekly rent	−28	−91	−07	91
Males	17	67	66	91
Maoris	08	−09	92	86
Per cent total variance	44·6	19·4	19·7	83·5

1936

Indicant	Factor				h^2
	I	II	III	IV	
Widowed	−90	21	−13	−23	92
Children	89	−23	−18	00	87
Married	80	−29	−28	−04	81
Males	−75	20	29	47	90
Sep.+divorced	−37	89	−13	05	96
Owner-occupier	06	−88	16	25	86
Single-family	63	−68	−02	−06	86
Unemployed	08	28	−84	−34	91
N.Z.-born	00	−17	83	00	72
Weekly rent	−08	45	69	−36	81
Maori	14	−12	02	93	90
Per cent total variance	30·7	23·4	19·3	13·2	86·6

1926

Indicant	Factor			h^2
	I	II	III	
Widowed	−90	−17	−25	89
Children	84	−25	−04	77
Married	78	−28	−31	78
Sep.+divorced	−78	−34	−32	82
Owner-occupiers	76	−18	14	63
Single-family	64	−60	12	79
Weekly rent	−08	95	03	91
House value	−03	97	04	95
Maoris	−04	−28	86	83
N.Z.-born	12	23	77	65
Males	51	07	53	54
Per cent total variance	36·4	24·2	17·4	77·9

the factors labelled as family status, social rank and ethnic status being joined by a factor which may be tentatively defined as urbanism-mobility. This latter construct exhibits high item-factor correlations with the proportion of separated and divorced females, the proportion of owner-occupiers (negative), and the proportion of single-family dwellings (negative). It distinguishes certain inner-city rooming-house districts. After 1936 there is no evidence that the factor remains salient in the ecological structure of Auckland at the boroughs and cities level of analysis. Its relationship with the economic upheavals of the 1930s is obscure. Between 1926 and 1966 there is a consistent trend for an ever-larger proportion of total variance to be explained by the retained factors (all components with an eigenvalue of unity and above). The significance of the finding is unclear, but it appears to suggest that the cities and boroughs of Auckland have undergone a progressive change in the direction of a more rigidly structured pattern of differentiation. It may be that the social area axes have provided the framework for a crystallization of the community's ecological structure.

The stability of social areas over time

If they are to provide generally useful categories, the social areas delimited using the Shevky–Bell technique should be reasonably constant over time. According to Tryon:

The constancy with which a social area retains its demographic and psychosocial character is a property that determines the degree to which it provides an enduring field for the social learning of its inhabitants and environmental supports to their social habits. It is difficult to believe that a social area, including a number of tracts of people having the same configuration of demographic and correlated psychosocial ways, would change much in a decade, or perhaps many decades. A change would be gradual. Individual persons may be born into the area, move out or die, but it should retain its subcultural homogeneity with considerable constancy, short of socially catastrophic events. Even those areas that undergo rapid growth through construction of new homes are likely to incorporate new groups of persons homogeneous with those already there.[1]

Using data on median schooling, Tryon finds little evidence of any shift in the homogeneity of social areas over the 1940–50 decade in San Francisco. He also reports a close correlation between the 1940 presidential election and the 1947 congressional election in San Francisco: census tracts take virtually the same position with regard to the proportion of Democratic votes recorded (r 0·94). Other evidence in favour of the stability of social areas is provided by McElrath who reports that use of the social areas thirteen years after their determination produces sample proportions which are congruent with their original scores on the social rank, family status, and ethnic status indexes.[2] After reviewing evidence on the stability of social area characteristics, Bell states: 'This is not to say that tracts do not change their social

---

[1] Tryon, *Identification of Social Areas by Cluster Analysis*, p. 31.
[2] D. C. McElrath, 'Prestige and esteem identification in selected urban areas', *Res. Studies, State College of Washington*, 23 (1955), 130–7.

area positions, but rather that most of them can be expected to maintain consistent social patterns for relatively long periods of time.'[1]

A comparison of the cities and boroughs data for Auckland over the period 1926-66 allows a further analysis of the stability of residential differentiation. Although differences in the data available, especially in the case of those relating to social rank, make exact comparisons difficult, there is a sufficiently similar set of data available to allow a fairly rigorous test of the constancy hypothesis. Table 4.28 shows the product-moment correlation coefficients obtained for the various standardized measures of family status and ethnic status in the Auckland area over the four study dates, 1926, 1936, 1951 and 1966. Problems in the availability of data limit the analysis of social rank changes to a single 1926-66 comparison.

TABLE 4.28 *Inter-year correlation coefficients for social area indexes: Auckland cities and boroughs, 1966-26*

I	Social rank				
		1966-26 *r* 57			
II	Family status				

	1966	1951	1936	1926
1966	–			
1951	90	–		
1936	82	92	–	
1926	70	81	90	–

III	Ethnic status				

	1966	1951	1936	1926
1966	–			
1951	73	–		
1936	63	90	–	
1926	63	91	93	

In general, the Auckland data support the assumption that any changes in the residential differentiation of the city will be gradual rather than rapid. The correlation between the family status scores of the cities and boroughs which comprise the Auckland urban area in 1926 and 1966 is 0·70. Between 1936 and 1951, a period of radical change in New Zealand, the family status correlation is 0·92. In the case of ethnic status, as measured by the proportion of Maoris in the population, the picture is somewhat blurred by the great increase in Maori population between 1951 and 1966. Although the 1951 distribution pattern of Maoris is very similar to that obtaining in 1926 and 1936 (*r* 0·91 and 0·90 respectively) there is a considerable shift in pattern in 1966. Thus the 1951-66 correlation between the

[1] Bell, 'Urban neighbourhoods', p. 253.

proportion of Maoris in the various cities and boroughs is only 0·73. Analysis of changes in the social rank position of the Auckland cities and boroughs is bedevilled by problems in the data. The only comparison that can be made with any confidence, that between the 1926 data relating to house values and rent and the 1966 data relating to occupational status and income, yields a correlation coefficient of 0·57. Change does occur, but it appears to occur gradually.

THE SOCIAL AREA TYPOLOGY AS AN EMPIRICAL TOOL

Whatever the details of the conceptual argument generated by an analytical instrument, the final decision on its significance rests on its operational utility. The social area model and, more particularly, the underlying theory relating the model to social change, possess undoubted heuristic value. The cross-cultural application of the model holds the promise of developing a genuinely comparative theory of urban social structure. For the moment, however, we are concerned less with the theoretical fruitfulness of social area analysis than with its contributions as an empirical device. The absence of suitable material from the less developed countries restricts our attention to the utility of the basic social area model in the modern city.

Social areas are aggregated of populations which form social types. In common with other constructed types they are based on the 'purposive, planned selection, abstraction, combination, and (sometimes) accentuation of a set of criteria with empirical referents that serves as a basis for comparison of empirical cases'.[1] Assessment of the significance of the social area scheme involves demonstrating both that the particular set of criteria which are selected as the bases of the classification process correspond with major structural properties in the empirical situation and that the social area typology forms a useful classification system.

The efficiency of the social area indexes

The similarity between the social area constructs and the factors uncovered in extensive factor analytic studies of the modern city has already been discussed. In Auckland the social rank index shows a correlation coefficient of 0·97 with the socio-economic status factor discovered in an extensive factor analytic study. The family status index exhibits a 0·96 item-factor correlation with a familism factor. The Shevky–Bell presentation of the relationship between the social area indicants and the underlying constructs closely parallels the empirical relationship revealed in direct tests of factor

[1] McKinney, *Constructive Typology and Social Theory*, p. 203.

structures. To this extent the social area indexes may be seen as simple approximations to the factor scores generated along the relevant factors.[1]

In their tests of the factorial validity of the Shevky–Bell constructs, Van Arsdol *et al.* express doubts about the utility of using the social area indexes rather than their individual components.[2] Assessing the utility of the social area measures in terms of their efficiency in predicting the criterion variables of population mobility and elderly persons, they find that none of the indexes is generally more predictive than are the individual indicants and that, when combined, the constructs account for significantly less variance in the criterion variables than do the combined indicants. Varying the weights attached to the indicants in the construction of the indexes, by utilizing factor coefficients, fails to alter the findings to any significant extent. Van Arsdol *et al.* report that the weights utilized in the Shevky–Bell scheme appear to do approximately as well as the more refined techniques. Their more general conclusions are less favourable to the social area indexes: 'The fact that criterion variables are more closely associated with independent variables not combined into the Shevky indexes indicates that the claims of pragmatic value of social area analysis must be discounted on empirical grounds.'[3] 'The multi-variable Shevky indexes appear to offer no empirical or logical advantages over the more traditional census measures in accounting for census tract variation of the selected criteria.'[4]

Somewhat similar findings emerge in an analysis of the ecology of criminality in Seattle reported by Schmid.[5] Employing the technique of ecological correlation, Schmid examines the relationship between differences in the residential patterning of various types of criminal and the variation between census tracts in terms of the social area indexes of social rank, family status, and ethnic status and in terms of a variety of specific census variables which are said to be related to the concept of social disorganization (masculinity, proportion married, median income, proportion unemployed). The social disorganization set bears many similarities to the urbanism-mobility factor discovered in factor analytic studies and to McElrath's migration status construct. Each of the Shevky–Bell indexes shows a moderate correlation with most types of crime. The correlation between social rank and crime varies between −0·37 (highway and car robbery) and −0·04 (indecent exposure). Fourteen out of 20 coefficients are significant at

---

[1] Factor scores can be perfectly measured only in those cases where unities are placed in the main diagonal of the correlation matrix. Otherwise various least squares estimates must be used. Especially in the case of oblique factor solutions, the computation of factor scores may be highly complicated. In practice, it is usual to employ simple estimates based on a small number of variables which have proved reliable indicants of the factor concerned. See Nunnally, *Psychometric Theory*, pp. 358–61; Harman, *Modern Factor Analysis*, chap. 16.

[2] M. D. Van Arsdol, Jr, *et al.*, 'An investigation of the utility of urban typology', *Pac. Sociol. R.* 4 (1961), 26–32.   [3] *Ibid.* p. 32.   [4] *Ibid.* p. 30.

[5] C. F. Schmid, 'Urban Crime Areas: Part II', *Am. Sociol. Rev.* 25 (1960), 655–78. See also B. S. Bloom, 'A census tract analysis of socially deviant behaviours', *Multivar. Beh. Res.* I (1966), 302–20.

better than the 0·05 level of confidence. The correlation between family status and criminality varies between −0·54 (auto theft) and 0·19 (bicycle theft). Seventeen of the correlations produce significant coefficients. The ethnic status dimension produces coefficients ranging between −0·50 (fighting) and 0·08 (bicycle theft). Fifteen of the coefficients are significant. Each axis of differentiation produces its own unique effect. In several instances the single census variables produce higher correlation coefficients than do the Shevky–Bell constructs. Thus, both per cent male and per cent unemployed exhibit eleven correlation coefficients of more than 0·70. As Schmid indicates this does not necessarily mean that for all purposes the typological indexes are inferior to single variables. The categories of crime involved in the high correlations with the disorganization variables – drunkenness, vagrancy, suicide, disorderly conduct, lewdness, and certain types of larceny – are highly concentrated in the skid row areas of the city. It may well be that the urbanism-mobility set of dimensions forms the prime background for this sort of criminal activity.[1]

In contrast to the relatively low correlations between the Shevky–Bell indexes and criterion variables in the Van Arsdol and Schmid studies, the analysis of Rome reported by McElrath produces consistently high co-efficients. The social rank index exhibits high correlations with crowding (−0·85), illiteracy (−0·95), and with a variety of variables relating to the industrial composition of the workforce. The family status index shows high correlations with a dependent population ratio (0·73), the proportion of aged persons (−0·71), and mean family size (0·61). McElrath shows that the social rank and family status indexes provide more complete descriptions of the variation in population characteristics when considered jointly than when taken alone. The multiple correlations between the two indexes and the various dependent variables are significantly higher than are the equivalent zero-order correlations for all except the case of the elderly persons variable. Moreover, the multiple coefficients are strikingly high. In the case of over-crowding the two social area indexes account for over 70 per cent of total variance. McElrath concludes that 'These findings demonstrate that the dimensions of social area analysis effectively describe distinctive population types.'[2]

An evaluation of the relative efficiency of the Shevky–Bell indexes as compared with 'traditional' ecological variables in controlling the variance in dependent properties involves a prior specification of the mathematical model being employed, of the generality being claimed and of the nature of the alternative measures. Leaving aside, for the moment, the legitimacy of using typological indexes as independent variables in linear correlation analysis, it is clear that considerable caution needs to be exercised in the selection of relevant criterion measures. As Schnore observes in a comment on the Van Arsdol *et al.* critique of the social area indexes, the particular

---

[1] Cf. chapter 1 above, pp. 20–1, 27–31.   [2] McElrath, 'The social areas of Rome', p. 384.

criteria selected by Van Arsdol *et al.* may not have been the best, may have behaved atypically, and may not have provided a representative test of the predictive validity of the Shevky–Bell scheme.[1] Moreover, the alternative variables suggested by Van Arsdol *et al.*, the Shevky–Bell indicants, are hardly the 'traditional' variables of human ecology. The significance of the variables outside the social area model is unclear. In any case, it is not at all clear that general structural characteristics will necessarily provide a better fit to outside criteria than will their components on all occasions. Problems or error and bias in the data are likely to upset even the most perfect relationships. At varying times differing combinations of indicants may provide the best measures of the underlying construct. In the absence of any model which can predict what these combinations will be in any particular case it seems that the causes of simplicity and power may best be served by general factors rather than *ad hoc* indicants. It is to this end that the social area scheme is directed.

The social area typology as a classification device

The social area typology is a multi-dimensional classification. Urban neighbourhoods or other sub-area communities are grouped together into social areas on the basis of their scores along the social area dimensions. It is somewhat unclear whether the typology is seen as an arbitrary division of continuous space or whether it is believed that the social areas are types corresponding to some empirical reality. As a classification device the least that is to be expected from the social area typology is that its classes are internally homogeneous and well-demarcated from each other. Neighbourhoods classified as being members of one social area rather than another should have more in common with the other members of their class than they do with any neighbourhoods belonging to a different social area. Little evidence is available on the validity of this assumption. In Brisbane, tests of significance using student's *t*, produce acceptable results across 15 out of 16 social areas in all indicants used in the computation of the social areas.[2] In contrast with nearest-neighbour or least-distance classifications, however, the social area typology is an imposed scheme.[3] Rather than following the

---

[1] L. F. Schnore, 'Another comment on social area analysis', *Pac. Sociol. R.* 5 (1962), 13–16. See also the exchange between Bell and Greer and Van Arsdol *et al.*, reported in the same issue, pp. 3–33.

[2] F. J. Powell, 'The Social Areas of Brisbane' (unpub. B.A. dissertation, University of Queensland, 1967).

[3] For other classification techniques see P. McNaughton-Smith, *Some Statistical and Other Numerical Techniques for Classifying Individuals* (London, 1965); R. R. Sokal and P. H. A. Sneath, *Numerical Taxonomy* (San Francisco, 1963); K. A. Kershaw, *Quantitative and Dynamic Ecology* (London, 1964); P. Greig-Smith, *Quantitative Plant Ecology* (London, 1964); W. T. Williams and G. N. Lance, 'Logic of computer-based intrinsic classifications', *Nature* 107 (1965),

natural clustering of populations in attribute space, the Shevky–Bell technique imposes arbitrary divisions. In any single city there is no guarantee that the social area boundaries will provide the most efficient delimitation of social space. It may be that the boundaries of the social areas pass through densely populated regions of social space rather than through the sparsely inhabited boundary zones. But a demand for natural classifications misses the main point of the Shevky–Bell technique: its insistence on the provision of a comparative framework. For comparative purposes, standardization of types is essential. Knowledge that neighbourhoods in different cities are both members of the same social area is meaningful only if the boundaries of the social areas are invariant across cities.

The concept of type implies that the properties on which it is based exhibit discontinuous rather than continuous distributions. Interaction effects in their relationship may destroy the simplicity assumed in linear models. To the extent that social areas possess 'unit' character, it may be anticipated that they will provide an efficient framework for contextual or structural analyses.[1] The more closely empirical reality follows the typological model rather than an ordination, the greater the significance of contextual techniques of analysis as compared with such linear techniques as product-moment correlation. Given the mosaic nature of the city, it may be anticipated that studies involving the intra-urban relationship between ecological variables should be based on contextual or structural methods. The use of correlational techniques, as exemplified in Schmid's study of the ecological patterning of criminality in Seattle, has been effectively criticized in these terms by Polk. Polk notes that, especially when higher-order correlation coefficients are used, ecological studies involving the social area indexes provide little support for the assumed relationship between the patterning of juvenile delinquency and the differentiation of the residential population of the city in terms of social rank. 'The failure to find a consistent and meaningful relationship between the economic status [social rank] characteristics of areas and delinquency presents a curious and major disjunction of "facts" and "theory" in delinquency research.'[2] Polk believes that the reason for the disjunction lies in the use of inappropriate research techniques. In particular, he suggests that the use of global correlational techniques in the study of the relationship between neighbourhood characteristics and behaviour is unwarranted:

the 'mosaic' nature of the organization of urban life is hopelessly blurred by product-moment correlations of census tract variables, and this blurring becomes especially confounded when higher order correlation terms such as partial cor-

---

159–61. A classification of Brisbane CD's, using a program developed by Williams and Lance, has been computed on the basis of the social area indicants but is not reported here. An example of a similar classification is to be found in Jones, 'Social area analysis', pp. 438–41.

[1] Cf. Riley, *Sociological Research*, vol. 1, pp. 700–39.

[2] K. Polk, 'Urban social areas and delinquency', *Soc. Problems*, 14 (1967), p. 321.

relation . . . are employed. More valid empirical and theoretical information will be obtained by looking at the nature of delinquency within specific kinds of urban social areas.[1]

Polk illustrates his argument with data on the social area distribution of juvenile delinquency in San Diego and Portland. He is able to demonstrate that although each of the Shevky–Bell axes contributes its own effect to the distribution of delinquency, the presence of a large interactional effect makes simple correlation techniques inappropriate to the full explication of the relationships involved. The highest delinquency rates occur in areas which combine low social rank and low family status; the lowest delinquency rates occur in areas which combine high social rank and high family status. However, at the lowest levels of family status, delinquency tends to increase with increasing social rank, whereas at all other levels of family status, delinquency rates decrease with increasing social rank. Correlation-based measures cannot hope to summarize such complicated findings. Instead, Polk makes a strong claim for the use of contextual or 'typological' analyses in which attention is directed 'at the nature of delinquency within specific kinds of urban social areas'.[2]

The interactional effect of the social area typology has been demonstrated in several studies dealing with such diverse phenomena as the distribution of demographic and ethnic variables, differences in social participation and differences in attitudes. We shall look at some examples of each in turn.

In one of the earliest applications of the social area typology Bell shows that there is an orderly but non-linear relationship between a census tract's scores on the social rank and family status indexes and the age and sex composition of its population.[3] In both Los Angeles and San Francisco the ratio of males to females varies inversely with family status at low levels of social rank, varies directly with family status at high levels of social rank, and shows a consistent inverse relationship with social rank at all family status levels. The greatest relative concentrations of women occur in the expensive apartment-house areas which combine high social rank with low family status. The greatest relative concentrations of men occur in the cheap rooming-house districts, in which low family status is combined with low social rank. Similar, albeit somewhat simpler, relationships exist between the family status and social rank indexes and the distribution of various age groups. Thus, the per cent of each social area population aged 0-14 years increases with family status at each social rank level and tends to decrease with social rank at every level of family status. The highest proportions of young people occur in areas combining high family status and

[1] *Ibid.* p. 322.　　　　　　　　　　　　　　　　　　　　　　　　　[2] *Ibid.*
[3] W. Bell, 'The social areas of the San Francisco Bay Region', *Am. Sociol. Rev.* 18 (1953), 39–47; Shevky and Bell, *Social Area Analysis*, pp. 37–42; Shevky and Williams, *Social Areas of Los Angeles*.

low social rank. Conversely, the highest proportion of elderly persons occurs in areas combining low family status and high social rank. The proportion of the population aged 50 years and over increases with social rank and decreases with family status. Systematic relationships are also found between the social rank and family status axes and the distribution of various ethnic groups. In San Francisco, the Russian-born group have the highest proportion of their population in the social area of highest social rank, followed, in order, by the native Whites, the Orientals, the Italians, the Mexicans, and finally, the Negroes. Whereas almost 50 per cent of the 1950 Russian-born population of San Francisco live in areas with a social rank score of more than 75, the equivalent proportion of Negroes is less than 5 per cent. The ordering of the groups in relation to the family status of the area of residence is, first, the native-born Whites, then, in order, the Mexicans, the Negroes, the Italians, the Russians and, finally, the Orientals.[1]

Analysis of the differential distribution of ethnic groups in the two-dimensional social areas formed along the social rank and family status axes helps to elucidate both the relationship between the various dimensions of the social area model and the bases of ethnic differences. Differences within the 'ethnic' population may be expected to result in different patterns of distribution. In Australian cities a well-marked distinction between British, Northern European and Southern European populations may be predicted. Table 4.29 shows the relative concentration of each of the seven largest overseas-born populations in Brisbane in terms of the 16 social areas formed on the social rank and family status indexes. For ease of comparison the data are presented in terms of location quotients based on the percentage of the Australian-born population resident in each cell. A group with a location quotient of 5 in a particular social area has proportionally five times as many of its members living there as does the Australian-born category. The smallness of the populations used in many of the computations cautions against over-great reliance on minor differences between the figures for the various groups.

There is no overall pattern of distribution which is characteristic of the overseas-born as a whole. Interpretation of the pattern requires that each migrant group be considered separately.

The New Zealand-born population is concentrated in those social areas which possess high social rank or low family status. It is the only migrant group which occurs relatively more frequently than the Australian-born population in the areas of highest socio-economic status. This probably reflects the dual nature of the New Zealand group as visitors on the one hand and high-ranking workers on the other. The United Kingdom-born population deviates less than any of the other migrant groups from the distribution pattern of the Australian-born majority. There is, however, a slight tendency

<hr>

[1] Shevky and Bell, *Social Area Analysis*, pp. 43–53.

TABLE 4.29 *Location quotients of overseas-born compared with Australian-born by social area types, Brisbane, 1961*

High	100					
		N.Z.	0·49	0·73	0·79	1·24
		U.K.	0·92	0·92	0·90	0·90
		Neth.	2·63	1·47	1·02	0·76
		Ger.	1·51	0·89	0·61	–
		Pol.	1·04	0·79	0·33	–
		It.	0·41	0·37	0·18	–
		Gr.	0·21	0·30	0·18	–
	75					
		N.Z.	0·80	0·80	0·99	2·16
		U.K.	1.10	0·98	0·91	0·94
		Neth.	1·31	0·69	0·48	0·66
		Ger.	2·46	0·80	0·54	0·69
		Pol.	2.79	0·81	0·48	0·42
		It.	1·38	0·66	0·23	0·09
Family		Gr.	0·81	0·77	0·36	0·36
status	50					
		N.Z.	2·13	1·68	2·03	2·77
		U.K.	1·23	1·26	1·17	0·93
		Neth.	0·91	1·02	0·79	0·48
		Ger.	2·00	1·09	0·64	0·62
		Pol.	3·28	1·32	0·79	0·38
		It.	8·62	3·77	1·59	0·31
		Gr.	4·48	3·83	4·56	0·44
	25					
		N.Z.	3·87	3·49	2·97	
		U.K.	1·42	1·61	1·37	
		Neth.	0.72	1.10	1·26	
		Ger.	1·43	1·77	1·14	Nil
		Pol.	3·27	2·29	1·17	
		It.	5·13	5·22	5·13	
		Gr.	6·13	6·09	2·32	
	0					
Low						

0	25	50	75	100
Low				High

Social rank

for United Kingdom migrants to occur relatively more frequently in areas combining low family status and low social rank. Again this finding is in line with what is known about the age and occupational characteristics of the U.K. group. The Netherlands-born, German-born and Polish-born groups are concentrated in social areas characterized by high family status and low social rank. Within this general pattern each group exhibits special patterns. The Netherlands-born are concentrated in the highest family status areas and are relatively under-represented in the low social rank–low family status districts. Geographically they are essentially a fringe population, living on the outskirts of the metropolitan area. The Dutch population contains many horticultural workers and is unique among the migrant groups in its demographic characteristics. The proportions of both the aged and the unmarried are low, while that of children is high. Its characteristics closely match those of the Australian-born population inhabiting the peri-urban fringe. The German migrants also tend to be most frequently represented in areas characterized by relatively high family status and low social rank. The influence of the socio-economic factor, however, is more pronounced in their distribution than it is in that of the Netherlands-born. The Polish migrants show an even greater tendency to locate in areas of low social rank, but still occur relatively more frequently than the Australian-born population in the areas which combine low social rank with high family status. The Greek-born and Italian-born on the other hand, are concentrated in areas which exhibit low scores on the family status index.[1] Within these areas they occur relatively more frequently than the Australian-born in all except those populations exhibiting the highest social rank. The data are consistent with the suggestion that socio-economic status factors may be relatively unimportant in the concentration of the Greek-born and Italian-born populations. Their inner-city location is a function of their ethnic identity rather than of their social rank.

As predicted, there are systematic differences in the distribution of the various migrant populations in social space. In aggregate the complex interplay of the relationships involved eventuates in a relatively low ecological association between ethnicity and the two other dimensions of the basic social area model as it applies to Brisbane. In detail, the differences in the social area patterning of the various migrant groups provides rich information on their position within the ethnic hierarchy of the local community.

The relevance of the social area typology for the behaviour of the urban population has been most directly explored in the area of social participation. In a series of studies set in Los Angeles, Greer examines the effects of differences in family status on the participation of census tract population in a series of local and city-wide associations.[2] In the initial study two neighbourhoods are selected for analysis, differing widely in their family status, but having essentially the same social rank and ethnic status. Samples of respondents from each neighbourhood closely reflect the census-derived social area indexes. The high family status sample differs sharply and consistently

---

[1] This does not, of course, imply that either group is characterized by low family status. The numbers involved in Brisbane are still too small for them to greatly affect overall CD characteristics.

[2] S. Greer, 'Urbanism reconsidered', *Am. Sociol Rev.* 21 (1956), 19–25; S. Greer, 'The social structure and political process of suburbia', *Am. Sociol. Rev.* 25 (1960), 514–26; S. Greer and E. Kube, 'Urbanism and social structure', in M. Sussman (ed.), *Community Structure and Analysis* (New York, 1959); S. Greer and P. Orleans, 'The mass society and the parapolitical structure', *Am. Sociol. Rev.* 27 (1962), 634–46.

from the low family status sample in the direction of more participation in the local community. The high family status samples have a higher neighbouring score, know more friends in the local area, have a greater proportion of their friendships locally, attend more local cultural events, belong to more local organizations and can nominate more local community leaders. No differences between the two samples are apparent in terms of their visits to kin or in terms of satisfaction with the neighbourhood. The reasons given for satisfaction, however, do tend to differ. The high family status sample 'describe their area as a "little community", like a "small town", where "people are friendly and neighbourly" '. The low family status sample, 'on the other hand, most frequently mention the "convenience to downtown and everything", and speak often of the "nice people" who "leave you alone and mind their own business" '.[1] Greer also finds some evidence of differential association with populations at a similar level of family status. The high family status sample tend to choose their out-of-neighbourhood friends from other high family status areas. The low family status sample tend to visit in other low family status neighbourhoods. On the basis of his findings, Greer suggests that the significance of locality for behaviour may vary systematically according to its family status. In areas characterized by high family status, participation in the local community is of major importance and the residents 'carry on a life in many ways similar to that of the small town described by Warner and his associates. At the other pole lie those areas of the city which are more heterogeneous, with fewer children and little interest in the local area as a social arena. Such areas may approach, in many ways, the ideal type of urban environment hypothesized by Wirth.'[2] An extension of the argument to a sample of four census tracts produces effectively identical results.[3]

The influence of variations in neighbourhood characteristics on the social participation of individuals is further examined in a series of studies by Bell and his collaborators conducted in four San Francisco census tracts which differ in terms of both social rank and family status.[4] Men living in neighbourhoods characterized by high social rank belong to more formal associations, attend more meetings, hold more offices, have a greater proportion of their memberships in general interest types of association, interact with their co-workers more frequently off the job, have more contacts with friends who are not neighbours or kin, are less likely to be calculating in their relationships with neighbours and show lower scores on the Srole

---

[1] Greer, 'Urbanism reconsidered', pp. 22–3. Greer uses the term 'urbanization' rather than family status. Tense of quote changed.

[2] *Ibid.* p. 24.   [3] Greer and Kube, 'Urbanism and social structure'.

[4] W. Bell, 'Anomie, social isolation, and the class structure', *Sociometry*, 20 (1957), 105–16; W. Bell and M. D. Boat, 'Urban neighbourhoods and informal social relations', *Am. J. Sociol.* 62 (1957), 391–8; W. Bell and M. T. Force, 'Urban neighbourhood types and participation in formal associations', *Am. Sociol Rev.* 21 (1956), 25–34; W. Bell and M. T. Force, 'Social structure and participation in different types of formal associations', *Soc. Forces*, 34 (1956), 345–50.

anomia scale, than do men who live in areas characterized by low social rank. Similar systematic differences occur in the participational behaviour of men living in neighbourhoods characterized by differing family status. The residents of the high family status neighbourhoods have more social contacts with neighbours and kin and are more likely to have met their friends locally.[1] Differences in participational behaviour between the two high social rank neighbourhoods are associated with differences in their family status. Men living in the high social rank–high family status area belong to more formal associations, attend meetings more frequently, are more likely to hold office and belong to more general-interest types of associations, than do men living in the high social rank–low family status neighbourhood. The 'neighbourhood effect' is still apparent when differences in individual characteristics are controlled. Although not all the inhabitants of the census tracts characterized as possessing high or low social rank are themselves of high or low rank, their participational behaviour has more in common with that of their neighbours than it does with that of their rank equals living in neighbourhoods characterized by lower or higher rank. On the basis of this finding, Bell and Force suggest 'that the economic characteristics of a neighbourhood population as a unit may be important indicators of the economic reference group of those living in the neighbourhood and may provide a set of expectations with respect to the residents' associational behaviour'.[2]

Data on the patterns of neighbourhood participation in Brisbane generally repeat the San Francisco and Los Angeles findings.[3] Table 4.30 shows the responses of 300 Brisbane housewives, living in CDs from seven different social areas, in terms of three main aspects of neighbourhood behaviour: the general friendliness of the neighbourhood as exhibited in knowledge of and attitude towards fellow residents, the extent of formal and informal interaction, and the practice of such forms of mutual help as borrowing and lending, and help in family crises.

The two inner-city neighbourhoods in the sample have low scores on the indexes of social rank and family status and high scores on the ethnic status variable. A high proportion of those interviewed live in atypical households; the number of the aged, the deserted or divorced, and the widowed is high. Each CD is in the centre of a major concentration of Southern or Eastern European migrants. Neither area exhibits any marked degree of 'friendliness'. The number of other residents known by name is small (average 3·4), fewer still are engaged in anything other than the most superficial of relationships.

---

[1] For a general summary see Bell, 'Urban neighbourhoods', pp. 248–51, 254–5.
[2] Reported in W. Bell, 'Social areas', in Sussman (ed.), *Community Structure and Analysis*, p. 85.
[3] Data based on a survey carried out in June 1964 by members of the Anthropology and Sociology II Class, University of Queensland. For further details see R. J. Fielding, 'Area Differences in Neighbourhood Interaction in Brisbane' (unpub. B.A. thesis, University of Queensland, 1964).

TABLE 4.30 *Neighbourhood interaction by housewives in selected social areas, Brisbane, 1964*

Social area	Location	General friendliness	Sociability	Mutual aid
1C	Inner city north	Little knowledge of neighbours. Unfavourable attitudes to neighbourhood. Ethnic resentments. Few neighbourhood friendships	Low. Few visits, few joint outings, no formal entertainment	Low: little practice of borrowing or lending. Isolated in crises
2C	Inner city south	Little knowledge of neighbours unless fellow member of ethnic minority. Australian-born have negative attitudes to neighbourhood. Few cross-ethnic neighbourhood friendships	Confined to fellow members of ethnic minorities. No cross-ethnic visits, entertainment, outings	Low: little practice of borrowing or lending. Isolated in crises
2B	Middle city north	Much knowledge of neighbours. Many neighbourhood friendships. Favourable attitudes to neighbourhood	Average: mainly informal visits, joint outings	Average: borrowing of small items subject to conditional approval. Mutual aid general
2B	Middle city north	Much knowledge of neighbours. Many neighbourhood friends. Favourable attitudes to neighbourhood	Above average: mainly informal visits	Above average: much borrowing, positive attitude towards mutual aid
3B	Middle city south	Much knowledge of neighbours. Acquaintances rather than friends. Favourable attitudes to neighbourhood	Above average: formal entertainment prominent, joint outings. Little informal activity reported	Average: borrowing tolerated if not abused. Mutual aid in crises
4B	Middle city north	Much knowledge and praise of neighbours. Express pride in traditions of neighbourhood	Above average: formal entertainment	Below average: negative attitude towards and little practice of borrowing and lending. Aid in crises from outside organizations
2A	Outer city south	Knowledge of neighbours but little contact. Many new arrivals. Ambiguous attitudes to neighbourhood	Below average: little interaction, few joint visits	Above average: much borrowing and lending. Mutual aid approved and practised

The majority of respondents are highly suspicious of borrowing and lending and many believe they would be totally isolated in a crisis (e.g. illness). Those friendships that do occur appear to be based on ethnic identities rather than any general liking for fellow residents. Amongst the Australian-born majority considerable resentment is expressed at the manner of living adopted by migrant groups.

The four middle-city neighbourhoods in the sample are all of middle to high scores on the index of family status, but differ from each other in terms of social rank. In all neighbourhoods there is a considerable amount of friendliness, but the exact form which this takes varies with the socio-economic status of the populations. In the two neighbourhoods with lower social rank there is a good deal of informal interaction and many of the respondents 'best friends' are drawn from amongst the neighbours. Lending and borrowing is practised widely although it is confined to small items and is the subject of conditional approval only. Mutual aid in crises is thought to be freely available. In the two neighbourhoods characterized by higher social rank there is a greater stress on formal interaction – coffee parties, dinner parties, bridge evenings, etc., and a less ready tolerance of borrowing and lending. It is noteworthy that in the area with the highest social rank help in crises is believed to be the province of professional agencies rather than that of neighbours or relations. The residents of the high social rank neighbourhoods know even more of their neighbours by name than do those of the lower rank category (13·2 *v.* 10·4) and, especially in the case of the respondents falling into the highest social rank type, are intensely proud of the traditions of their neighbourhood as a home of 'leaders of the community'.

The final neighbourhood in the sample is a new area on the southern fringes of Brisbane. Its family status is high, it contains practically no non-British migrants and is of rather low social rank. Attitudes towards the neighbourhood are marked by ambivalence and, although considerable knowledge of the neighbours is exhibited, there is little interaction between them, apart from borrowing and lending. The main impression of the neighbourhood is one of newness. The present lack of interaction may plausibly be explained in terms of the demands of young families and the necessity to invest considerable effort in such activities as making a garden.

Summarizing the findings produced in the various studies which have examined the relationship between the social area typology and participational behaviour, Bell concludes

These ... studies, taken together, offer convincing evidence that the social character of local areas within a city as defined by economic, family, and ethnic characteristics is an important predictor of individual attitudes and behaviours, subcultural patterns, and the social organization. It is crucial in determining the extent to which a local area in a city can even be considered a community in the sense of having flows of communication, interaction, community identification, and social integration among its residents.[1]

The significance of social areas as contexts for social behaviour is given further weight in the study of adolescent groups in a series of south-western U.S. cities reported by Sherif and Sherif.[2] Employing a sophisticated 'individual behaviour—small group—neighbourhood model', the Sherifs demonstrate that the social areas of the city provide an important setting in the unfolding of both individual and group activities.

For example, the range and standards of living in a neighbourhood where adolescents live and meet indicate a patterned set of circumstances. These circumstances are pertinent to what youth do, how they spend their time, where they spend it, and even what they consider suitable activities during leisure hours. Boys in favoured neighbourhoods of high socio-economic rank own cars, have comfortable homes, and ample spending money. They will think of leisure related to their cars, their visits and parties in each others' homes, and outlays of money for dates and professional entertainment. They are extremely mobile . . . The contrast in mobility and attitudes is striking in an urban neighbourhood where cars are not available, homes poor and crowded, and money lacking.[3]

Similar differences are spelt out in connexion with the family status and ethnicity of neighbourhoods. Not only does the neighbourhood structure the opportunities available to the adolescent, but differences in the characteristics of the urban mosaic form part of his world view and provide stimulus conditions for the development of his attitudes and behaviours. At the most general level, 'social areas are real, not only in the sheer perceptual sense of being part of the map of reality carried about in individuals' heads, but also in the sense of providing individuals with significant reference groups for gauging their own behaviour as well as the behaviour of others'.[4] The use of the social area framework in connexion with comparative contextual analyses is likely to prove one of the most profitable avenues for the study of social behaviour.

The social area typology and comparative analyses

The main virtue of the Shevky–Bell typology, as contrasted with more sophisticated and less arbitrary techniques of classification, is that it provides a ready framework for comparative analyses. Full realization of this potential awaits the development of truly cross-national and cross-terminal indicants and indexes, but some indication of the possibilities is already apparent.

[1] Bell, 'Social areas', p. 80.   [2] Sherif and Sherif, *Reference Groups*.
[3] M. Sherif and C. W. Sherif, 'The adolescent in his group in its setting', in M. Sherif and C. W. Sherif (eds.), *Problems of Youth* (Chicago, 1965), p. 298.
[4] Bell, 'Urban neighbourhoods', p. 256.

TABLE 4.31 *Population distribution by social area types: Auckland, Brisbane, San Francisco, Newcastle-under-Lyme, Rome*

Auckland, 1966
(per cent population each type)

	Low			High	
High	20·3	11·5	1·8		(33·6)
Family status	20·6	11·7	8·8	3·9	(45·0)
	9·7	5·4	2·9	0·7	(18·7)
	0·6	2·1			(2.7)
Low	(51·2)	(30·7)	(13·5)	(4·6)	(100)
	Low	Social rank		High	

Brisbane, 1961
(per cent population each type)

	Low			High	
High	7·3	12·7	3·7	0·2	(23·9)
Family status	9·1	35·2	15·2	1·7	(61·2)
	1·4	7·7	2·4	0·9	(12·4)
	0·7	0·8	1·0		(2·5)
Low	(18·5)	(56·4)	(22·3)	(2·8)	(100)
	Low	Social rank		High	

San Francisco, 1940
(per cent population each type)

	Low			High	
High		0·2	0·6		(0·8)
Family status	3·7	17·0	13·8	5·7	(40·3)
	1·0	15·1	17·6	5·1	(38·8)
		3·2	10·4	6·5	(20·1)
	(4·7)	(35·5)	(42·4)	(17·4)	(100)
	Low	Social rank		High	

San Francisco, 1950
(per cent population each type)

	Low			High	
High			1·1	1·4	(2·5)
Family status		14·0	21·0	12·6	(47·6)
	0·1	9·7	15·1	9·0	(33·9)
			7·0	9·0	(16·0)
	(0·1)	(23·7)	(44·2)	(32·2)	(100)
	Low	Social rank		High	

Newcastle-under-Lyme, 1961
(per cent census areas each type)

	Low			High	
High	1	2			(3)
Family status	13	10	3	2	(28)
	27	16	11	5	(59)
Low	7	4			(11)
	(48)	(32)	(14)	(7)	(100)
	Low	Social rank		High	

Rome, 1951
(per cent census areas each type)

	Low			High	
High	9	3	1		(13)
Family status	8	19	21	4	(52)
	1	18	16		(35)
		1			(1)
	(17)	(23)	(41)	(20)	(100)
	Low	Social rank		High	

Table 4.31 presents data on the relative composition of Brisbane, Auckland, San Francisco, Newcastle-under-Lyme, and Rome in terms of the two-dimensional social areas formed by quartering the social rank and family status indexes.[1] The Brisbane data are generated from CD material, the Auckland data from statistical subdivisions and boroughs and the San Francisco data from census tracts. In each case the percentages plotted are

[1] Data from Shevky and Bell, *Social Area Analysis*; Herbert, 'Social area analysis: a British study'; McElrath, 'The social areas of Rome'.

in terms of total population. The data for Newcastle and Rome, on the other hand, refer to statistical sub-areas rather than to populations. Each index is standardized to the range characteristic of the city concerned. Comparisons are, therefore, of a relative rather than an absolute nature.

The two Australasian cities are unique in the extent to which their populations are concentrated in those social areas characterized by high family status and low to middle social rank. Only in Rome is there an approximation to the high family status of the Brisbane and Auckland populations. Sixty-five per cent of the *gruppi di sezione* in Rome fall into the upper division of the family status index as compared with 85 per cent of the Brisbane population and 79 per cent of that of Auckland. Newcastle-under-Lyme reveals the lowest proportion of high family status populations in its composition, with only 30 per cent of its enumeration districts falling into the upper half of the index range. The contrast between the cities in the top quarter of the family status range is even more marked. In terms of the social rank index the most notable feature of the Australasian cities is the low proportion of their population falling into the highest category. Less than 3 per cent of the Brisbane population and 5 per cent of the Auckland population live in areas with a social rank index of more than 75; the equivalent figures are 32 per cent in San Francisco (1950), 20 per cent in Rome, and 7 per cent in Newcastle. The latter city has a social rank spread remarkably similar to that of Auckland.

The degree of heterogeneity exhibited by the cities varies widely. In Brisbane over one-third of the population lives in CD's falling in social area 2B, which combines high-middle family status with low-middle social rank. A further 15 per cent of the population live in CD's in social area 3B. In Auckland 20 per cent of the population live in subdivisions falling into each of social areas 1A and 1B – areas combining low social rank with high and high-middle family status. The dominant social areas in San Francisco are types 3B and 3C combining high-middle and low-middle family status with high-middle social rank. A somewhat similar pattern is revealed by Rome. In Newcastle, on the other hand, social areas 1C and 2C are dominant, accounting for 27 per cent and 16 per cent respectively of enumeration districts.

Further explication of the differences in the population structures of various cities must await greater standardization of measures. With the development of such standard measures it may be hoped that the social area typology may be used as a framework for comparative contextual analyses. As yet it remains an open question whether the social areas possess similar 'meanings' in different cities.

Other uses of the social area scheme

The social area indexes and typology have proved to be useful instruments in several ways other than those mentioned. As a sampling frame they have allowed the efficaceous selection of samples at both the individual and the aggregate level.[1] They have been used to facilitate the planning of social welfare services,[2] in the analysis of political attitudes[3] and in studies of the relationship between churches and neighbourhoods.[4] As a tool for comparative analyses they have been used to study changes over time[5] as well as changes over societies. Social areas distinguished in terms of social rank, family status, ethnic status and, given the relevant data, migration status, contain populations which differ in many characteristics other than those used in computing the axes of differentiation. Separately and jointly each axis contributes a significant effect to the ecological structuring of the modern urban population. The social areas of the modern city are systematically related to differences in social participation and political attitudes, in the patterning of crime, and in the distribution of suicide. As parts of the individual's mental map of the city, they provide a backdrop for much human behaviour. The case for their utility as an efficient means of systematizing the modern urban mosaic seems soundly based.

CONCLUSION

Social area analysis has been the object of heated argument. Virtually every aspect of the technique and of its underlying theory has been examined, criticized, and found wanting. But to every assault there has been an equally impassioned defence. It seems clear that the basic social area model, outlined by Shevky and Bell, lacks the universal validity which its popularizers originally claimed. On the other hand, it appears to fit the structure of the modern city well. Its axes emerge in the predicted fashion and differentiate populations of systematically varied characteristics. The social area typology provides a simple if arbitrary framework for contextual and comparative analyses. The most important contribution which Shevky and his colleagues

[1] E.g. W. Bell, 'The utility of the Shevky typology for the design of urban subarea field studies', *J. Soc. Psychol.* 47 (1958), 71–83; R. C. Williamson, 'Socio-economic factors and marital adjustment in an urban setting', *Am. Sociol. Rev.* 19 (1954), 213–16; P. R. Wilson, 'Immigrant Political Behaviour' (unpub. Ph.D. dissertation, University of Queensland, 1970).

[2] E. Bange, *et al.*, 'A Study of Selected Population Changes and Characteristics with Special Reference to Implications for Social Welfare' (unpub. Master's thesis, University of California, Berkeley, 1955), esp, pp. 265–329.

[3] W. C. Kaufman and S. Greer, 'Voting in a metropolitan community', *Soc. Forces*, 38 (1960), 196–204.

[4] R. L. Wilson, 'The Association of Urban Social Areas in Four Cities and the Institutional Characteristics of Local Churches in Five Denominations' (unpub. Ph.D. dissertation, Northwestern University, 1958); J. H. Curtis, *et al.*, 'Urban parishes as social areas', *Am. Cath. Social. Rev.* 18 (1957), 1–7; T. Sullivan, O.S.B., 'The application of Shevky-Bell indices to parish analysis', *Am. Cath. Sociol. Rev.* 12 (1961).

[5] Shevky and Bell, *Social Area Analysis*.

have made, however, lies not so much in the details of their argument as in the emphasis they place on the relationship between the city and the wider society of which it is a part. In sensitizing the student of the city to the reciprocal relations which exist between the characteristics of the urban community and those of the encompassing society Shevky and Bell have helped bridge the gap which exists between urban and general sociologies.

The residential differentiation of the urban population reflects the basic social differentials extant in the society concerned. These will vary according to the particular mix of values characteristic of the society and, more generally, according to its degree of modernization. The process of modernization is associated with the emergence of new axes of differentiation and with a loosening of the bonds which connect one institutional sphere with another. In societies which approximate to the urban-industrial culture exemplified by the West coast of the United States urban sub-communities may be distinguished in terms of their social rank, their preferred family styles, their ethnic background, and their mobility experiences. Elsewhere systematic variations may be predicted in the way these dimensions and their associated indicants inter-relate. The possibility of outlining general 'urban types', distinguished by the particular patterns of item-construct relationships which they exhibit, is one of the more exciting prospects in urban sociology.

CHAPTER 5

THE SPATIAL PATTERNING OF
RESIDENTIAL DIFFERENTIATION

The residential differentiation of the urban population, a function of the axes of social differentiation extant in the society concerned, is reflected in a sifting and sorting of populations and locations. As the city develops typical patterns of differentiation become apparent. Different areas become associated with particular types of population and certain systematic relationships between geographical space and social space appear. The concern of the present chapter is with the spatial aspects of residential differentiation and, more particularly, with the validity of certain general models of this spatial structure which have appeared in the literature.

Discussions of the spatial aspects of urban structure generally concern themselves with three general models of urban form: the zonal, the sectoral, and the multiple nuclei. In the present case only the two former approaches will be examined. In contrast to the multiple nuclei model both the zonal and the sectoral analogies are concerned with the structural connotations of a particular set of differentiating processes, predict particular patterns of residential differentiation, and lend themselves readily to empirical test. The multiple nuclei 'theory' may be regarded as a caveat to the more general zonal and sectoral models.

THE ZONAL MODEL OF URBAN GROWTH AND STRUCTURE

The concern of the early Chicago ecologists with the differences in environment and in behaviour between different parts of the city led not only to descriptive studies of the ways of life to be found in particular natural areas, but also to a concern with the general features of urban structure. The classical ecologists were especially interested in the relationship between community structure and developmental history, seeing in this a parallel with the processes of evolution found in the animal and plant worlds. Many of the concepts used by the classical ecologists in discussing the evolution of urban structure – 'dominance', 'succession', and 'invasion' – are direct borrowings from plant and animal ecology.[1] The conclusions reached, however, are concerned primarily with the patterns of development and

---

[1] See the discussion in chapter 3 above.

structure to be found in one particular type of human settlement, the large industrial city as exemplified by Chicago.

The roots of much of the later work by the Chicago ecologists may be traced back to the early theories of urban expansion developed by Hurd. Writing in 1903, Hurd outlined a theory of urban growth which stressed the simultaneous operation of two general principles: central growth and axial growth.[1] The zonal hypothesis developed by Burgess, some two decades later, is concerned primarily with the reorganization of urban structure which is consequent on the operation of one of these principles alone, that of radial or central expansion.[2] The Burgess scheme is intimately related to the general ecological assumptions about the role of impersonal competition and about the dominance of the central business district in determining the pattern of residential differentiation. The zonal model of urban structure is introduced almost as an aside in the course of a general discussion of the effects of urban expansion: 'The typical process of the expansion of the city can best be illustrated, perhaps, by a series of concentric circles, which may be numbered to designate both the successive zones of urban extension and the types of areas differentiated in the process of expansion.' To accompany the presentation Burgess produces a chart illustrating the five main zones of urban expansion (Figure 5.1). 'This chart represents an ideal construction of the tendencies of any town or city to expand radially from its central business district.'[3]

The first and smallest zone is the central business district. This is the focus of the commercial, social and cultural life of the city and corresponds with the area of highest land values. Only those activities whose profits are high enough to pay high rents can locate in the area. The heart of the zone is the downtown retail district with its large department stores and smart shops, but the area also contains the main offices of financial institutions, the headquarters of various civic and political organizations, the main theatres and cinemas, and the more expensive hotels. The central business district is the most generally accessible area in the city and has the greatest number of people moving into and out of it each day. The main transport terminals are located there. Encircling the central area and forming its outer ring is a wholesale business district with warehouses, light industries, and, perhaps,

---

[1] Hurd, *Principles of City Land Values*.
[2] The first statement of the zonal model is contained in a paper which Burgess delivered to the 1923 convention of the American Sociological Society. See E. W. Burgess, 'The growth of the city', reprinted in Theodorson (ed.), *Studies in Human Ecology*, pp. 37–44. Later versions of the scheme appear in E. W. Burgess, 'The new community and its future', *Ann. Am. Ac. Pol. Soc. Sci.* 149 (1930) and in E. W. Burgess, 'The ecology and social psychology of the city', in D. J. Bogue (ed.), *Needed Urban and Metropolitan Research* (Oxford, Ohio, 1953). Much of the relevant material is contained in an article by L. F. Schnore, 'On the spatial structure of cities in the two Americas' in P. M. Hauser and L. F. Schnore (eds), *The Study of Urbanization* (New York, 1965), pp. 347–98.
[3] Burgess, 'The growth of the city', p. 38.

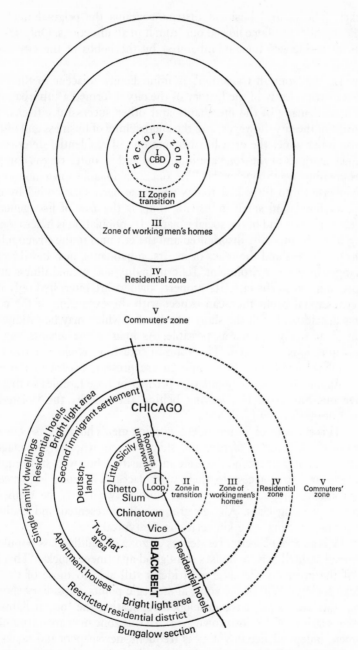

Fig. 5.1. Burgess' spatial model (source: 'The growth of the city', pp. 39, 41)

a market. The central business district contains the original nucleus of settlement which has since flowed out from it in all directions. Only scattered pockets of residences remain, inhabited by the hobos of the city and by caretakers.

Zone II, the 'zone in transition', is immediately adjacent to the central business district. Early in the history of the city it formed a suburban fringe which housed many of the merchants and other successful citizens. With the growth of the city, however, and the encroaching of business and industry from the inner zone, the area has become one of residential deterioration. The inner margins of the zone are industrial and its outer ring is composed of retrogressing neighbourhoods. The once-fashionable town houses have been converted into furnished rooms and have been surrounded by cheap bars, pawnshops, and small industries. This is the area of first-generation immigrant colonies and of the social isolates. Its population is heterogeneous, ranging from the mentally disoriented and the criminal to the cosmopolitans, the ethnic villagers and the relics of its first inhabitants, now bewildered by the changes in their environment. Its criminality and mental illness are the most pronounced in the city. Its property owners are interested only in the long-term capital profit they can expect with the expansion of the central business district and with the short term profits which may be produced by packing in as many tenants as possible. As long as the tenants pay their rent, no questions are asked. The zone in transition is characterized by a highly mobile population. Few children are present, except in the ethnic villages. As members of the population prosper or raise families so they tend to move out into zone III, leaving behind the elderly, the isolated, the 'defeated, leaderless, and helpless'.

Zone III is the zone of 'independent working men's homes'. Its population consists of the families of factory and shop workers who have managed to prosper sufficiently to escape the zone in transition but who still require to have cheap and easy access to their workplaces. The zone is focused on factories and its population forms the bulk of what may be termed the respectable working class. All age groups are represented and traditional family forms stressing wide kin relations are typical.

Zone IV is an area of 'better residences', a zone of middle-class populations living in substantial private houses or in good apartment blocks. 'This is the home of the great middle class with ideals still akin to those of the rural American society.' Within the zone, at strategic points, subsidiary shopping centres, 'satellite loops', have developed replicating the 'bright lights' and expensive services of the downtown area. 'In this zone men are outnumbered by women, independence in voting is frequent, newspapers and books have wide circulation, and women are elected to the state legislature.'

Still further out from the inner city is zone V, the commuters' belt, within a journey time of 30-60 minutes of the central business district. This is essentially a suburban zone, characterized by single-family dwellings. In the main it is a dormitory area because the majority of its men spend the day at work in the offices of the central business district, returning only for the night.

Thus, the mother and the wife become the centre of family life. If the Central Business District is predominantly a homeless-men's region, the rooming house district, the habitat of the emancipated family, the area of first-immigrant settlement, the natural soil of the patriarchal family transplanted from Europe; the Zone of Better Residences with its apartment houses and residential hotels, the favourable environment for the equalitarian family; then the Commuters' Zone is without question the domain of the matricentric family.'

The commuters' zone is not, however, homogeneous, instead 'the communities in this . . . zone are probably the most highly segregated of any in the entire metropolitan region, including in their range the entire gamut from an incorporated village run in the interests of crime and vice . . . to (communities) with . . . wealth, culture and public spirit'.[1]

Beyond the five urban zones, Burgess sometimes recognizes two additional sets of areas: 'The sixth zone is constituted by the agricultural district lying within the circle of commutation . . . The seventh zone is the hinterland of the metropolis.'[2]

The nature and assumptions of the zonal model

The zonal model of urban growth and structure is put forward as an ideal or constructed type rather than as a substantive generalization. It gives a picture of urban development as this would occur if only one factor, radial expansion from the city centre, determined the pattern of urban growth. Burgess is explicit about the constructed nature of the model in a 1953 statement:

My name has been identified with a zonal theory of growth of the city as it would be interpreted graphically *if only one factor, namely, radial expansion, determined city growth*. The critics of the theory have been rather obtuse in not realizing that this theory is an ideal construction, and that in actual observation many factors other than radial expansion influence growth . . . At no time in advancing this ideal construct of the effect of radial growth have I denied the existence of other possible factors which might also be regarded as ideal constructs. For example, sectors, climatic conditions, types of street plan, barriers (hills, lakes, mountains, rail-roads) can each have an effect upon the formation of city structure.[3]

1 The best general description of the five zones is given in E. W. Burgess, 'Urban areas,' in T. V. Smith and L. D. White (eds), *Chicago : An Experiment in Social Science Research* (Chicago, 1929), pp. 114–23. All quotations are from this source.
2 Burgess, 'The new community', pp. 130–1.
3 Burgess, 'The ecology and social psychology', p. 178.

Thus, while 'all American cities which I have observed or studied approximate in greater or less degree this ideal construction; no one . . . perfectly exemplifies it'.[1]

The essence of the scheme lies in the tendency of each inner zone to expand its territory outwards by invading the next outer zone. The model depicts a process rather than a static structure and may be compared with a depiction of the expanding ripples which result from dropping a stone into water. The chart depicting the zones which result from urban expansion is a 'frozen' picture of a dynamic situation. Nonetheless, Burgess appears to believe that at any given time it will be possible to delimit the five urban zones: 'So universal and powerful is the force of expansion outward from the centre that in every city these zones can be more or less clearly delimited.'[2]

Attempts to apply the zonal model of urban growth and form to empirical data have frequently ignored the assumptions, implicit or explicit, on which the scheme is based.[3] As with any ideal type, the zonal model assumes a very particular and a very extreme configuration of circumstances.[4] Attempts to use it as a substantive generalization where these circumstances do not hold are of dubious legitimacy.

The Burgess scheme assumes a very particular demographic background. The model is based on a theory of rapid and untrammelled urban expansion and demands a rapidly increasing and large population. The prototype for the model, Chicago, increased its population almost twenty-fold in the fifty years between 1860 and 1910. Moreover, much of this increase is assumed to be the result of overseas and ethnically diverse immigration. The model assumes the presence of a heterogeneous population, differentiated in terms of migration experience, ethnic background, and occupation.[5] It is unclear how the model should be adapted to fit a city with a static or declining population or which is culturally homogeneous. It is also unclear how the model should be varied to take account of population size. Although even a village exhibits a non-random ecological structure, the development of zones demands a relatively large population.

The Burgess scheme is also based on a particular set of economic and political factors. To a large extent the zonal model is based on the classical ecological concept of impersonal competition and assumes private ownership of property and the absence of city planning. Power is equated with wealth. The rich may locate where they will, the poor where they have to. Property owners are free to use their property in whatever way they think best,

[1] E. W. Burgess, 'The determination of gradients in the growth of the city', *Pubs. Am. Sociol. Soc.* 21 (1927), p. 178.
[2] E. W. Burgess, 'Residential segregation in American cities', *Ann. Am. Ac. Pol. Soc. Sci.* 140 (1928), p. 108.
[3] For an excellent critique along this line, see Schnore, 'On the spatial structure of cities'.
[4] On the characteristic of 'ideal' or 'constructed types', see McKinney, *Constructive Typology and Social Theory.*
[5] Many of the underlying assumptions of the Burgess model are spelt out in Quinn, *Human Ecology.*

regardless of planning ordinances or other non-economic political considerations. The institution of city planning processes and the direct intervention of government into the housing market may well halt and even reverse the processes which provide the dynamics of the model. Thus, the zone in transition, a 'natural' consequence of unbridled economic competition in an expanding city, may be transformed in bureaucratic society as the result of redevelopment schemes and the growth of large-scale planning. The model also assumes a wide variety of commercial and industrial undertakings in the city each operating under private enterprise conditions. Its relevance to cities which are of different economic character is uncertain.

The mainspring of the zonal model is the expansion of the inner zones forced by the excessive demand for central city locations. The underlying assumptions are that accessibility is greatest in the city centre, that it declines regularly with increasing distance from the centre and that it is associated with important evaluative criteria. Transportation facilities are assumed to be relatively efficient, so that all inhabitants of the city can reach the centre with ease. It is also assumed that transportation is equally easy, rapid, and cheap in every direction within the city. Thus the more central the location, the greater the accessibility and the greater the demand, as reflected in land values. The dominance of the city centre and the gradient of land values towards the outskirts are seen as the main determinants of residential zonation. There is a striking resemblance between the Burgess presentation and the Von Thünen model of agricultural zonation developed a century earlier.[1] The most extensive forms of land use are those which are likely to locate on the outskirts of the system: single-family dwellings in the case of the city, grazing enterprises in the case of the country. Although the Burgess scheme is presented in terms of economic processes, much of the descriptive emphasis in the treatment of the five urban zones is laid on the family form and the style of life characteristics of the inhabitants. To a large extent, it appears that Burgess considers differences in style of life to be a direct function of differences in wealth. Thus, the zonal variation in styles of life reflects the ability of the wealthy to pre-empt the newer and more desirable housing areas, typically those at the periphery of the city. The association between distance and wealth is based on the assumption that high value is given to residence in areas which are close to open country and which possess 'garden city' characteristics. It is by no means clear that this assumption holds true for all members even of Anglo-American society and it is clearly untrue for many groups in other culture areas.[2] At the same time,

[1] J. H. von Thünen, *Der Isolierte Staat* (Hamburg, 1826). Like the Burgess model, the Von Thünen conception rests on a rent-distance function. For a general introduction to the Von Thünen model, see M. D. I. Chisholm, *Rural Settlement and Land Use* (London, 1962).

[2] Cf. our earlier discussion of the various life-styles to be found in the inner city. On the other hand, the belief that 'garden city' characteristics are desired may structure the market so that little choice of alternatives is left.

H

The urban mosaic

Burgess' remarks about the heterogeneous nature of the settlements in the outer zone indicate that he must have been aware that peripheral location was by no means a privilege of the wealthy alone. Indeed, the simple geometry of area suggests that the very size of the outer zone will make it open to a large proportion of the population – perhaps any who desire the suburban way of life.

Criticism of the Burgess scheme

A detailed review of the argument initially generated by the Burgess model is available in an article by Quinn.[1] In the present section only some of the more important general criticisms will be outlined.

Probably the most severe misgivings about the utility of the Burgess scheme have been generated over the empirical status of the zone as a meaningful classificatory device. Each zone in the Burgess scheme is presented as if it were a relatively homogeneous area, notwithstanding the fact that a number of different types of land use and population are said to characterize zones I and II and that zone V is said to include a wide variety of subcommunities, differing considerably in income. Empirical tests of zonal homogeneity have generally been negative.[2] Moreover, Alihan has suggested that the concept of the zone is directly contradictory to another concept used by Burgess, that of the gradient.[3] After demonstrating that many variables demonstrate a typical gradient form, Alihan goes on to state that:

A relatively continuous progression or regression of rates is manifested along radial lines that cut the successive zones. In other words, the five zones, as presented by Burgess, cease to be sharply demarcated from each other, as they appear to be when described in terms of qualitative factors, such as economic and educational standards or types of profession, and so forth. The standard zonal boundaries do not serve as demarcations in respect of the ecological or social phenomena they circumscribe, but are arbitrary divisions. They can be treated only as convenient methodological devices for the classification of data under smaller divisions than the total area included in a particular study. The zone can have significance only if it marks a distinction of gradients or between gradients. Otherwise, if the gradients are continuous as the name implies, the zonal lines can be drawn indifferently at any radius from the centre. Yet Burgess' description of the five zones clearly indicates that ecologists envisage these zones as distinct units, differentiated in terms of numerous factors.[4]

[1] J. A. Quinn, 'The Burgess zonal hypothesis and its critics', *Am. Sociol. Rev.* 5 (1940), 210–18. See also Quinn, *Human Ecology*, pp. 116–37.
[2] E.g. M. R. Davie, 'The pattern of urban growth', reprinted in Theodorson, *Studies in Human Ecology*, pp. 77–92.
[3] M. A. Alihan, *Social Ecology* (New York, 1938).   [4] *Ibid.* pp. 224–5.

She makes similarly strong criticisms on the basis of the lack of consistency in the distribution pattern of family types and of other factors mentioned by Burgess, and suggests that the discrepancies indicate

that either (*a*) the two zonal arrangements are not of the same universe; or (*b*) one general zonal pattern does not hold for all factors and therefore more than one zonal arrangement is possible. In the latter case, zones should be treated, not as entities, but as arbitrary abstractions in terms of any one factor. This, however, would contradict Burgess' definitive delimitation of the zones.[1]

The argument is similar to the debate generated by the concept of the natural area. On the one hand, it involves the question of the theoretical status of the zone and, on the other, its utility as a general or as a specific tool. In neither case is Burgess particularly enlightening. Although he states that the zonal chart is an ideal construction and that it represents a static abstraction from a dynamic process, at other times he clearly seems to regard the zone as a real entity. Similarly, although his description of zonal characteristics is heavily biased towards style of life and family type considerations, his treatment of radial expansion is couched in general terms.

A further source of confusion and critical comment has been the extent of the claims made for the Burgess scheme. In an early statement Burgess claims that the zonal model is applicable to any town or city, but in later works he limits its scope to North American cities and, more particularly, to those which are of a commercial-industrial nature. Notwithstanding these limitations, the Burgess model has been subjected to a great deal of cross-cultural testing. It is to the evidence produced in these cross-cultural studies that we now turn.

Cross-cultural evidence and the zonal model

The Burgess model of urban growth and structure has probably been subjected to more cross-cultural examination than any other sociological statement about the city. Case studies in Europe, Asia, Latin America, and Africa, and historical reconstructions of earlier forms of urban development, have provided a mass of material for testing the universality of the zonal scheme. With few exceptions, however, the material produced is only relevant for one of the more ambiguous aspects of the zonal model: the spatial patterning of socio-economic status groups. There is very little information available on the spatial patterning of styles of life or family types. This bias in the material restricts the power of the cross-cultural test. On the other hand, the fact that a distinct style of life dimension appears to come into existence at only a relatively advanced stage of modernization helps to

[1] *Ibid*. p. 222.

219

restore the significance of the social rank data. In the pre-industrial city, at least, it may be anticipated that style of life variations will accompany those occurring in the social rank data.

It is implicit in the Burgess model that the social rank of a population varies directly with distance from the city centre. Since the wealthy are assumed to buy the newest housing and to pay a premium for space they are assumed to locate at the periphery of the community. The further from the city centre, the higher should be social rank. The results of the cross-cultural testing of this proposition are relatively unambiguous. Notwithstanding differences in methodology, in definitions, and in the aims of the research, the consensus of evidence is that throughout most of urban history and throughout most of the world the general relationship between urban zonation and social rank has been the reverse of that outlined by Burgess. Writing about the pre-industrial city in general, Sjoberg states that 'the elite typically has resided in or near the centre, with the lower class and outcast groups fanning out toward the periphery'.[1] A similar conclusion has been reached in studies of several European towns, of various cities in Latin America, and of several Asian cities.[2]

Recurring themes in many studies of the spatial patterning of the pre-industrial city are the symbolic value of residence near the centre of power and the fact that this can be manipulated by those who constitute or have access to the power elite. According to Violich the distance of a family's residence from the city centre in pre-conquest Peru was a function of the degree of kinship relation it could show to the Inca ruler.[3] A similar finding is presented in a study of urban ecology in pre-contact Japan:

The ecological structure of the castle town placed the administrative organs of the feudal regimes at the centre, and its structure was planned according to the related defence and status systems ... The *diamyō* (feudal lord) resided in the castle, the centre for political and military integration. The upper military class resided within easy access of the castle, and the lower military class, shrine and temple buildings were located in the surrounding area for defence of the town. In the

---

[1] Sjoberg, 'Cities in developing and in industrial societies', in Hauser and Schnore, p. 216. See also the same author's *The Preindustrial City*.

[2] E.g. McElrath, 'The social areas of Rome'; T. Caplow, 'Urban structure in France', *Am. Sociol. Rev.* 17 (1952), 544–9; E. D. Beynon, 'Budapest: an ecological study', *Geog. Rev.* 33 (1943), 256–75; A. T. Hansen, 'The ecology of a Latin-American city', in E. B. Reuter (ed.), *Race and Culture Contacts* (New York, 1934); N. S. Hayner, 'Mexico City: its growth and configuration', *Am. J. Sociol.* 50 (1945), 295–304; T. Caplow, 'The social ecology of Guatemala City', *Soc. Forces*, 28 (1949), 113–33; F. Dotson and L. O. Dotson, 'Ecological trends in the city of Guadalajara, Mexico', *Soc. Forces*, 32 (1954), 347–74; P. F. Cressey 'Ecological organization of Rangoon', *Sociol. Soc. Res.* 40 (1956), 166–9; N. P. Gist, 'The ecology of Bangalore, India', *Soc. Forces*, 35 (1957), 356–65; Yazaki, *The Japanese City*; S. K. Mehta, 'Patterns of residence in Poona', *Am. J. Sociol.* 73 (1968), 496–508. For a general review, see Schnore, 'On the spatial structure of cities'.

[3] F. Violich, *Cities of Latin America* (New York, 1944), pp. 22–5. Ref. in Schnore, 'On the spatial structure of cities'.

centre of the city were located the townsmen of the first rank under the rule of the military . . . after which came in order the merchant and artisan householders . . . Labourers lived in the back streets, and finally the outcasts (*eta*) resided on the city's periphery.[1]

In pre-nineteenth-century Europe a similar pattern is described by Comhaire and Cahnman:

In the European baroque town, everything is oriented around the palace. As in the middle ages the prestige-accented quarters of the burghers were located around the market place because it was the focal point in the city, so had the baroque-age aristocracy its townhouses erected in the vicinity of the palace. In both instances the middle classes lived farther away from the centre of town and the lower classes settled in the least desirable locations . . . On the outskirts were miserable hovels.[2]

In the absence of an efficient mass transportation system it is necessary to locate within easy walking distance of desired facilities. For the elite this means locating around the organs of government. As Sjoberg puts it,

Assuming that upper-class persons strive to maintain their prerogatives in the community and society . . . they must isolate themselves from the non-elite and be centrally located to ensure ready access to the headquarters of the governmental, religious, and educational organizations. The highly valued residence, then, is where fullest advantage may be taken of the city's strategic facilities; in turn these latter have come to be tightly bunched for the convenience of the elite.[3]

The elitist control of city government enables the elite to plan the city for their own ends. Population groups can be located according to their positions within the power and status hierarchies. In Colonial Africa, Pons observes that

The physical lay-out of the town could be seen as both an expression and a symbol of the relations between Africans and Europeans. European residential areas were situated close to, and tended to run into, the area of administration offices, hotels, shops and other service establishments, while African residential areas were strictly demarcated and well removed from the town centre.[4]

Similar observations have been reported for other colonial territories. In the post-colonial era the departure of the overseas elites has generally merely heralded a change-over in the composition of the elite central residents. Thus, in Guatemala City, Caplow reports that

the attachment of the upper-class population to the centre of the community arose from the planned location of the ruling group in colonial times, and persisted in

---

[1] Yazaki, *The Japanese City*, pp. 70–1.

[2] J. Comhaire and W. J. Cahnman, *How Cities Grew* (Madison, N. J., 1959), p. 40. Ref. in Schnore, 'On the spatial structure of cities'.

[3] Sjoberg, *The Preindustral City*, pp. 88–9.

[4] V. G. Pons, 'The growth of Stanleyville and the composition of its African population', in D. Forde (ed.), *Social Implications of Industrialization and Urbanization in Africa South of the Sahara* (Paris, 1956).

terms of both the symbols of status represented by central location and the social habits which became associated with the palacio, the cathedral, and the plaza.[1]

In many European cities the persistence of traditional rank considerations has allowed a continuance of the association between high status inner-city residence and may have inhibited trends toward the massive suburban growth characteristic of cities in the new world.[2]

The Burgess scheme of urban growth and structure was developed to fit the pattern of rapidly growing cities, with industrial bases, efficient transport, heterogeneous populations, free-market housing conditions and a value system which stressed newness and spaciousness. None of these character-istics was typical of most pre-nineteenth-century cities and many remain untypical in most parts of the world. In the absence of growth the conditions of obsolescence, invasion and succession which provide the dynamic to the Burgess model and which are assumed to make the zone in transition so unattractive to high status populations no longer apply. An economic concentration on cottage or small scale industries obviates the necessity for a functional segregation of residences and workplaces. The absence of an efficient transportation and communication system increases the relative advantage of proximity to the city centre and makes geographical distance a direct function of social distance. Fringe dwellers are marginal not only in a spatial sense but also in an organizational context. The concept of an essentially free market in housing has always been largely fictional, but nowhere more so than in societies in which elitist control of city government goes hand-in-hand with city planning. In the modern world the spread of the planning ideology has further limited the role of impersonal competition even though the planners may be agents of the middle classes.[3] The influence of competition in human societies is, in any case, largely guided by broad cultural considerations – and the culture of early twentieth-century Chicago may have had little in common with that characteristic of most other cities, either before or since.

With the modernization of traditional societies, and the concomitant changes in economic bases, transport and communication techniques, and value systems, it is tempting to predict a tendency for the distribution of status groups within the cities of the developing countries to approximate more and more to the Burgess model. There is considerable evidence in support of such a prediction. Thus, in Poona, Mehta observes that over the 1940-60 decades there has been a tendency for the highest income groups to decentralize.[4] In Latin America, Caplow observes that 'if we arrange . . .

[1] Caplow, 'Social ecology of Guatemala City', reprinted in Theodorson, *Studies in Human Ecology*, p. 344.

[2] Sjoberg, 'Cities in developing and industrial societies'.

[3] See Gans, 'Planning for people, not buildings'; Meadows, 'The urbanists'.

[4] Mehta, 'Patterns of residence in Poona', p. 502.

the Middle American cities upon which some ecological data are available in order of size, it is at once apparent that the larger the community the further it has departed from the traditional colonial pattern'.[1] As Schnore notes, however, in his review of Latin-American studies, the assumption that modernization is associated with development towards the Burgess pattern is as yet based on very dubious material. The example of such countries as the Union of South Africa or Sweden where physical and social planning have so close a relation, of much of Africa and Asia, with their peripheral slums, and even of the present-day Anglo-American societies with their increasing use of urban redevelopment policies, would argue great caution in any assumption that the Burgess model represents an inevitable form of development as far as the distribution of socio-economic status groups is concerned. The return of certain high status populations to the inner city, as the problems of transportation take on a more costly appearance may yet herald a return to the traditional pattern – albeit at a vastly increased scale.

The position with regard to the distribution of other population characteristics remains obscure. In general, what little cross-cultural evidence there is argues in favour of the Burgess zonation as a framework for the distribution of different family types wherever these emerge as a separate dimension of social differentiation. Thus in Calcutta, Berry and Rees find 'a clear and strong land-use and familism gradient . . . from commercial core to residential periphery'.[2] As yet, however, the evidence is too scant to warrant generalization.

A final verdict on the utility of the Burgess model as an empirical instrument must await the provision of further cross-cultural material. The data to hand only allow the conclusion that it is by no means a universal framework for the distribution of socio-economic status groups. This by no means rules out its potential value as an analytical framework for the description of other forms of social differentiation, such as that composed by the familism dimension. In Quinn's words:

If . . . a zonal system is to be accepted it must be conceived as a device of limited value in the interpretation of the city. It will not be a composite, universal frame of reference for the interpretation of all urban phenomena but will be limited to such single factors or combinations of them as correspond in distribution to the zonal pattern.[3]

THE SECTOR MODEL OF URBAN GROWTH AND STRUCTURE

The Burgess model of urban growth and structure was evolved in connexion with the wide-ranging interests of the Chicago ecologists. Despite its emphasis on family status and style of life considerations, it was put forward as a

---

[1] Caplow, 'Social ecology of Guatemala City' in Theodorson, *Studies in Human Ecology*, p. 347.
[2] Berry and Rees, 'The factorial ecology of Calcutta', *Am. J. Sociol.* 74 (1969), 490.
[3] Quinn, *Human Ecology*, p. 135.

general model, summarizing much of urban life. The sector model developed by Hoyt has a much narrower focus: the distribution of rental classes.[1] Basing his model on an intensive block-by-block analysis of changes in a variety of housing characteristics in 142 U.S. cities, Hoyt concludes:

The high rent neighbourhoods do not skip about at random in the process of movement, they follow a definite path in one or more sectors of the city. Apparently there is a tendency for neighbourhoods within a city to shift in accordance with what may be called the 'sector theory' of neighbourhood change . . . the different types of residential areas tend to grow outward along rather distinct radii, and new growth on the arc of a given sector tends to take on the character of the initial growth in that sector.[2]

As in the case of the zonal model, the spatial expression of Hoyt's theory is presented almost as an aside. The main *raison d'être* of the thesis is exposition of a theory of changes in the patterning of rental areas over time.

Movement of the high-rent neighbourhoods and a subsequent 'filtering' effect provide the main dynamic of the sector model. In the high-rent neighbourhoods live the elite of the city. As they move outwards so the lower and intermediate status groups filter into their abandoned houses. Sometimes the high-rent areas jump to a new location in a different part of the city, but usually the new districts of high-status homes are in the line of growth of the high-rent areas.

(The) high-grade residential neighbourhoods must almost necessarily move outward towards the periphery of the city. The wealthy seldom reverse their steps and move backward into the obsolete houses which they are giving up. On each side of them is usually an intermediate rental area so they cannot move sideways. As they represent the highest-income group, there are no houses above them abandoned by another group. They must build new houses on vacant land. Usually this vacant land lies available just ahead of the line of march of the area because, anticipating the trend of fashionable growth, land promoters have either restricted it to high-grade use or speculators have placed a value on the land that is too high for the low-rent or intermediate rental group. Hence the natural trend of the high-rent area is outward, towards the periphery of the city in the very sector in which the high-rent area started.[3]

The origins of the high-status residential sector are traced back to the retail office centre of the city which provides the main employment area for the higher income groups and is the point farthest removed from the side of the city that has industries or warehouses.

In each city the direction and pattern of further growth then tends to be governed by some combination of the following considerations: (1) High-grade residential

---

[1] The basic statement of the sector theory is contained in H. Hoyt, *The Structure and Growth of Residential Neighbourhoods in American Cities* (Washington, 1939). See also the same author's 'Recent distortions of the classical models of urban structure', *Land Econ.* 40 (1964), 199–212.
[2] Hoyt, *The Structure and Growth*, p. 114.　　　　　[3] *Ibid.* p. 116.

growth tends to proceed from the given point of origin, along established lines of travel or toward another existing nucleus of buildings or trading centres . . . (2) The zone of high-rent areas tends to progress toward high ground which is free from the risk of floods and to spread along lake, bay, river, and ocean-fronts, where such water-fronts are not used for industry . . . (3) High-rent residential districts tend to grow toward the section of the city which has free, open country beyond the edges and away from 'dead end' sections which are limited by natural or artificial barriers to expansion . . . (4) The higher-priced residential neighbourhood tends to grow toward the homes of the leaders of the community . . . (5) Trends of movement of office buildings, banks and stores, pull the higher-priced residential neighbour-hoods in the same general direction . . . (6) High-grade residential areas tend to develop along the fastest existing transportation lines . . . (7) The growth of high-rent neighbourhoods continues in the same direction for a long period of time . . . (8) De-luxe high-rent apartment areas tend to be established near the business centre in old residential areas . . . This exception is a very special case . . . (9) Real estate promoters may bend the direction of high-grade residential growth . . .[1]

The movement of the higher-status populations outwards from the city centre along the main transport routes has coincided in time with changes in transport technology which have allowed more expansive settlement forms. Thus, the high-status areas grow outwards not linearly, but in a fan- or wedge-shaped pattern.

As a result of the growth process a particular pattern of residential areas emerges which may be summarized in terms of five generalizations:

(1) The highest rental areas are in every case located in one or more sectors on the side of the city.

(2) High-rent areas take the form of wedges extending in certain sectors along radial lines from the centre to the periphery.

(3) Intermediate rental areas or areas falling just below the highest rental areas tend to surround the highest rental areas on one side.

(4) Intermediate rental areas on the periphery of other sectors of the city besides the ones in which the highest rental areas are located are found in certain cities.

(5) Low rent areas extending from the centre to the edge of settlement are found in practically every city.[2]

The nature and assumptions of the sector model

The sector model of urban growth was developed during the course of an investigation of housing trends sponsored by the U.S. Federal Housing Administration. In contrast to the zonal model it was designed as a practical, rather than as a theoretical, instrument. Rather than being an ideal-type construction it was put forward as an empirical generalization, which could be used as the basis for making practical decisions about future developments.

[1] *Ibid.* pp. 117–19.   [2] *Ibid.* chap. VI *passim.*

Since these decisions were to be primarily of a financial nature the whole emphasis of the theory is on rental levels and on the ability to pay.

Many of the assumptions on which the sector theory is based are held in common with Burgess's zonal model. The theory envisages a growing population, a wide range of commercial and industrial undertakings in the city, a single dominant nucleus, and, most specifically, a laissez-faire, private enterprise economy, in which impersonal competition can have full play. In an impassioned defence of this position in 1950, Hoyt contrasts the sector theory with what he claims are theories based on hybrid mixtures of economics, social welfare and politics, which have as their real objective not the advancement of knowledge but the over-throw of the free market economy and its substitution by 'the complete socialization of the United States'. There is, according to Hoyt,

[A] fundamental conflict between the nature of city growth in the type of society in which the sector theory was formulated and the welfare state . . . It is conceded that if the new social welfare state triumphs completely, the sector theory will be only a historical account of city growth in the capitalistic society in the early twentieth century.[1]

The original exposition of the sector theory coincided with the first burgeonings of the automobile age. Although it took into account the effects of road transport on the siting of industry, it paid little attention to its potential effects on residential location. As presented the theory was, of course, based on the evidence of the past and thus related to conditions which have since been radically altered. In a 1964 statement Hoyt writes,

The automobile and the resultant belt highways encircling American cities have opened up large regions beyond existing settled areas, and future high-grade residential growth will probably not be confined entirely to rigidly defined sectors. As a result of the greater flexibility in urban growth patterns resulting from these radial expressways and belt highways, some higher income communities are being developed beyond low income sectors, but these communities usually do not enjoy as high a social rating as new neighbourhoods located in the high income sector.[2]

Prior to the advent of mass private transport, the demands of the wealthy for space combined with accessibility to the city centre, resulted in the concentration of high rent development along the lines of most rapid transport. With the advent of mass ownership of automobiles, however, the once favoured avenues, now filled with petrol fumes, noisy, and dangerous to children, cease to be attractive as home sites. The new trend is for seclusion, for garden suburbs with winding streets, woods, and their own community

[1] M. Hoyt, 'Residential sectors revisited', *The Appraisal J.* (Oct. 1950), p. 450.
[2] Hoyt, 'Recent distortions', p. 209.

centres. These are located off the main axial routes, but are still to be found in the original high-grade sectors.

Criticism

The prime mover in the pattern of residential growth outlined in the sector theory appears to be attraction to the leaders of society. The identity of these leaders is, however, somewhat indistinct, as is the nature of their appeal. Rodwin has pointed out that the Hoyt scheme rests on an ambiguous and over-simplified view of the stratification system characteristic of the city. The homes of the leaders of society are variously equated with the highest-rental areas, the high-grade districts, and the most fashionable areas. As Rodwin states 'these areas are not always synonymous'.[1] The operational measure of social rank adopted by Hoyt is rent. This is used 'because exact data were available and there was no way of accurately defining social classes or social leaders on a block by block basis'.[2] The maps which Hoyt uses to illustrate his thesis show five rental classes, but in his text he speaks generally of only three: an upper class, those who pay the highest rent, a lower class consisting of those in the lowest rental areas, and an intermediate class containing the remainder. The exact nature of the relationship between rent, income, and prestige is not explored. Nor is there any discussion of the relationship of stratification and ethnic variables in residential location apart from passing comments about the desire of people of the same ethnic background to live together and about 'the segregation of sectors populated by different races'.[3] No mention is made of stratification or ecological patterns within these groups. In a discussion of the movement of various ethnic and status populations in Boston, Rodwin concludes:

These tendencies suggest that lower and middle-income groups often move not only to the leaders of society but also to the leaders of their class or nationality, many of whom are located in other quarters of the city . . . these class relationships are much more subtle and complicated than the rent gradations employed by Hoyt.[4]

The analysis is further clouded by the vague definition given to the intermediate class. It covers such a broad spectrum of the population that it is clearly impossible for more than a fraction to live adjacent to the leaders of society. Many must of necessity live in districts far removed from the areas of highest rent. In these cases factors other than the attractiveness of the

[1] Rodwin, 'The theory of residential growth and structure', p. 308.
[2] Hoyt, 'Residential sectors', p. 448.
[3] Hoyt, *The Structure and Growth*, p. 62.
[4] L. Rodwin, 'Rejoinder to Dr Firey and Dr Hoyt', *The Appraisal J.* (Oct. 1950), p. 455.

elite must be brought into the argument. This Hoyt conspicuously fails to do.

Probably the most ambiguous aspect of the sector model is the definition of sectors. Part of this ambiguity flows from the vagueness with which the main dynamic of residential differentiation is outlined in the theory. Since much of the model derives from the assumed attractiveness of the elite it might be assumed that proximity to the areas of highest rental would provide the required indicant. On the other hand, in the application of the model Hoyt seems to have emphasized direction, suggesting that sectors might be seen as the combination of zones and radial axes. It is this latter geometric property which has generally been used in the empirical application of the model. Even here, however, there remains much scope for ambiguity. In the original exposition of the model the term sector is loosely allocated to areas which range in size from single blocks to whole quadrants of the city. On the detailed city maps showing the distribution of rent areas which appear in the main exposition of the model the data are given block by block. As Rodwin states these maps are not altogether in line with the 'theoretical' maps which appear later in the work.[1] Here, sectors become the areas defined by the intersection of zones and radial axes. Later still sectors are referred to in terms of general direction, for example the south-western or the northern sectors. According to Rodwin:

The sector then may be formally defined as a radial residential grouping, usually capable of expansion along or close to an avenue of transportation and comprising enough families able to afford a comparable type of housing to establish a pattern ... The broader pattern, that is the southwestern, western or northwestern suburban trends really reflect only a general direction of expansion, not a sector...[2]

If Rodwin's position be adopted, however, there seems little apart from shape to distinguish the sector from the natural area. According to Firey, Rodwin's attempt to reformulate the concept 'has granted so much, for the sake of empirical adequacy, that it has left little room for an imaginable converse'.[3] Firey's views on the concept may be gathered from some earlier comments in the same article:

Shall it be said, for instance, that when approximately one-third of a city's circumference lies in water that any radial divisions in the remaining land portion comprise sectors? Shall it be said that when hills and topographical features lay down only a few possible courses for outward residential extension that these courses then constitute a sector or series of sectors? Can it be said that when some fifty per cent of the circumference of a city is occupied with various segments of a particular type of residential land use that the resulting mosaic truly answers to a sector theory? When, in one city, a sector emerges as a result of outward extension of an

[1] *Ibid.*
[2] Rodwin, 'The theory of residential growth', pp. 307–8.
[3] W. Firey, 'Residential sectors re-examined', *The Appraisal J.* (Oct. 1950), p.452.

upper-income area due to suburban platting, can these two discrete phenomena be legitimately assimilated to the same theory? The author's own answer to these questions must be in the negative.[1]

Such a pessimistic view seems overstated. In view of the emphasis in the model on the radial extension of residential areas a delineation of sectors in terms of their relationship to major arterial roads would seem the proper and potentially useful technique. Many so-called 'sectoral analyses' are based on no more than an arbitrary geometric division of the city area, each sector being defined by radial axes at some arbitrary angle away from each other. It is difficult to see what relevance this sort of analysis has to the sector model as outlined by Hoyt. Little improvement is offered by those analyses which take main roads as the boundaries of sectors. Hoyt clearly envisages that development on either side of main routes is likely to be similar in character: main roads are unifying rather than divisive features in the model. Much of the empirical evidence produced in studies which are said to use the Hoyt framework are, in fact, irrelevant to it.

Hoyt makes few explicit claims for the generalization of the sector model outside the empirical universe on which it is based. In a 1964 review of the model Hoyt concludes:

The principles of city growth and structure, formulated on the basis of experience in the United States prior to 1930, are ... subject to modification not only as a result of dynamic changes in the United States in the last few decades but these principles ... are subject to further revisions when it is sought to apply them to foreign cities.[2]

TOWARDS AN INTEGRATION OF THE ZONAL AND SECTORAL MODELS
OF URBAN STRUCTURE

Much of the initial discussion concerned with the absolute or the relative merits of the zonal and sectoral models of urban structure took place in terms of an implicit assumption that the two schemes were oriented towards the same universe of content: something called the 'ecological structure of the city'. Both models were presented and discussed as if they were total schemes capable of capturing all, or nearly all, of the significant variation in urban residential structure. Differences between different parts of the city were conceptualized in vague and amorphous terms and the underlying model seems to have been unidimensional rather than multidimensional. Tests of the utility of the zonal and sectoral models were based on a great variety of data. Not surprisingly there were data enough to suggest that neither model possessed the total utility which its supporters claimed.

[1] *Ibid.*   [2] Hoyt, 'Recent distortions', p. 212.

The urban mosaic

The realization that urban residential differentiation is a multidimensional phenomenon has brought about a more sophisticated approach to the study of its geographical expression. Separate analyses of the distribution patterns followed by social rank, familism and ethnicity have suggested that rather than being competing approaches, the zonal and sectoral models of urban structure may actually be concerned with different sets of properties. In a review of studies concerned with the internal structure of the modern city, Berry claims that the zonal and sectoral models may be considered 'independent, additive contributors to the total socio-economic structuring of city neighbourhoods'.[1] Berry suggests that the basic organization of the city's residential fabric may be seen in terms of (*a*) 'the axial variation of neighbourhoods by socio-economic rank [and] (*b*) the concentric variation of neighbourhoods according to family structure'. Neighbourhood characteristics involving such social rank indicants as type of occupation, educational attainment, income, and house value, vary according to a sectoral pattern: 'High status sectors search and follow particular amenities desired for housing, such as view, higher ground, and so on. Lower status sectors follow lower lying, industrial-transportation arteries that radiate from the central business district and which, together with that district, form the exogenously-determined skeleton of the city.'[2] Conversely, the distribution of such variables as age structure, women in the workforce, single-family houses, and the other family-linked characteristics varies with distance from the centre:

Thus, at the edge of the city are newer, owned, single-family homes, in which reside larger families with younger children than nearer the city centre, and where the wife stays at home. Conversely, the apartment complexes nearer the city centre have smaller, older families, fewer children, and are more likely to be rentals; in addition, larger proportions of the women will be found to work.[3]

Berry suggests that

If the concentric and axial schemes are overlaid on any city, the resulting cells will contain neighbourhoods remarkably uniform in their social and economic characteristics. Around any concentric band communities will vary in their income and other characteristics, but will have much the same density, ownership, and family patterns. Along each axis communities will have relatively uniform economic characteristics, and each axis will vary outwards in the same way according to family structure. Thus, a system of polar co-ordinates originating at the central business district is adequate to describe most of the socio-economic characteristics of city neighbourhoods.[4]

The evidence relating to Berry's conclusions is by no means unanimous. The major source of relevant material consists of a series of studies which

[1] B. J. L. Berry, 'Internal structure of the city', *Law Contemp. Probs*, 3 (1965), p. 115.
[2] *Ibid.*   [3] *Ibid.* pp. 115–16.   [4] *Ibid.* p. 116.

have used analysis of variance techniques in an attempt to unravel the separate effects of zones and sectors in the distribution of social rank and family status scores. Less attention has been paid to the distribution of ethnicity and virtually none to that of mobility or migration status. The generality of the findings has been further limited by problems in the delineation of the analytical frameworks.

In one of the earliest attempts to apply the analysis of variance technique to data on the spatial patterning of urban residential differentiation, Anderson and Egeland examine the role of zonal and sectoral variation in the spatial patterning of the Shevky–Bell social rank and family status constructs in the U.S. cities of Akron, Dayton, Indianapolis, and Syracuse.[1] Sectors are defined geometrically and zones are marked off by a series of circles concentric to the city centre. Sixteen census tracts, one for each zone-sector combination, are selected for analysis in each city. The results of the ensuing analyses of variance are presented in Table 5.1.

The presence of considerable city-sector interaction with regard to the distribution of the social rank index leads to the presentation of separate social rank analyses for each city. In three of the four cases – Akron, Dayton, and Syracuse – the analyses reveal significant sectoral and insignificant zonal effects. In the fourth city, Indianapolis, both spatial effects reach significance, although the sectoral effect is still associated with the greater F-ratio. The distribution of the family status index follows a zonal pattern. Reporting a similar pattern in the distribution of social rank and family status factors in Toronto, Murdie concludes that 'economic status and family status tend to be distributed in sectoral and concentric patterns respectively'.[2]

Evidence from other studies is less consistent. Analyses of Rome and of Chicago suggest that the spatial patterning of social rank and family status characteristics may be considerably more complicated than is suggested in Berry's additive model. Although neither set of analyses find evidence of any marked interaction effects, each uncovers a distribution pattern in which zonal and sector effects are apparent for both sets of socio-economic characteristics.

In Rome, McElrath uses contiguity to three major transportation arteries to define sectors.[3] Within each sector, zones are distinguished according to traditional administrative lines. Eighty-four *gruppi di sezione* are included in the analysis. Results of the two-way analyses of variance are shown in Table 5.2.

The analysis shows that each set of socio-economic data varies both zonally and sectorally. Social rank varies inversely with distance from the city

---

[1] T. R. Anderson and J. A. Egeland, 'Spatial aspects of social area analysis', *Am. Sociol. Rev.* 26 (1961), 392–9.

[2] R. A. Murdie, *The Factorial Ecology of Metropolitan Toronto, 1951–1961* (Chicago, 1969). Quoted in Rees, 'Factorial ecology of metropolitan Chicago'.

[3] McElrath, 'The social areas of Rome'.

TABLE 5.1 *Analyses of variance for social rank and family status by zones and sectors in Akron, Dayton, Indianapolis and Syracuse, 1950*

A. Social rank

Source	Sum of squares	df	Variance estimate	F	H_o i
Akron					
Between zones	898	3	299	1·93	Accept
Between sectors	5,408	3	1,803	11·64	Reject
Remainder	1,393	9	155	–	–
Total	7,699	15	–	–	–
Dayton					
Between zones	608	3	203	2·88	Accept
Between sectors	3,576	3	1,192	16·97	Reject
Remainder	632	9	70	–	–
Total	4,816	15	–	–	–
Indianapolis					
Between zones	1,695	3	565	5·77	Reject
Between sectors	2,435	3	812	8·29	Reject
Remainder	881	9	98	–	–
Total	5,011	15	–	–	–
Syracuse					
Between zones	482	3	161	0·54	Accept
Between sectors	9,642	3	3,214	10·74	Reject
Remainder	2,694	9	299	–	–
Total	12,817	15	–	–	–

B. Family status

Source	Sum of squares	df	Variance estimate	F	H_o i
Between cities	4,816	3	1,605	5·68	Reject
Between sectors	948	3	361	1·12	Accept
Between zones	28,419	3	9,473	33·49	Reject
Cities × sectors	3,864	9	429	1·62	Accept
Cities × zones	1,692	9	188	0·71	Accept
Sectors × zones	2,757	9	306	1·16	Accept
Remainder	7,143	27	265	–	–
Pooled error	15,276	54	283	–	–
Total	49,639	63	–	–	–

SOURCE. Anderson and Egeland, 'Spacial aspects of social area analysis', pp. 397–8.
NOTE. i 0·01 level of significance adopted.

centre, while family status varies directly with distance. The three sectors exhibit marked differences in both sets of variables.

The joint influence of zonal and sectoral effects on the distribution of social rank and family status is also evidenced in Rees's study of the factorial

TABLE 5.2 *Analyses of variance for social rank and family status by zones and sectors in Rome, 1951*

A. Social rank

Source	Sum of squares	df	Variance estimate	F	H_o i
Between zones	11,485	2	5,743	29	Reject
Between sectors	11,549	2	5,775	29	Reject
Zones × sectros	2,980	4	745	3·69	Accept
Remainder	15,139	75	202	–	–
Total	41,153	83	–	–	–

B. Family status

Source	Sum of squares	df	Variance estimate	F	H_o i
Between zones	6,234	2	3,117	39	Reject
Between sectors	4,018	2	2,009	25	Reject
Zones × sectors	852	4	213	2·66	Accept
Remainder	6,002	75	80	–	–
Total	17,106	83	–	–	–

SOURCE. McElrath, 'The social areas of Rome', p. 389.
NOTE. i 0·01 level of significance adopted.

ecology of Chicago.[1] Factors identified as referring to social rank and to family status vary significantly by both zones and sectors. The relative strength of the two effects varies according to the bounds of the study universe. When the analysis is conducted within the extensive area formed by the Chicago metropolitan area the zonal effect is the greater for both factors. When the analysis is conducted within the smaller area comprising the effective labour and housing markets of the city, the zonal effect is less important than the sectoral in the distribution of social rank, but becomes more important in the distribution of family status.

Rees suggests that there may be a relationship between the relative strengths of the zonal and sectoral effects and city size. He points out that the larger the city, the greater appears to be the relative importance of zonal variations in social rank and of sectoral variations in family status, even though each remains the subsidiary effect. Table 5.3 presents the relevant information.

Rome appears somewhat out of line, but the major exception concerns the high sector: zone F ratio for social rank in Toronto. Rees suggests that this may be a statistical artefact of the particular combination of variables which correlate highly with the Toronto social rank factor. More generally, it

[1] Rees, 'Factorial ecology of metropolitan Chicago: II, Social and physical space of the metropolis' (mimeo. Chicago, 1968).

The urban mosaic

TABLE 5.3 *City size and 'F' ratios for social rank and family status*

City	Population	Social rank Sectors/zone ratio	Family status Zone/sector ratio
Chicago	5,959,000	1·15	2·60
Toronto	1,824,000	30·00	10·70
Rome	1,530,000	1·00	1·56
Indianapolis	639,000	1·44	*ii*
Brisbane *i*	594,000	1·30	4·17
Dayton	502,000	5·89	⎫
Akron	458,000	6·03	⎬ 29·9 *ii*
Syracuse	333,000	19·89	⎭

SOURCE. Rees, p.129.
NOTES. *i* For Brisbane, see below.
ii Indianapolis included in Dayton, Akron, Syracuse set.

appears that the larger the city the more complicated its spatial structure. Although the evidence is scant it seems likely that one of the reasons for this lies in the greater heterogeneity of the large city population. The presence of large ethnic or other minorities, especially where these are strongly differentiated from the core society, may be expected to have a considerable impact on the structure of the city. In the American situation the lower degree of differentiation found amongst the Negro population as compared with the White is evidenced in the lack of independence in Negro areas of variables relating to the social rank and family status dimensions. It is not entirely the case that 'the segregated area is a microcosm of the whole, compressed spatially, reproducing in miniature the metropolitan-wide pattern'.[1] Rather, the segregated area represents a different order of urban society. The larger the city the more likely it is to include populations marked off by ethnic or migration experiences. Since it appears that such disadvantaged populations are generally confined to certain disadvantaged inner-city locations their presence is likely to upset the simple nature of the zonal and sectoral effects.[2] Successive invasions of new minorities may be expected to complicate the pattern yet further. The axial movement of minorities may be expected to increase the sectoral component in distribution of family status. The infilling of inner-city areas may be expected to increase the zonal component in the distribution of social rank. It may be that the more homogeneous a population in terms of its degree of modernity and differentiation the more its spatial patterning will approximate to the simple, additive model suggested by Berry.

[1] *Ibid.* p. 12.
[2] E.g. Taeuber and Taeuber, *Negroes in Cities*; D. N. Jeans and M. I. Logan, 'A reconnaissance survey of population change in the Sydney metropolitan area', *Aust. Geog.* 13 (1961); Duncan and Lieberson, 'Ethnic segregation and assimilation'.

THE SPATIAL PATTERNING OF THE SOCIAL AREA INDEXES IN
BRISBANE AND AUCKLAND

Further evidence on the interplay between zonal and sectoral modes of
spatial organization is provided by the distribution of social rank, family

Fig. 5.2. Distribution of social rank in Brisbane, 1961

status and ethnicity in Brisbane and Auckland. Figures 5.2 to 5.7 illustrate
the patterns in map form. The indexes are computed according to the
procedures outlined in the last chapter with categories at 25-point intervals.

Social rank exhibits a complicated geographical pattern in both cities.
In Brisbane low social rank characterizes much of the inner city and of the
southern and eastern outskirts. High social rank characterizes a western
sector with the highest values occurring at middle distances from the city
centre. Scattered pockets of high rank CDs occur immediately to the east

235

of the city centre and in the mid–south.[1] Collectors' districts bordering the river upstream from the inner city also tend to exhibit relatively high social rank values. Only the western high rank sector, however, is able to develop

Fig. 5.3. Distribution of social rank in Auckland, 1966

towards open country. In Auckland there is evidence of a more general sectoral pattern. The main area of high social rank occurs in an eastern sector hugging the coast. Secondary areas of high–middle rank occur in a southern sector, on the north shore of the Waitemata harbour and in an isolated area in the east. In each case well–marked topographic features are

[1] The 1961 pattern is remarkably similar to that obtaining in the 1890's. All the districts possessing high social rank in 1961 were of high prestige at the turn of the century. See R. Lawson, 'The Social Structure of Brisbane in the late Nineteenth Century' (unpub. Ph.D. dissertation, University of Queensland, 1969).

followed. Low rank sectors characterize much of the south and west. There is little evidence of a zonal pattern.

If the main impression of the maps showing the distribution of social rank in Brisbane and Auckland is one of sectors that of those showing the

Fig. 5.4. Distribution of family status in Brisbane, 1961

pattern of family status scores is one of zones. In Brisbane low values on the family status index are concentrated in the inner-city, within a one-mile radius of the GPO. The surrounding zone, to a radius of two miles, consists largely of CDs scoring in the 25–49 range. In general these are areas characterized by old and relatively stable populations. The innermost zone, on the other hand, contains a heterogeneous mixture of boarding-house residents and other largely non-family units.[1] The outer areas of Brisbane exhibit

[1] The family dissolution or non-family factor discussed in chapter 2 shows its only high scores in the inner-city area.

almost uniformly high values on the family status index. Both private and
Housing Commission areas are characterized by young families, many
children, single-family dwellings and few women in the workforce. The
Auckland material exhibits a closely similar pattern. Low values characterize

Fig. 5.5. Distribution of family status in Auckland, 1966

the inner-city sub-divisions to the south of the harbour. Surrounding these
to a radius of four to five miles is a zone of high-middle scores, with consistently high family status indexes further out. In both cities family status
exhibits a remarkably simple spatial pattern.

The distribution of those populations which provide the basis for the
ethnic status index in the two cities shows a bipolar pattern. In Brisbane
major concentrations of the foreign-born occur in the inner city and on the
southern outskirts. The inner-city area contains major concentrations of

Italian-born migrants, north of the river, and of Greek-born migrants south of the river. Both groups are in the process of invading and renovating run-down areas of turn-of-the-century housing. The southern concentration is much more heterogeneous in ethnic background. Its development reflects

Fig. 5.6. Distribution of ethnicity (foreign-born) in Brisbane, 1961

Housing Commission policy, proximity to a heavy industry complex, and market gardening. The distribution of non-Europeans in Auckland repeats the spatial pattern of the foreign-born in Brisbane. Major concentrations occur in the inner city and on the southern outskirts. The inner city is a receiving area for Maori and Island migrants; the southern concentration centres on State Housing areas and the proximity of heavy industry.[1]

[1] It is noteworthy that 75 per cent of new State tenancies taken up in Auckland during 1969 were by Maori or Islander families. Considerable educational and attitudinal problems are resulting from the concentration of Maoris and Islanders in the State Housing areas.

The rapid increase in the density of Polynesian settlement in both areas has been perhaps the most radical development in the recent ecological history of Auckland.

A more detailed examination of the role played by distance and direction in the spatial patterning of the social area indexes involves the use of analysis

Fig. 5.7. Distribution of ethnicity (non-European) in Auckland, 1966

of variance techniques. Regrettably, the large size and small number of sub-areas in Auckland limits the analysis to Brisbane.

The geographical framework for the analysis of the Brisbane material is provided by a series of six concentric zones, each one mile wide, centred on the GPO in the city centre, and nine sectors defined along the major arterial roads. It is believed that this latter delimitation is more in keeping with Hoyt's presentation of the sector model than are frameworks using a simple geometrical definition. Collectors' districts included in the analysis were selected in terms of their contiguity to the zone-sector intersections. One hundred and eight CDs are included in the analysis, two for each possible

Fig. 5.8. Sectors used in Brisbane analyses of variance, 1961

distance-direction intersection. The area framework used is illustrated in Fig. 5.8. The results of the basic two-way analysis of variance for each of the social area indexes are shown in Table 5.4.

TABLE 5.4 *Analysis of variance for social rank, familism, and ethnicity by zones and sectors, Brisbane, 1961*

Source	Sum of squares	df	Variance estimate	F	H_o i
		Social rank			
Between zones	3,852	5	770	7·6	Reject
Between sectors	7,997	8	1,000	9·9	Reject
Zones × sectors	7,377	40	184	1·8	Accept
Remainder	5,429	54	101	–	–
Total	24,655	107	–	–	–
		Familism			
Between zones	8,242	5	1,648	50	Reject
Between sectors	3,227	8	403	12	Reject
Zones × sectors	3,070	40	77	2·3	Reject
Remainder	1,769	54	33	–	–
Total	16,308	107	–	–	–
		Ethnicity			
Between zones	5,564	5	1,113	23	Reject
Between sectors	2,380	8	297	6·2	Reject
Zones × sectors	5,854	40	146	3·0	Reject
Remainder	2,608	54	48	–	–
Total	16,406	107	–	–	–

NOTE. i 0·01 level of significance adopted.

241

Each social area construct exhibits both zonal and sectoral patterns. In the case of two of the indexes, family status and ethnicity, a significant interaction effect is also present. A more detailed picture of the varying influence of distance and direction as they affect social rank, family status and ethnicity is provided by the cell-means for each zone-sector intersection. Tables 5.5 to 5.7 provide the relevant information.

TABLE 5.5 *Cell means of the social rank index, Brisbane, 1961*

Zones	Sectors									Zone means
	1	2	3	4	5	6	7	8	9	
I	31·0	24·0	49·0	42·0	45·5	30·0	34·5	30·0	60·5	38·5
II	43·5	35·5	45·0	30·0	46·5	39·5	48·0	41·0	57·9	42·9
III	42·0	49·0	62·5	40·5	77·0	53·0	48·0	67·5	58·5	55·3
IV	47·5	62·5	44·0	18·0	53·5	44·0	36·0	50·5	64·0	46·7
V	28·0	39·0	24·0	30·0	36·5	34·0	49·5	52·0	54·0	38·6
VI	19·5	50·5	33·5	14·5	45·5	44·5	30·5	47·5	71·5	39·7
Sector means	35·3	43·4	43·0	29·2	50·8	40·8	41·1	48·1	61·0	

The prime spatial effect in the patterning of social rank in Brisbane is sectoral. The ratio of the between sectors F to the between zones F, 1·30, is markedly similar to that reported for Indianapolis, a city of approximately the same size as Brisbane (Table 5.3). Consistently high social rank scores occur along sector 9 and consistently low scores characterize sector 4. The remaining sectors exhibit fluctuating scores in the middle social rank range. Superimposed on the sectorial pattern is a marked zonal effect. In general, social rank arises with distance from the GPO to zones III or IV and then declines to zones V and VI. All the northern sectors, numbers 5–9, with the exception of sector 9, show a peak in zone III. The southern sectors tend to peak in zone IV. The difference in the location of the peaks north and south of the river probably reflects the choice of the GPO as the point of origin. Since it is located on the northern edge of the main commercial area, measurements taken from it exaggerate the effective distance of the southern CDs from the city centre.

Interpretation of the spatial patterning of family status in Brisbane is complicated by the necessity of coping with the zone-sector interaction effect. The main cause of this effect appears to lie in the peculiar behaviour of sectors 4, 5 and 8. In contrast to the general tendency for scores on the family status index to increase with increasing distance these three sectors show erratic fluctuations with distance. Sector 4 peaks in zone III (a State Housing area) and then declines to the outskirts; sector 5 increases in family status to zone II, drops to zone III, increases to a high peak in zone V and then

TABLE 5.6 *Cell means of the familism index, Brisbane, 1961*

Zones	Sectors									Zone means
	1	2	3	4	5	6	7	8	9	
I	49·5	49·5	46·0	62·0	56·0	52·5	55·5	54·5	42·5	52·0
II	50·0	52·0	60·5	65·5	38·0	44·5	57·5	72·0	51·0	54·6
III	57·0	59·5	65·5	75·0	42·0	55·0	66·5	62·0	61·0	60·4
IV	57·0	64·5	71·5	73·5	66·5	58·5	68·0	74·5	68·5	66·9
V	66·5	69·5	68·5	72·0	64·0	67·0	87·0	88·0	73·5	72·9
VI	71·0	81·0	72·5	73·0	65·5	67·5	83·0	76·0	87·0	75·2
Sector means	58·5	62·7	64·1	70·2	55·3	57·5	69·6	71·2	63·9	

drops again to zone VI. With the exception of these fluctuations the major spatial effect in the patterning of family status is zonal. The ratio of the between zones F to the between sectors F is 4·17, a considerably greater figure than those reported for Rome or Chicago, but considerably less than those reported for the four U.S. cities set and for Toronto (Table 5.3). In aggregate there is a steady increase in family status with increasing distance from the city centre.

TABLE 5.7 *Cell means of the ethnicity index, Brisbane, 1961*

Zones	Sectors									Zone means
	1	2	3	4	5	6	7	8	9	
I	67·0	45·5	18·5	12·5	32·5	18·5	29·0	26·0	19·5	29·9
II	19·5	20·0	11·0	11·5	22·5	22·0	10·0	19·5	16·0	16·9
III	15·5	14·0	5·5	12·0	9·5	9·0	11·0	1·5	7·0	10·6
IV	7·0	8·5	9·0	12·0	3·5	6·5	2·5	12·5	8·0	7·7
V	9·0	12·5	14·5	12·0	6·0	3·0	7·5	20·0	21·0	11·7
VI	44·0	12·5	14·5	12·0	7·5	6·5	16·5	10·0	10·5	14·9
Sector means	27·0	18·8	12·2	12·0	13·6	10·9	12·8	14·9	15·3	

The interpretation of the spatial patterning of ethnic status in Brisbane follows along very similar lines to those employed in the case of family status. Again the zonal effect is by far the strongest. There is a general U-shaped pattern in the zonal distribution of the non-British born, high rates characterizing the inner and outer zones and low rates characterizing the intermediate zones. It is apparent that the populations involved in the two peaks differ: the inner city peak results from the concentration of Italian, Greek, and East European migrants, the peripheral peak reflects the location of German and Dutch migrants. The major interactional effects result from the consistent ethnic status scores in sector 4 and the very high values which occur in zones I and VI of sector 1. The inner city peak in sector 1 occurs in the main Greek settlement in Brisbane; the other peak occurs in a major industrial area which draws on a large migrant workforce.

In general, the Brisbane and Auckland data support the assumption that zonal and sectoral patterns of spatial organization are complementary to each other. Social rank varies primarily by sectors, while family status and ethnicity vary primarily in terms of zones. The Brisbane materials indicate, however, that there are strong secondary effects in each case.

THE SPATIAL PATTERNING OF RESIDENTIAL DIFFERENTIATION AND DEVIANT BEHAVIOUR IN LUTON AND DERBY

One of the main analytical offshoots of the Burgess zonal scheme is the gradient, a cross-sectional profile based on the ecological assumption that the community is organized in terms of a dominant centre. Use of gradients has been particularly common in studies of the ecological distribution of deviant behaviour. Thus, examples of gradients are to be found in the delinquency studies of Shaw and McKay and in the Faris and Dunham analysis of psychiatric disorders.[1] Implicit in the use of the technique is the assumption that the zonal model captures much of the variation in the environmental factors that are related to differences in the rate of deviant behaviour. In general this assumption has been accepted as an article of faith rather than being the object of investigation.

Two of the most widely discussed environmental variables in the ecology of deviant behaviour are social rank and community integration–mobility.[2] Singly and in combination both factors have been used in the attempt to explicate the residential patterning of individuals who have been labelled as deviants. If it may be assumed for the moment that differences in social rank and mobility are causally related to the pattern of deviant residence, then the spatial variation in the two factors should be reflected in that of the community's deviants. An opportunity to assess this proposition is provided by data on the ecological structure and patterns of deviant residential differentiation in the two English towns of Luton and Derby.[3]

Although Luton and Derby are almost identical in size they have experienced very different patterns of development. Luton is a creation of the motor-car; Derby of the railway. The development of Luton closely follows the Hoyt outline; the development of Derby may best be understood in

---

[1] Shaw and McKay, *Juvenile Delinquency and Urban Areas*; Faris and Dunham, *Mental Disorders in Urban Areas*.
[2] E.g. Shaw and McKay, *ibid.*; Faris and Dunham, *ibid.*; Morris, *The Criminal Area*.
[3] Timms, 'The Distribution of Social Defectives in Two British Cities'.

terms of the Burgess hypothesis.[1] As a result of the differences in their pattern of development it is anticipated that Luton and Derby will exhibit different ecological organizations. In particular, it is hypothesized that sectoral patterns are likely to be more important in the ecological organization of Luton and zonal patterns are likely to be more important in that of Derby. These differences should be apparent not only in the distribution of neighbourhood characteristics, but also in that of various forms of behaviour. Use of the analysis of variance technique on data relating to social rank, mobility, criminality and mental illness allows these assumptions to be tested. Social rank is indexed by the variable rateable value per elector; mobility is indexed by the variable electoral stability.[2] Criminality and mental illness data are based on police and hospital records respectively and are expressed in terms of annual rates per thousand population at risk. The area framework for the analysis of variance in each city is provided by a combination of three one-mile zones and four arterial roads. Twenty-four 'residential areas' are included in the analysis for each city, two for each zone-sector intersection.[3] Results of the two-way analyses of variance applied to rateable value per elector and electoral stability are shown in Table 5.8.

In Luton, rateable value per elector varies sectorally; in Derby, it varies zonally. Neither city exhibits a significant interaction effect, but, in each, the secondary areal factor, zonal in Luton and sectoral in Derby, approaches significance ($p < 0.05 > 0.01$). Electoral stability shows no significant relation with either areal framework in Luton although the zonal effect approaches significance ($p < 0.05 > 0.01$). In Derby, electoral stability varies zonally. The fact that the two indexes show such a different areal patterning in Luton reinforces the belief that neither the Burgess nor the Hoyt models can serve as total frameworks. While both the general pattern of growth and the social status differentiation of Luton appear to follow the Hoyt model, the role of zonal effects appears to be the more important in the distribution of electoral stability. The 'zone in transition' appears in both communities.

The analyses of zonal and sectoral effects in the distribution of criminals and mental patients in the two towns produce less consistent results than do those concerned with the variation in rateable values and electoral stability. Table 5.9 shows the relevant information.

Adult criminality rates show pronounced zonal tendencies in both cities. No evidence is forthcoming of a significant sectoral effect. There is a steady gradient from high rates of criminal residence around the town centres to

---

[1] For details, see Timms, *ibid.*
[2] The indicant rateable value per elector forms part of a general socio-economic status dimension established by the use of the Guttman scaling technique. See Timms, 'Quantitative techniques'.
[3] The residential areas comprise streets which fall into the same social rank-mobility types as determined by the scaling procedure. See Timms, *ibid.*, for further details of the operations involved.

TABLE 5.8 *Analyses of variance for rateable value per elector and electoral stability by zones and sectors, Luton and Derby, 1961*

Source	Sum of squares	df	Variance estimate	F	H_o i
Luton – Rateable value per elector					
Between zones	74	3	25	5·82	Accept
Between sectors	124	2	62	14·7	Reject
Zone × sectors	50	6	8·4	1·98	Accept
Remainder	51		4·2	–	–
Total	199	12	–	–	–
		23			
Derby – Rateable value per elector					
Between zones	130	3	43	13·5	Reject
Between sectors	37	2	18	5·72 ii	Accept
Zones × sectors	33	6	5·5	1·70	Accept
Remainder	38	12	3·2	–	–
Total	238	23	–	–	–
Luton – Electoral stability					
Between zones	265	3	88	4·43 ii	Accept
Between sectors	14	2	7·2	0·36	Accept
Zones × sectors	69	6	11	0·57	Accept
Remainder	240	12	20	–	–
Total	588	23	–	–	–
Derby – Electoral stability					
Between zones	322	3	107	10·9	Reject
Between sectors	4	2	2	0·203	Accept
Zones × sectors	83	6	13	1·40	Accept
Remainder	119	12	9·9	–	–
Total	528	23	–	–	–

NOTE. *i* 0·01 level of significance adopted.
ii Significant at 0·05 level but not at 0·01 level.

low rates in the peripheral zones. The prediction that the greater importance of zonal effects in the residential structuring of Derby will be accompanied by a greater zonal effect in the distribution of the city's criminals as compared with that of those in Luton is not borne out by the analyses of variance. The ratio of the between zones F to the between sectors F is 6·4 in the case of Luton and 3·8 in the case of Derby. On the other hand, construction of gradients based on the whole-city data does support the prediction. With 15 per cent of the adult population of Luton, the half-mile zone contains 43 per cent of its adult offenders. The equivalent figures for Derby are 8 per cent and 28 per cent. Areas in the outermost zone of the two towns contain 24 per cent of the Luton adult population, 32 per cent of the Derby adult population and 11 and 14 per cent, respectively, of their criminals. The gradient of criminality rates is much steeper in Derby than it is in Luton.

A similar hiatus between the result of the analyses of variance and the

TABLE 5.9 *Analyses of variance for adult criminality and mental illness rates by zones and sectors, Luton and Derby, 1959–61*

Source	Sum of squares	df	Variance estimate	F	H_o i
		Luton – Adult criminality			
Between zones	1·170	3	0·390	7·673	Reject
Between sectors	0·123	2	0·062	1·205	Accept
Zones × sectors	0·637	6	0·106	2·085	Accept
Remainder	0·610	12	0·051	–	–
Total	2·540	23	–	–	–
		Derby – Adult criminality			
Between zones	4·405	3	1·468	12·677	Reject
Between sectors	0·776	2	0·388	3·350	Accept
Zones × sectors	0·447	6	0·075	0·648	Accept
Remainder	1·390	12	0·116	–	–
Total	7·018	23	–	–	–
		Luton – mental illness			
Between zones	0·613	3	0·204	7·034	Reject
Between sectors	0·193	2	0·097	3·345	Accept
Zones × sectors	0·614	6	0·102	3·517 *ii*	Accept
Remainder	0·348	12	0·029	–	–
Total	1·768	23	–	–	–
		Derby – mental illness			
Between zones	3·745	3	1·248	5.304 *ii*	Accept
Between sectors	1·877	2	0·939	3·991 *ii*	Accept
Zones × sectors	0·733	6	0·122	0·518	Accept
Remainder	2·823	12	0·235	–	–
Total	9·178	23	–	–	–

NOTE. *i* 0·01 level of significance adopted.
ii Significant at the 0·05 level but not at 0·01 level.

gradients constructed on whole-city data occurs in the case of mental patients. The analyses of variance conducted on the data on mental hospital admissions produce a significant zonal effect in Luton but find no other effects significant. In Derby both zonal and sectoral effects approach, but not do reach, the one per cent level of significance. The ratio of the between zones F to the between sectors F is 2·1 in the case of Luton and 1·3 in the case of Derby. The zonal gradients constructed on the basis of full data, however, suggest that the gradient in mental illness rates is steeper in Derby than in Luton. Thus, whereas in Luton there is a twofold difference in first admission rates between inner and peripheral zones, the Derby data show a threefold increase. No explanation of the differing results other than chance sampling factors is forthcoming.

Neither the zonal nor the sectoral model provides a satisfactory framework for detailed ecological analyses. Although the analyses of variance carried out on the data relating to social rank and mobility in Luton and Derby produce results that are consistent with the pattern of development characteristic of the two towns, the lack of correspondence between these results and those relating to criminality and mental illness suggests that considerable caution needs to be exercised in any attempt to use the zonal and sectoral models, singly or in combination, as analytical frameworks for the explication of ecological relationships.[1] The differential distribution of behaviour in the city reflects the detailed differentiation of its population along several axes. Conceived as general models, neither the zonal nor the sectoral scheme is well adapted to uncovering the particular relationships involved.

THE SPATIAL STRUCTURE OF THE CITY

In general, social rank is distributed within the city along sectoral lines, while family status, ethnic status, and variables relating to community integration, follow essentially zonal patterns. Each index, however, shows some tendency to exhibit a secondary form of patterning: zonal in the case of social rank, sectoral in the case of family status and ethnic status. Some evidence is available which suggests that the relative importance of each spatial factor may be a function of city size and of population heterogeneity.

The emergence of distinct zonal and sectoral patterns must depend on the stage of modernization characteristic of a society and a complex of factors relating to residential differentiation. In a laissez-faire city, situated in a pre-industrial society, it seems likely that a zonal arrangement will be the characteristic spatial framework. Since in such a society there is unlikely to be a major division between social rank and family status axes of differentiation, both will follow the zonal pattern. High social rank will be characteristic of the central areas, particularly those adjacent to governmental and religious edifices. The peripheral zones of the city, especially those areas outside the city walls, will be inhabited by those possessing the lowest ranks in the local stratification system. Frequently these groups will include major ethnic minorities. Other ethnic differences will provide the basis for self-contained interior quarters or wards. Differences in family patterns and associated styles of life will vary according to social rank. As modernization corrodes the ties between social rank and styles of life, and as developments in technology stimulate and allow new patterns of residential

---

[1] Cf. the claim by Castle and Gittus: 'If the main trend of city development is from the centre to the periphery, areas in the city centre . . . show the highest incidence of physical deterioration and conditions precipitating family breakdown.' I. M. Castle and E. Gittus, 'The distribution of social defects in Liverpool', *Sociol. Rev.* 5 (1957), 64. The situation is, in fact, much more complicated. While the pattern of growth may be reflected in the physical characteristics of the inner city the patterning of the social environment may follow a different template.

land use, so one may expect to find a diversification of urban residential structure. The attractions of the newer and more spacious neighbourhoods on the city outskirts may occasion the development of a gradient in family types. The old attractiveness of central city residence for the elite will lose much of its force and a reversal of the old social rank gradient may be predicted with the inner city being increasingly left to the lowest ranking members of the society. 'Islands' of high rank populations may, however, survive in the inner city given sufficient symbolic value or topographic protection. With the expansion of the urban area a point may eventually be reached where the outer-fringes are too far distant from the central city amenities to maintain their desirability. If it proves impossible to attract the desired amenities to the suburbs this may occasion a return of the elite to the inner city. More generally, however, it appears that a sectoral growth of high rank neighbourhoods may be predicted, with development proceeding towards open country and, preferably, towards areas of high topographic or social prestige. The increasing independence of the bases of social differentiation gives rise not only to a fine-scale mosaic of social worlds, but is also reflected in the overall spatial structure of the city.

SUMMARY AND CONCLUSION

Like the society in which it exists, the modern city is highly differentiated. Different parts of the city are associated with different populations, with different opportunity structures, and with different reputations. The geographical framework of the city provides the basis for the emergence of a mosaic of social worlds. The increasing movement characteristic of modern society has almost certainly lessened the salience of location in the day-to-day lives of city-dwellers, but it remains the case that residence in one part of the city rather than in another has implication for a wide range of behaviours and biographies. The effects of location may be expected to be most pronounced on those whose daily movements are more or less confined to the bounds of their immediate neighbourhood – the young, the old, and the 'care-takers' – but the role of the local community in the initial socialization process and in the provision of a reference for social comparison purposes, ensures that the influence of the 'neighbourhood effect' is felt across a variety of activities and groups. Different populations have different relationships to their locale and areas which are suitable for one group may be quite unsuitable for another. The diversity of urban life and society both reflect and demand a diversified community.

People living in one part of the city differ from those resident in other areas in innumerable ways. These differences are reflected in the variation in a great variety of demographic, socio-economic and cultural indexes across neighbourhood populations. Underlying the detailed variation, however, it is possible to discern the effects of a relatively small number of general differentiating properties. In the modern Western city, at least, much of the detailed differentiation between neighbourhood populations is accountable for in terms of no more than three or four underlying axes of differentiation: social rank, family status, ethnicity, and urbanism-mobility. The ecological structure of the city is formed by the inter-action of these properties as this is acted out in the locational decisions of the urban population and in the physical constructions of the city-builders.

The differentiation of the urban community is the result of a complex interplay of forces. The attempts to understand the differentiation must span a wide range of systematic levels and must transgress many traditional disciplinary boundaries. Given present knowledge no attempt to produce an integrated theory of residential differentiation is likely to be successful. It is possible, however, to indicate some of the lines which such a theory should take. Residential differentiation involves both the overall structure of society and the decision-making activities of individual households. The attempt to understand the resulting urban structure must encompass aspects both of macro-sociology and social psychology.

At the individual level the choice of one residential location rather than another is the product of an involved sequence of aspirations, searches, and evaluations. In the hunt for a suitable address the preferences of the household for social rank, ethnicity identity and way of life assume considerable prominence. Residential location may be seen as a mechanism for satisfying identity aspirations. Within the limits imposed by the information at their disposal and the economic resources which they possess, households attempt to attain their desired identities by locating amongst those who already possess the relevant statuses. At the cognitive level, it appears that information about the city may be organized in terms of those major social differentia which provide the bases for differential evaluation and reward and which provide the cores of self-identities. Different parts of the city are associated with different constellations of statuses and provide the foundations for different sets of identities. Where a person lives is a symbol of the type of person he is. Aspirations for social rank may be satisfied by locating in neighbourhoods which have the repute desired. Aspirations for a given ethnic identity may be satisfied by residing amongst those whom one wants to be taken as being 'of one's own kind'. In either case, protection from undesirable contact and loss of desired statuses may be sought by removing oneself from the vicinity of the threatening group. Residential distance becomes a symbol of social distance and a means of preserving existing differentia. Different locations provide different facilities. Preferences for different ways of life – differences which may be summarized in terms of such orientations as 'familism', 'careerism', and 'urbanism' – involve an evaluation of the facilities which are offered by the available locations. Such characteristics as the size and type of housing, the density of development, the age characteristics of the population and the accessibility of the site, assume considerable salience. Aspirations and outcomes rarely coincide in precise detail, but, as the result of feed-back loops involving information flows and market processes, the aspirations of households and the supply of locations provide the parameters of a reasonably stable residential system whose structure reflects that of the encompassing society. Residential differentiation may be seen as a symbol of social differentiation.

The urban community does not exist in isolation. The city is both the creator and the creature of urban society. Changes in the structure of that society produce changes in the structure of the city. The limited differentiation characteristic of pre-modern society is reflected in the relative simplicity of the ecological structure characteristic of the pre-modern city. Both social and residential differentiation are based on a small number of closely-correlated criteria. Ascribed characteristics are uppermost and position in one status system is highly predictive to position in others. Different neighbourhoods are associated with populations which differ from each other in consistent ways across each of the status dimensions. Social rank is a prime determiner of way of life and provides the major axis of differentiation. With modernization and social mobilization the congruence between differentiating criteria breaks down. Traditional associations between statuses are upset. New bases of differentiation emerge and there is a growing structural independence between them. In the urban-industrial society universalistic, achievement-oriented criteria become major bases of status-allocation although the influence of such ascribed characteristics as ethnic origin may still remain important. Very generally, however, the process of modernization may be seen as eventuating in a shift from traditional forms of social differentiation and evaluation in which social rank, family characteristics, ethnic identity and migration experiences are all interrelated to systems in which each set of characteristics exercises its own independent effect. The ecological separation between social rank and family status indicants is believed to provide a sensitive measure of the degree of modernization to be found in the society concerned.

The spatial order of the city is founded on the desires and resources of its inhabitants as these are constrained and directed by the encompassing society. In the pre-modern city the simplicity of the social and ecological systems is reflected in that of the resulting spatial pattern. Self-contained quarters and a general zonal arrangement, with central-city location being the preserve of the elite, provide the basic plan. In the modern city a more complicated spatial order is apparent. Each differentiating property tends to follow its own distinct spatial pattern. The need to be within reasonable access to work and the attraction of the elite areas are reflected in the sectoral distribution of social rank. Once identified with a particular rank, developments in a given direction tend to perpetuate that identity. The attraction of new suburbs, with new houses and new standards of amenities, is reflected in a zonal arrangement of family status. The younger the area, the more young people; the older the area, the more old people and the fewer families with young children. The zones in transition around the central business district and on the rural-urban periphery provide a haven for despised minorities and an attractive location for all those who welcome the anonymity and freedom from traditional social controls characteristic of the urban way of life. Since each set of differentiating properties is, to a greater or lesser extent, independent of all the others, the resulting spatial pattern is highly complex. It is unlikely that any simple model, stressing the influence of one or other spatial arrangement, will provide an acceptable description of the modern city.

Human society is, increasingly, an urban phenomenon. The city is becoming the principal setting for human behaviour. In the attempt to understand that behaviour or to plan for its control it is essential that the characteristics of the urban setting are themselves understood. Neither the individual nor the community can be fully understood without knowledge of the other. The city not only shapes human behaviour but is, itself, the result of human behaviour. The urban mosaic is the matrix for urban society.

BIBLIOGRAPHY

The principal primary sources used in the original analyses reported in the present work are as follows.

Brisbane: Commonwealth Bureau of Census and Statistics, *Census of the Commonwealth of Australia, 1961*. Collectors' district tabulations for Brisbane metropolitan area. Electoral Office, Queensland State Government, *State Electoral Roll, 1961*. Valuer-General's Department, Queensland State Government, average house and land values.

New Zealand: Department of Statistics, *Census of New Zealand*. Reports for 1926, 1936, 1951 and 1966.

Cook Islands: Premier's Department, Government of the Cook Islands, *Population Census, 1966*.

Luton: Register of electors, Luton M.B., 1959.
Valuation list, Luton M.B.
Magistrate's Court Record, 1959–61.
Case register, Three Counties Hospital, Arlesey, 1955–9.

Derby: Register of electors, Derby C.B., 1959.
Valuation list, Derby C.B.
Files of the *Derby Evening Telegraph*.
Case register, Kingsway Hospital, 1955–9.

REFERENCES

The references which follow are classified under two headings – general references, and social area analysis and factorial ecology.

Several of the articles mentioned are reprinted in G. A. Theodorson (ed.), *Studies in Human Ecology* (Evanston, Ill., 1961). Where appropriate, this is indicated by the suffix, Theodorson (1961).

GENERAL REFERENCES

Abrams, M. 'Consumption in the year 2000', in M. Young (ed.), *Forecasting and the Social Sciences* (London, 1968).

Abu-Lughod, J. 'The emergence of differential fertility in urban Egypt', *Millbank Memorial Fund Quart.*, 43 (1965), 235–53.

Alihan, M. A. *Social Ecology* (New York, 1938).

Alonso, W. *Location and Land Use* (Cambridge, Mass., 1964).

'The form of cities in developing countries', *Papers and Proc. Reg. Sci. Ass.* 13 (1964).

Anderson, N. *The Hobo* (Chicago, 1923).

Baer, G. (trans. H. Szöke), *Population and Society in the Arab East* (London, 1966).

Barton, A. H. 'The concept of property space in social research', in P. F. Lazarsfeld and M. Rosenberg (eds), *The Language of Social Research* (New York, 1955), pp. 40–53.

Bendix, R. and Lipset, S. M. (eds), *Class, Status and Power: Social Stratification in Comparative Perspective* (New York, 1966).

Berry, B. J. L. and Horton, F. E. (eds), *Geographic Perspectives on Urban Systems* (Englewood Cliffs, N.J., 1970).

Beshers, J. M. 'Statistical inferences from small area data', *Soc. Forces* 38 (1960), 341–8.

Urban Social Structure (New York, 1962).

Beynon, E. D. 'Budapest: an ecological study', *Geog. Rev.* 33 (1943), 256–75. Reprinted in Theodorson (1961).

Blake, J. and Davis, K. 'Norms, values, and sanctions', in R. E. L. Faris (ed.), *Handbook of Modern Sociology* (Chicago, 1964), pp. 456–84.

Bossard, J. H. S. 'Residential propinquity as a factor in marriage selection', *Am. J. Sociol.* 38 (1933), 219–27.

Brown, L. A. and Moore, E. G. 'Intra-urban migration: an actor-oriented framework' (mimeo., Northwestern University, 1968).

Burgess, E. W. 'The growth of the city', in R. E. Park, E. W. Burgess, and R. D. McKenzie (eds), *The City* (Chicago, 1925). Reprinted in Theodorson (1961), pp. 37–44.

(ed.), *The Urban Community* (Chicago, 1926).

'The determination of gradients in the growth of the city', *Pubs. Am. Sociol. Soc.* 21 (1927), 178–84.

'Residential segregation in American cities', *Ann. Am. Ac. Pol. Soc. Sci.* 140 (1928).

'Urban areas', in T. V. Smith and L. D. White (eds), *Chicago: An Experiment in Social Science Research* (Chicago, 1929).

'The new community and its future', *Ann. Am. Ac. Pol. Soc. Sci.* 149 (1930).

'The ecology and social psychology of the city', in D. J. Bogue (ed.), *Needed Urban and Metropolitan Research* (Oxford, Ohio., 1953).

'Natural area', in J. Gould and W. L. Kolb (eds), *A Dictionary of the Social Sciences* (New York, 1964), p. 458.

Burgess, E. W. and Locke, H. J. *The Family* (New York, 1953).

Burgess, E. W. and Bogue, D. (eds), *Contributions to Urban Sociology* (Chicago, 1964).

Caplow, T. 'The social ecology of Guatemala City', *Soc. Forces* 28 (1949), 113–33. Reprinted in Theodorson (1961).

'Urban structure in France', *Am. Sociol. Rev.* 17 (1952), 544–9. Reprinted in Theodorson (1961).

Bibliography

Caplow, T. and Forman, R. 'Neighbourhood interaction in a homogeneous community', *Am. Sociol. Rev.* 15 (1950), 357–67.

Castle, I. M. and Gittus, E. 'The distribution of social defects in Liverpool', *Sociol. Rev.* 5 (1957), 43–64. Reprinted in Theodorson (1961).

Cavan, R. S. *Suicide* (Chicago, 1928).

Chisholm, M. D. I. *Rural Settlement and Land Use* (London, 1962).

Clinard, M. B. (ed.), *Anomie and Social Structure* (New York, 1964).

Cloward, R. A. and Ohlin, L. E. *Delinquency and Opportunity* (New York, 1961).

Cohen, A. K. *Delinquent Boys* (New York, 1955).

Collison, P. and Mogey, J. 'Residence and social class in Oxford', *Am. J. Sociol.* 64 (1959), 599–605.

Comhaire, J. and Cahnman, W. J. *How Cities Grew* (Madison, N.J., 1959).

Congalton, A. A. *Status Ranking of Sydney Suburbs* (Sydney, 1964).
Status and Prestige in Australia (Melbourne, 1969).

Cooley, C. H. *Social Organization* (New York, 1962).

Cressey, D. R. 'Epidemiology and individual conduct', *Pac. Sociol. Rev.* 3 (1960), 47–54.

Cressey, P. F. 'Ecological organization of Rangoon', *Sociol. Soc. Res.* 40 (1956), 166–9.

Cronbach, L. and Meehl, P. 'Construct validity in psychological tests', *Psych. Bull.* 52 (1955), 281–302.

Davie, M. R. 'The pattern of urban growth', in G. P. Murdock (ed.), *Studies in the Science of Society* (New Haven, 1938). Reprinted in Theodorson (1961), pp. 77–92.

Davis, A., Gardner, B. B. and Gardner, M. R. *Deep South* (Chicago, 1941).

Deutsch, K. W. 'Social mobilization and political development', *Am. Pol. Sci. Rev.* 55 (1961), 493–514.

Dickinson, R. E. *The West European City* (London, 1951).

Dobriner, W. M. *Class and Suburbia* (New York, 1963).

Dohrenwend, B. P. 'Social status and psychological disorder: an issue of substance and an issue of method', *Am. Sociol. Rev.* 31 (1966), 14–34.

Dotson, F. and Dotson, L. O. 'Ecological trends in the city of Guadalajara, Mexico', *Soc. Forces* 32 (1954), 347–74.

Drake, St C. and Clayton, H. R. *Black Metropolis* (New York, 1945).

Duncan, O. D. and Davis, B. 'An alternative to ecological correlation', *Am. Sociol. Rev.* 18 (1953), 665–6.

Duncan, O. D. and Duncan, B. 'A methodological analysis of segregation indexes', *Am. Sociol. Rev.* 20 (1955), 210–17.
'Residential distribution and occupational stratification', *Am. J. Sociol.* 60 (1955), 493–503. Reprinted in Theodorson (1961).
The Negro Population of Chicago (Chicago, 1957).

Duncan, O. D. and Lieberson, S. 'Ethnic segregation and assimilation', *Am. J. Sociol.* 64 (1959), 364–74.

Duncan, O. D. and Reiss, A. J. *Social Characteristics of Urban and Rural Communities 1950* (New York, 1956).

Dunham, H. W. 'Current status of ecological research in mental disorder', *Soc. Forces* 25 (1947), 321–6.

'Comment on article by Kohn and Clausen', *Am. J. Sociol.* 60 (1954), 151–3.
Eisenstadt, S. N. 'Social change, differentiation and evolution', *Am. Sociol. Rev.* 29 (1964).
Modernization: Protest and Change (Englewood Cliffs, N.J., 1966).
Ellis, R. H. 'A Behavioural Residential Location Model' (mimeo., Evanston, Ill., 1966).
Faris, R. E. L. 'Cultural isolation and the schizophrenic personality', *Am. J. Sociol.* 40 (1937), 456–7.
Faris, R. E. L. and Dunham, H. W. *Mental Disorders in Urban Areas* (Chicago, 1939).
Feldman, A. S. and Tilly, C. 'The interaction of social and physical space', *Am. Sociol. Rev.* 25 (1960), 877–84.
Festinger, L., Schachter, S. and Back, K. *Social Pressures in Informal Groups* (London, 1950).
Fielding, R. J. 'Area Differences in Neighbourhood Interaction in Brisbane' (unpublished B.A. dissertation, University of Queensland, 1964).
Firey, W. 'Sentiment and symbolism as ecological variables', *Am. Sociol. Rev.* 10 (1945), 140–8. Reprinted in Theodorson (1961).
Land in Use in Central Boston (Cambridge, Mass., 1947).
'Residential sectors re-examined', *The Appraisal J.* (Oct. 1950), 451–3.
Foley, D. L. 'Census tracts and urban research', *J. Am. Stat. Ass.* 48 (1953), 733–42.
Form, W. H. 'The place of social structure in the determination of land use', *Soc. Forces* 32 (1954), 317–23.
Form, W. H., Smith, J., Stone, G. P. and Cowhig, J. 'The compatibility of alternative approaches to the delimitation of urban sub-areas', *Am. Sociol. Rev.* 19 (1954), 434–40. Reprinted in J. P. Gibbs (ed.), *Urban Research Methods* (Princeton, 1961), pp. 176–87.
Freedman, R. 'Cityward migration, urban ecology, and social theory', in E. W. Burgess and D. Bogue (eds), *Contributions to Urban Sociology* (Chicago, 1964).
Galtung, J. *Theory and Methods of Social Research* (Oslo and London, 1967).
Gans, H. J. 'Planning and social life', *Journ. Am. Inst. Planners*, 27 (1961), 134–40.
'Urbanism and suburbanism as ways of life', in A. M. Rose (ed.), *Human Behaviour and Social Processes* (London, 1962), pp. 625–48.
'Planning for people, not buildings', *Envir. and Planning*, 1 (1969), 33–46.
Gettys, W. E. 'Human ecology and social theory', *Soc. Forces*, 18 (1940), 496–76. Reprinted in Theodorson (1961).
Gibbs, J. P. (ed.), *Urban Research Methods* (Princeton, N.J., 1961).
(ed.), *Suicide* (New York, 1968).
Gist, N. P. 'The ecology of Bangalore, India: an east-west comparison', *Soc. Forces*, 35 (1957), 356–65.
Glass, R. 'The structure of neighbourhoods', in M. Lock (ed.), *Middlesbrough Survey and Plan* (Middlesbrough, 1947).
The Social Background to a Plan (London, 1948).
Goodman, L. A. 'Ecological regressions and behaviour of individuals', *Am. Sociol. Rev.* 18 (1953), 663–4.
Gordon, M. M. *Assimilation in American Life* (New York, 1964).

Bibliography

Gould, J. 'Neighbourhood', in J. Gould and W. L. Kolb (eds), *A Dictionary of the Social Sciences* (New York, 1964), p. 464.

Gould, P. R. 'On Mental Maps' (mimeo., Ann Arbor, Mich., 1966).

Gray, P. G. *et al. The Proportion of Jurors as an Index of the Economic Status of a District* (London, 1951).

Greer, S. *The Emerging City* (New York, 1962).

Greig-Smith, P. *Quantitative Plant Ecology* (London, 1964).

Guilford, J. *Psychometric Methods* (New York, 1954).

Hagerstrand, T. 'Migration and area', in D. Hannerberg, T. Hagerstrand and B. Odeving (eds), *Migration in Sweden: A Symposium* (Lund, 1957). 'A Monte Carlo approach to diffusion', *Arch. Europ. Sociol.* 6 (1965), 43–67.

Hansen, A. T. 'The ecology of a Latin-American city', in E. B. Reuter (ed.), *Race and Culture Contacts* (New York, 1934).

Hare, E. H. 'Mental illness and social conditions in Bristol', *J. Ment. Sci.* 102 (1956), 349. 'Family setting and the urban distribution of schizophrenia', *J. Ment. Sci.* 102 (1956), 753.

Harman, H. H. *Modern Factor Analysis* (Chicago, 1960).

Hatt, P. K. 'The concept of natural area', *Am. Sociol. Rev.* 11 (1946), 423–8. Reprinted in Theodorson (1961).

Hauser, P. M. and Schnore, L. F. (eds), *The Study of Urbanization* (New York, 1965).

Havighurst, R. J. *Education in Metropolitan Areas* (Boston, 1966).

Hawley, A. H. *Human Ecology* (New York, 1950).

Hayner, N. S. 'Mexico City: its growth and configuration', *Am. J. Sociol.* 50 (1945), 295–304.

Hempel, C. G. 'Fundamentals of concept formation in empirical science', in O. Neurath *et al.* (eds), *Internat. Encycl. of Unified Science* (Chicago, 1952), vol. 2, no. 7.

Hiller, E. T. *Principles of Sociology* (New York, 1933).

Hollingshead, A. B. 'A re-examination of ecological theory', *Sociol. Soc. Res.* 31 (1947), 194–204. Reprinted in Theodorson (1961). 'Community research: development and present condition', *Am. Sociol. Rev.* 13 (1948), 136–55.

Hoover, E. M. and Vernon, R. *Anatomy of a Metropolis* (Cambridge, Mass., 1959).

Horst, P. *Factor Analysis of Data Matrices* (New York, 1965).

Hoyt, H. *The Structure and Growth of Residential Neighbourhoods in American Cities* (Washington, 1939). 'Residential sectors revisited', *The Appraisal J.* (Oct. 1950), 445–50. 'Recent distortions of the classical models of urban structure', *Land Econ.* 40 (1964), 199–212.

Hughes, C. C., Tremblay, M. A., Rapoport, R. N. and Leighton, A. H., *People of Cove and Woodlot* (New York, 1960).

Hurd, R. M. *Principles of City Land Values* (New York, 1903).

Isard, W. (with G. A. P. Carrothers), 'Migration estimation', in W. Isard, *Methods of Regional Analysis* (Cambridge, Mass., 1960), pp. 53–79.

Jeans, D. N. and Logan, M. I. 'A reconnaissance survey of population change in the Sydney metropolitan area', *Aust. Geog.* 13 (1961).

Johnson, C. S. *Patterns of Negro Segregation* (New York, 1943).
Jonassen, C. T. 'Cultural variables in the ecology of an ethnic group', *Am. Sociol. Rev.* 14 (1949), 32–41. Reprinted in Theodorson (1961).
'A revaluation and critique of some of the methods of Shaw and McKay', *Am. Sociol. Rev.* 14 (1949), 608–15.
Jones, E. *A Social Geography of Belfast* (London, 1960).
Jones, F. L. 'Ethnic concentration and assimilation: an Australian case study', *Soc. Forces*, 45 (1965), 412–23.
Kaine, J. F. 'The journey to work as a determinant of residential location', *Papers Reg. Sci. Ass.* 9 (1962), 137–60.
Kaiser, H. F. 'The varimax criterion for analytic rotation in factor analysis', *Psychometrika*, 23 (1958), 187–200.
Kantor, M. B. (ed.), *Mobility and Mental Health* (Springfield, Ill., 1965).
Kaplan, A. *The Conduct of Inquiry* (San Francisco, 1964).
Katz, A. M. and Hill, R. 'Residential propinquity and marital selection', *Marr. and Fam. Living*, 20 (1958), 27–34.
Keller, S. 'The role of social class in physical planning', *Internat. Soc. Sci. J.* 18 (1966).
    The Urban Neighbourhood: A Sociological Perspective (New York, 1968).
Kerlinger, F. N. *Foundations of Behavioural Research* (New York, 1964).
Kershaw, K. A. *Quantitative and Dynamic Ecology* (London, 1964).
Kish, L. 'Differentiation in metropolitan areas', *Am. Sociol. Rev.* 19 (1954), 388–98.
Knos, D. S. 'The distribution of land values in Topeka, Kansas', in B. J. L. Berry and D. F. Marble (eds), *Spatial Analysis* (Englewood Cliffs, N.J., 1968) pp. 269–89.
Kobrin, S. 'The conflict of values in delinquency areas', *Am. Sociol. Rev.* 16 (1951), 653–61.
Kohn, M. L. and Clausen, J. A. 'The ecological approach in social psychiatry', *Am. J. Sociol.* 60 (1954), 140–51.
Kuper, L. (ed.), *Living in Towns* (London, 1953).
Kuper, L., Watts, H. and Davies, R. *Durban: A Study in Racial Ecology* (London, 1958).
Lasswell, T. E. *Class and Stratum* (Boston, 1965).
Lawson, R. 'The Social Structure of Brisbane in the Late Nineteenth Century' (unpublished Ph.D. dissertation, University of Queensland, 1969).
Lazarsfeld, P. F. 'Some remarks on the typological procedures in social research', *Zeitschrift für Sozialforschung*, 6 (1937), 119–39.
    'Concept formation and measurement in the behavioural sciences', in G. J. Direnzo (ed.), *Concepts, Theory, and Explanation in the Behavioural Sciences* (New York, 1966).
Lazarsfeld, P. F. and Barton, A. H. 'Qualitative measurement in the social sciences', in D. Lerner and H. Lasswell (eds), *The Policy Sciences* (New York, 1951).
Leighton, A. H. *My Name is Legion* (New York, 1959).
Leighton, P. C., Harding, J. S., Macklin, D. B., Macmillan, A. M. and Leighton, A. H. *The Character of Danger* (New York, 1963).
Lerner, D. *The Passing of Traditional Society: Modernizing the Middle East* (New York, 1958).

Bibliography

'Toward a communication theory of modernization', in L. C. Pye (ed.), *Communications and Political Development* (Princeton, 1963).

Lewis, O. 'The culture of poverty', *Sci. Amer.* 215 (1966), 19–25.

Lieberson, S. 'The impact of residential segregation on ethnic assimilation', *Soc. Forces*, 40 (1961), 52–7.

Ethnic Patterns in American Cities (New York, 1963).

Linge, G. J. R. 'The Delimitation of Urban Boundaries for Statistical Purposes' (mimeo. Australian National University, Canberra, 1966).

Lynch, K. R. *The Image of the City* (Cambridge, Mass., 1960).

Mabry, J. H. 'Census tract variation in urban research', *Am. Sociol. Rev.* 23 (1958), 193–6.

Maccoby, E. E., Johnson, J. P. and Church, R. M. 'Community integration and the social control of juvenile delinquency', *J. Soc. Issues*, 14 (1958).

McGee, T. M. 'The social ecology of New Zealand cities', in J. Forster (ed.), *Social Process in New Zealand* (Auckland, 1969), pp. 144–80.

McKenzie, R. D. *Neighbourhood* (Chicago, 1923).

'The scope of human ecology', *Pubs. Am. Sociol. Soc.* 20 (1926), 141–54. Reprinted in Theodorson (1961).

McKinney, J. C. *Constructive Typology and Social Theory* (New York, 1966).

McNaughton-Smith, P. *Some Statistical and Other Numerical Techniques for Classifying Individuals* (London, 1965).

McNemar, Q. 'On the number of factors', *Psychometrika*, 7 (1942), 9–18.

Marble, D. F. 'Transport inputs at urban residential sites', *Papers Reg. Sci. Ass.* 5 (1959), 253–66.

Margenau, H. *The Nature of Physical Reality* (New York, 1950).

Martin J. I. *Refugee Settlers* (Melbourne, 1965).

Mayhew, H. *The Criminal Prisons of London* (London, 1862).

London Labour and the London Poor (London, 1864).

Mays, J. B. *On the Threshold of Delinquency* (Liverpool, 1958).

Education and the Urban Child (Liverpool, 1962).

Meadows, P. 'The urbanists', in *1963 Yearbook* (School of Architecture, Syracuse, 1965).

Mehta, S. K. 'Patterns of residence in Poona', *Am. J. Sociol.* 73 (1968), 496–508.

Menzel, H. 'Comment on Robinson's "Ecological correlations and the behaviour of individuals" ', *Am. Sociol. Rev.* 15 (1950), 674.

Merton, R. *Social Theory and Social Structure* (New York, 1957).

Metge, J. *A New Maori Migration* (Melbourne, 1964).

Miller, W. B. 'Lower class culture as a generating milieu of gang delinquency', *J. Soc. Issues* 14 (1958), 5–19.

Moore, E. G. 'Residential Mobility in an Urban Context' (unpublished Ph.D. dissertation, University of Queensland, 1966).

Morris, R. N. and Mogey, J. *The Sociology of Housing* (London, 1965).

Morris, T. *The Criminal Area* (London, 1957).

Mowrer, E. W. *Disorganization, Personal and Social* (New York, 1942).

Mumford, L. *The City in History* (New York, 1961).

Myers, J. K. 'Note on the homogeneity of census tracts', *Soc. Forces* 32 (1954), 364–6.

'Assimilation to the ecological and social systems of a community', *Am. Sociol. Rev.* 15 (1950), 367–72. Reprinted in Theodorson (1961).

Nunnally, J. *Psychometric Theory* (New York, 1967).

Park, R. E., Burgess, E. W. and McKenzie R. D. (eds), *The City* (Chicago, 1925).

Park, R. E. *Human Communities* (New York, 1952).

Parsons, T. *Essays in Sociological Theory, Pure and Applied* (New York, 1949).

Petersen, G. L., 'A model of preference: quantitative analysis of the perception of the visual appearance of residential neighbourhoods', *J. Reg. Sci.* 7 (1967), 19–32.

'Measuring visual preferences of residential neighbourhoods', *Ekistics*, 23 (1967), 169–73.

Petersen, W. 'A general typology of migration', *Am. Sociol. Rev.* 23 (1958), 256–66.

Plant, J. S. 'The personality and an urban area', in P. K. Hatt and A. J. Reiss (eds), *Cities and Society* (New York, 1957), pp. 647–66.

Pons, V. G. 'The growth of Stanleyville and the composition of its African population', in D. Forde (ed.), *Social Implications of Industrialization and Urbanization in Africa South of the Sahara* (Paris, 1956).

Price, C. A. *Southern Europeans in Australia* (Melbourne, 1964).

Australian Immigration: A Bibliography and Digest (Canberra, 1966).

Priest, R. F. and Sawyer, J. 'Proximity and peership: bases of balance in interpersonal attraction', *Am. J. Sociol.* 72 (1967), 633–49.

Queen, S. A. 'Ecological study of mental disorders', *Am. Sociol. Rev.* 5 (1940), 201–9.

Quinn, J. A. 'The Burgess zonal hypothesis and its critics', *Am. Sociol. Rev.* 5 (1940), 210–18.

Human Ecology (New York, 1950).

Ramsøy, N. R. 'Assortative mating and the structure of cities', *Am. Sociol. Rev.* 31 (1966), 773–86.

Riley, M. W. *Sociological Research*: Vol. 1, *A Case Approach* (New York, 1963).

Robinson, A. H. 'The necessity of weighting values in correlation analysis of areal data', *Ann. Ass. Am. Geog.* 46 (1956), 233–6.

Robinson, W. S. 'Ecological correlations and behaviour of individuals', *Am. Sociol. Rev.* 15 (1950), 351–7.

Rodwin, L. 'The theory of residential growth and structure', *The Appraisal J.* 18 (1950), 295–317.

'Rejoinder to Dr Firey and Dr Hoyt', *The Appraisal J.* (Oct. 1950), 454–7.

Rogers, E. M. (with L. Svenning). *Modernization Among Peasants: The Impact of Communication* (New York, 1969).

Ross, H. L. 'The local community: a survey approach', *Am. Sociol. Rev.* 27 (1962), 75–84.

Rossi, P. H. *Why Families Move: A Study in the Social Psychology of Urban Residential Mobility* (New York, 1955).

Sainsbury, P. *Suicide in London* (London, 1955).

Schmid, C. F. 'The theory and practice of planning census tracts', *Sociol. and Soc. Res.* 22 (1938). Reprinted in J. P. Gibbs (ed.), *Urban Research Methods* (Princeton, 1961), pp. 166–75.

Bibliography

Schmid, C. F., MacCannell, E. H. and Van Arsdol, M. D. Jr. 'The ecology of the American city: Further comparison and validation of generalizations', *Am. Sociol. Rev.* 23 (1958), 392–401. Reprinted in Theodorson (1961).

Schnore, L. F. 'On the spatial structure of cities in the two Americas', in P. M. Hauser and L. F. Schnore (eds), *The Study of Urbanization* (New York, 1965), 347–98.

'Social class segregation among non-whites in metropolitan centres', *Demography*, 2 (1965), 126–33.

Schroeder, C. W. 'Mental disorders in cities', *Am. J. Sociol.* 48 (1942), 40–7.

Schultz, T. W. *The Economic Organization of Agriculture* (New York, 1953).

Schwimmer, E. G. (ed.), *The Maori People in the 1960's* (Auckland, 1968).

Shaw, C. R. *The Jackroller* (Chicago, 1930).

Shaw, C. R. and McKay, H. D. *Juvenile Delinquency and Urban Areas* (Chicago, 1942).

Social Factors in Juvenile Delinquency (Washington, 1931).

Shaw, C. R., McKay, H. D. and McDonald, J. F. *Brothers in Crime* (Chicago, 1938).

Shaw, C. R., Zorbaugh, F. M., McKay, H. D. and Cottrell, L. *Delinquency Areas* (Chicago, 1929).

Shibutani, T. *Society and Personality* (Englewood Cliffs, N.J., 1961).

Sjoberg, G. *The Preindustrial City* (New York, 1960).

'Cities in developing and industrial societies', in P. M. Hauser and L. F. Schnore (eds), *The Study of Urbanization* (New York, 1965), 213–63.

'Theory and research in urban sociology', in *ibid.*

Sokal, R. R. and Sneath, P. H. A. *Numerical Taxonomy* (San Francisco, 1963).

Srole, L. 'Social integration and certain corollaries', *Am. Sociol. Rev.* 21 (1956), 709–16.

Sterne, R. S. 'Components and stereotypes in ecological analyses of social problems', *Urb. Aff. Quart.* 3 (1967), 3–21.

Stevens, S. S. 'Mathematics, measurement, and psychophysics', in S. S. Stevens (ed.), *Handbook of Experimental Psychology* (New York, 1951).

Stewart, J. Q. 'Demographic gravitation', *Sociometry*, 11 (1948), 31–58.

Stouffer, S. A. 'Intervening opportunities: a theory relating mobility and distance', *Am. Sociol. Rev.* 5 (1940), 845–67.

Sutch, W. B. *Poverty and Progress in New Zealand* (Wellington, 1969).

Sutherland, E. G. and Cressey, D. R. *Principles of Criminology* (Philadelphia, 1960).

Svalastoga, K. *Social Differentiation* (New York, 1964).

Taeuber, K. E. and Taeuber, A. F. *Negroes in Cities* (Chicago, 1965).

Theodorson, G. A. 'Human ecology and human geography', in J. S. Roucek (ed.), *Contemporary Sociology* (New York, 1959).

(ed.), *Studies in Human Ecology* (Evanston, Ill., 1961).

Thrasher, F. M. *The Gang* (Chicago, 1927).

Thurstone, L. L. *Multiple-factor Analysis* (Chicago, 1947).

Tietze, C., Lemkau, P. and Cooper, M. 'Personal disorders and spatial mobility', *Am. J. Sociol.* 43 (1942), 29–39.

Tilly, C. 'Occupational rank and grade of residence in a metropolis', *Am. J. Sociol.* 67 (1961), 323–9.

Timms, D. W. G. 'The Distribution of Social Defectives in Two British Cities: A Study in Human Ecology' (unpublished Ph.D. dissertation, University of Cambridge, 1963).

'The spatial distribution of social deviants in Luton, England', *Aust. N.Z. J. Sociol.* 1 (1965), 38–52.

'Quantitative techniques in urban social geography', in R. J. Chorley and P. Haggett (eds), *Frontiers in Geographical Teaching* (London, 1965).

'Occupational stratification and friendship nomination: a study in Brisbane', *Aust. N.Z. J. Sociol.* 3 (1967), 32–43.

'The dissimilarity between overseas-born and Australian-born in Queensland', *Sociol. and Soc. Res.* 53 (1969), 363–74.

'Anomia and social participation amongst suburban women' (mimeo. University of Auckland, 1969).

Tolman, E. C. 'Cognitive maps in rats and men', *Psych. Rev.* 55 (1948), 189–208.

Torgerson, W. S. *Theory and Methods of Scaling* (New York, 1958).

Townshend, P. *The Family Life of Old People* (London, 2nd ed., 1963).

UNESCO, *Urbanization in Africa South of the Sahara* (New York, 1957).

Van Arsdol, M. D. Jr, Sabagh, G. and Butler, E. W. 'Retrospective and subsequent metropolitan residential mobility', *Demography* (forthcoming).

Van Hoey, L. 'The coercive process of urbanization', in S. Greer *et al.* (eds), *The New Urbanization* (New York, 1968).

Violich, F. *Cities of Latin America* (New York, 1944).

Von Thünen, J. H. *Der Isolierte Staat* (Hamburg, 1826).

Warner, W. L., Meeber, M. and Eells, K. *Social Class in America: A Manual of Procedure for the Measurement of Social Status* (New York, 1960).

Weinberg, S. K. 'Urban areas and hospitalized psychotics', in S. K. Weinberg (ed.), *The Sociology of Mental Disorders* (Chicago, 1967), pp. 22–6.

Whyte, W. F. *Street Corner Society* (Chicago, 1955).

Willhelm, S. M. *Urban Zoning and Land Use Theory* (New York, 1962).

Williams, W. T. and Lance, G. N. 'Logic of computer-based intrinsic classifications', *Nature, Lond.* 107 (1965), 159–61.

Wilson, A. B. 'Residential segregation of social classes and aspiration of high school boys', *Am. Sociol. Rev.* 24 (1959), 836–45.

Wilson, G. and Wilson, M. *The Analysis of Social Change* (Cambridge, 1945).

Wilson, R. 'Difficult housing estates', *Tavistock Pamphlets*, no. 5 (London, 1963).

Wirth, L. *The Ghetto* (Chicago, 1928).

'Human ecology', *Am. J. Sociol.* 50 (1945), 483–8. Reprinted in Theodorson (1961).

'Urbanism as a way of life', *Am. J. Sociol.* 44 (1938), 1–24. Reprinted in P. K. Hatt and A. J. Reiss (eds), *Cities and Society* (New York, 1957), pp. 46–63.

Wolfgang, M. E., Savitz, L. and Johnston, N. (eds), *The Sociology of Crime and Delinquency* (New York, 1962).

Wolpert, J. 'Behavioural aspects of the decision to migrate', *Papers Reg. Sci. Ass.* 15 (1965), 159–69.

'Migration as an adjustment to environmental stress', *J. Soc. Issues* 22 (1966), 92–102.

Wootton, B. *Social Science and Social Pathology* (London, 1959).

Bibliography

Wurster, C. B. 'Social questions in housing and community planning', in W. L. Wheaton *et al.* (eds), *Urban Housing* (New York, 1966).

Yazaki, T. *The Japanese City* (Tokyo, 1963).

Young, M. and Willmott, P. *Family and Kinship in East London* (London, 1957).

Zorbaugh, H. W. 'The dweller in furnished rooms: an urban type', in E. W. Burgess (ed.), *The Urban Community* (Chicago, 1926), pp. 98–105.

'The natural areas of the city', *Publs. Am. Sociol. Soc.* 20 (1926), 188–97. Reprinted in Theodorson (1961).

The Gold Coast and the Slum (Chicago, 1929).

Zubrzycki, J. 'Ethnic segregation in Australian Cities', *Proc. Internat. Pop. Conf.* (Vienna, 1959), 610–16.

Immigrants in Australia (Melbourne, 1960).

STUDIES IN SOCIAL AREA ANALYSIS AND FACTORIAL ECOLOGY

Abu-Lughod, J. 'Testing the theory of social area analysis: the ecology of Cairo, Egypt', *Am. Sociol. Rev.* 34 (1969), 189–212.

Anderson, T. R. and Bean, L. 'The Shevky–Bell social areas: confirmation of results and a reinterpretation', *Soc. Forces* 40 (1961), 119–24.

Anderson, T. R. and Egeland, J. A. 'Spatial aspects of social area analysis', *Am. Sociol. Rev.* 26 (1961), 392–9.

Bange, E. *et al.* 'A Study of Selected Population Changes and Characteristics with Special Reference to Implications for Social Welfare'. A group research project submitted in partial fulfilment of requirements for the MSW degree (Berkeley, 1955).

Bell, W. 'A Comparative study in the Methodology of Urban Analysis' (unpublished Ph.D. dissertation, University of California, Los Angeles, 1952).

'The social areas of the San Francisco Bay Region', *Am. Sociol. Rev.* 18 (1953), 39–47.

'Economic, family, and ethnic status: an empirical test', *Am. Sociol. Rev.* 20 (1955), 45–52.

'Comment on Duncan's review of "Social Area Analysis" ', *Am. J. Sociol.* 61 (1955), 260–1.

'Anomie, social isolation and the class structure', *Sociometry*, 20 (1957), 105–16.

'The utility of the Shevky typology for the design of urban subarea field studies', *J. Soc. Psychol.* 47 (1958), 71–83. Reprinted in Theodorson (1961).

'Social areas: typology of urban neighbourhoods', in M. Sussman (ed.), *Community Structure and Analysis* (New York, 1959), pp. 61–92.

'Urban neighbourhoods and individual behaviour', in M. Sherif and C. W. Sherif (eds), *Problems of Youth* (Chicago, 1965), pp. 235–64.

'The city, the suburb, and a theory of social choice', in S. Greer *et al.* (eds), *The New Urbanization* (New York, 1968), pp. 132–68.

Bell, W. and Boat, M. D. 'Urban neighbourhoods and informal social relations', *Am. J. Sociol.* 62 (1957), 391–8.

Bell, W. and Force, M. T. 'Urban neighbourhood types and participation in formal associations', *Am. Sociol. Rev.* 21 (1956a), 25–34.

'Social structure and participation in different types of formal associations', *Soc. Forces*, 34 (1956*b*), 345–50.

'Religious preference, familism and the class structure', *Midwest Sociol.* 19 (1957), 79–86.

Bell, W. and Greer, S. 'Social area analysis and its critics', *Pac. Sociol. Rev.* 5 (1962), 3–9.

Bell, W. and Moskos, C. C., Jr. 'A comment on Udry's "Increasing scale and spatial differentiation" ', *Soc. Forces*, 42 (1964), 414–17.

Bell, W. and Willis, E. M. 'The segregation of Negroes in American cities', *Soc. Econ. Studies*, 6 (1957), 59–75.

Berry, B. J. L. 'Internal structure of the city', *Law Contemp. Probs* 3 (1965), 111–19.

Berry, B. J. L. and Murdie, R. *Socioeconomic Correlates of Housing Condition* (Toronto, 1965).

Berry, B. J. L. and Rees, P. H. 'The factorial ecology of Calcutta', *Am. J. Sociol.* 74 (1969), 447–91.

Beshers, J. M. 'Census Tract Data and Social Structure: a Methodological Analysis' (unpublished Ph.D. dissertation, University of North Carolina, 1957).

'The construction of "social area" indices: an evaluation of procedures', *Proc. Soc. Stats. Section, Am. Stat. Ass.* (1959), 65–70.

Bloom, B. S. 'A census tract analysis of socially deviant behaviours', *Multivar. Beh. Res.* 1 (1966), 302–20.

Boggs, S. L. 'Urban crime patterns', *Am. Sociol. Rev.* 30 (1965), 899-908.

Bollens, J. C. *Exploring the Metropolitan Community* (Berkeley, 1961).

Borgatta, E. F. and Hadden, J. K. 'An analysis of tract data by regions' (mimeo. University of Wisconsin, 1964).

Brody, S. A. 'Urban characteristics of centralization', *Sociol. Soc. Res.* 46 (1962), 326–31.

Broom, L., Beem, H. P. and Harris, V. 'Characteristics of 1,107 petitioners for change of name', *Am. Sociol. Rev.* 20 (1955), 33–9.

Broom, L. and Shevky, E. 'The differentiation of an ethnic group', *Am. Sociol. Rev.* 14 (1949), 476–81.

Buechley, R. W. 'Review of "Social Area Analysis" ', *J. Am. Stat. Ass.* 51 (1956), 195–7.

Carey, G. W. 'The regional interpretation of population and housing patterns in Manhattan through factor analysis', *Geog. Rev.* 56 (1966), 551–69.

Carpenter, D. B. 'Review of "Social Area Analysis" ', *Am. Sociol. Rev.* 20 (1955), 497–8.

Cartwright, D. S. and Howard, K. I. 'Multivariate analysis of gang delinquencies: I, ecologic influences', *Multivar. Beh. Res.* 1 (1966), 321–69.

Clignet, R. and Sween, J. 'Accra and Abidjan: a comparative examination of the theory of increase in scale' (mimeo. Northwestern University, 1968).

Curtis, J. H., Avesing, F. and Klosek, I. 'Urban parishes as social areas', *Am. Cath. Sociol. Rev.* 18 (1957), 1–7.

Duncan, O. D. 'Review of "Social Area Analysis" ', *Am. J. Sociol.* 61 (1955), 84–5.

Bibliography

'Reply to Bell', *Am. J. Sociol.* 61 (1955), 261–2.

'Review of "Identification of Social Areas by Cluster Analysis" ', *Am. Sociol. Rev.* 21 (1956), 107–8.

Erickson, E. G. 'Review of "The Social Areas of Los Angeles" ', *Am. Sociol. Rev.* 14 (1949), 699.

'Rejoinder to Greenwood and Schmid', *Am. Sociol. Rev.* 15 (1950), 296.

Farber, B. and Disonach, J. C. 'An index of socio-economic rank of census tracts in urban areas', *Am. Sociol. Rev.* 24 (1959), 630–40.

Gagnon, G. 'Les zones sociales de l'agglomération de Quebec', *Recherches Sociogr.* 1 (1960).

Gittus, E. 'An experiment in the definition of urban sub-areas', *Trans. Bartlett Soc.* 2 (1964), 109–35.

'The structure of urban areas', *Town Pl. Rev.* 35 (1964), 5–20.

Goheen, P. *The North American Industrial City in the Late Nineteenth Century: The Case of Toronto* (Department of Geography Research Paper, Chicago, 1969).

Goldstein, S. and Mayer, K. 'Population decline and the social and demographic structure of an American city', *Am. Sociol. Rev.* 29 (1964).

Greer, S. 'Urbanism reconsidered: a comparative study of local areas in a metropolis', *Am. Sociol. Rev.* 21 (1956), 19–25.

'The social structure and political process of suburbia', *Am. Sociol. Rev.* 25 (1960), 514–26.

'The social structure and political process of suburbia: empirical test', *Rural Sociol.* 27 (1962), 438–59.

Greer, S. and Kube, E. 'Urbanism and social structure: a Los Angeles study', in M. Sussman (ed.), *Community Structure and Analysis* (New York, 1959).

Greer, S. and Orleans, P. 'The mass society and the parapolitical structure', *Am. Sociol. Rev.* 27 (1962), 634–46.

Greer, S., McElrath, D. C., Miner, M. W. and Orleans, P. (eds), *The New Urbanization* (New York, 1968).

Greenwood, E. 'Comment on Erickson's review of "The Social Areas of Los Angeles" ', *Am. Sociol. Rev.* 15 (1950), 108–9.

Hawley, A. H. and Duncan, O. D. 'Social area analysis: a critical appraisal', *Land Econ.* 33 (1957), 337–45.

Herbert, D. T. 'Social area analysis: a British study', *Urban Studies*, 4 (1967), 41–60.

Hyderabad Metropolitan Research Project. *Social Area Analysis of Metropolitan Hyderabad* (Hyderabad, 1966).

Imse, T. and Murphy, A. 'Metropolitan Buffalo Perspectives' (mimeo. Buffalo n.d., *c.* 1960).

Janson, C.-G. 'The spatial structure of Newark, New Jersey. Part I: the central city', *Acta Sociol.* 11 (1968), 144–69.

Johnston, R. J. 'Residential space or residential spaces in American cities?' (mimeo. Canterbury University, Christchurch, N.Z., 1969).

Jonassen, C. T. and Peres, S. H. *Interrelationships of Dimensions of Community Systems: A Factor Analysis of Eighty-two Variables* (Columbus, Ohio, 1960).

Bibliography

Jones, F. L. 'A social profile of Canberra, 1961', *Aust. N.Z. J. Sociol.* 1 (1965), 107–20.

'Population growth and population distribution, Melbourne, 1954–1961' (mimeo. Australian National University, 1965).

'Social area analysis: some theoretical and methodological comments illustrated with Australian data', *Brit. J. Sociol.* 19 (1968), 424–44.

Dimensions of Social Structure (Canberra, 1969).

Kaufman, W. C. 'Social Area Analysis: An Explication of Theory, Methodology and Techniques with Statistical Tests of Revised Procedures, San Francisco and Chicago, 1950' (unpublished Ph.D. dissertation, Northwestern University, 1961).

Kaufman, W. C. and Greer, S. 'Voting in a metropolitan community: an application of social area analysis', *Soc. Forces*, 38 (1960), 196–204.

Krech, D., Crutchfield, R. S. and Ballackey, E. L. 'Social areas', pp. 319–26 in *Individual in Society: A Textbook of Social Psychology* (New York, 1962).

Lammana, R. 'The Influence of Place of Residence on the Attitude Towards School Desegregation. A Social Area Analysis of Norfolk, Virginia' (unpublished M.A. dissertation, Fordham University).

McCannell, E. 'An Application of Urban Typology by Cluster Analysis to the Ecology of Ten Cities' (unpublished Ph.D. dissertation, University of Washington, 1957).

McElrath, D. C. 'Prestige and esteem identification in selected urban areas', *Res. Studies, State College of Washington*, 23 (1955), 130–7.

'The social areas of Rome: a comparative analysis', *Am. Sociol. Rev.* 27 (1962), 376–91.

'Urban differentiation', *Law Contemp. Probs* 3 (1965), 103–10.

'Societal scale and social differentiation', in S. Greer *et al.* (eds), *The New Urbanization* (New York, 1968), pp. 33–52.

McElrath, D. C. and Barkey, J. W. 'Social and physical space: models of metropolitan differentiation' (mimeo. Centre for Metropolitan Studies, Northwestern University, n.d., *c.* 1964).

Metropolitan St Louis Survey, various reports (St Louis, Mo., 1956–7).

Moush, E., Scrivens, J. and Avesing, F. 'Social Area Analysis of Cleveland Metropolitan Area, 1950' (mimeo. Cleveland, 1960).

Murdie, R. A. *The Factorial Ecology of Metropolitan Toronto, 1951–1961: An Essay on the Social Geography of the City* (Dept of Geography Research Paper, University of Chicago, 1969).

Pedersen, P. O. *Modeller for Befolkningsstruktur og Befolkningsudvikling i Storbyområder-specielt med Henblik på Stockøbenhavn* (Copenhagen, 1967).

Polk, K. 'The Social Areas of San Diego' (unpublished M.A. dissertation, Northwestern University, 1957*a*).

'Juvenile delinquency and social areas', *Soc. Problems*, 5 (1957*b*), 214–7.

'Urban social areas and delinquency', *Soc. Problems*, 14 (1967), 320–5.

Powell, F. J. 'The Social Areas of Brisbane' (unpublished B.A. dissertation, University of Queensland, 1967).

Reeks, O. 'The Social Areas of New Orleans' (unpublished M.A. dissertation, University of California, Los Angeles, 1953).

Bibliography

Rees, P. H. 'The factorial ecology of metropolitan Chicago', 1960 (unpublished M.A. dissertation, University of Chicago, 1968).

'The factorial ecology of metropolitan Chicago', in B. J. L. Berry and F. E. Horton (eds), *Geographic Perspectives on Urban Systems* (Englewood Cliffs, N.J., 1970).

Robson, B. *Urban Analysis: A Study of City Structure* (Cambridge, 1969).

Schmid, C. F. 'Comment on Erickson's review of "The Social Areas of Los Angeles" ', *Am. Sociol. Rev.* 15 (1950), 109–10.

'Urban crime areas: Part I', *Am. Sociol. Rev.* 25 (1960), 527–42.

'Urban crime areas: Part II', *Am. Sociol. Rev.* 25 (1960), 655–78.

Schmid, C. F. and Tagashira K. 'Ecological and demographic indices: a methodological analysis', *Demography*, 1 (1964), 194–212.

Schnore, L. F. 'Another comment on social area analysis', *Pac. Sociol. Rev.* 5 (1962), 13–16.

Sherif, M. and Sherif, C. W. *Reference Groups* (New York, 1964).

(eds), *Problems of Youth* (Chicago, 1965).

Shevky, E. and Bell, W. *Social Area Analysis: Theory, Illustrative Application and Computational Procedures* (Stanford, 1955).

Shevky, E. and Williams, M. *The Social Areas of Los Angeles* (Berkeley, 1949).

Sullivan, T. 'The application of Shevky–Bell indices to parish analysis', *Am. Cath. Sociol. Rev.* 12 (1961), 168–71.

Sweetser, F. L. *The Social Ecology of Metropolitan Boston, 1950* (Boston, 1961).

The Social Ecology of Metropolitan Boston, 1960 (Boston, 1962).

Patterns of Change in the Social Ecology of Metropolitan Boston, 1950–60 (Boston, 1962).

'Factor structure as ecological structure in Helsinki and Boston', *Acta Sociol.* 8 (1965), 202–25.

'Factorial ecology: Helsinki, 1960', *Demography*, 2 (1965), 372–86.

'Ecological factors in metropolitan zones and sectors', in M. Dogan and S. Rokan (eds), *Quantitative Ecological Analysis in the Social Sciences* (Cambridge, Mass., 1969), pp. 413–56.

Tiebout, C. M. 'Hawley and Duncan on social area analysis: a comment', *Land Econ.* 34 (1958), 182–4.

Tryon, R. C. *Identification of Social Areas by Cluster Analysis: A General Method with an Application to the San Francisco Bay Region* (Berkeley, 1955).

'Biosocial constancy of urban social areas' (paper read before *Am. Psych. Ass.*, 1955).

'The social dimensions of metropolitan man (revised title)' (paper read before *Am. Psych. Ass.*, 1959).

Udry, J. R. 'Increasing scale and spatial differentiation: new tests of two theories from Shevky and Bell', *Soc. Forces*, 42 (1964), 403–13.

Van Arsdol, M. D. Jr. 'An Empirical Evaluation of Social Area Analysis in Human Ecology' (unpublished Ph.D. dissertation, University of Washington, 1957).

Van Arsdol, M. D. Jr, Camilleri, S. F. and Schmid, C. F. 'A deviant case of Shevky's dimensions of urban structure', *Res. Studies State College of Washington*, 25 (1957), 171–7.

'The generality of the Shevky social area indexes', *Am. Sociol. Rev.* 23 (1958*a*), 277–84. Reprinted in Theodorson (1961).

'An application of the Shevky social area indexes to a model of urban society', *Soc. Forces*, 37 (1958*b*), 26–32.

'An investigation of the utility of urban typology', *Pac. Sociol. Rev.* 4 (1961), 26–32.

'Further comments on the utility of urban typology', *Pac. Sociol. Rev.* 5 (1962), 9–13.

Wendling, A. 'Suicide in the San Francisco Bay Region 1938–1942 and 1948–1952' (unpublished Ph.D. dissertation, University of Washington, 1954).

Wendling, A. and Polk, K. 'Suicide and social areas', *Pac. Sociol. Rev.* 1 (1958), 50–3.

Williamson, R. C. 'Selected urban factors in marital adjustment', *Res. Studies State College of Washington*, 21 (1953), 237–41.

'Socio-economic factors and marital adjustment in an urban setting', *Am. Sociol. Rev.* 19 (1954), 213–16.

Willie, C. V. 'The relative contribution of family status and economic status to juvenile delinquency', *Soc. Problems*, 14 (1967), 326–35.

Wilson, P. R. 'Immigrant Political Behaviour' (unpublished Ph.D. dissertation, University of Queensland, 1970).

Wilson, R. L. 'The Association of Urban Social Areas in Four Cities and the Institutional Characteristics of Local Churches in Five Denominations (unpublished Ph.D. dissertation, Northwestern University, 1958).

INDEX

271

Index

Index

Index